# CONTEXTUAL
# TRAUMA
# THERAPY

# CONTEXTUAL TRAUMA THERAPY

Overcoming Traumatization and Reaching Full Potential

STEVEN N. GOLD

AMERICAN PSYCHOLOGICAL ASSOCIATION
Washington, DC

Copyright © 2020 by the American Psychological Association. All rights reserved. Except as permitted under the United States Copyright Act of 1976, no part of this publication may be reproduced or distributed in any form or by any means, including, but not limited to, the process of scanning and digitization, or stored in a database or retrieval system, without the prior written permission of the publisher.

The opinions and statements published are the responsibility of the authors, and such opinions and statements do not necessarily represent the policies of the American Psychological Association. The Author has worked to ensure that all information in this book is accurate at the time of publication and consistent with general mental health care standards. As research and practice continue to advance, however, therapeutic standards may change. Moreover, particular situations may require a particularized therapeutic response not addressed or included in this book.

Published by
American Psychological Association
750 First Street, NE
Washington, DC 20002
https://www.apa.org

Order Department
https://www.apa.org/pubs/books
order@apa.org

In the U.K., Europe, Africa, and the Middle East, copies may be ordered from Eurospan
https://www.eurospanbookstore.com/apa
info@eurospangroup.com

Typeset in Meridien and Ortodoxa by Circle Graphics, Inc., Reisterstown, MD

Printer: Sheridan Books, Chelsea, MI
Cover Designer: Beth Schlenoff, Bethesda, MD

**Library of Congress Cataloging-in-Publication Data**

Names: Gold, Steven N., author.
Title: Contextual trauma therapy : overcoming traumatization and reaching full potential / Steven N. Gold.
Description: Washington, DC : American Psychological Association, [2020] | Includes bibliographical references and index.
Identifiers: LCCN 2019050941 (print) | LCCN 2019050942 (ebook) | ISBN 9781433831997 (paperback) | ISBN 9781433832000 (ebook)
Subjects: LCSH: Contextual therapy. | Psychic trauma—Treatment.
Classification: LCC RC488.55 .G653 2020  (print) | LCC RC488.55 (ebook) | DDC 616.85/21—dc23
LC record available at https://lccn.loc.gov/2019050941
LC ebook record available at https://lccn.loc.gov/2019050942

http://dx.doi.org/10.1037/0000176-000

*Printed in the United States of America*

10 9 8 7 6 5 4 3 2 1

*With love and gratitude:*

*To my mother, Shirley Lee Bernstein-Gold,
whose constant growth, inner strength, and zest for life
have been an inspiration to me and to many others.*

*To my children, Andrea, Lylah, and Adam,
whose big hearts and nimble minds
are a continual source of joy and pride.*

*And especially to my wife, Doris,
whose love and companionship have enriched my life immeasurably,
and who from the earliest days of our relationship insisted,
"You have to write another book!"*

# CONTENTS

| | |
|---|---|
| Acknowledgments | xi |
| Introduction | 3 |

### 1. The Context of Complex Traumatization: Overview and Conceptual Foundations — 11

| | |
|---|---|
| *The Experiential and Existential Nature of Trauma and Trauma-Focused Therapy* | 12 |
| *Definition of Complex Traumatization and Rationale for Differential Treatment* | 15 |
| *The Importance of Respecting Complex Trauma Survivors' Experience and Input* | 18 |
| *Limitations of Intervention-Focused Therapy for Survivors of Complex Trauma* | 23 |

### 2. In the Foreground: The Presence of Trauma — 27

| | |
|---|---|
| *The Paradoxical Nature of Traumatization* | 28 |
| *The Surge in Recognition of Trauma and Traumatization* | 31 |
| *Obstacles to Accessing Trauma Therapy* | 34 |
| *The Defining Characteristics of Trauma as an Event* | 38 |

### 3. In the Background: Inadequate Interpersonal Developmental Resources — 49

| | |
|---|---|
| *Role of Developmental Deprivation* | 50 |
| *Adverse Childhood Experiences as Markers of an Ineffective Family Environment* | 53 |
| *Features and Consequences of Growing Up in an Ineffective Family* | 57 |
| *The Contextual Trauma Therapy Model: Differentiating the Impact of Abuse Trauma and Neglect* | 65 |
| *Reconceptualization of the Distinction Between PTSD and C-PTSD* | 67 |
| *Characteristics of Families of Abused Children: The Context of Maltreatment* | 70 |

### 4. Integrating Figure and Ground: A Major Shift in Perspective — 77
A Model of Dual Cause and Effect — 77
Bidirectional, Circular Causation Between Diagnostic Syndromes and Functional Impairment — 80

### 5. Initial Contact, Assessment, and Case Formulation: Setting the Stage for Success — 89
Initiating Conceptually Guided Treatment — 89
Establishing an Orientation Toward Success — 98
Assessing Traumatization in an Interpersonal/Developmental Context — 99
Including the Pivotal Role of Client Strengths in Contextual Trauma Therapy — 102
Constructing a Provisional Case Formulation — 105
Incorporating the Three Spheres of Contextual Trauma Therapy — 107

### 6. Forging a Collaborative Relationship: Fostering Connection and Growth — 113
Contextual Trauma Therapy's Relational Philosophy for Remediating Developmental Gaps and Warps — 114
Challenges to the Formation of a Collaborative Therapeutic Alliance — 117
The Necessity of Therapist Self-Care — 143
The Centrality of the Relational Sphere in Contextual Trauma Therapy — 145

### 7. Collaborative Conceptualization: Jointly Constructing Cognitive Understanding — 149
The Combined Negative Impact of Deprivation and Threat on Sound Reasoning — 150
Principles of the Collaborative Conceptualization Process in Contextual Trauma Therapy — 151
Delineation of the Procedure of "Following the Thread" — 157
Two Major Areas of Application of Collaborative Conceptualization — 159
Two Domains of Understanding: Facilitating Deduction Versus Providing Information — 162
Intersection of the Relational, Conceptual, and Practical Intervention Spheres — 164

### 8. Establishing a Sense of Safety and Contentment: Overcoming Chronic Dysphoria — 167
Reducing Baseline Distress — 169
Relieving Immediate Spikes in Distress — 178
Overcoming Depression — 179

### 9. Learning to Modulate Dissociation: Expanding Focus and Awareness — 183
Varieties of Problematic Dissociative Experiences — 184
Dissociation as Experiential Distance and Disconnection — 186
A Contextual Conceptualization of Dissociation — 187
Strategies for Modulating and Extinguishing Dissociative Reactions — 191

### 10. Identifying Complex Dissociation: Annotated Transcript of an Initial Assessment Interview — 203
The Assessment Interview — 204

## 11. Relinquishing Addictions and Compulsions: Acquiring Adaptive Coping Abilities    **233**

*A Contextual Understanding of Trauma-Related Addictive and Compulsive Behaviors*    233

*SCAN-R: A Contextual Trauma Therapy Strategy for Resolving Addictive and Compulsive Behavior Patterns*    235

## 12. Resolving Trauma: Exorcising the Destabilizing Past    **245**

*Cognition-Centered Trauma Processing*    247
*Cue-Centered Trauma Processing*    258
*Event-Centered Trauma Processing*    259
*Final Considerations About Trauma Processing*    267

## 13. Enhancing the Life Trajectory: Trauma Integration and Competency Consolidation    **269**

*Taking Stock: Phases 1 and 2 of Treatment*    270
*Enhancing the Life Trajectory: Phase 3*    271
*Helping Survivors of Complex Traumatization Embark on a More Favorable Life Trajectory*    279

Epilogue: Applying Contextual Trauma Therapy to Short-Term Treatment    281
References    285
Index    309
About the Author    319

# ACKNOWLEDGMENTS

A central premise of the contextual model presented in this book is that none of us is separate from those around us. We are the product of the society and culture in which we live and of those we are closest to. Our very identity is shaped—both in our formative years and throughout our lifetime—by those we are in relationship with. My professional and personal identity and my perspective on and approach to conducting therapy for survivors of complex traumatization have been influenced by innumerable mentors, colleagues, students, and clients. I am certain that not all of their names appear on this page, but these are the ones who readily come to mind:

- My mentors, Al Rabin and Bert Karon at Michigan State University and Don Beere at Central Michigan University; professional colleagues Judy Alpert, Gonzalo Bacigalupe, Laura Brown, William "Joe" Burns, Lisa Butler, Eduin Caceres, Etzel Cardeña, Catherine Classen, Chris Courtois, Constance Dalenberg, Jennifer Davidtz, Mary Ann Dutton, Jan Faust, Charles Figley, Steve Frankel, Esther Giller, Annita Jones, Andres Laddis, Laurie Pearlman, Elizabeth Power, David Reitman, Margo Rivera, Beth Rom-Rymer, Eli Somer, Marlene Steinberg, Lenore Walker; and others who have been active in the International Society for the Study of Trauma and Dissociation and APA Division 56, Trauma Psychology

- Former students and now colleagues Robert Allred, Raquel Andrés, Kelly Araujo, Jennifer Beckjord, Steve Beckjord, Jeremy Bidwell, Maddy Cabrera, James Campbell, Yenys Castillo, Anthony Castro, Kelly Chrestman, Jon Cleveland, Scott Creighton, Joan Cook, Jani Cuono, Jon Elhai, Amy Ellis, Robert Finlay, Seth Grobman, Jason Henle, Laura Hohnecker, Scott Hyman,

Dawn Hughes, Lyndsey Karns, Mary Kelly, Brandon Korman, Louis LaPorta, Judy Lasher, Jackie Lefebre, Lisa Lewis, Barb Lucenko, Cristina Mahhelaes, Lori Merling, Landon Michaels, Michael Morreale, Gisela Padrón, Maria Panero, Beverley Pedroche, Bryan Reuther, Nicole Richardson, Django Rogers, Rebeca Ergas Scherman, Dan Schoenwald, Stacy Seibel, Heidi Schaetz Sigmund, Dennis Slate, Lindsay Stewart, Jan Swingle, Sheree Tarver, Leah Taylor, and Mischa Tursich, and other alumni of the Nova Southeastern University Trauma Resolution & Integration Program

- Current student collaborators Michael Quiñones, Nathan Daly, and Ryan Strosser

- Numerous clients who taught me more than any professional possibly could about complex traumatization

- And especially former student, current colleague, longtime collaborator, and assistant director of the Trauma Resolution & Integration Program, Amy Ellis (and her husband, Jeff "Aquaman" Ellis)

- And for their kindness, patience, encouragement, and feedback: American Psychological Association (APA) Acquisitions Editor Susan Reynolds; APA Development Editor Kristen Knight; and my colleague in the APA Council of Representatives, Marta Miranda

Thank you all! Your stamp is on these pages.

# CONTEXTUAL TRAUMA THERAPY

# Introduction

This volume presents a detailed account of a form of psychotherapy for survivors of extensive childhood maltreatment that I first introduced exactly 20 years ago in the book *Not Trauma Alone: Therapy for Child Abuse Survivors in Family and Social Context* (*NTA*; Gold, 2000). At the time, I was struggling to formulate and articulate a framework for working with individuals who were extensively abused early in life that differed in essential ways from the prevailing, trauma-centered form of treatment. I eventually came to refer to this alternate perspective as contextual trauma therapy (CTT).

The core insight that distinguishes CTT from other treatment approaches is that survivors of prolonged childhood trauma suffer not just from the impact of the damaging things that happened to them but also from the consequences of the beneficial conditions that were not provided for them. These are people who have not only been beaten down by repeated encounters with trauma and violence but have also been deprived of the most fundamental interpersonal developmental resources that children require—ones that many of us have trouble imagining any child growing up without. It is this factor that constitutes the context of repeated traumatization from which CTT derives its name, and that distinguishes this model and its attendant treatment strategies from other trauma-relevant therapies. Once we have recognized the existence of the deficient interpersonal/developmental conditions that almost invariably accompany (and foster) repeated traumatization in childhood and adolescence, we will be in a substantially better position to appreciate the

---

http://dx.doi.org/10.1037/0000176-001
*Contextual Trauma Therapy: Overcoming Traumatization and Reaching Full Potential,*
by S. N. Gold
Copyright © 2020 by the American Psychological Association. All rights reserved.

far-reaching consequences of these surrounding circumstances. They render the individual vulnerable to recurring acts of manipulation and coercion, dramatically compound the impact of traumatic events, and, most important, contribute to difficulties displayed by the survivor that extend well beyond those attributable to traumatic experiences themselves.

When I wrote *NTA*, I found that stepping outside the predominant paradigm, glimpsing a different way of understanding complex traumatization, and communicating it to others proved to be an inordinately challenging task. At the time that *NTA* was published, the prevailing model for working with survivors of all types of trauma was to make the central focus of treatment the confrontation of the traumatic events that the survivor had lived through. This was the case even though, almost a decade earlier, psychiatrist Judith Herman (1992b) had proposed an alternate approach to working with people who had lived through especially pervasive trauma, one that could be traced back as far as the pioneering work of French psychologist Pierre Janet in the late 19th century. She argued that prolonged, pervasive trauma is qualitatively different and leads to much more fundamental and wide-ranging psychological damage than single discrete traumatic events, a syndrome that she labeled complex posttraumatic stress disorder (C-PTSD).

CTT initially arose from my own clinical experience and my supervision of scores of doctoral trainees at a university-based trauma training clinic, the Trauma Resolution & Integration Program, where the survivor population overwhelmingly fits Herman's (1992b) C-PTSD conception. These were people for whom treatment that primarily or exclusively focused on traumatic events did not yield improvement, was insufficiently helpful, or, in some instances, was unequivocally harmful. CTT builds on Herman's model by proposing that prolonged early adversity differs from circumscribed types of trauma that occur later in life not merely because it is ongoing or repeated but because of the additional impact of the developmentally inadequate family context in which it occurs.

A great deal has changed in the 2 decades since *NTA* was released. Only recently has the C-PTSD diagnosis been officially recognized in the most recent edition of the *International Classification of Diseases* (World Health Organization, 2018). In concert with this milestone, empirical research is greatly extending our understanding of the nature of C-PTSD. In conjunction with other lines of research, these findings compose a robust empirical panorama consistent with CTT theory. These findings, in combination of with an additional 20 years of clinical and supervisory experience, make it possible to more clearly delineate the CTT model and its rationale than when *NTA* was written.

## GUIDING PRINCIPLES OF CONTEXTUAL TRAUMA THERAPY

In contrast to many forms of therapy for survivors of psychological trauma, interventions do not compose the essence of CTT. It is, rather, a conceptually driven treatment approach. Thorough familiarity with the CTT theoretical formulation, therefore, is indispensable for treatment effectiveness. CTT recognizes that among survivors of prolonged child maltreatment, each individual comes to therapy with a unique constellation of factors. Each has been influenced by a distinct personal history; family background; trauma history; pattern of diverse gender, racial, sexual orientation, national origin, and religious identifications and experiences; psychological difficulties; developmental deficits; and adaptive strengths. A defining feature of CTT is arriving at an awareness of these aspects of the client's experiential background and how they shape the client's functioning and sense of self—rather than structuring treatment primarily around diagnostic categories and corresponding predetermined interventions. Although CTT regularly draws on treatment objectives and strategies, they are suggested rather than mandated. Therapy does not consist of a prescribed series of procedures delivered in a set sequence. Although major areas of focus and associated interventions are offered here as a guide, in CTT, therapeutic goals and strategies are arrived at, modified, sequenced, paced, and executed primarily through an ongoing process of collaborative negotiation between client and practitioner.

The tremendous practical consequence of absorbing and applying the CTT model is that it not only allows survivors to overcome their debilitating experiences of traumatization but also enables them to acquire, bolster, and extend the capacities for productive and gratifying adult living denied to them as a result of the developmentally inadequate interpersonal environment in which they were reared. What this means is that survivors of complex traumatization come to be able to exercise capacities and capitalize on potentials that they were unaware they possessed. Ultimately, with the types of interpersonal support, experiential connection, and practical guidance that were relatively absent while growing up and that they may have not realized they were deprived of, they are able to establish a quality of relational, educational, occupational, and spiritual attainment they may have previously yearned for but did not fully believe was within their reach. This orientation to treatment outcome is consistent with the conclusion of Andresen, Caputi, and Oades (2010) that "mental health consumers view recovery as leading a meaningful life, and have criticised traditional clinical measures for being too disability-oriented" (p. 309).

The full expanse of these types of therapeutic gains, this rich quality of life, and the associated transformations in self-perception, emotional equilibrium, and interpersonal connectedness are not and cannot be achieved in time spans of weeks or months. They also are not attainable via an exclusive reliance on rote implementation of unmodified, preexisting interventions that are meant to be applied regardless of the idiosyncratic histories, experiences, understanding, and difficulties presented by each survivor. Treatment goals this ambitious require dedication and follow-through by both practitioner and client, and a willingness to creatively tailor therapy to match the individual and their past and present circumstances.

Despite the time and effort entailed by this type of treatment approach, it is inexpressibly rewarding when someone who has lived a life steeped in pervasive terror, shame, and despair not only overcomes their trauma-related symptoms but radically improves their quality of life. These improvements in quality of life can, for example, include attainments such as going off disability, becoming gainfully employed and self-supporting, and earning the solid respect and confidence of superiors and coworkers; breaking out of isolation and self-loathing to form deep and enduring relationships embedded in a broader a sense of community; and moving from a sense of emotional desolation and pervasive meaninglessness to a profound experience of living a life imbued with purpose and spiritual significance.

## OBJECTIVE AND STRUCTURE OF THE BOOK

This book is designed to explain the CTT model, how it differs in fundamental ways from other trauma-relevant approaches, its conceptual and practical applications, the three major components of CTT treatment, and particular interventions routinely used in this approach. Although the primary target audience is practicing therapists, clinical researchers, graduate students, and others are likely to find it useful. Survivors of extensive childhood trauma may find in these pages clarity about life circumstances other than trauma that have powerfully affected them but of which they may have been only dimly aware. Friends and loved ones may better understand survivors' difficulties that transcend those attributable to traumatization.

The first four chapters lay out in detail the conceptual model that informs CTT. Chapter 1 provides an overview of the CTT model and emphasizes the experiential nature of trauma and the importance of and basic principles regarding the treatment relationship in CTT. It also introduces the proposed construct of complex traumatization (CTr), a variety of forms of impairment related to prolonged or repeated trauma that includes C-PTSD but extends well beyond it. Chapter 2 discusses the nature of trauma; the crucial conceptual distinction between the terms *trauma* and *traumatization*; how research findings have refined our understanding of traumatization over the past several decades; common obstacles encountered by survivors in attempting to access effective trauma treatment; distinctions among posttraumatic stress disorder, C-PTSD, and CTr; and the differing treatment requirements of these three forms of traumatization. In contrast, Chapter 3 explores the context in which prolonged childhood maltreatment regularly occurs and from which CTT derives its name: an ineffective family environment that fails to provide the interpersonal supports essential for adequate psychological development, socialization, and enculturation. Recognizing these circumstances and how they limit and warp the child's psychological functioning in ways that transcend the effects of traumatization can greatly enhance the effectiveness of therapy for CTr. The trauma-focused perspective presented in Chapter 2 and the contextual model covered in Chapter 3 are integrated in Chapter 4 into a comprehensive conceptual framework. That framework draws on newly emerging lines of research that converge with and validate a host of clinical observations garnered from decades of clinical experience working with adult survivors of prolonged childhood trauma.

Chapter 5 marks a transition from conceptual and empirical material to consideration of the practical clinical implications of the CTT model. It focuses on how the CTT conceptual framework guides the initiation of treatment: being alert for difficulties not directly attributable to traumatization that arise from having been reared in a developmentally insufficient interpersonal environment, approaching the initial contact with the client in a way that enhances establishment of a resilient therapeutic relationship and promotes robust treatment outcomes, conducting a pretreatment assessment that goes beyond a consideration of trauma history to encompass the client's interpersonal/developmental context, and formulating an initial case conceptualization to be collaboratively revised with the client as treatment progresses. Chapter 5 concludes with an overview of the three major spheres of CTT:

- the evolution of a collaborative therapeutic relationship designed to provide the type of development-enhancing interpersonal environment that was not an adequately consistent feature of the survivor's family of origin;

- collaborative conceptualization of the material the client brings to treatment; that conceptualization is aimed at both (a) assisting the survivor to make sense of their confusing history and its continuing debilitating effects and (b) guiding survivors through the reasoning process to help them develop more refined judgment and decision-making skills; and

- collaboratively identifying adaptive living capacities that the client needs to acquire or bolster and jointly negotiating the methods via which these competencies will be mastered.

This triadic model makes it explicit that CTT consists of concrete interventions and also the intentional evolution of a type of a treatment relationship and conceptual understanding that are key contributors not only to trauma resolution but also to psychological maturation.

Chapter 6 consists of a detailed delineation of how the relational component of CTT is implemented. It includes coverage of the indispensable role of this component in the transmission of developmental capacities, socialization, and enculturation, and it examines the conditions necessary for establishing a productive treatment alliance with survivors of CTr. It also provides a survey of potential obstacles to forming a collaborative alliance with complex trauma survivors, offers recommendations for productively navigating these challenges, and considers the key role of therapist self-care in supporting the evolution of a productive survivor-responsive therapeutic relationship.

Chapter 7 describes the manner in which the conceptual aspect of CTT is executed. It explains how experiences of threat (i.e., trauma) and experiences of deficit (i.e., developmental deprivation) conjointly act to hinder capacities for sound reasoning. This discussion is followed by coverage of principles to be applied in the collaborative reasoning process jointly engaged in by client and therapist, and the cognitive capacities attainable via this enterprise.

The chapters that follow each offer methods for carrying out a particular treatment objective commonly addressed in CTT. Chapter 8 focuses on overcoming the intense ongoing *dysphoria*, an umbrella term for various forms of distress, that is a core component of CTr. Dysphoria often needs to be tackled early in therapy to prevent it from diverting attention from other treatment goals and sapping motivation needed to fuel progress.

Chapters 9 and 10 deal with the intricate topic of dissociative experiences and helping survivors learn to modulate them. CTT proposes that at their core, dissociative phenomena are expressions of what is colloquially referred to as "spacing out" or "zoning out." Like dysphoria, these experiences can radically impede work toward other treatment goals. Chapter 9 discusses strategies for helping clients learn to establish greater mastery over dissociative experiences. Chapter 10 presents an extended annotated transcript of an initial assessment session with a client who had reason to believe that many of his difficulties were dissociative in nature.

As a means of avoiding and desperately trying to temper their dysphoric mood and distance themselves from intrusive traumatic thoughts and recollections, survivors of CTr frequently rely on addictive and compulsive behaviors. Chapter 11 explores the relationship between traumatization and these counterproductive attempts at coping and how to help clients reduce their reliance on and ultimately relinquish them.

Methods for processing traumatic material—frequently considered the core if not the totality of trauma-related treatment—are surveyed in Chapter 12. The chapter delineates the conditions that render survivors of CTr ready to approach this potentially destabilizing task in a way that will be productive rather than seriously detrimental to them. It provides an overview of programs of intervention for processing trauma and elaborates on a model for classifying them to help the practitioner decide which program may be best suited for a particular situation.

Throughout CTT, an overriding objective is to equip the survivor to enjoy a more adaptive, effective, and gratifying adult life. As other treatment goals up to and including resolving trauma via processing methods have been achieved, client and therapist can increasingly focus on improving the survivor's quality of life. Chapter 13 examines this territory and presents a case history[1] that illustrates in detail how the components of this overarching objective can be identified and attained.

The Epilogue provides a dramatic case example of the circumscribed but critical accomplishments that can be produced when CTT is applied under conditions of limited time and correspondingly restricted treatment resources.

---

[1] All client names and many of the potentially identifying elements of their circumstances in the case histories presented in this volume have been altered to protect their privacy and adhere to the tenets of confidentiality. None of the quotations in this volume attributed to clients are from external sources. All are derived either from the author's own cases or from doctoral trainees he has supervised. For this reason there are no citations applicable to these quotes.

This case history demonstrates that CTT, although usually long term because of its ambitious objectives, can be adapted as a short-term approach when circumstances require it. It also illustrates that capacities of enduring value can be attained in as little as a few weeks.

It is my hope that the approach delineated in this volume will equip and inspire therapists to travel breadths of this scope and consequence with their intensely traumatized and functionally restricted clients. It is a privilege to accompany survivors of complex traumatization on this journey. I cannot think of any work that is more rewarding.

to recognize this inherent quality of trauma can severely compromise the ability to be helpful, whereas a willingness to do so can benefit both therapist and client (e.g., Gold, 2017).

The aversion to looking squarely at trauma and its impact can help explain why, for the better part of the late 20th century, recognition of the topic altogether disappeared from view (Herman, 1992b). Despite the prevailing skepticism on the part of society as a whole, as well as on the part of mental health professionals, throughout that era about the reality and profound psychological impact of traumatic occurrences, clients were periodically reporting them to therapists. They frequently were not heard, though, because they were not believed. Descriptions of incest were often assumed to be expressions of delusional thinking. Accounts of domestic violence or rape were regularly discounted as hysterical reactions. Traumatization related to hideous experiences in combat was written off as an expression of cowardice. In essence, cause and effect were reversed. Rather than recognizing the events being conveyed as the cause of psychological disturbance, reports of their occurrence was too often assumed to be expressions of it.

Sadly, despite much more widespread acknowledgment of the reality of trauma over the past few decades, the tendency to disbelieve accounts of certain forms of interpersonal violence persists to this day. Too many people refuse to entertain the possibility, to name just a few examples, that accusations of sexual violation by powerful men are anything more than a bid for attention or financial gain, that rape is something that happens to men and transgender individuals as well as to women, that neither perpetrators of intimate partner violence nor their victims are universally represented by a particular gender, or that there are children who grow up in cults in which they are ritually abused. Too often, when survivors of child sexual abuse or adult sexual assault ⟨⟩ their victimization many years after it occurred, their veracity is questi⟨⟩ body of empirical literature that indicates that delayed reporting is ⟨⟩ndon, Bruck, Ceci, & Shuman, 2007). Most likely, survivors' ⟨⟩'s due to their anticipation that they will not be believed, or tha⟨⟩·lieved, no one will do anything decisive to end the abuse, a su⟨⟩'l too often confirmed if they do disclose what they are being ⟨⟩ ner, Brown, Rae-Grant, & Loughlin, 1999; Swingle et al., 2016⟨⟩

However, a willingness to acknowle⟨⟩·f traumatic events is merely a first step in working with survivors. ⟨⟩·nts in treatment, the practitioner must be prepared to listen to ⟨⟩ ccounts of the traumatic events that survivors have endured. Sev⟨⟩ st respected treatments for traumatization, such as prolonged expos⟨⟩ Hembree, & Rothbaum, 2007), cognitive processing therapy (CPT; ⟨⟩·son, & Chard, 2017), and eye-movement desensitization and repro⟨⟩ DR) therapy (Shapiro, 2017), consist largely of having the survivor ⟨⟩ traumatic events he or she has undergone or salient elements of the⟨⟩ ences to extinguish the symptoms triggered by cues associated with the⟨⟩

Recognizing and accepting one's kinship with the trauma survivor can go a long way toward bolstering one's ability to be helpful in such situations. But too often, practitioners disidentify with their clients; they do their best to reassure themselves that the people they treat are fundamentally different from themselves. It is too easy to intellectually divide humanity into the mentally ill and the well adjusted, an inclination that is frequently intensified by professional training that is implicitly anchored in this distinction.

Trauma, though, is a great equalizer. As discussed in the following chapter, the vast majority of adults in the general population have encountered at least one, and often more than one, traumatic incident in their lifetime. The minority who have eluded direct encounters with trauma have almost certainly been affected by one or more close friends or loved ones who have, through one circumstance or another, been traumatized—people they know intimately and who therefore cannot be easily reduced to "them" in contradistinction to "us."

As L. S. Brown (2008) reminded us, the widespread reach of trauma ensures that many trauma therapists are at the same time trauma survivors. If we draw on that commonality or at least on our shared humanity and the corresponding vulnerability we share with our traumatized clients, we will be radically better equipped to be helpful to them. Conversely, if we retreat into the rote execution of treatment strategies, are overcome by the illusion that therapy is something we do *to* our clients rather than a joint enterprise we participate in *with* them, or fall into the role of rescuer, both they and we will suffer grim consequences, and treatment will likely result in severely limited substantive gains.

Effective trauma work requires the humility of recognizing that no matter how much we learn about trauma, our survivor clients carry the most indispensable knowledge: firsthand experience that we cannot be privy to unless they share it with us. Only they have access to their memories of past events. Only they endure the current reverberations of those horrific episodes. In this respect, no matter how much we may think we have learned about trauma, our survivor clients are more expert about their particular traumatization than we could ever hope to be. They may be unable to escape being haunted by those traumatic incidents and their psychological fallout on their own. But we, as practitioners, are unlikely to be adequately equipped to help them resolve their impact unless we are willing to patiently, attentively, and compassionately join with them, listen to them, and be educated by them in the process.

As clinicians, we can be helpful when we do the difficult work of putting aside our assumptions to clearly hear and appreciate what our clients are telling us. It is difficult to resist the belief that we know better. Isn't that what our training, experience, and expertise culminate in: knowing what is best for our survivor clients? I would strenuously argue that the answer is a resounding "No!" A trauma therapist's effectiveness lies not in knowing better than the people the therapist works with what is good for them but in the therapist's willingness to be informed by his or her clients so that the therapist can work jointly with them to help them figure out what is in their best interest.

## DEFINITION OF COMPLEX TRAUMATIZATION AND RATIONALE FOR DIFFERENTIAL TREATMENT

As unsettling as facing the intensity of a circumscribed traumatic experience can be for both client and practitioner, for several decades now, many experts in trauma treatment have recognized that people who have lived through and been adversely affected by prolonged trauma exhibit a much broader and more intricate clinical picture. This presentation was dubbed by a number of trauma investigators, most prominently, Judith Herman (1992a, 1992b), as *complex posttraumatic stress disorder* (C-PTSD). Herman proposed that as opposed to PTSD, which can occur in response to a single or circumscribed traumatic event, C-PTSD is a reaction to repeated or ongoing trauma that consists of a constellation of psychological difficulties that include but extend beyond those composing PTSD (Herman, 1992b; World Health Organization, 2018).

The defining features of PTSD are closely tied to the traumatic event itself: reexperiencing the event, for example, in the form of nightmares; avoiding thoughts and circumstances associated with the event; having persistent negative thoughts and emotional states that arose subsequent to the event; and having heightened reactivity (American Psychiatric Association, 2013). In contrast, recent empirical findings have identified three additional factors, referred to collectively as disturbances in self-organization (DSO), that differentiate C-PTSD from PTSD: an intensely negative self-image, poor interpersonal functioning, and impaired emotional and impulse control (Brewin et al., 2017; Hyland et al., 2017; Karatzias et al., 2016).

In addition, it is well known that a wide range of syndromes other than PTSD are associated with a history of trauma (Gold, 2004b; Herman, 1992b; Luyten et al., 2017), such as trauma-related depression, dissociation, and substance use disorder. My colleagues' and my clinical observation at the Nova Southeastern University Trauma Resolution & Integration Program has been that some survivors of extended childhood trauma present with the three components of DSO in combination with trauma-related disorders other than PTSD. To distinguish these instances from C-PTSD throughout this volume, I use the term *complex traumatization*, or CTr, to refer to an overarching domain that includes not only the co-occurrence of PTSD and DSO (i.e., C-PTSD) but any disorder that arises in response to traumatic events and is accompanied by the three components of DSO.

A diagnostic category is of value to the extent that it points to the need for modes of treatment that differ from those that are effective for other diagnoses. This raises the question of whether C-PTSD, in particular, and CTr, in general, warrant forms of therapy distinct from the form required for PTSD.

In contrast to C-PTSD, the central strategy for treating PTSD falls under the general rubric of *exposure therapy*: helping the survivor to repeatedly mentally revisit the traumatic event or salient elements of it until it no longer elicits the adverse psychological reactions that compose the disorder. This treatment approach is based on the principles of classically conditioned responses and their extinction (Foa et al., 2007). The fight–flight–freeze response that becomes sensitized in some people who encounter a traumatic event and that underlies many of the symptoms of PTSD becomes desensitized and extinguished through planned, systematic encounters with recollections of the event. Proponents of exposure therapy as the treatment of choice for PTSD insist that C-PTSD is essentially indistinguishable from PTSD and that treatment for it should therefore be the same (e.g., De Jongh et al., 2016). Given the proposed mechanism underlying C-PTSD—extensive or prolonged experiences of trauma—their position seems quite reasonable. If PTSD is a reaction to a traumatic event, and its manifestations can be extinguished by repeatedly reviewing the event, shouldn't the same procedure be effective for resolving the consequences of prolonged trauma?

Specialists from Herman (1992b) onward have argued that this formulation is flawed. They have long contended that treatment for C-PTSD needs to be appreciably different from that for PTSD. Direct confrontation of recollections of traumatic events, they have insisted, must be proceeded by a phase of stabilization to fortify survivors' coping skills. But if the cause of C-PTSD is essentially the same as that of PTSD, why should this be the case?

What my colleagues and I have witnessed clinically at the Trauma Resolution & Integration Program is that when survivors of C-PTSD are led prematurely into exposure therapy without a period of stabilization, detrimental reactions can occur. For example, they may lapse into flashbacks of the traumatic event (Gold & Brown, 1997). A flashback is appreciably different from a memory. When people remember an incident, they think about or picture it but are firmly oriented to the present moment and their immediate surroundings, and are well aware that it is in the past and is not something occurring now. In contrast, a flashback is reexperienced in a way that compellingly feels as if it is occurring in the present. In the midst of an intense flashback, the trauma survivor, at best, has difficulty registering what is happening at the moment and, at worst, has little or no awareness of what is going on around them. This state of affairs, obviously, prevents the therapist from intervening.

A second possible response is that the survivor may fall into a profound dissociative state. In everyday language, the survivor may zone out to such an extent that, in effect, everything goes blank. Like the individual encapsulated in an intense flashback, the person is oblivious to attempts to communicate with him or her and therefore is cut off from therapeutic input.

Although such reactions often can be relied on to eventually dissipate, they have the potential to seriously disrupt treatment. If the therapist is unprepared for their occurrence and thus panics, he or she might respond in a way that is counterproductive. For example, the practitioner might compound the intensity of the adverse reaction by yelling at an unresponsive client in the midst of a flashback or dissociative reaction in a desperate attempt to reorient the client. Handling the situation in this way can intensify their terror and exacerbate the client's retreat into unresponsiveness.

Sometimes the consequences of leaping into trauma-focused approaches without adequately preparing the survivor with C-PTSD are appreciably more dire. Ill-timed processing of traumatic material leads not to a temporary decline in functioning from which the client rebounds but to long-standing impairment. Although these reactions may not occur in the majority of cases, when they do, they can have serious consequences. The case of Jeanette that appears at the end of this chapter and the case of Valerie in Chapter 3 vividly illustrate the negative impact that can result from premature or ill-advised engagement in trauma exposure with CTr survivors.

One possible explanation for the deleterious outcomes in these cases is that the therapists may have attempted trauma processing without having been sufficiently trained in or adhering to standard protocols for trauma exposure, such as PE (Foa et al., 2007), CPT (Resick et al., 2017) or EMDR therapy (Shapiro, 2017). Proponents (Foa et al., 2007; Resick et al., 2017; Shapiro, 2017) of these approaches have sometimes argued that treatment failures, whether they consist of detrimental effects or a lack of positive treatment outcomes (referred to as *nonresponsiveness*), are attributable to inadequate therapist training. The Veterans Administration (VA) system has strongly advocated for the use of PE and CPT and has made extensive efforts to train VA practitioners in these approaches. It is particularly striking, therefore, that a first-person account of treatment by a clinician trained in PE within the VA system—an account provided by an articulate and accomplished author—depicts severe symptom exacerbation. David Morris, a former Marine infantry officer and war correspondent, described his course of PE for PTSD in his book *The Evil Hours* (Morris, 2015). As treatment proceeded, his posttraumatic symptoms grew increasingly worse. Eventually, in his struggle to contain the distress that emerged in response to therapy, Morris developed a serious alcohol problem.

Unfortunately, few researchers have investigated symptom exacerbation or other adverse reactions to exposure to traumatic material. In a review of 55 evidence-based treatments for PTSD, Schottenbauer, Glass, Arnkoff, Tendick, and Gray (2008) found only three empirical studies that examined symptom exacerbation such as that described by Morris (2015) in response to this type of intervention; one study showed rates as high as 28% (Foa, Zoellner, Feeny, Hembree, & Alvarez-Conrad, 2002). Pitman et al. (1991) reported on six cases of men with PTSD who responded to trauma-focused exposure (i.e., flooding) with adverse effects, such as increased depression, relapse into alcohol abuse, and onset of panic disorder. Zayfert and Black (2000) found that a little more than 10% of clients at their outpatient clinic who dropped out of trauma exposure-based treatment indicated that they did so because it led to suicidal or dissociative reactions.

Cook, Schnurr, and Foa (2004) acknowledged that few clinicians in actual practice regularly use PE or other empirically supported treatments for PTSD. They opined that this is most likely attributable to the low proportion of therapists who receive extensive training in PE or other evidence-based treatments. However, Najavits (2015a) proposed a different explanation: In contrast to randomized control trials of PE and CPT for the treatment of PTSD, studies of their implementation in actual clinical practice reflect considerably higher rates of treatment dropout. Schottenbauer et al. (2008) observed that across investigations, both dropout rates and nonresponsiveness to treatment often approached and, at times, exceeded 50%. They concluded that these findings indicated that treatments such as PE and CPT are not effective for everyone.

It is to be expected that distress will often increase in response to confronting traumatic material, but when decisive exacerbations in risky and self-harming behaviors or maladaptive functioning occur, they need to be heeded as signs that other treatment objectives must be attended to first. Herman (1992b), building on the premise that CTr is the result of prolonged rather than circumscribed traumatic experiences, characterized these efforts as ones aimed at increasing "safety" (p. 153). But, as is discussed extensively in Chapter 3, CTT proposes that the origins of C-PTSD (and CTr, in general) lie not just in prolonged trauma but in traumatic events in childhood that occur in conjunction with and within a context of deprivation. Vulnerability to repeated encounters with traumatic events, CTT suggests, is exacerbated and accompanied by the absence of adequate care and responsiveness to support psychological development, enculturation, and socialization. This developmentally inadequate interpersonal environment is related to the DSO component of C-PTSD and radically compounds trauma-related disturbance (see Figure 1.1). The resulting functional deficiencies seriously compromise the survivor's coping ability and therefore his or her ability to benefit rather than become destabilized by confronting past trauma. This is why experts on C-PTSD prescribe a period of stabilization before addressing trauma directly. But, as Chapters 3 and 4 reveal, CTT suggests that the impact of growing up in a developmentally deficient interpersonal environment is much broader than that identified thus far in the professional literature. I return to and expand on the topics of trauma and complex traumatization in Chapter 2. Before proceeding, however, it is useful to first consider practical implications of treating complex traumatization.

## THE IMPORTANCE OF RESPECTING COMPLEX TRAUMA SURVIVORS' EXPERIENCE AND INPUT

Complex trauma survivors who grew up with repeated trauma in the midst of an interpersonal environment that failed to meet their emotional, psychological, and developmental needs often are invalidated by the very people they should be able to rely on: the parents and other family and community members who reared them. They were indoctrinated to believe that they do not know their own minds and that others knew what the survivors thought, felt, and needed better than they themselves did. Their childhood caretakers did not respond to the survivor's needs, thus leaving the survivor with the conviction that his or her own needs are unimportant. An absolutely essential aspect of treatment for complex trauma survivors, therefore, is to proceed in ways that counter rather than reinforce these deep-seated convictions. In cases of CTr, in particular, the skill of the clinician is not in unilaterally imposing conclusions and solutions on the client but in working jointly with the client to help the client come to their own conclusions and identify or

**FIGURE 1.1. Schematic Diagram Showing the Complex Trauma Therapy Model of Two-Pronged Causation of Complex Traumatization**

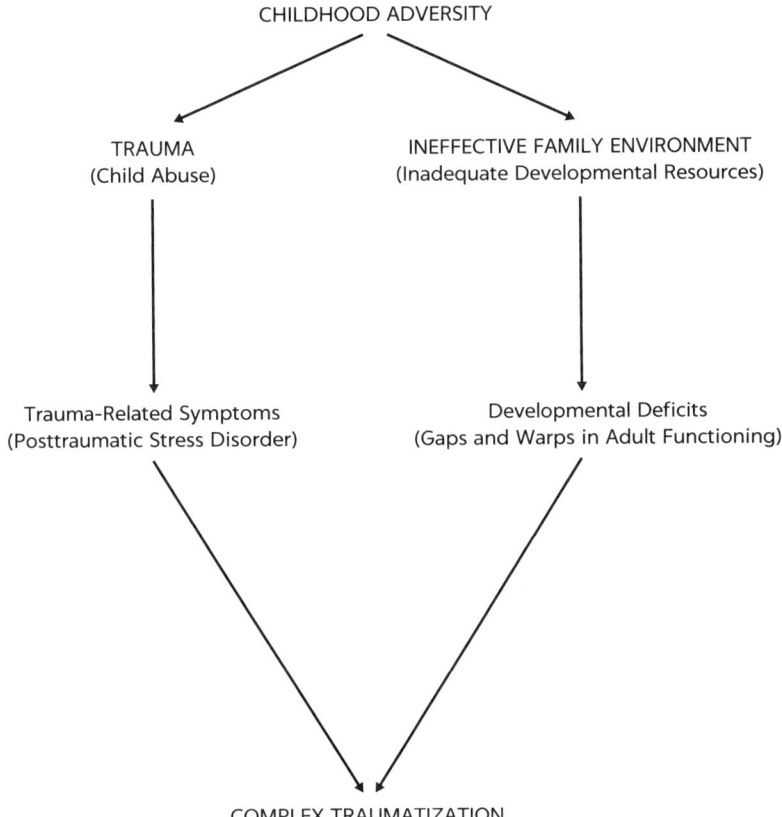

collaboratively formulate the solutions that are most likely to work for the client as an individual. In this way, the client's unique set of inadequately met developmental needs can be identified and remediated.

I emphasize these points because, like much of the most important and useful material in these pages, I was taught them by the survivors of CTr with whom I have worked. What I have heard from these clients and witnessed among psychology trainees I have supervised is that even clinicians who possess extensive trauma-related knowledge and experience are unable to be helpful to survivors of CTr if they are not receptive to joining them in identifying, attending to, and compassionately addressing these gaps in development. Those clinicians with considerably less experience who are open to recognizing that they cannot hope to "get it" unless they are willing to be educated by their clients are poised to assist their clients in reaching much more extensive and lasting treatment outcomes. Admittedly, these observations contradict our usual thinking about what constitutes expertise in therapy. Practitioners may not only believe that they understand their clients (and what they need) better than their clients understand themselves but may assume that it is this very ability that is the hallmark of clinical skill.

Imagine the impact it has on survivor clients who grew up hearing variations of statements such as "I know you better than you know yourself," "I can always tell what you are thinking and feeling," or "No matter where you go, I can see what you are doing" to interact with a therapist whose work is permeated by the conviction that his or her expertise lies in informing the client what is best for that client and explaining the client to themselves. At best, such an approach will be helpful in some respects but, in others, will reinforce the client's self-image of ineptitude and powerlessness. At worst, it will intensify the client's abiding distrust in themselves and others.

While growing up being negated leads survivors of CTr to harbor an intensely negative self-image sustained by constant self-criticism, often the adults in the household they were reared in also frequently ignored them. As one survivor remarked to his therapist,

> You can't be a person in yourself unless somebody sees you or hears you. Growing up alone is the most painful feeling. To watch life and not be in it [as a child because you are not included in it by those around you, and later, as an adult, because you never learned how to join in effectively participating in life with others] is a horrible feeling.

For these reasons, CTr survivors have in effect been trained to defer to the opinions of others. Clinicians, therefore, need to be particularly careful not to ignore, fail to solicit, or unthinkingly override the input of survivors regarding the nature of their difficulties and how to overcome them. The following case shows, among other things, the potentially disastrous consequences of disregarding the survivor's understanding of their own experience.

**Case Example: The Risky Consequences of Ignoring Client Input**
The case history presented here illuminates two crucial points. One is the unintended harmful consequences that can stem from an ill-informed approach to trauma therapy. The other is the importance of recognizing that traumatic experiences can lead to outcomes other than either PTSD or C-PTSD. Jeanette,[1] a White woman in her early 30s, had created a life for herself that most people her age would envy. She was a successful business executive working for a company in which she had steadily rose from an entry-level, middle management position to become a highly respected member of the leadership team. She was engaged to be married to a caring and attentive young man with a similar level of professional attainment. On top of the demands of her work life and the time and energy she devoted to maintaining her relationship with her fiancé, she gladly and lovingly assumed primary responsibility as the caretaker for her aged maternal grandmother. She unquestionably was functioning exceptionally well.

---

[1] All client names and many of the potentially identifying elements of their circumstances in the case histories presented in this volume have been altered to protect their privacy and adhere to the tenets of confidentiality.

It caught both Jeanette and those close to her completely off guard when she fell into a severe depressive state following her grandmother's death. Although she was unusually close to her grandmother, the extent of her emotional decline plainly exceeded the intensity of uncomplicated bereavement. The depths of her melancholy struck both Jeanette and those around her as out of proportion to her loss. Her occupational functioning and her relationship with her fiancé noticeably suffered. Jeanette therefore decided to seek therapy to help her through this difficult period.

At the end of her first therapy session, the clinician announced that the source of Jeanette's difficulty was clear to him. She was a trauma survivor; she had PTSD. Jeanette was shocked and offended by the therapist's pronouncement. She protested that she had never experienced a trauma. "Really?" the clinician replied, sounding stunned. "Your entire history is filled with trauma. You told me yourself that you witnessed your best friend being shot and killed when you were only 10 years old!" He continued to enumerate other difficult circumstances in Jeanette's history.

Jeanette, still skeptical, tried to dispute the therapist's formulation. She was seeking treatment because she was well aware that her functioning was compromised by depression. But the therapist persisted in his argument that she was a trauma survivor. Her mother had a serious drinking problem. Her father frequently stayed out until the early morning hours and gambled away money needed to cover household expenses. It was common for her parents to burst into prolonged yelling matches.

Although she had always known in the periphery of her awareness that her homelife was troubled, she had never thought of herself as traumatized. Two forces seemed to contradict that characterization. One was her own overfunctioning, a habit pattern she had firmly established by the time she entered kindergarten. The other was the love and protection of her grandmother, who lived a few short blocks from her house. She often went straight to her grandmother's house from school and stayed there until well after dinner. Whenever things grew too tense and volatile between her parents, she could always throw together some belongings and spend the night at her grandmother's house.

As she listened to the therapist recount the dramatic circumstances of her history, however, Jeanette found his argument hard to contradict. To recover from her PTSD, the clinician explained, she would have to face each of the disturbing events she had been through by repeatedly describing them in session. They would begin with the shooting death of her best friend in their next meeting.

In less than a month, it became apparent both to Jeanette and her therapist that her condition was rapidly worsening. She began to experience nightmares about her friend's murder and her grandmother's death. Each time she dozed off, the nightmares seemed to resume. She became phobic about falling asleep and feared that doing so would trigger nightmares that had awakened her in a panic. The lack of sleep compounded her already faltering work performance. She grew increasingly tense and unable to concentrate.

In response to her downward slide, Jeanette began to question her therapist about whether continuing the course of exposure-based treatment was indicated. She complained that she left each session feeling and functioning worse instead of better. In response, the therapist grew increasingly irritated and impatient. "You're not doing it right," he insisted. "You need to try harder and face what you've been through. If you're not committed, you won't make progress."

Jeanette redoubled her efforts during session but found it increasingly challenging to stay focused. About a month and a half into treatment, in the midst of describing the shooting death of her friend, her gaze became vacant, her body became immobile, and she fell silent. The clinician quickly realized that Jeanette was unresponsive. He called Jeanette's name, his tone louder and more insistent as the minutes passed. No response. Sometime after the therapist stopped shouting, Jeanette slowly reoriented. It was difficult for her to tell whether the therapist was more alarmed or infuriated. "You're just not doing it right," he fumed. "I can't work with you."

In less than a week after this last session, Jeanette concluded that she had no better option than to take a leave of absence from work. She was barely able to get dressed and show up at the office. Once she got there, she was distracted and unable to get much done. Perhaps if she took some time off, she thought, she would be able to recuperate. By now, her nightmares seemed to extend into her waking hours. She was experiencing flashbacks. And all of this was layered on top of the severe depressive state that had begun soon after her grandmother's death.

She quickly found another practitioner and resumed treatment. By the end of the initial meeting, the new clinician was concurring with the previous one: "You've definitely been through trauma. You have to face what you've been through. It's the only way you'll recover."

Her fiancé had done his best to be supportive, but, over time, he had run out of patience. Jeanette no longer even remotely resembled the lively, confident woman he had dated and asked to marry him. She was undoubtedly getting worse, and he saw no sign that she would ever be that person again. With considerable remorse, he ended the engagement and broke off communication with her. By this time, Jeanette had been let go from her firm. After an extended job search, she felt lucky to find a minimally demanding position as an administrative assistant at another company at close to a quarter of her previous income.

It took 3 months of prodding for her new practitioner to get Jeanette to agree to resume exposure. But almost as soon as Jeanette began describing the murder of her friend, she again lapsed into a deep dissociative state. Like the previous practitioner, he reacted angrily at her failure to respond as expected to the procedure. This scenario recurred about another 3 months and 6 months later, at which point, intensely frustrated, the therapist referred her to another clinician.

### Implications of the Case of Jeanette
Through the lens of CTT, Jeanette had both been misdiagnosed and offered a form of treatment that was inappropriate for her. Although she had

encountered a number of traumatic events throughout her childhood and adolescence, her traumatization had not taken the form of either PTSD or C-PTSD. In addition to the traumatic events she had lived through, experiences of deprivation figured prominently in her history and its effect on her. When she originally entered treatment, she did not report any symptoms of PTSD. Her difficulties indicated the presence of a severe major depressive episode that, in light of her history, was a comprehensible response to the loss of the only figure in her childhood who had provided stability, predictability, consistent love, and reliable nurturance.

From an early age, Jeanette had over-functioned, but apparently her ability to do so had been predicated on the foundation of a sense of safety and validation she had experienced in her relationship with her grandmother. Once that scaffolding was removed, she faltered. In an already psychologically vulnerable state, the inappropriate introduction of trauma-focused exposure that had her focus in her emotionally weakened condition on experiences of threat appears to have iatrogenically triggered PTSD. Sadly, the cost to her of immersion in an ill-timed and inappropriate form of intervention was tremendously high. Her mental status declined, her career was derailed, and her relationship with her fiancé was lost.

Although her depression was likely trauma related, one of the considerations illustrated by this case vignette is that traumatization is not always expressed as PTSD or C-PTSD. As her coping ability eroded in response to ill-advised exposure, and in the absence of the support she experienced in response to her grandmother's presence, the negative self-image, interpersonal difficulties, and impaired emotional regulation capacities that had been obscured by her pattern of over-functioning became evident. Recognition of CTr in the form of trauma-related depression accompanied by DSO may have led to a different approach to treatment.

Sadly, both of Jeanette's clinicians seem to have been so single-minded in their pursuit of an intervention-based approach to addressing her difficulties that they do not appear to have taken into account the importance of the therapeutic alliance. Jeanette had just lost the person who was her most steadfast source of support from early childhood onward: her grandmother. By the time she began treatment with the second practitioner, she had also lost her fiancé. Yet both clinicians seem to have neglected to pay much attention to the quality of the therapeutic relationship—the aspect of treatment that likely would have been most helpful to her in the immediate aftermath of her interpersonal losses. Instead, the two clinicians had fallen into an antagonistic style of interaction when Jeanette did not respond as expected to what they both presumed was the only avenue of recovery available.

## LIMITATIONS OF INTERVENTION-FOCUSED THERAPY FOR SURVIVORS OF COMPLEX TRAUMA

Jeanette's response to the therapy she received compellingly depicts how substantially limiting formulaic treatment for survivors of CTr can be. Certainly, effective psychotherapeutic work with this population entails the acquisition of trauma-specific knowledge and skills that many experts in the field have argued must encompass awareness of how CTr differs from PTSD (Courtois & Ford, 2013; Herman, 1992a; Kinsler, 2017). As discussed extensively in Chapter 3, CTT emphasizes that beyond this distinction, effective treatment for CTr survivors necessitates identifying the particular insufficiencies in the household in which they grew up and the developmental capacities that require remediation because of those insufficiencies. These areas of deficit can vary considerably among individuals. And as Jeanette's situation illustrates, without careful assessment, the difficulties associated with CTr as opposed to those composing PTSD may sometimes be obscured by clients with otherwise impressive functioning.

The capacity to identify what in particular was missing during the CTr survivor's formative years and the gaps in knowledge and functioning resulting from these areas of deprivation simultaneously requires that practitioners have the ability to transcend their own cultural biases. As one survivor client put it, therapists need to

> be able to step outside your ego. Realize you don't know what the client knows and you often don't know what's best for them. You have to be willing to empathize, to see things from the client's point of view. I want to experience normality, but I'm angry that people think that it's the only experience.

What this client is referring to is not normality as contrasted with psychopathology. It is, rather, perceptions and modes of experience that are widely embraced not because they are necessarily adaptive or effective, or the only "accurate" way to see and understand things, but because most members of the larger society have been culturally conditioned to see them that way. Normality in this sense is not an objective, universal given. It differs from one culture and one society to the next, and is inculcated in its members with such force and depth that it takes on the appearance of self-evident fact. The limitations in functioning created by traumatization and developmental deprivation can easily obscure the sophistication and strengths that many survivors exhibit, often precisely because they have endured adversity or been hampered in their participation in the mainstream. Being alert for these assets can aid the practitioner to maintain healthy respect for survivors' input in case formulation and treatment planning, and appreciate how their personal strengths and aspects of diversity in their backgrounds can be drawn on to enrich therapy.

Recognizing the importance of perspectives such as the one expressed by this client highlights the difficulties that can be raised by treatment approaches that exclusively or primarily center on interventions. Approaches such as these are based on rigid presumptions about what composes "normal" and "desirable" forms of adjustment. Because their life experiences have led them to question and mistrust "mainstream" perspectives, clients are likely to be alienated by this orientation and are likely to refuse to participate in these types of treatment, especially if a relatively single-minded focus on interventions eclipses other considerations, such as building a therapeutic relationship that promotes a sense of safety and trust. (See Chapter 6 for a detailed consideration of managing the therapeutic relationship with clients with CTr.) As in many other areas of contemporary psychotherapy, much of the literature on treating the chronic effects of having encountered a traumatic event consists of prescribed sequences of intervention techniques (Guideline Development Panel for the Treatment of PTSD in Adults, American Psychological Association, 2019; Lancaster, Teeters, Gros, & Back, 2016). It has been my observation in training doctoral-level clinical psychologists and in various leadership roles at the American Psychological Association that increasingly, practitioners have come to equate therapy in general with interventions—preferably "empirically supported interventions," ones that are backed by research evidence that substantiates their efficacy.[2] Especially for many clinical psychologists trained in the past 10 to 15 years, to suggest that therapy might consist of much beyond concrete, manualized techniques is highly likely to be perplexing. In the past several decades, the training of doctoral clinical psychologists has taken a remarkable shift. Attention to skills such as (a) carefully observing clients' verbal and nonverbal behavior as a basis for making sound inferences to help guide various aspects of treatment; (b) conceptualizing case material within a coherent theoretical framework rather than merely arriving at a *Diagnostic and Statistical Manual of Mental Disorders* (fifth ed.; American Psychiatric Association, 2013) diagnosis and matching it with a prefabricated, standardized treatment; and (c) navigating the obstacles to establishing a resilient therapeutic relationship with clients who may present appreciable interpersonal challenges have increasingly faded from the education of professional psychologists. I regularly find that doctoral trainees up to and including postdoctoral residency have only superficial or almost no familiarity with these elements of clinical practice.

Whether therapy is being conducted for trauma-related difficulties or to address other types of problems, interventions alone cannot always be relied on to produce solid therapeutic outcomes. Despite the pervasive exhortations about the power of empirically supported interventions, what psychology research has long shown is that specific clinical techniques account for a small proportion of the variance in treatment outcome: only about 15% (Asay & Lambert, 1999). Other aspects of treatment are equal or much greater contributors to outcome. Expectancy that treatment is likely to be effective accounts for about the same percentage of outcome variance as intervention techniques: about 15%. Not only in the mental health fields but in medicine, too, it is increasingly acknowledged that the outcome of treatment can and often is strongly influenced by the degree to which the person receiving the treatment believes it will work (Benson & Friedman, 1996). In comparison to the specific interventions used and the influence of expectancy, the quality of the treatment alliance contributes approximately as much to psychotherapy outcome as these other factors combined: about 30% (Asay & Lambert, 1999). And

---

[2]*Efficacy* refers to how well a treatment works under controlled ("laboratory") conditions in contrast to *effectiveness*, which refers to how well a treatment works under real-world conditions.

extratherapeutic factors, such as the client's life circumstances and events that occur outside of therapy during the course of treatment, compose the largest contributor: about 40% (Asay & Lambert, 1999).

As most of the chapters in the later part of this volume reflect, intervention techniques are an integral part of CTT. But they are far from its entirety. One of the meanings of the term *context* is that CTT is a form of therapy that places at least as much importance on the elements that compose the framework within which interventions are implemented—client characteristics, forming a collaborative treatment alliance, working together with clients to understand the nature and origins of their difficulties, and tailoring therapy in concert with clients by taking into consideration their unique strengths, preferences, and perspective—as the specific techniques used. Rather than being primarily technique- or intervention-based, CTT is a conceptually guided form of treatment. Therapy proceeds not through a predetermined sequence of treatment techniques but on the basis of a conceptual framework that is applied to and adapted in response to the specific current circumstances, personal and social history, demographic and cultural background, difficulties, resources, and strengths of each individual.

# 2

# In the Foreground
*The Presence of Trauma*

Contextual trauma therapy (CTT) proposes that awareness of and responsiveness to the repercussions for complex traumatization (CTr) survivors of having been reared in an ineffective family environment can appreciably improve therapeutic outcomes and help clinicians to avoid grave missteps in treatment. Before exploring the impact of family context directly, however, it is important to be conversant with the territory of trauma itself. The very nature of traumatization is counterintuitive: The trauma survivor is haunted in various ways by recollections of trauma and simultaneously struggles vigorously not to think about it. In this chapter, I provide a broad survey of central topics to understanding the nature of trauma. A clear understanding of what trauma consists of is an essential foundation for later consideration of the territory that CTT proposes is the other major component of CTr—developmental deprivation, including neglect—that often is equated with trauma but, from the vantage point of CTT, is in consequential ways distinct from trauma. Included are a description of the opposing forces that compose traumatization: an inability to break free of thoughts about the traumatic event and intense attempts to avoid being reminded about it. The chapter also discusses how trauma has gone from an almost entirely forgotten-about topic to one that has generated a vast body of scientific and professional literature. Despite this explosion of knowledge about trauma, survivors continue to face roadblocks to obtaining treatment for the debilitating effects of trauma. I also clarify the essential characteristics of a traumatic event.

---

http://dx.doi.org/10.1037/0000176-003
*Contextual Trauma Therapy: Overcoming Traumatization and Reaching Full Potential,*
by S. N. Gold
Copyright © 2020 by the American Psychological Association. All rights reserved.

## THE PARADOXICAL NATURE OF TRAUMATIZATION

Psychological trauma, an event that can overwhelm or seriously strain the limits of a person's coping ability, is by its very nature shot through with paradox. It is a powerful, disruptive, and sometimes shattering experience that can be unspeakably painful to think about. Consequently, that traumatic experience is often incentive enough for the survivor to avoid making the effort to think about or be reminded of it.

And, yet, the impact of a traumatic experience can be, when expressed in everyday language, "haunting." It frequently and disturbingly may occupy the survivor's attention or continually loom below the surface of focal awareness before it periodically and suddenly breaks into consciousness in an unbidden and certainly unwanted fashion. Despite (or more accurately because of) their unnerving intensity, it is not unusual for traumatic events to be recalled through a jumbled haze. On a perceptual and sensory level, past traumatic events can abruptly intrude with little or no warning on awareness with a ferocity so tremendous that trauma survivors compellingly experience those events as occurring in the present moment, and the events obscure survivors' awareness of their immediate surroundings.

In some instances, reminders of traumatic events are steeped in overt terror, rage, shame, or other extreme affects. In others, however, there is a notable absence of an emotional response, so that when survivors encounter situations similar to the traumatic events they have experienced, they are imbued with a degree of emotional numbness that can easily be confused with indifference by both outside observers and survivors themselves. To further complicate the clinical picture, these apparently opposing reactions—intense reactivity and marked unresponsiveness—frequently alternate in the same person. In some cases, it can seem difficult or nearly impossible to assemble the resultant kaleidoscope of acute sensations and perceptions into a coherent, comprehensible narrative. In contrast, other survivors may remember the traumatic event in considerable detail but with a detached coolness that is markedly inconsistent with the reactions one would expect in the face of a catastrophic incident.

How can we explain these apparently contradictory effects of having lived through traumatic circumstances? It is essential to appreciate that, in large part, the psychological experiences associated with the impact of trauma are rooted in bodily processes. A traumatic event is, above all, a threat to physical survival and well-being. All human beings (and other animals) are equipped with a built-in mechanism to increase the likelihood that they will endure such a threat. Many people are familiar with the name of this mechanism: the fight–flight–freeze response. Just like any other reflex, the fight–flight–freeze response is automatic and cannot be simply and easily overridden by logical reasoning or an act of will. Its automatic and immediate triggering in response to perceived danger is an intrinsic characteristic directly tied to its effectiveness. In an emergency situation, one often cannot afford to stop and think about how to respond; one must react with immediacy and without hesitancy, and must operate primarily on instinct.

A key purpose of the fight–flight reflex is to instantaneously mobilize the body to react to danger and bypass the interference of the considerably slower processes of thinking and deliberating to produce an immediate and decisive response. This mobilization generally takes the form of intense and instantaneous physiological arousal. Heart rate suddenly elevates, muscles tense, and respiration rate increases, all in the service of preparing the body to react with split-second efficiency.

Consider, for example, that someone is walking down the street when a vehicle suddenly jumps the curb and comes barreling toward the person at high speed. By the time the individual cognitively registers what is occurring and determines how to respond, it could easily be too late. They would be at risk for being run over, an outcome that obviously carries an inordinately and almost certain probability of serious injury or, even more likely, death. In an emergency situation, therefore, the considerably slower responsiveness of deliberative thinking gives way to nearly instantaneous behavior. Deliberative processes are overridden by reflexive responsivity accompanied by powerful affect that, in large part, circumvents, blunts, or entirely eclipses rational thought. Experientially, therefore, the event itself may appear both at the time and in retrospect to consist of a perceptual and sensory blur that is exceedingly difficult to translate into a cohesive, sequential narrative.

In dangerous circumstances, split-second reactivity can mean the difference between death or serious bodily mutilation and evading danger. If someone is being attacked and a reasonable probability exists that resistance will be effective, the reflex is likely to trigger the body to fight back. If it is not possible to effectively resist an attack, or if the danger exists in some form other than an attack as in a natural disaster such as an earthquake, then the reflex is likely to trigger the body to flee to a position of relative safety.

However, consider a third potential outcome of the triggering of this "survival" reflex. In the event that it is not possible or practical to either fight or flee in response to danger, the reflex might set off a decidedly different type of response: a freezing of reactivity. The freeze response is thought to be analogous to the behavior one sees in infrahuman animals when they are attacked by a predator and manifest the reaction that is commonly referred to as "playing dead" (Ataria, 2015; Nijenhuis, Vanderlinden, & Spinhoven, 1998). In reality, the endangered animal is not "playing." Its body responds to a potentially lethal attack with an immediate suppression of physiological arousal that, like the fight-or-flight responses, is reflexive, instantaneous, and not mediated by deliberative thinking. Heart rate plummets. Profound immobility sets in. Respiration rate plunges so that breathing becomes essentially undetectable to the predator. The survival value of the freeze response is that if the predator perceives the targeted animal as already being dead, it might abort its attack and leave, increasing the likelihood that its prey will survive. The recognition of the existence of this third response pattern as a reaction that functions to increase the likelihood of surviving potentially lethal circumstances has led to an expansion of the term for the reflex, now sometimes referred to as *fight–flight–freeze system* (e.g., Hannan & Orcutt,

2013; Schmidt, Richey, Zvolensky, & Maner, 2008; Thompson, Hannan, & Miron, 2014).

When someone who has experienced a traumatic event goes on to develop posttraumatic stress disorder (PTSD), the fight–flight–freeze response either remains chronically elevated long after the traumatic incident is over or continues to be set off and instantaneously spike whenever the person encounters cues associated with the traumatic event or, in some instances, merely thinks about the event. It is as if, having encountered a highly hazardous set of circumstances, the body is now primed to either constantly scan and be prepared for similar situations (in the case of chronically elevated fight–flight–freeze) or to react instantaneously whenever it apprehends the presence of elements associated with the original threatening situation. Although this "overreactivity" can create intense distress and act as a tremendous impediment to adaptive functioning in the present, its purpose as an aspect of the fight–flight–freeze response is to increase the likelihood of detecting potential sources of danger and rapidly responding to them to increase the chances of survival. Sober reasoning, which is purposefully overridden by the reflex in what are perceived as hazardous circumstances, continues to be superseded by the physiologically more fundamental instinct for survival that is governed by impulse and emotion rather than logic.

There are practical reasons for recognizing that an automatic reflexive reaction is a large part of what drives many of the manifestations of PTSD. Well-intentioned people who do not understand this aspect of traumatic reactions may exhort the PTSD sufferer to "forget about it," "put it all in the past," or "just stop thinking about it." People who are unaware of this underlying mechanism of the disorder may misperceive the person with PTSD as behaving unreasonably or being overly dramatic and self-indulgently attention-seeking. Even the person experiencing PTSD firsthand may become frustrated with themselves for "dwelling" on the incident and being unable to simply marshal the resolve to put it out of their mind.

Many of the manifestations of PTSD, both experiential and behavioral, are rendered comprehensible when perceived through the framework of the fight–flight–freeze response and its function as a mechanism for eluding serious threats to safety and survival. It becomes understandable that recollection of a perilous situation may be fragmentary and cloudy. To the degree that one recognizes that PTSD reactions in a particular individual may be driven by instinctual reflexes, it grows more obvious that attempts to directly suppress or somehow talk oneself or others out of those reactions are unlikely to be successful.

And when we understand that much of what composes PTSD is under the influence of an intrinsic and purposeful reflex, we can appreciate that treatment for effects that are largely psychological in nature are to an appreciable degree directed by an expression of bodily reactions. The emotional arousal (experienced as anxiety, anger, or some other form of distress), affective and perceptual blunting, immersion in vivid trauma-related sensations, and jumbled, incoherent trauma-related recollections that often accompany posttraumatic responses can be recognized as the psychological concomitants of physiological processes. Therefore, it becomes apparent that effective treatment often must include intervention on the physiological, bodily plane to defuse many of the manifestations of PTSD (van der Kolk, 2014). Undoubtedly, cognitive distortions are both based on the original experience of the traumatic event and emanate from the physiological reactions to a recollection of the event. Certainly, therefore, treatment strategies that intervene at the levels of cognition and behavior can be helpful when thoughtfully applied. However, failure to recognize the automatic, physiological component that often is central to PTSD is likely to promote dead ends and counterproductive efforts in therapy.

## THE SURGE IN RECOGNITION OF TRAUMA AND TRAUMATIZATION

For all its dramatic power, psychological trauma has long remained hidden in plain sight. Undergraduate and graduate students frequently are surprised to learn that, not long ago, *trauma* was a term rarely used by psychologists or other mental health professionals compared with its use today. Awareness of the potentially life-altering impact of traumatic events only emerged from relative obscurity in the late 20th century.

Before the publication in 1980 of the third edition of the *Diagnostic and Statistical Manual of Mental Disorders* (third ed. [*DSM–III*]; American Psychiatric Association, 1980), the term *posttraumatic stress disorder* and its commonly used acronym, PTSD, did not exist. Even more fundamentally, the concept of trauma itself was by no means a focus of attention among the vast majority of psychologists. Before that landmark occurrence in 1980, acknowledgment, for example, of the widespread incidence of domestic violence or the various forms of child abuse and of their often agonizing, lingering psychological consequences went almost entirely unrecognized.

I encountered a striking example of the lack of awareness of the existence of traumatic events in my role as clinical director at a psychological facility in the 1980s. Although it had been several years since the PTSD diagnosis had appeared in the *DSM–III* (American Psychiatric Association, 1980), understanding among mental health professionals of how prevalent trauma is and the impact it can have was still extremely limited. The case of a boy in his early teens was referred to the facility and was accompanied by a lengthy assessment report written by his psychiatrist. The evaluation included a detailed description of the boy's allegations that his father had repeatedly sexually molested him. From the vantage point of our current knowledge about trauma, child abuse, and its psychological impact, the boy's report was internally consistent and entirely plausible. However, the report's conclusion, which seemed markedly at odds with the account and psychological difficulties expressed by the boy, was that he was "clearly" delusional. The only apparent evidence for this deduction was the assessor's assumption that by their very nature, the boy's allegations could not be construed as credible. At the time, few practitioners would have considered accusations such as those made by the boy as lying within the realm of possibility. This example helps explain why trauma remained largely invisible for much of the 20th century. Even today, some may have serious enough questions about the likelihood of such allegations to be hesitant placing credence in them.

Societal recognition of the existence of trauma and its capacity to severely compromise psychological functioning has steadily grown since the 1980s. We now know on the basis of research findings that traumatic events, especially in the form of interpersonal violence, are exponentially more common than previously believed. According to our best current empirically based estimates regarding child sexual abuse, for example, one out of every four to five girls and approximately one out of every six to 12 boys (the reported findings for boys vary much more widely than those for girls) have been subjected to at least one instance of sexual molestation before reaching adulthood (Barth, Bermetz, Heim, Trelle, & Tonia, 2013; Dong, Anda, Dube, Giles, & Felitti, 2003; Pereda, Guilera, Forns, & Gómez-Benito, 2009; Stoltenborgh, van IJzendoorn, Euser, & Bakermans-Kranenburg, 2011). Similarly, about one out of every three women has encountered at least one episode of battering by an intimate partner in her lifetime (Black et al., 2011). Still, many people, including therapists, find it unfathomable that adult men can be victims of domestic violence. However, research-based approximations of the lifetime prevalence of this form of violence among men suggest that it is between 15% and 20% (Breiding, Black, & Ryan, 2008; Desmarais, Reeves, Nicholls, Telford, & Fiebert, 2012).

Similarly, the traumatic impact of exposure to the violence, carnage, and death that are intrinsic to combat was in previous times almost entirely invisible among most mental health professionals and the general public (Herman, 1992b). Although terms such as *soldiers' heart, shell shock*, and *combat neurosis* (Paulson & Krippner, 2007) were in use by some mental health professionals affiliated with the military in the Civil War, World War I, and World War II, respectively, they frequently were either thought of as purely medical rather than psychological in nature or were not recognized as legitimate ailments. It was widely assumed that any reasonably "normal" man (until recently, women combatants were almost completely unheard of) could weather the stressors of combat without any appreciable, lasting negative psychological effects. However, recent empirical findings have indicated that PTSD prevalence rates among combat veterans may be as high as 30% (Kulka et al., 1990; Thomas et al., 2010).

Clearly, awareness of traumatic events and their consequences has expanded radically since the 1980s. The most recent version of the *Diagnostic and Statistical Manual of Mental Disorders* (fifth ed. [*DSM–5*]; American Psychiatric Association, 2013) contains not merely the PTSD classification but an entire chapter titled "Trauma and Stressor-Related Disorders." And both within and beyond the realm of the mental health professions, it is now commonplace to encounter the terms *trauma* and *PTSD*. They frequently arise in everyday conversation, social media, and the news. Given this radical transformation among both professionals and the general public in attitudes toward and acceptance of the reality of trauma and its impact, it is little wonder that students of psychological trauma have difficulty imagining a time not too long ago when this was not the case.

Among the pivotal findings in the constantly mushrooming literature on psychological trauma are these:

- The majority of individuals in the general population—between 55% and more than 90% in various studies—have encountered at least one traumatic event during their lifetime (Kilpatrick, Badour, & Resnick, 2017). In a survey of a nationwide probability sample of adolescents and adults ages 15 to 54, about 34% of men and 25% of women reported having encountered more than one traumatic event in their lifetime (Kessler, Sonnega, Bromet, Hughes, & Nelson, 1995).

- Although the proportion of survivors who go on to develop PTSD varies from one type of traumatic event to another, for most types of traumatic events, fewer than one in 10 people in the general population who have encountered an instance of trauma will go on to develop PTSD at some point in their lifetime (Kilpatrick et al., 2017).

- A wide range of psychological diagnoses beyond those in the *DSM–5* (American Psychiatric Association, 2013) chapter "Trauma- and Stressor-Related Disorders" are associated with a history of having encountered a traumatic event, including depression, substance use disorders, eating disorders, dissociative disorders, and psychosis (Gold, 2004b; Luyten et al., 2017).

- Although the negative psychological consequences of having lived through a traumatic event can be extremely debilitating and long lasting, a number of treatment approaches have been supported as effective by scientific research (Foa, Keane, Friedman, & Cohen, 2009).

And, yet, despite the rapid expansion of knowledge about traumatic events, their psychological impact, and how to effectively treat the consequences of living through them, myths and misconceptions about traumatic events and their impact remain commonplace. For instance, individuals who have experienced an incident of trauma, whether as recently as the past few weeks or as remotely as decades ago, may hear either from laypeople or professionals that they "must" have PTSD or that they will unavoidably develop the disorder at some point. This pronouncement is strongly contradicted by the research findings just summarized. Even among victims of rape trauma, the form of traumatic event most likely to result in PTSD and that has prevalence rates more than 50% (Resnick, Kilpatrick, Dansky, Saunders, & Best, 1993; Rothbaum, Foa, Riggs, Murdock, & Walsh, 1992), the disorder is still far from universal. Studies have repeatedly shown that for most types of traumatic events, fewer than one out of 10 people will go on to exhibit the PTSD (e.g., Kessler et al., 1995; Kilpatrick et al., 2013).

For this reason, it is important to use terminology that clearly distinguishes trauma as an event from the adverse psychological impact of that event. Doing so provides an important reminder that encountering a traumatic event and developing PTSD are far from equivalent phenomena. To make this distinction clear, throughout the remainder of this volume, I use the term *trauma* to denote a traumatic incident and the designation *traumatization* to refer to the resulting negative psychological outcomes. The key point to remember is that although the vast majority of the population encounters at least one traumatic event in their lifetime, only a minority will be traumatized by the experience. Most people who encounter a traumatic situation will not be traumatized by it in the sense of experiencing ongoing adverse psychological consequences from it (Kilpatrick et al., 2017).

Other misunderstandings abound regarding treatment for PTSD. Survivors may be told there is no "cure" for PTSD and that they "will just have to learn to live with it." Alternately, they may be urged by a therapist to simply describe the traumatic event and assured that if they "just get it off your chest," a single recounting will dissipate their distress and dispel their related posttraumatic symptoms. It is not unusual for trauma survivors with PTSD to be informed that in a single session or, failing that, in a relatively brief number of sessions, certain therapies are guaranteed to successfully banish their trauma-related symptoms. A much more accurate claim would be that the manifestations of traumatization can certainly be resolved, and in some select instances with appropriate treatment, that resolution can occur in as little as one session. However, in the vast majority of cases, therapy continuing for much more than a handful of sessions is required to appreciably alleviate traumatization symptoms and for the survivor to establish a stable, productive, and gratifying work and social adjustment. Unfortunately, it is not an easy matter to access therapy designed to address traumatization. The difficulty in doing so is considerably greater when treatment for CTr is required. In the following section, I discuss the reasons for this state of affairs.

## OBSTACLES TO ACCESSING TRAUMA THERAPY

### Shortage of Trauma-Trained Therapists

Given how widespread erroneous convictions about trauma and traumatization are, it is easy to understand why prospective therapy clients—whether they live in a sparsely populated rural area or a large metropolitan setting—often report that it is daunting task to find a knowledgeable and skilled trauma therapist with whom to secure an appointment. Undoubtedly, even though the professional scientific literature has revealed a high degree of prevalence of traumatic events and consequent trauma-related psychological disorders, this state of affairs is related to the reality that few professional educational programs in the mental health disciplines provide sufficient training in how to work effectively with traumatized individuals (Courtois & Gold, 2009).

Too often, mental health practitioners assume that they are adequately equipped to conduct therapy with trauma survivors on the basis of reading a few books or attending a professional workshop. At decisive points in treatment, they may discover that the reactions their clients exhibit in response to poorly timed and unartfully executed interventions prove to be appreciably beyond their capacity to effectively address. As noted in the previous chapter, clients may be prematurely encouraged to discuss their traumatic experiences in detail only to be overwhelmed and subjected to vivid traumatic flashbacks and severe emotional or even sensory shutdown. Such incidents may result not only in retraumatization but also in a determination on the part of the client to immediately terminate treatment. Furthermore, such incidents may engender phobic avoidance of resuming therapy with a new practitioner for extended periods and, in some instances, a determination to forgo treatment forever.

In the most egregious instances, in response to uninformed attempts at trauma-related therapy, clients' difficulties substantially worsen to the point at which their symptoms appreciably increase and their capacity for educational, occupational, or social functioning is severely compromised. Individuals with PTSD who previously had little or no difficulty meeting their responsibilities on the job may end up having to go on disability. Some pursuing an education may find that they have no alternative other than to drop out of school. Others whose traumatization did not previously interfere with their social lives may begin to severely limit their interactions with other people or nearly entirely isolate themselves.

Not every helping professional can be expected to be conversant in the treatment of trauma-related difficulties. However, it is important for those in the helping professions to be trauma informed. Being *trauma informed* does not refer to being able to conduct therapy with trauma survivors; it means knowing enough about trauma to be sensitive and avoid doing harm by not intensifying the distress a traumatized individual might be experiencing (e.g., Ardino, 2014). The following case portrays an unfortunately common type of situation that occurs even in mental health treatment centers.

**Case Example: Retraumatizing Treatment**

A White woman in her 40s with severe PTSD and dissociative symptoms had an extensive history of physical and sexual abuse by her father, who would be extremely violent toward her when he was angry and consistently framed his abusive behavior as "punishment" because she had been "bad." Even though, as an adult, she realized that his allegations were groundless, she would become terrified and feel like a little child when she believed others were angry with her. She was convinced that she was going to be "punished" for being "bad."

In response to her perception that her husband was angry at her, she grew highly anxious, began having intrusive suicidal thoughts, and had tremendous difficulty staying oriented to the present. To ensure her own safety, she admitted herself at a psychiatric hospital despite being afraid that she would be seen as "crazy" and committed to a long inpatient stay. When she arrived at the hospital, even though she went there to voluntarily admit herself, she was treated roughly and involuntarily committed, which increased her anxiety even further and radically intensified her fears that she would be "incarcerated" in a long-term psychiatric facility indefinitely. Her husband came to the hospital from work in an effort to support her and explain to the staff what she was experiencing, but staff ignored him. The woman was placed in isolation for several hours, which further exacerbated her distress, before she was admitted about 8 hours after her arrival to the hospital.

On admission to the psychiatric unit, the patient briefly talked to a nurse there, the first person on staff who had spoken to her gently and had treated her kindly. The nurse took the time to listen to her account and provided her with a form to complete that changed her admission from involuntary to voluntary. By treating her humanely, the nurse was following the tenets of trauma-informed care.

The next day, the patient and her husband asked that her outpatient clinician call her primary therapist at the hospital to explain that she was a survivor of extensive, serious childhood trauma and was easily triggered. When the outpatient practitioner called to explain the situation, the inpatient therapist, a doctoral-level psychologist, assured her in an irritable tone of voice that she would complete a thorough, multiple-page assessment of the patient and see her for individual therapy, and that groups would be running all day for the patient to attend.

None of these efforts occurred. Instead, as soon as she got off the phone, the inpatient psychologist went to a location where the patient was sitting with a number of other patients and yelled at her: "Did you tell your therapist to call me? I don't have time for that! Didn't I tell you that I'm busy?" Of course, because the patient had self-admitted due to suicidal ideation aroused by her fear of anger, having the inpatient therapist yell at her was intensely disturbing. Fortunately, after the inpatient therapist has left, one of the other patients sitting nearby turned to her and asked, "Why is she being so mean to you?" This small acknowledgment from another patient helped to calm her down by confirming that she was being treated in an unwarranted manner.

Many in the mental health professions would not find this anecdote either surprising or unusual. Sadly, not only are few in the profession sufficiently trained in trauma therapy, but it is almost as rare in many settings to find therapists who are trauma informed. It is a sad irony when the very people who are expected to provide a safe haven for people with psychological distress conduct themselves instead in a way that exacerbates a crushing sense of danger.

It would not be an overstatement to frame this woman's experiences in the hospital as abusive. Ultimately, an interaction that warrants this label is the abuse of power. Those of us in the role of helping professionals are inherently invested with power in that those who seek our assistance intrinsically rely on us. This is a great responsibility, and it is incumbent on those of us who take on the roles of treaters and helpers to be attuned to the potential to act oppressively toward others—in some instances, without being focally aware of it—by virtue of failing to be mindful of the authority invested in us. To the extent that we fail to do so, we run the risk of acting in a way that is traumatizing rather than healing.

**Lack of Familiarity With Complex Posttraumatic Stress Disorder**

As we saw in the previous chapter, there is considerable contention among experts in trauma psychology whether complex posttraumatic stress disorder (C-PTSD) is a distinct syndrome requiring a substantially different treatment approach from that for PTSD. The disparity between the intricate and challenging problems of many trauma survivors and the availability of knowledgeable, well-trained practitioners grows considerably greater when the client's traumatic history extends well beyond a single, circumscribed catastrophic incident. One explicit impetus for Herman's (1992b) proposed C-PTSD diagnosis was that a number of frequently stigmatizing syndromes—including borderline personality disorder, the somatoform disorders, and the dissociative disorders—are commonly applied to individuals in therapy, especially women, in the absence of the recognition that the difficulties composing these and other disorders are often trauma related. Consequently, a major point emphasized by Herman in delineating the C-PTSD construct was that a broad array of symptoms and syndromes could be and often were an expression of an extensive, ongoing history of traumatic experiences. She proposed that these difficult-to-treat disorders could be much more effectively addressed once practitioners were alerted to the possibility that underlying these presentations was an extensive history of trauma. For example, previously seemingly inexplicable behaviors, such as the rage reactions, nonsuicidal self-injury, dissociative episodes, erratic interpersonal relationships, and fear of abandonment emblematic of borderline personality disorder, immediately become more comprehensible when we become aware that an individual's childhood was marked by pervasive ongoing maltreatment.

In the intervening decades since Herman (1992b) first introduced the construct of C-PTSD, it has become the source of intense controversy between two factions of trauma experts. One of these constituencies has found in their experience of conducting therapy for people who have undergone trauma powerful confirmation of the intricate network of psychological difficulties composing C-PTSD. The other group has strongly disputed the validity of C-PTSD as a diagnostic entity distinct from the PTSD diagnosis as it appears in the *DSM* (De Jongh et al., 2016). Proponents of the validity of C-PTSD as a syndrome distinct from PTSD as it appears in the *DSM* warn that exposure-based intervention approaches, especially when entered into early in the treatment process and without titration, can do appreciably more harm than good (Cloitre et al., 2012). Moreover, these approaches have been shown to have substantial dropout rates, to frequently lead to only marginal improvement in PTSD-related difficulties, and to fail to address the wide range of other serious and disabling problems many traumatized clients exhibit (Steenkamp, Litz, Hoge, & Marmar, 2015; Yehuda & Hoge, 2016).

Despite the contention that C-PTSD is not distinct from PTSD, a substantial and burgeoning body of research supports the validity of the C-PTSD diagnosis (Karatzias, Cloitre, et al., 2017; Karatzias et al., 2016; Litvin, Kaminski, & Riggs, 2017) and even suggests that it is more commonly occurring than PTSD as more narrowly defined (Karatzias, Shevlin, et al., 2017). The standard psychological or psychiatric diagnostic manual used in many countries outside of North America, the *International Classification of Diseases* (ICD; World Health Organization [WHO], 2018), currently in its 11th edition (ICD–11) and published by WHO, an affiliate of the United Nations, formally recognizes PTSD and C-PTSD as discrete diagnostic entities.

Beyond concerns that standard exposure-based treatment can be detrimental to individuals with an extensive trauma background, a compelling counterargument to the contention that it is unnecessary to conduct treatment for C-PTSD any differently than one would for PTSD is that the psychological difficulties that compose C-PTSD extend appreciably beyond the criteria for PTSD per se. The manual for the most extensively researched and widely respected form of exposure therapy for PTSD, prolonged exposure, explicitly states that it specifically aims to treat the symptoms of PTSD. Thus, given the much broader series of impairments associated with C-PTSD, there is no reason to expect that prolonged exposure or other exposure-based therapies would sufficiently address the entire gamut of difficulties composing C-PTSD. Moreover, the additional symptoms other than those attributable to PTSD can easily complicate attempts to address C-PTSD in the same fashion one would for survivors with PTSD alone.

## THE DEFINING CHARACTERISTICS OF TRAUMA AS AN EVENT

In all likelihood, a source of confusion regarding this point is related to the way in which Herman (1992a, 1992b) formulated the diagnostic criteria for C-PTSD. Her conceptualization, in some respects, drew from a relatively unique aspect of the PTSD diagnosis itself. Unlike other *DSM–5* diagnoses (with the exception of some of those in the "Neurodevelopmental Disorders" chapter of the *DSM–5*; American Psychiatric Association, 2013), the criteria for which focus on the symptoms of those disorders, the cause of PTSD—exposure to a traumatic event—is not only one of the diagnostic criteria but the cardinal one. Having encountered a traumatic event is a prerequisite for the diagnosis of PTSD. It is the first criterion listed in the *DSM–5* (American Psychiatric Association, 2013) under the PTSD diagnosis. This criterion, therefore, is routinely referred to as *Criterion A*, which defines traumatic events as those encompassing actual or threatened death, serious physical injury, or sexual violation.

### The Adoption of Criterion A as the Standard Definition of Trauma as an Event

Throughout the field of trauma psychology, Criterion A is considered the standard definition of what constitutes a traumatic event. Even if an individual experiences all the symptoms of PTSD, the diagnosis cannot be applied in the absence of that person's having encountered a traumatic event as defined in Criterion A—which raises an interesting issue from an empirical perspective. In instances in which research may show that events outside the parameters of Criterion A regularly are associated with the full symptom picture of PTSD, the presence of that full symptom picture may, at some point in the future, come to be construed as evidence-based grounds for extending the commonly accepted definition of what constitutes a traumatic event (Gold, Dalenberg, & Cook, 2017).

So, how did it come about that the diagnostic criteria for PTSD, in contrast to the other syndromes in the *DSM*, with the exception of certain neuropsychological developmental disorders related to demonstrable organic abnormalities, are unique in that they require the identification of a particular etiology as an essential criterion? In the years leading up to the proposal that PTSD be incorporated into the *DSM–III* (American Psychiatric Association, 1980), it was recognized that relatively independent investigations into diverse forms of violence—including child kidnapping (Terr, 1979), combat (Figley, 1978), domestic violence (Walker, 1979), and rape (Burgess & Holmstrom, 1974)—identified similar psychological effects of these experiences. The press to make the causal element of having experienced a traumatic event a prerequisite for diagnosing PTSD was a means of highlighting that divergent types of events led to essentially identical psychological consequences (Figley, 2006). At least as consequential, however, was the imperative to make it clear that the constellation of symptoms associated with these various types of trauma, ones that often had been dismissed as histrionics, faking, or, in the case of combat veterans, cowardly and desperate attempts to elude a return to the war zone, composed a cohesive, definable, and, above all, genuine diagnostic entity.

As Herman (1992b) and others (Blackwell, 2005; L. S. Brown, 2017; McKenzie-Mohr, Coates, & McLeod, 2012) have emphasized, trauma, and especially interpersonal violence trauma, is an inherently political issue because it is inextricably intertwined with power. In general terms, the perpetrators of interpersonal violence are overwhelmingly those affiliated with demographic groups that are privileged in terms of power, and those who are most often targeted for coercive control and violence belong to relatively powerless cohorts. Accordingly, men, members of ethnic majorities, and adults are more likely to engage in interpersonal violence, whereas sexual and gender minorities, ethnic minorities, and children have an inordinately greater risk of being the targets of coercion, domination, and explicit violence.

Accordingly, Herman's (1992a, 1992b) construct of C-PTSD paralleled the original PTSD diagnosis; it was framed to highlight the traumatic source of the disturbance. The primary distinction posed by Herman was that instead of representing a reaction to a single or circumscribed event as in PTSD, C-PTSD was a response to repeated or ongoing trauma (Herman, 1992a, 1992b). The psychological difficulties composing C-PTSD include those that constitute PTSD but extend well beyond them. Herman herself (1992a) seemed to suggest that

C-PTSD either can manifest as a range of other syndromes, such as borderline personality disorder, somatoform disorders, or dissociative disorders, or that these diagnoses are often mistaken for or coexist with C-PTSD. As I explain in the next chapter, CTT proposes that it is the considerably broader scope of dysfunction beyond and other than traumatization that differentiates C-PTSD from PTSD. It asserts that factors frequently accompany and are associated with a history of repeated, ongoing, or prolonged trauma. These factors can have overlapping effects with those of trauma but are distinguishable from trauma and make an independent contribution to the potentially broad array of difficulties that characterize C-PTSD.

## Divergent Patterns of Impairment in Posttraumatic Stress Disorder and Complex Posttraumatic Disorder

Thus far, we have primarily considered the differentiation in causation between PTSD and C-PTSD. Although both are manifestations of having been impacted by traumatic events, PTSD is associated with a single instance of trauma or a circumscribed traumatic situation. In contrast, C-PTSD is associated with a history of ongoing, prolonged, or repeated trauma (Herman, 1992a, 1992b). To fully appreciate the distinction between PTSD and C-PTSD, however, it is essential to be conversant with the differing traumatic effects associated with each of these diagnostic entities.

Once it is established that an individual has experienced an event that fits the Criterion A definition of trauma, four categories of symptoms must be present to diagnose PTSD as described in the *DSM–5* (American Psychiatric Association, 2013):

1. intrusion, being "haunted" by thoughts, recollections, sensations, and physiological reactions associated with the traumatic event; *flashbacks*, in which the person reexperiences the event so vividly that it compellingly feels as if it is occurring in the present, are especially unique to and emblematic of PTSD;

2. avoidance of reminders of the traumatic event or of thinking or talking about it;

3. negative beliefs or moods that first arose or intensified following the traumatic event; and

4. intensified arousal, commonly expressed in manifestations such as difficulty sleeping, impaired ability to concentrate, sensitization of the startle response, increased irritability or aggressiveness, or habitually scanning one's surroundings for signs of danger.

In addition to the presence in the person's history of a Criterion A event and symptoms from the four categories listed previously, to diagnose PTSD, the symptoms must persist for at least 1 month following the traumatic incident. The reason is that an appreciable proportion of people who encounter a traumatic incident will experience symptoms from one or all four categories representative of PTSD, but for most of them, those disturbances will subside on their own without treatment (Bryant, 2017). To avoid conflating transient posttraumatic reactions with persistent ones that are indicative of PTSD, when the symptoms of PTSD last for at least 3 days but have not persisted for a month, they fall under the designation of acute stress disorder. If they continue past 1 month, then the PTSD diagnosis is applied.

The criteria for C-PTSD originally proposed by Herman (1992b) overlap those of PTSD to some degree but are organized appreciably differently. In the first diagnostic criterion, analogous to Criterion A in PTSD, she specified that the type of traumatic experience associated with C-PTSD consists specifically of "a history of subjection to totalitarian control over a prolonged period (months or years)" (p. 121). Although she used the term *totalitarian*, Herman stipulated that this nomenclature includes such control "in sexual and domestic life" (p. 121), such as child abuse or intimate partner violence. (I prefer the term *coercive control* rather than ones such as *totalitarian*, which usually are associated with control at a systemic, especially governmental, level.) Six categories of symptoms compose the remaining criteria, each of which begins with the phrase "Alterations in. . . ." The implication contained in this phrase is that each class of symptoms is causally tied, and arises in response to, trauma. The six varieties of C-PTSD symptoms are alterations in

1) affect, such as suppressed or impulsive anger, suppressed or impulsive sexual expression, or persistent negative mood;
2) consciousness, consisting of various forms of dissociative experiences;
3) self-perception, such as shame and alienation from others;
4) perceptions of the perpetrator, such as viewing the perpetrator as possessing an inordinate degree of power;
5) interpersonal relationships, including enduring mistrust; [and]
6) sense of meaning in life, such as the absence of a sense of purpose. (p. 121)

Herman (1992b) noted at the time that the framers of the ICD were considering a syndrome similar to C-PTSD that was provisionally referred to as "personality change from catastrophic experience" (p. 122). A quarter of a century later, the current version of that diagnostic manual, the ICD–11 (WHO, 2018), recognizes both PTSD and C-PTSD as diagnostic entities, a distinction that has long been proposed for inclusion in the *DSM–5* but has yet to be accepted. Herman and the framers of the ICD conveyed that the nature of the difficulties encompassed by C-PTSD is much more fundamental than those difficulties composing PTSD; they consist of impairment at the level of the survivor's very sense of self and expression of character (consistent with the current ICD–11 term *disturbances in self-organization*).

An essential consideration in formulating treatment for individuals with PTSD or C-PTSD is that there is an especially high frequency of co-occurrence with other disorders. A clear majority of those who meet criteria for PTSD exhibit at least one other mental disorder, and a substantial proportion qualify for three or more coexisting diagnoses (Brady, Killeen, Brewerton, & Lucerini, 2000). Disorders that commonly co-occur with PTSD include depression (Creamer, Burgess, & McFarlane, 2001; Hauffa et al., 2011; Pietrzak,

Goldstein, Southwick, & Grant, 2012), substance use disorders (Bhalla, Stefanovics, & Rosenheck, 2019; Ouimette & Brown, 2003), dissociative disorders (Bremner, Steinberg, Southwick, Johnson, & Charney, 1993; Brende, 1987), somatization disorders (Escalona, Achilles, Waitzkin, & Yager, 2004), and psychotic disorders (Seedat, Stein, Oosthuizen, Emsley, & Stein, 2003). A study of African American women found an even higher prevalence of substance use, major depression, and dissociation among participants with C-PTSD than those with PTSD (Powers et al., 2017).

Obviously, the coexistence of these other symptom patterns in the clinical picture complicate therapy; intervention is not merely a matter of applying a series of individual treatments for separate diagnoses. For example, substance use disorders often co-occur with PTSD. Reliance on substances is frequently a means by which people with PTSD attempt to suppress trauma-related distress and intrusive recollections of trauma (Najavits, 2015b). The reliance on substances to manage traumatic reactions regularly results in an exacerbation of the symptoms of PTSD when substance use is appreciably reduced or eliminated. Conversely, there is reason to suspect that marked exacerbation of reliance on substances or relapse into active substance abuse if abstinence has been attained often occurs if trauma-focused interventions are introduced too early or too forcefully. Sharkansky, Brief, Peirce, Meehan, and Mannix (1999) found that a greater level of substance abuse was related to situations involving unpleasant emotions in participants with PTSD. Similarly, Norman, Tate, Anderson, and Brown (2007) reported a greater likelihood for relapse among those in their sample with PTSD accompanied by anger, anxiety, fear, and depression.

As the example of co-occurring PTSD and substance abuse illustrates, the interconnection between coexisting disorders is an intricate one that complicates treatment considerably and requires careful planning and execution of interventions and their sequencing. The same is true for CTr, clinical presentations in which the disturbances in self-organization component of C-PTSD co-occurs not with PTSD but with other disorders that are traceable to past traumatic experiences.

The case vignette that follows illustrates the extremely severe and disabling consequences that the combined impact of an ineffective family background and an exceptionally violent traumatic event had on a young woman. Several courses of treatment either did not result in amelioration of her difficulties or appreciably intensified her traumatization. Such situations underscore why these types of cases are accurately labeled *complex*—ones for which approaches that attempt to immediately address traumatization or are not individualized are highly unlikely to be helpful and instead carry considerable risk of compounding existing psychological impairment.

**Case Example: The Risks of Prematurely Trauma-Focused Treatment for Complex Traumatization**

Valerie, a Latinx, was in her mid-30s and living in California when she began CTT-oriented treatment. Her parents were divorced when she was 9 years old. As is often the case, they were awarded joint custody, and she spent alternating weeks at each of her parents' homes. Both parents were extremely critical of Valerie; perhaps they were, in part, deflecting onto her their anger at each other. Soon after the divorce, her father, a small business owner, insisted that Valerie begin working at his office. Although she was only 9 years old at the time, she was placed in a complex role in the work environment that would have been demanding for a fully grown adult. Nevertheless, her father expected her to perform at an unrealistically flawless level with little training or guidance. He would berate her mercilessly any time she did not live up to the unrealistic standards he had set for her, and he frequently cursed at her and characterized her as "hopeless," "inept," and "a total idiot." In reality, she was performing well beyond what could reasonably be expected of most people her age; by 12 years old, she had assumed many of the functions of an office manager. Her mother, for her part, was self-absorbed and emotionally overreactive.

Just as important but not nearly as obvious, neither of Valerie's parents provided her with consistent affection, structure, or guidance. They both seemed so preoccupied with their resentment toward each other and their own pursuits that Valerie did not capture much of their attention other than when they were irritated and let out their frustrations on her. Valerie was unusually bright, had excelled academically from the earliest grades, and seemed so competent that perhaps her parents did not recognize that no matter how gifted, every child needs parental support and direction. In contrast, her older sister, who in adolescence acted out impulsively, garnered a great deal of attention from both parents. Valerie's verbal facileness and sharp intellect seemed to work against her. In the light of these superior abilities, her parents expected her to operate at a level of functioning that would have been unrealistic for any child.

One evening, when she was in her early teens, her father flew into a tirade and repeatedly screamed at her that she was a "slut" and a "whore," rebukes she had heard from him many times before even though her behavior had never been remotely consistent with this characterization. His rage ended with her father yelling at her to "get out of my house" and "go stay with your mother." Valerie ran into her room in tears. She began assembling her belongings to go to her mother's house when her phone rang. It was her friend Tina. Sobbing, Valerie confided in Tina what had just happened. Tina, sounding sympathetic, suggested that she come spend the night at her house. Her own parents, she explained, were away, so it was a perfect night for Valerie to stay over. In a radical break from a long-standing history of submissive compliance, Valerie finished packing and left her father's to go spend the night at Tina's.

When she arrived at Tina's house, Valerie felt grateful that there were no parents in the house. Only Tina's brother, Rick, who was in his mid-20s, was there. For some time now, Valerie had admired him. She, Tina, and Rick gathered in Rick's room, and soon afterward, Tina announced that she was going to the kitchen to fix the three of them something to eat. Almost immediately once Tina was out of the room, Rick sat down on the bed next to Valerie and placed his arm around her shoulder in a gesture that seemed to radiate consolation and comfort. In that moment, she felt a sense of solace and peace that she had rarely encountered previously.

An instant later, everything suddenly shifted. Rick began nuzzling and then kissing Valerie, who reacted with alarm and froze. In a flash, Rick pulled her off the bed and down onto the floor, straddling her and ripping off her clothes. Valerie struggled frantically, but despite her determination to get Rick off of her, his considerably greater weight and larger frame made it impossible for her to accomplish anything beyond exhausting herself. Rick's face alternately registered annoyance, amusement, and chilling resolve as Valerie continued to futilely try to wriggle her way out from under him and get away.

Before she could fully absorb what was happening, two men who appeared to be about that same age as Rick rushed into the room, laughing derisively and joining Rick in overpowering and sexually assaulting her. It did not take Valerie long to discover that the more intensely she fought back and the more loudly she screamed to Tina to come help her, the more severe and painful were the blows she received in response. Worse still, there was no sign of Tina. Valerie had no idea where Tina had gone and later came to wonder whether she was aligned with the assailants and had therefore intentionally lured her there. Soon the wind was knocked out of Valerie, and her muscles ached so badly that she could hardly move. In the meantime, Rick and the other two assailants verbally mocked her with humiliating taunts that resonated and seemed to merge with her father's sneering accusations earlier that same evening that she was a "slut" and a "whore." To a great extent, their ridicule, infused with coarse and humiliating obscenities, was as deeply lacerating as the physical and sexual aspects of the attack. It was as if they were confirming all the demeaning insults her father had hurled at her over the years. "Come on, you pig, you know want this." "Hey, slut, stop pretending you're not enjoying it." In Valerie's mind, what she was hearing from her assailants was proof not that she was being victimized but that she deserved what was happening to her. Hadn't she elected, instead of going to her mother's house, to stay over at her friend Tina's house—a place without adult supervision—without letting her parents know where she was going?

Terrified and incapacitated, Valerie floated in and out of consciousness. In retrospect, she had trouble discerning whether she had repeatedly fainted, sustained a blow to the head, or was simply overwhelmed by the enormity of what was taking place. In any event, her recollection afterward consisted of a series of disconnected horrifying episodes during which she floated up into consciousness and was unable to track how much time had passed or to knit what she did remember into an intelligible order. The shades in Rick's room were drawn, so there was no way for her to distinguish day from night. She had no idea whether hours or days had passed.

At one point, a sharp blade was held against her neck, releasing a warm, sickening rivulet of blood. At that juncture, faced with the certainty that she was about to die, her frantic panic was suddenly replaced with a deep and pervasive emotional numbness. At various times, she was aware of the presence of all three men; at other times, just one or two. The longer the ordeal continued, the clearer it was to her that she was not going to leave the house alive.

Then, at a certain point, she came to, surrounded by darkness and silence. Afraid to move, petrified that her assailants would return at any minute, she listened anxiously for any sounds indicative of others moving about the house. Hearing nothing, dazed and aching, she slowly pulled herself to a sitting position a little bit at a time. As her eyes adjusted to the darkness, she thought she could make out articles of her clothing scattered about her. Sluggishly but deliberately, doing her best not to alert the others, she located her undergarments, top, and jeans, and painfully and haltingly pulled them on. Although she was sure she would be intercepted before she could make it outside, once she was dressed, she resolved to at least make an effort to escape. In a frantic dash for the front door, she arrived at the threshold to the outside and was astounded to discover that no one was there to stop her from fleeing. As she reached the outside, the lighting suggested to her that it was early dawn. After that, all she could recall was spotting the rear wheel of her car and racing blindly toward it.

The next thing she knew, she was in school. As far as she could gauge, several months had elapsed. She remembered nothing between the time she made it out of Tina's house and when she found herself sitting in a high school classroom. It was obvious that, somehow, she had been going about her day-to-day routine for all that time, but she had absolutely no recollection of anything subsequent to emerging from Tina's house.

For the remaining 2 years of high school, she somehow did well academically despite living in a blurry twilight state of mind that continued a year or so into college. Even as she gradually returned to a more alert state of consciousness, she rarely thought about the terrifying events that had occurred at Tina's house for quite some time. Yet, if she had stopped to consider it, she would have realized that something was profoundly different about her. The dazed and emotionally shut down state that had overcome her when she was sure she was approaching the moment of her death had never receded. She often felt that she was operating on automatic pilot, mechanically going through the motions of life without really being present.

It was another year, as a college junior, before she even entertained the possibility of seeing a therapist. She had become so accustomed to her blunted emotional state that it did not occur to her that psychological help was needed. Toward the end of her junior year, Valerie began seeing a clinician; she seemed kind and well-intentioned. However, other than oblique references to something too disturbing to talk about that had happened to her a few years earlier, Valerie adamantly resisted encouragement to unburden herself by opening up about what had happened.

Somewhere between 2 and 3 years into the treatment, Valerie's therapist suggested that they use hypnosis. Despite some apprehension, Valerie agreed to give it a try. But in the midst of the hypnosis, she fell silent and unresponsive, and stared blankly ahead—at least that is what the therapist saw. From Valerie's vantage point, everything went black. The next thing she knew, she was fighting to catch her breath and struggled to focus on her surroundings. The following day, the therapist called her and explained that she did not consider herself equipped to be helpful to Valerie. Apparently unnerved by the unresponsive state Valerie had suddenly fallen into and at a loss to know how to respond to it, the clinician informed Valerie that she would have to refer her elsewhere.

After that session, Valerie became profoundly more distressed than she had been previously. She was now unable to get images of the assault out of her mind, and she found herself beginning to have nightmares and flashbacks about it. She made a vow to herself to bury herself in her college studies and actively cultivate the numbness that she had been immersed in ever since the assault at Tina's house as a means of managing her distress. She made it through to graduation, applied to law schools, and was accepted.

Although extremely hesitant to reenter treatment, by the second semester of her legal studies, Valerie's worsening condition led her back to therapy with a clinician whom a knowledgeable friend assured her had the reputation of being a trauma specialist. In session, at his prompting, Valerie was able to marshal enough courage to gradually assemble a written account of the assault. Despite her best efforts to compose a coherent narrative, she was hampered by a number of gaps in her memory and remained uncertain about the sequence of events. However, writing about what had happened didn't seem to lead to any noticeable improvement in her trauma-related difficulties. Instead, her self-doubt and self-reproach about her now much more acute reaction to the incident was appreciably compounded when this therapist told her, "I don't know what you're so upset about." He continued, "I've seen other people go through much worse without being as distressed by it as you are." This statement only served to intensify Valerie's self-reproach that she was making too big a deal about an event that was now several years in the past and should, as far as she was concerned, no longer be bothering her.

Despite her appreciably elevated distress after two courses of counterproductive treatment, Valerie had completed law school and started working for a law firm in the Midwest, several states away from where she had grown up and gone to college. Although she was suffering greatly, she still was able to successfully complete her legal studies, pass the bar exam, and obtain a job with a law firm. These accomplishments reflect the presence of abilities and a level of emotional stamina that could serve as powerful resources in treatment. Given her level of distress and impairment, this is a point that could be easily overlooked.

Nevertheless, as the stress of her new job intensified, Valerie found her anxiety quickly escalating to the point where she was experiencing protracted flashbacks that, at times, lasted several hours a day and kept her from sleeping at night. Periodically, she would find herself on the floor of her bedroom in the early morning hours, terrified, unable to move, reexperiencing excruciating pain, and buffeted by the derisive taunts her attackers had bombarded her with echoing in her head. She felt she had no choice but to seek treatment with yet another therapist, her third attempt at receiving help for her trauma-related disturbances. That therapy seemed to neither worsen nor ameliorate her distress. Eventually, she begrudgingly accepted that she could not maintain her job at the law firm. Between the many days she had missed due her flashbacks and insomnia, and her degree of difficulty focusing, she was amazed that the firm had not already let her go before she elected to resign and return to her hometown in California.

Valerie had hoped that relief from the pressures of employment as an attorney and a return to the familiarity of the town where she had grown up and gone to college would lead to a reduction in her distress, flashbacks, and difficulty sleeping. Sadly, this was not the case. Vivid images of the assault that lasted for much of the day continued to be a frequent occurrence, and Valerie began to wonder how long she could tolerate living this way. She grew preoccupied with suicide, and, at one point, blurted out to her friend Diane how miserable she was and alluded to having gone through a hellish experience that she could not push out of her mind. Valerie immediately regretted having confided in Diane, but, fortunately, rather than probing for details, Diane urged her to return to therapy.

It was at this point that Valerie began CTT. By now, even the most limited mention of the assault she had endured as a teenager risked triggering intense flashbacks and dissociative states. The inadequate parental support during her formative years took their own toll and appreciably compounded the debilitating impact of the assault. Valerie's previous therapy was trauma focused but did not seem to consider the contribution of developmental deprivation to her difficulties, a factor likely obscured by Valerie's high level of intelligence and academic and professional attainment.

Trauma and its impact compose intricate territory. We have examined the nature of trauma: how traumatic events can sensitize the fight–flight–freeze response to promote continued reverberations of the trauma experience and simultaneously motivate strenuous attempts to avoid those traumatic echoes. We also explored the important conceptual distinction between trauma as event and traumatization as the negative psychological consequences of traumatic incidents. We also have seen how this and other decisive understandings have emerged from empirical research, and we have considered the reasons why, despite our growing knowledge, receipt of effective treatment for traumatization remains elusive. We now have a foundation from which to explore this guiding principle of CTT—that developmental adversity often goes hand in hand with prolonged childhood trauma and accompanies and markedly compounds its crippling effects. The role of this developmental deprivation is the central topic of the next chapter.

# 3

# In the Background
*Inadequate Interpersonal Developmental Resources*

Chapter 2 of this volume provided an overview of how psychological trauma surfaced from relative obscurity to become a continually expanding focus of study. As a result, psychological trauma has gained wide acceptance as a source of serious psychological impairment. The establishment of the posttraumatic stress disorder (PTSD) diagnosis clearly was a turning point in this process. Approximately a decade after the construct of PTSD was introduced via the *Diagnostic and Statistical Manual of Mental Disorders* (third ed. [*DSM–III*]; American Psychiatric Association, 1980), Herman (1992a, 1992b) and, soon afterward, others (Allen, Coyne, & Huntoon, 1998; Roth, Newman, Pelcovitz, van der Kolk, & Mandel, 1997; Zlotnick et al., 1996) vastly extended our understanding of traumatization via the diagnostic construct of complex posttraumatic stress disorder (C-PTSD; Herman, 1992a, 1992b), which pointed to the potential of prolonged subjugation trauma to even more radically alter psychological functioning.

This chapter explains how contextual trauma therapy (CTT) differs from other trauma-related treatment approaches by highlighting aspects of the childhood backgrounds of complex traumatization (CTr) survivors not as explicitly addressed in other models. At its core, CTT builds on and further extends the concept of CTr by drawing attention to the developmental deprivation that regularly accompanies ongoing childhood trauma. Just as Herman and others (e.g., Allen et al., 1998; Herman, 1992a, 1992b; Roth et al., 1997; Zlotnick et al., 1996) have expanded our understanding of the symptomatic reach that traumatic events could have, CTT proposes that ongoing or repeated childhood maltreatment almost invariably occurs within a larger context of a developmentally inadequate upbringing, and that the developmentally deficient environment both compounds the destructive consequences of trauma and creates difficulties over and above those attributable to trauma itself. The practical implication of this perspective is that the gaps and warps that result from this interpersonal/developmental context require treatment approaches appreciably different from those that are effective for trauma resolution, and that, therefore, therapy for CTr needs to explicitly target these sources of impaired functioning.

## ROLE OF DEVELOPMENTAL DEPRIVATION

Careful exploration in this volume of the accounts of many survivors of CTr reveals key elements in their backgrounds beyond trauma that powerfully contribute to their difficulties in psychological adjustment. It is these clients, such as Valerie, whose traumatization and first few attempts at treatment were described in Chapter 2, that CTT was designed to help. These are people who not only have been faced with multiple traumatic experiences in their lifetimes, often beginning early in childhood, but who grew up in circumstances that did not adequately provide for their developmental needs.

It is awareness of and responsiveness to this second element—gaps and warps in learning, socialization, enculturation and psychological development; a legacy of a paucity of support, guidance, and instruction during childhood and adolescence—that distinguish the theory and practice of CTT from other approaches. Just as recognizing the very existence of trauma and its adverse impact on adjustment entailed a perceptual shift (discussed in Chapter 2 in the section The Surge in Recognition of Trauma and Traumatization) with a myriad of beneficial consequences, becoming aware of the context in which ongoing childhood maltreatment trauma commonly occurs—growing up in a deficient family environment—entails and promotes a transformation in outlook.

The irony is that the powerful influence of a trauma-informed understanding of psychological functioning can be so profound that it can easily obscure the more subtle but equally decisive impact of the interpersonal developmental context that promotes child abuse trauma. From a CTT framework, CTr is not merely the result of multiple traumatic events but of the dual impact of those events and of having been reared in circumstances that did not adequately equip the survivor to navigate the intricate demands of adult functioning. When this dual impact is fully appreciated, the resulting perspective provides a solid framework for discerning its consequences and effectively addressing them to substantially improve treatment in a way that better meets the needs of survivors of CTr. In practical terms, what is crucial about awareness of the interpersonal/developmental context of ongoing early trauma is that its resolution requires approaches other than trauma-focused exposure techniques or other forms of trauma processing. Strategies that help survivors remediate what they missed out on developmentally are required.

Consider, for example, Valerie's situation (see case example in Chapter 2). Her brutal sexual and physical assault in adolescence by three men was extremely violent and, at certain points, appeared life-threatening. It unquestionably could be expected to have long-lasting traumatic effects. However, what may be less obvious, and could even be overlooked without taking a careful history, was the degree to which Valerie's upbringing did not adequately prepare her for the demands of adulthood. Her parents not only were verbally abusive toward her but also failed to be sufficiently supportive or affectionate toward her. Valerie's intelligence and academic ability was misconstrued by them as reflecting a level of self-sufficiency and practical functioning way beyond what could reasonably be expected from someone her age. As a result, despite her considerable academic and practical abilities, the impact of the ordeal she suffered was greatly compounded by her limited capacity for coping emotionally and a firm conviction that her only option was to manage on her own any difficulties she encountered in life. She firmly believed that if she were unsuccessful in handling problematic situations by herself, it was due to nothing other than her own inherent incompetence.

Like Valerie, survivors themselves are rarely aware of the source of their limited abilities to function effectively in the adult world. Because they have little or no basis for comparison, they often have no way of recognizing that unlike their more fortunate peers, they did not receive the affection, direction, attention, or opportunities to learn by example from adults proficient in life skills that would have rendered them more capable. They are unlikely to have had extensive contact with families other than their own and therefore unable to observe cohesive family life and consistently responsive parenting.

Although trauma survivors such as Valerie may be unaware of why they experience difficulties in adapting to adult living, they frequently are painfully cognizant that they are struggling mightily with matters that appear easy for other people to master. Almost always, they blame themselves for being less competent at managing life than others seem to be and denigrate themselves for being so inept. Often a childhood marked by a lack of reliably consistent affection and guidance practically guarantees that a survivor has been deprived of other aspects of adequate parenting that will lead to difficulty managing life. At times, survivors of CTr pointedly express that they not only feel inept, but that their experience is one of never having grown up and become effective adults. The following vignette is a particularly compelling example of this phenomenon.

**Case Example: Prominent Deficits in Functional Adaptation**
Chet, a homeless White man in his 50s, was referred for psychotherapy by a government agency that paid for his treatment. He had been sexually molested repeatedly as a child and had grown up with distant and uninvolved parents, neither of whom had graduated high school and both of whom precariously maintained at a barely adequate level of adjustment. Although he had considerable problems doing so, he struggled mightily to live the way other people did by trying to establish consistent employment, financial

stability, an organized household, and a structured lifestyle. Repeatedly, however, he would find these objectives beyond his grasp and slide into homelessness. Each time this occurred, he would resolutely dedicate himself to finding a job, getting hired, maintaining employment, saving the money to secure a place to live, and establishing a household. Often his efforts would be subverted by his inadequate emotional restraint and limited social skills, which would make it extremely difficult to get along with supervisors and coworkers or otherwise manage the routine tasks of daily living. Consequently, within a few weeks of obtaining work, he would find himself in an altercation on the job or engage in some other form of rash behavior that would result in his being fired, leaving him with no income and landing him back on the street. Once he was homeless again, Chet responded to the stress of having lost what he had struggled so intensely to establish by abusing alcohol for a time until he dedicated himself again to stopping drinking so he could make another attempt to work toward a more secure life.

This cycle continued: Chet would attain sobriety, find employment, establish enough financial stability to be able to rent a place to live, and then impulsively do something that would lead him back into homelessness. On one occasion, he had been working for several weeks, found a place to live, and seemed to be establishing a stable lifestyle. On his day off from work, idle and bored, it occurred to him to buy a television to relieve the monotony and give him something to do when he was not at work. (This was at a time when one could use an antenna to receive a television signal rather than rely on cable or the Internet.) He remembered seeing an electronics store within walking distance of his apartment. He walked to the store, purchased a portable television set, brought it home, and got it working. Later in the day, as dinnertime approached, it occurred to him that he had nothing to eat in the house. Only then did he realize that he had spent all but his last few dollars on the television, his rent was due in a few days, and he would not be receiving his next paycheck for more than a week. Unable to pay his rent and with little money to even purchase groceries, Chet was soon homeless again.

During this episode, Chet continued to unfailingly and promptly attend his scheduled psychotherapy sessions even though it was a hardship for him to get to the therapy office, which required travel across town and transfers along three bus routes. Lack of motivation to benefit from treatment and overcome his difficulties, therefore, clearly was not a factor in explaining his repeated cycles of striving and backsliding.

Sometime after his purchase of the television had landed him back in a state of homelessness, in the midst of addressing an unrelated issue during a therapy session, Chet suddenly fell silent and gazed at the floor. After a few minutes he raised his head, looked at the therapist, and said, "You know, you really don't know who I am. You look at me, and you see a man in his 50s. But inside, I'm a 9-year-old boy."

Imagine sending a 9-year-old child off to get a job, rent an apartment, maintain it, and be completely responsible for taking care of himself. To do so would simply be unreasonable or unrealistic. But what Chet was conveying was a type of self-experience shared by many people who grew up with both ongoing maltreatment and a lack of developmental support. They do not perceive themselves as fully grown, competent adults. In desperate or unguarded moments, they may reveal that they feel like "a child in an adult's body" or that they have "never have felt like an adult."

In certain respects, they are correct. From the perspective of CTT, this self-perception and the constraints on their ability to function are not merely reflections of their trauma-related symptoms, nor are they even exclusively the result of trauma-related interference with psychological development.[1] They are also and often primarily a consequence of having grown up in an interpersonal environment that did not adequately foster and support the attainment of the full array of capacities—emotional, social, intellectual, knowledge-based, practical—needed to negotiate day-to-day life as an adult. The particular areas of inadequacy may differ considerably from one survivor of childhood adversity to another in light of the particular capacities for adult functioning that the household they grew up in failed to support. However, whatever the areas of adaptation are that need remediation, they frequently are extremely pronounced in their impact and yet largely unrecognized by others. Paradoxically, this is especially likely to be the case for survivors such as Valerie, whose areas of exceptional ability or functioning acted to obscure her adaptive deficits. In general, we tend to assume that anyone who has the physical appearance of being an adult will function accordingly. If we do notice anomalies in behavior, we are likely to attribute them to some form of psychopathology rather than to a simple absence of knowledge, skills, socialization, or enculturation ascribable to having been reared in interpersonally impoverished[2] circumstances. It is this factor that extends well beyond traumatization itself that CTT draws attention to and seeks to address.

## ADVERSE CHILDHOOD EXPERIENCES AS MARKERS OF AN INEFFECTIVE FAMILY ENVIRONMENT

Careful clinical assessment of the forms of psychological problems and of the historical background of therapy clients who have extensive past trauma frequently reveals that these psychologically overwhelming incidents occurred within a larger context characterized by the relative absence of psychologically constructive influences that, for one reason or another, were unavailable to

---

[1] Some theorists, such as van der Kolk (2005) and Ford, Pinazzola, van der Kolk, and Grasso (2011), consider trauma itself to be the source of developmental deficiencies in survivors of prolonged childhood trauma.

[2] The hardships of financial deprivation on both parents and children may increase the risk that a child's developmental environment is interpersonally inadequate, but there is wide variation in the child-rearing abilities in impoverished households. Conversely, ineffective child rearing can and unquestionably does exist in households at all economic strata, including in those at the highest levels of wealth (Luthar & Latendresse, 2005).

them. Children do not grow up to be functional, content, productive adults without the investment of appreciable time and dedication of their parents, other family members, and the larger community in which they are embedded. If one is attuned to exploring only the dramatic and severely damaging occurrences in traumatized clients' lives but not to the much more subtle matter of what was missing from their interpersonal environment during their formative years, many of their difficulties and the factors responsible for those difficulties are highly likely to be overlooked. Chet's repeating cycle of homelessness, drinking, stabilization, and a return to homelessness, for instance, could readily be assumed to be a direct outgrowth of his traumatization, his alcohol problem, or the interaction of the two, rather than also being recognized largely as manifestations of having been poorly equipped to handle the functional requirements of adulthood.

In the late 1990s, a truly revolutionary, unusually large-scale study—the Adverse Childhood Experiences Study—appeared in the psychological research literature (Felitti et al., 1998; Stevens, 2012). More than 17,000 participants were recruited for this investigation from among residents of the San Diego, California, area who had received their medical services from the Kaiser Permanente Foundation. The study grew out of the experiences of Vincent Felitti, who oversaw a weight loss program designed to improve the health and longevity of people suffering from extreme obesity, especially those weighing more than 400 pounds. What led Felitti to initiate the study was the observation that some program participants appeared to have been successful, losing large amounts of weight in a short period, only to quickly return to their former size even more rapidly than they had shed pounds.

An astute professional, Felitti was determined to explain the apparent paradox that those patients who seemed to have been most successful during the course of the program were among those who were the quickest to return to their previous overweight status (Stevens, 2012). He therefore set about interviewing these patients with the aim of resolving this mystery (Stevens, 2012). What he was told by several of them was that after completing the program, they felt uncomfortable at their lower weight and intentionally turned their efforts toward approximating their previous weight status. Among this group were a number of respondents who explained to Felitti that they had been molested as youngsters. These episodes of childhood sexual abuse had left them feeling that they would be safer from sexual advances if they were heavy because they believed this would make them less attractive to other people, or that at their higher weight, they would be better equipped to fight off potential assailants. In response to one or both of these motivations, born of a history of childhood abuse, they had intentionally scrambled to return to their former weight status.

Felitti was powerfully affected by the implications of these follow-up interviews. He realized that the weight loss program and similar attempts to help at-risk patients establish and maintain habits that could help them prevent future disease and extend their lifespans could be rendered useless if early detrimental experiences fueled patterns of behavior antithetical to healthy lifestyles (Stevens, 2012). Consequently, rather than pursue his previous interest in developing such programs, he became determined to empirically assess the impact of adverse experiences in childhood on later health-related habits (Stevens, 2012). With funding from the Centers for Disease Control and Prevention, he assembled a team with several other physician-researchers and recruited as many adult health care recipients at Kaiser Permanente San Diego as possible to participate in the investigation (Stevens, 2012). Study participants were administered a lengthy, detailed interview about their health histories (Felitti et al., 1998), including questions about types of traumatic and otherwise adverse experiences they may have encountered before age 18.

The study findings were profound and disturbing, and had momentous implications for the medical and mental health professions. Felitti and his colleagues identified 10 adverse childhood experiences (ACEs; Dong et al., 2004; see also Dong, Anda, Dube, Giles, & Felitti, 2003), each of which in and of itself increased the likelihood of engaging in a sizable number of health-risk behaviors, exhibiting a broad range of medical difficulties, or manifesting any of a considerable array of psychological syndromes (Chapman, Dube, & Anda, 2007). These results were especially remarkable because the average age of the participants in the study was in the fifties; what this suggested was that environmental factors encountered before age 18 could lead to lasting constellations of poor health habits, medical disorders, and debilitating psychological impairment decades later.

Felitti and his coinvestigators (Dube et al., 2001) noted that the 10 ACEs detected by the research can be grouped into three different categories: abuse (i.e., verbal, physical, sexual); neglect (i.e., emotional, physical); and household dysfunction (i.e., losing a parent to death, separation, or divorce before age 18; witnessing domestic violence; growing up in a household in which at least one member had a serious mental illness or depression, or attempted suicide; growing up in a household in which at least one member abused alcohol or street drugs; having a household member go to prison). Indicators of child abuse trauma, child neglect, and household dysfunction were found to be interrelated (Dong et al., 2003). In addition, all were associated with the increased probability of the same wide range of psychological and medical disorders later in life (Anda, Butchart, Felitti, & Brown, 2010; Felitti, 2002).

Moreover, the effect of the ACEs was found to be cumulative, constituting a dose–response relationship (Felitti et al., 1998). The presence of one ACE in someone's background heightens the likelihood that person will exhibit one or several of a large collection of health risk behaviors, psychological difficulties, and medical problems. A childhood marked by two ACEs further augments the probability of the same damaging outcomes. Three ACEs additionally increases the possibility of these harmful consequences, and so on.

A pattern of the escalating probability of a wide variety of forms of impairment in adulthood as the number of types of adversity in a person's childhood rises is explicitly and vividly illustrated by the statistical output of the ACEs explorations. It is the basis for one of the most startling findings of the ACEs research: The average life expectancy of someone with six or more ACEs is almost 20 years less than someone with no ACEs in his or her background (D. W. Brown et al., 2009). At a certain critical mass, the data suggested, childhood adversity could ultimately prove lethal. This finding both confirms the suspected relationship that originally intrigued Felitti and conveys how dire the consequences of that association can be.

How, then, are we to construe the nature of those ACEs that are not traumas but that have comparable effects? What do these two conceptually distinct types of childhood adversity have in common that might account for their mutual association with the same damaging outcomes? The answer is contained in the following observation by Felitti (2002) about a central implication of the ACEs investigation:

> Given an exposure to one [ACE] category, there is 80% likelihood of exposure to another category. . . . One may miss the forest for the trees if one studies these categories individually. They do not occur in isolation; for instance, a child does not grow up with an alcoholic parent or with domestic violence *in an otherwise supportive and well-functioning household* [emphasis added]. (p. 361)

This succinctly worded observation is, at the same time, more subtle and more expansive in its implications, and of at least as much import as the dose–response relationship revealed by the ACE study. It highlights that the ACEs are not just deleterious influences that exist independently of each other and have additive impact. What Felitti (2002) is drawing our attention to is that the ACEs are indicators or markers of a comprehensive context of ineffective household functioning in which parenting abilities are inadequate so that there is a failure to provide sufficient support for psychological development, socialization, and enculturation. As a result, adult functioning is impaired, an outcome that, if not addressed, is likely to persist indefinitely.

In the preceding quote, what Felitti (2002) conveyed is of momentous import and appears to have overshadowed for a long time another implication of the ACEs investigations frequently overlooked. It is not a surprising or novel finding that childhood trauma can have a profound impact on psychological functioning in adulthood. It is certainly noteworthy that the ACEs also have serious medical consequences. But there is a more subtle inference to be drawn from the study's findings related to the fact that not all 10 of the ACEs factors are traumas. Although at least half of the ACEs do not constitute forms of trauma, these nontraumatic ACE factors have similar long-term damaging consequences.

This point was explicitly recognized by Kalmakis and Chandler (2014) in a review of 128 published articles on the topic of ACEs (although not all of the articles used that particular designation). They emphasized how the ACEs composing neglect have similar consequences for the child as those consisting of child abuse:

> Childhood maltreatment, including child abuse and neglect, is often used interchangeably with adverse childhood experiences, although it differs from the latter term in not capturing family dysfunction or the influence of the social environment. (p. 1492)

Elsewhere in the same article, they stated,

> The concept of adverse childhood experiences represents a larger, more overarching concept than the terms child abuse, neglect and maltreatment. Adverse childhood experiences encompass not only harmful acts to a child or neglect of a child's needs but also familial and social-environmental influence. (Kalmakis & Chandler, 2014, p. 1493)

## FEATURES AND CONSEQUENCES OF GROWING UP IN AN INEFFECTIVE FAMILY

The more ACEs that are present in a household, the greater the probability that a pervasive interpersonal atmosphere exists that fails to provide the constructive conditions necessary for robust or even barely sufficient psychological development. What might such a household look like? The ways in which a child-rearing environment can be deficient are potentially endless. To imagine just a few of these possible permutations requires that we transcend our often deeply rooted assumptions of the minimally sufficient conditions under which many of us imagine practically all children grow up.

It can be a particular challenge to recognize, beyond the presence of damaging elements, the absence of supportive and beneficial ones. We so often take these positive influences for granted that it can be hard to fathom that in many households, children never encounter them. It is beyond many people's imagining that children grow up with various forms of deprivation that may have nothing to do with the household's financial status. Some of these children may never have been thrown a birthday party or been given a birthday present. Others may never have been taken to the dentist or received adequate medical care. Some may have been expected, again independently of the household's financial status, to somehow be completely responsible for purchasing or otherwise obtaining their own clothing, shoes, or other necessities, including food, by late childhood or early adolescence.

For many children, however, the elements that are missing from their experience are much less concrete and affect considerably more extensive essential areas of functioning and adaptation. It is difficult if not impossible to identify and convey all the fundamental aspects of an effective interpersonal developmental environment that can potentially be missing or flawed in a child's household. Nevertheless, in an attempt to capture a sampling of the features necessary to enable a child to acquire the capacities required to productively manage the intricacies of day-to-day living in the adult world, we turn to a discussion of the more common flawed or missing sources of support.

### Structure

Consider, for example, the matter of routine and structure. In an adequate to ideal household with children, a relatively set bedtime is accompanied by a pattern of more or less clearly defined bedtime rituals. These rituals may vary from household to household and may consist of different elements and take place in different orders. The overridingly essential factor is that a structure of events and activities culminates in going to bed and is conducive to falling asleep, and maintaining regular hours is conducive to getting adequate rest. In some households, particularly with children between toddlerhood and the early elementary school grades, part of the sequence may be reading a bedtime story, or, for older children in this age group, perhaps having the child read a book aloud to the parent. Another component may be bathing or showering and putting on pajamas. Hopefully, the series of rituals also includes having a child brush their teeth.

Many of us would like to think that this description approximates the series of events that takes place nightly in almost all children's homes. But for children who grow up with various forms of maltreatment trauma (and remember that the abuse they encounter may, in some instances, be at the hands of someone unrelated to family members), there may be no semblance of such regularity. In some of these households, children may grow up without ever being required to brush their teeth, or, in some instances, they may never have been taught how to brush their teeth or been provided with a toothbrush. Whether it is in the evening or first thing in the morning, they may not be expected to shower or bathe regularly. And in quite a few families, anything approximating a bedtime ritual may be entirely absent because there may be no regular bedtime. For example, on one evening, the elementary school child may be sent to bed whenever the parents happen to notice that the child is still awake, say, at 10 p.m. or 11 p.m., or later. On another occasion, bedtime for the same child in the same household might be as early as 6 p.m. or 7 p.m. because the parents find the child to be particularly annoying or because they use sending the child to bed at an exceptionally early hour as a misguided consequence for misbehavior or simply for behavior they find irritating.

This is just one example of the numerous ways in which structure and routine may be inconsistent or entirely lacking in a child's household environment. Detailed interviewing of survivors of extensive, long-term childhood abuse may reveal not only that these features were not a part of the person's upbringing, but that the survivor may be almost completely unaware that routine and structure are often an integral aspect of the way that children are reared. They may therefore arrive at adulthood unacquainted with how to structure their time and oblivious that doing so is one commonplace mechanism by which adults manage life's complexities. Inevitably, they are completely oblivious that a major missing element from their lives that may account for much of their impaired functioning is that, unlike most other people, habitual patterns of effective behavior have never been modeled for or transmitted to them.

The many positive consequences of a life infused with routine and structure would be difficult to adequately enumerate. Once the sequences of behavior that shape a person's day become so second nature that they are hardly noticed, the productivity that emanates from them becomes easy, unforced, and largely automatic. Psychotherapists tend to be well aware of the destructive nature of maladaptive habits, such as substance abuse or various forms of compulsive behavior that become so firmly entrenched that they can be exceedingly difficult to relinquish. But they are less prone to having been oriented to how invaluable habitual behaviors can be that support productivity and effectiveness. Along with the repetitive nature of such behavioral patterns comes discipline and a sense of effortlessness. This is one of the many reasons why people who grow up in favorable interpersonal environments find adult living so much less stressful and more navigable than those who do not.

**Interpersonal Relationships**

Another major area that is likely to present a myriad of difficulties for people reared in ineffective family environments is the ability to approach, get along with, work productively with, and feel connected to others. Growing up in a household characterized by interpersonal and emotional distance and high levels of interpersonal conflict is far from a productive training ground for developing the complex skills required for interpersonal relating. A range of social capacities—being aware of and becoming conversant with behaviors that are considered socially appropriate, knowing how to approach someone new and establish a type of interaction that is a conducive foundation for an ongoing relationship, mastering how to manage the inevitable conflicts that arise in human relationships in a way that is likely to lead to mutually agreeable resolution and the continuation of the relationship, acquiring a familiarity with emotional intimacy and how to initiate and sustain it—is highly unlikely to become part of the behavioral repertoire of someone whose childhood household was emotionally distant, interpersonally unpredictable, and filled with discord and rancor. Like the capacity for routine, structure, and the establishment of habitual, productive patterns of behavior, interpersonal abilities or the relative lack of them have a profound effect on almost all areas of adjustment.

The ability to handle the disagreements and conflicts that are an unavoidable component of human relations in a way that is likely to lead to a productive resolution is one that frequently is especially elusive for this cohort. Growing up in a household that is high in conflict and low in cohesiveness almost inevitably means that the survivor has frequently witnessed instances of people being at odds with each other without reaching a satisfactory outcome. In a family environment of this type, instead of being able to witness examples of mutually agreeable conflict resolution, what is often demonstrated are counterproductive interpersonal strategies. Patterns of mutually escalating anger and verbal or physical aggression leading to conflict intensification are common. Alternately, one or both parties may exhibit marked unassertiveness and retreat into interpersonal distancing characterized by impassive, tearful, or resentful silence. In this way, the children in the family are regularly exposed to examples of counterproductive approaches to managing disagreements, even if the adults in the household do not lapse into explicitly maladaptive responses, such as substance abuse or domestic violence.

Simultaneously, the relative lack of family cohesion and emotional expressiveness make it highly unlikely that children from such backgrounds will encounter many, if any, appropriate models of affection and intimacy directed either toward them or between the adults in the household. Instead, parents in such a household may in one way or another set inappropriate examples of affection for their children. They may, for instance, maintain a posture of relative interpersonal distance from each other. Alternately, they may exhibit patterns of behavior in which lustful displays that are inappropriate to engage in while in the presence of children substitute for genuine expressions of affection. Or they may make a show of physical affection when out in public but remain physically and emotionally detached in the privacy of home.

Parental interactions with the children in such settings are likely to be inappropriate or capricious. Affectionate physical contact with the child may alternate sporadically with expressions of anger and unwarranted criticism. The unpredictability of parental behavior makes it especially difficult for children from these backgrounds to develop the ability to discern others' motivations, predict their behavior on that basis, and modulate their own responses accordingly.

Even when the child is relatively young, physical or verbal expressions of affection toward the child might be exceedingly rare or entirely absent. In some of the more extreme instances, the parent may consistently seem so oblivious that the child may come to experience themselves as unimportant or even as entirely nonexistent. As a result, the child who comes from such a household may lack even the most fundamental sense of self or identity and will almost inevitably find it exceedingly difficult later in life to feel connected to others emotionally and thereby love or feel loved.

Outside of the family constellation, the parents might entirely lack friendships, may maintain relationships that are volatile and conflict laden, or may have friendships that are superficial and organized around behaviors such as alcohol or substance abuse. Contact with all or certain extended family members may be so sparse to nonexistent that the children in the household never get to know their grandparents, aunts, uncles, or cousins. Alternately, periods of consistent interaction with extended family may be punctuated by long stretches of animosity and emotional distance. In some instances, parental separation or divorce may result in the children's losing contact and an ongoing relationship with either or both parents or with being shunted from the household of one extended family member or family acquaintance to another.

A frequent consequence of spending one's formative years in circumstances that fail to model or transmit the intricate abilities required for developing effective social skills is that even if survivors do not intentionally retreat into isolation, they wander through life alone, feeling as if they are "strangers in a strange land." As adults, even though they may have relationships of various kinds—with immediate and extended family, friends, and romantic partners—they are unlikely to experience a sense of being accepted, belonging. or interpersonal connection. It may not even occur to them that it is an option to rely on others when they, like any human being, need emotional or practical support. Some may be painfully aware of a sense of aloneness and the conviction that they have no one to rely on but themselves. Some may feel that they are forever doomed to remain excluded from a circle of humanity that other people partake of effortlessly. For others, it may not even occur to them that it could be otherwise; they may assume that this is the way it is for everyone. The notion that making it through life effectively and comfortably entails interdependence with other people may remain completely beyond their imagining.

**Judgment and Reasoning**

The types of family environments that render children vulnerable to maltreatment trauma are also likely to lead to breaches in the children's ability to exercise effective judgment and reasoning. These competencies, especially when applied to the situations encountered in daily living, are far from equivalent to either intelligence or education. Although the ability to reason is one aspect of the multifactorial nature of intelligence, some very bright people find it exceedingly difficult or nearly impossible to invoke logical reasoning and engage in sound judgment in the course of everyday life. The type of educational system that actively encourages critical thinking seems to be growing increasingly rare, given a push for coverage of concrete information and skills and to measure the quality of schools by students' scores on content-focused standardized tests. Practical, real-world situations require a type of cognitive ability that differs from that usually encountered in a classroom setting. It is distinct from the highly conceptual, theoretical application of logic and reasoning called for in academia in that it is often regarding matters in which emotions play a large part and can derail or subvert rational considerations, and that can have palpable consequences.

Ineffective family environments are almost never productive arenas for modeling sound reasoning and decision making. Parents and other adults in such households are likely to act capriciously and unpredictably. Reasoning is likely to be strongly colored by emotion and impulse. Children in such households, therefore, have no basis for discerning a consistent underlying rationale for their parents' actions, decisions, and choices. In such an interpersonal atmosphere, the child is unable to abstract out any reliable, coherent principles to guide his or her own reasoning, judgment, and decision-making processes. Instead, the child is likely to unwittingly mimic the flawed reasoning exhibited by those he or she is surrounded by growing up.

**Modulation of Emotions and Curbing of Impulses**

One of the greatest struggles of daily living for adults is being faced numerous times every day with situations that challenges us to forgo the immediacy of giving in to the constantly arising impulses and emotions of the moment. If we yield to the temptations that these urges entice us to gratify, we are likely to be drawn down the path of least resistance in the short run while risking serious negative consequences in the long term. We may awaken in the morning to realize that it's a weekday and that regardless of how sleepy or unenthusiastic we are to spend the day at work, failing to appear there will result in losing our source of income. In the heat of anger at a boss, romantic partner, friend, or child, it may seem easy to rashly strike out verbally or even physically, but exercising the restraint to take time to rationally consider the situation helps remind us that we risk damaging or even losing a relationship that we value.

Children who grow up in a household of adults who regularly allow their impulses to rule their behavior rather than exercise restraint are confronted with two types of influence that make it especially difficult for them to grow up with the ability to satisfactorily curb their impulses and emotions. The adults around them may actually model the types of imprudent patterns of behavior that will serve them badly both currently and once they reach adulthood. The role models in their environment may respond to stressful situations by indulging in substance abuse, surrender to rage by striking out at others, or mismanage their finances by yielding two temporary desires rather than soberly thinking ahead. At the same time, they may insist that their children act in a more disciplined way than they themselves can manage. The case vignette of Estelle that follows shortly is a striking instance in which a child's behavior that was perceived as problematic was actually being modeled by the adults in the household.

It is increasingly becoming recognized that children with insufficient impulse control who are commonly viewed as exhibiting chronic misconduct or frank delinquency may actually be manifesting the fallout from abuse and emotional deprivation (Alain, Marcotte, Desrosiers, Turcotte, & Lafortune, 2018; Mersky & Reynolds, 2007). When these behavior patterns evoke punitive reactions from others, it only intensifies the likelihood that the problems stemming from their history of maltreatment and deprivation will be perpetuated and compounded rather than accurately identified and productively addressed. Conversely, when these children are viewed within the context of their past experiences of deprivation and threat, it opens up potential avenues for remediating their impaired impulse control and emotionality, and, therefore, for prosocial adjustment.

### Case Example: Modeling Impaired Functioning

Estelle, a White woman in her late 30s, sought out family therapy with her 5-year-old son, Bobby, and her live-in boyfriend, Max, who was in his late 20s. She sought treatment at Max's prompting because he had been strongly expressing his concern that Bobby was unruly and disrespectful. From early in the first session, Max, who quickly became visibly annoyed, repeatedly and sharply barked at Bobby, "Don't interrupt!" each time Bobby attempted to join the discussion.

The therapist observed what was occurring without comment. She sensed that if she were to express concern about the counterproductive pattern of interaction she was seeing too directly or too soon, Max would feel offended, respond defensively, and refuse to return for further sessions. Instead, she asked questions of both Estelle and Max in the hope of forming a more detailed account of their concerns about Bobby's behavior, the changes they were seeking, and the family system overall. Each time she turned to Estelle to address her, however, Max would answer for her. It became increasingly evident that Max's intrusive behavior was implicitly supported and intensified by Estelle's tendency, despite that she was several years older, to defer to him. Estelle rarely spoke, but each time she did, Max would quickly resume taking charge of the discussion.

About two thirds of the way into the session, the therapist began to offer feedback to Estelle and Max. Each time she started to speak, though, Max would immediately talk over her. To avoid pointless escalation, the therapist fell silent each time and allowed Max to continue before she resumed speaking. When there finally was enough of a pause for her to ask, "Max, have you noticed that each time I begin to say something, you start talking before I can finish?" Max seemed intensely ashamed and immediately and profoundly apologized with apparent sincerity. Nevertheless, what was especially disturbing was that, even after this interchange, he seemed to have no awareness that he had been engaging in the same pattern of behavior for which he had repetitively (and unwarrantedly) been admonishing Bobby. Moreover, Estelle seemed to be just as oblivious to the parallel between Max's behavior and Bobby's, and showed no signs of being dismayed by or objecting to Max's constant badgering of Bobby.

It would be difficult to precisely predict the effect that Max's interruptions and reproaches would have on Bobby over a prolonged period. However, despite the overt feedback parental figures such as Max express toward a child, their behavior is likely to convey a more powerful message: that acting in an impetuous and inconsiderate manner is not in itself objectionable but rather is a privilege of adulthood. Moreover, conducting themselves in the very same manner that they criticize the child for leaves the child without examples of how to exercise the restraint that the adults in the household demand of him or her. What is being modeled for the child is the very behavior for which he or she is being censured. This state of affairs not only leaves the child uncertain about how to act in the way he or she is being pressured to but is likely to also leave the child feeling inept and self-critical. The resulting feelings of frustration are likely to only compound the child's proclivity to respond to situations recklessly. Although this outcome is undoubtedly unintentional on the part of the adults in the household, it has the effect of failing to transmit to children the skills required for self-restraint and leading them to be more rather than less likely to act impulsively.

**Maintenance of Attention and Focus**

In general terms, the familial characteristics and organization typical of children who are exposed to ongoing or repeated abuse trauma, whether perpetrated by relatives or those outside the family, compose an unpredictable atmosphere of alternation between detachment and emotional chaos. For the developing child, an interpersonal environment such as this represents a breeding ground for disorganized attachment, which is related to dissociative difficulties with maintaining attention and focus (Siegel, 2012).

The developmental framework central to CTT suggests that being reared in an interpersonal environment approaching either end of the detachment/chaos dimension veers far from the optimal conditions that facilitate the ability to maintain attention and focus. Consequently, it is not unusual for children subjected to childhood abuse and neglect to exhibit attention-deficit disorder (Conway, Oster, & Szymanski, 2011; Schilpzand et al., 2017; Semiz, Öner, Cengiz, & Bilici, 2017). It has been observed in the literature that it can be difficult to differentially diagnose PTSD and attention-deficit disorder partly because their diagnostic criteria, although worded differently, are substantively similar (Ford et al., 2000; Szymanski, Sapanski, & Conway, 2011).

As discussed in Chapter 4 and in coverage of the topic of dissociation in Chapter 9, although traumatization is associated with difficulty focusing and sustaining attention, CTT proposes that the unpredictable interpersonal atmosphere in which complexly traumatized children often grow up makes its own contribution to problems with attentional processes. Dissociation is often framed in terms of relatively dramatic-appearing symptoms: amnestic episodes, not feeling real or experiencing one's surroundings as unreal, or the experience of shifting between various senses of self. As Chapter 9 reveals, however, CTT suggests that often beyond and underlying these exotic-seeming experiences are weaknesses or absences in fundamental developmental attainments, such as of having a stable sense of self or consistently feeling a connection to or ownership of one's one body.

**Impaired Brain Development**

Many of the difficulties of people reared in an inadequate developmental/interpersonal environment are due to either not having been transmitted essential functional capacities via effective parenting or having learned maladaptive patterns in the household in which they grew up. However, not all of their adaptive limitations are environmental. A developmentally inadequate environment can result in impairments and delays at the level of the central nervous system. An entire body of research literature, for example, identifies how maternal depression adversely affects brain development and behavior in their offspring (e.g., DeRose, Shiyko, Levey, Helm, & Hastings, 2014; Hughes, Roman, Hart, & Ensor, 2013; Yan, Zhou, & Ansari, 2016), presumably because depression in the mother truncates her attentiveness to and interaction with the developing child.

On a broader level, an extensive body of research indicates that being reared in conditions of ongoing trauma and deprivation have substantial and measurable delirious effects on brain development. Child maltreatment has been found to be related to reduced brain volume, which in turn has been associated with abuse onset and inversely related to abuse duration (De Bellis et al., 1999). Adverse childhood experiences were identified as being related to reduced volume and functional connectivity of the inferior frontal gyrus, a region of the brain that modulates emotions and impulses (Barch, Belden, Tillman, Whalen, & Luby, 2018). Childhood emotional maltreatment also was found to be related to reduced volume of the medial prefrontal cortex, an area of the brain associated with emotion regulation (van Harmelen et al., 2010). A number of studies (Bremner et al., 1997; Driessen et al., 2000; M. B. Stein, Koverola, Hanna, Torchia, & McClarty, 1997) have shown that adults with a history of child maltreatment exhibit decreased volume of the hippocampus, which regulates stress, but this pattern has not consistently been detected in maltreated children themselves. Whittle et al. (2013), therefore, hypothesized that the impact of child maltreatment on the brain may be delayed and first emerge during adolescence. Their findings were consistent with this supposition. As a whole, these investigations indicated that child maltreatment impacts brain development in a way that compromises the ability to modulate emotions and impulses on one hand and, on the other, compromises reasoning ability and decision making, including the abilities to think ahead and consider the consequences of one's actions.

## THE CONTEXTUAL TRAUMA THERAPY MODEL: DIFFERENTIATING THE IMPACT OF ABUSE TRAUMA AND NEGLECT

A central point in CTT is the conceptual importance of distinguishing harmful experiences in general from traumatic ones in particular. Parental neglect can certainly be emotionally hurtful to a child and also cause harm by having enduring negative consequences for practical functioning. CTT asserts, however, that neglect does not fit the definition of trauma encapsulated in Criterion A of the *DSM–5* (American Psychiatric Association, 2013) diagnostic criteria of PTSD. Instead of engendering trauma, neglect fosters developmental deficits. The importance of this distinction is a practical one. Trauma processing will not repair the developmental warps and deficits created by either physical or emotional neglect. Trauma-focused interventions such as prolonged exposure (Foa, Hembree, & Rothbaum, 2007) or eye-movement desensitization and reprocessing (Moos & Moos, 1986) will not repair the damage done by feeling unloved, unimportant, or unprotected, or by having been reared without adequate food or clean clothes.

The consequences of developmental deprivation require forms of intervention markedly distinct from trauma-focused strategies. What is needed are therapeutic strategies directly aimed at remediating the developmental deficits that result from neglect. When CTr is conceptualized exclusively in trauma-related terms, this distinction can easily be overlooked, and gaps and warps in development are more likely to go unaddressed.

Some are likely to find it extremely disturbing to think that there are children who grow up under the debilitating circumstances that practically always accompany ongoing or repeated traumatization. They may be strongly inclined to judge the parents in such households as "negligent" and therefore to construe what the children in such situations are experiencing as "neglect." However, it seems to me that it can be conceptually confusing and potentially misleading to categorize instances such as these as negligence. For one thing, the term *negligence* usually carries the connotation that the negligent person could choose to do otherwise. Neglect is often construed as a failure to do something out of laziness or lack of investment. Often (although certainly not always), parents and other caretakers who do not provide an environment conducive to promoting children's psychological development and adaptive functioning do so not out of maliciousness, intentional abrogation of responsibility, or lack of motivation. Rather, they themselves often grew up without effective parenting so that among their own deficits is a lack of models for effective child-rearing practices and as an inability to set an example of reasonable adult functioning given their own gaps and warps in development and adjustment. (The case of Estelle, Max, and Bobby presented earlier in this chapter is an excellent illustration of such a situation.) Alternately, a single parent who is the primary or sole source of family income may have to spend long hours working just to provide for the household's physical needs, which prevents the parent from having adequate time to spend at home with his or her children so he or she can execute other aspects of parenting. Similarly, a seriously ill, severely depressed, or psychologically disabled parent may be limited in providing for the physical and emotional needs of his or her children, not because the parent is disinterested or uncaring but because of the unavoidable restrictions created by these conditions. Although it may be the case in these circumstances that the child suffers from neglect, this does not necessarily imply that the parents have been negligent in the sense of choosing not to sufficiently meet their children's needs.

The reason this understanding is important is that when we consider neglect the result of willful, malicious intent, it is easy to assume that neglect is a trauma in the same sense that the perpetration of childhood verbal, physical, or sexual abuse is a trauma. These forms of child maltreatment differ from neglect in that they are both acts of commission and comprise identifiable events. Parental neglect most often consists not of discrete acts but of entire areas of omission that are not usually reduceable to discrete episodes. A history of neglect, therefore, requires a different therapeutic response than strategies for resolving particular instances of abuse and of other forms of trauma. Although confronting and discussing traumatic experiences in a prolonged or repeated structured fashion can lead to the resolution of the symptoms associated with them, such approaches to processing neglect will not provide the client with the capacities they lack because of neglect. Similarly, empathically commiserating with the survivor of childhood neglect undeniably has some therapeutic value, but it will not in itself remediate the weak or absent functional capacities that result from parental neglect.

There is no question that childhood emotional or physical neglect is detrimental regardless of whether it is the result of intentional abrogation of parental responsibility, but there is a crucial distinction to make between adverse childhood circumstances in general and circumscribed or even continuous, ongoing traumatic events. McLaughlin (2017) conceptualized this distinction as that between "experiences of threat" and "experiences of deprivation." In a passage completely consistent with the CTT theoretical model, she described her research on the differential impact of subcategories of ACEs:

> My early work demonstrated the importance of disruptions in emotional processing as a developmental pathway linking a wide range of adverse childhood experiences to the onset of psychopathology. But as this work progressed, both in my lab and elsewhere, I became concerned about the general tendency for research in this area to lump together a wide range of disparate experiences as indicators of the same underlying construct. It seemed unlikely that the vastly different social experiences encompassed by this construct—ranging from violence exposure to food insecurity to neglect—influenced development through the same underlying mechanisms. ("Are the Pathways Linking Adversity," para. 1)

She went on to delineate that "our model differentiates between experiences of threat—experiences involving harm or threat of harm, and deprivation—experiences involving an absence of expected inputs from the environment" (McLaughlin, 2017, "Are the Pathways Linking Adversity," para. 2). Her program of research and the empirical findings of others support the clinical observation that experiences of threat result in a marked exacerbation of the tendency to scan for and perceive potential danger—often in situations in which it does not exist. In contrast, the findings suggest that deprivation is related to impairments in cognitive and social development.

The Adverse Childhood Experiences Study (Felitti et al., 1998; Stevens, 2012) and the work of researchers such as McLaughlin and her coinvestigators have yielded findings that are highly consistent with the conceptual tenets of CTT. Adverse childhood experiences research has led to the identification of abuse trauma, neglect, and household dysfunction as distinct forms of adversity. The investigations and theory of McLaughlin and her coauthors delineated the divergent consequences of experiences of threat (i.e., trauma) and experiences of deprivation (i.e., neglect and household dysfunction). In the next section, I discuss how their findings are consistent with and supportive of the conceptual distinction proposed by CTT between PTSD and C-PTSD.

## RECONCEPTUALIZATION OF THE DISTINCTION BETWEEN PTSD AND C-PTSD

How, then, do the lines of research executed by Felitti and McLaughlin converge with the conceptual model of CTr proposed by CTT? Careful examination of the diagnostic criteria for PTSD and C-PTSD has shown that the symptoms composing PTSD are constellated around perceptions of and reactions to perceived danger, such as intrusive emotional and physiological reactions to cues reminiscent of traumatic events, hypervigilance, an exaggerated startle response, and the dissociative numbing emblematic of the freeze components of the fight–flight–freeze response (*DSM–5*; American Psychiatric Association, 2013). The characteristics encompassed by the syndrome of C-PTSD extend beyond those related to threat. They consist of difficulties with emotional regulation, the quality of consciousness, self-perception (i.e., identity), and relations with others (Brewin et al., 2017).

Herman (1992a, 1992b) conceptualized these difficulties as a direct consequence of ongoing or repeated trauma, but McLaughlin's (2017) research findings, which were grounded in and expanded on the ACEs investigations, may be construed to suggest otherwise. What McLaughlin's (2017) work may be taken to indicate, and what CTT theory proposes, is that C-PTSD is as much or perhaps even more a reflection of deprivation with resulting developmentally based cognitive and social difficulties than of the experiences of threat that compose trauma. Although it is likely to some degree a function of both threat and deprivation, the prominent presence among its diagnostic criteria of problematic orientations to areas such as emotional regulation, consciousness, self-perception (i.e., identity), and interpersonal relationships may be taken to indicate that a major contribution of C-PTSD is developmental deficits rather than trauma-related sequelae exclusively.

Because childhood neglect, whether physical or emotional, is construed by many to be a form of trauma, designating parental failings as neglect and therefore lumping them together with other forms of trauma misidentify them as primarily constituting forms of threat. The research of McLaughlin and her colleagues (e.g., McLaughlin, 2017; McLaughlin & Sheridan, 2016; McLaughlin, Sheridan, & Lambert, 2014; Sheridan & McLaughlin, 2014) strongly suggested otherwise. Construing neglect as a form of trauma misleads therapists about how to differentially respond to these two distinct forms of childhood adversity. Although having been subjected to neglect can certainly be stress inducing, trauma-focused interventions, such as exposure techniques, do not address the limited functional capacities that stem from neglect. Failure to recognize the developmental nature of the difficulties that McLaughlin (2017) referred to as deficit adversity draws their attention away from the types of skills deficits, that is, developmental gaps and warps, associated with experiences of deprivation.

In a finding reminiscent of and consistent with the ACEs investigation, children subjected to abuse and neglect were more likely than nonvictimized children to be from problem-ridden families with features such as parents who have been arrested, abused substances, or had five or more children (Widom, 1999). As Widom noted, "Abused and neglected children often come from multiple-problem families, and these results reinforce the need to begin to disentangle consequences specifically associated with childhood victimization from other risk factors" (p. 1227).

Symptoms of several trauma-related psychological disorders (including PTSD, depression, and dissociation) were found to be appreciably more pronounced among individuals who have experienced child abuse than those who reported neglect in the absence of overt abuse (Wechsler-Zimring & Kearney, 2011). Dorahy, Corry, et al. (2009) reported that being emotionally disconnected from family and friends was associated with C-PTSD, which they noted has been conceptualized as a relational disorder. In a study that examined the association of forms and levels of intensity of child maltreatment to PTSD and

ADHD symptom severity, only child emotional neglect was found to not be related to these two disorders (Evren, Umut, Bozkurt, Evren, & Agachanli, 2016).

Although Herman (1992a) originally suggested that C-PTSD is the consequence of any form of ongoing subjugation trauma, mounting empirical evidence has indicated that areas of impairment composing the disorder are especially related to child maltreatment as opposed to traumatic events in adulthood (Briere & Rickards, 2007; Cloitre, Scarvalone, & Difede, 1997; Powers et al., 2017; Wamser-Nanney & Vandenberg, 2013). This finding is consistent with the CTT conception that the areas of impaired adjustment composing C-PTSD are a function of deficits in developmental capacities and of trauma rather than solely trauma related. Palic et al. (2016) also found C-PTSD to be associated with prolonged severe interpersonal trauma in adulthood, such as political torture, but acknowledged that because they did not systematically assess for the presence of childhood trauma, they could not rule out that childhood trauma was a predisposing antecedent.

A measure expressly designed to assess the 11th edition of the *International Classification of Diseases* (ICD–11; World Health Organization, 2018) diagnoses of PTSD and C-PTSD is the International Trauma Questionnaire (ITQ; Cloitre et al., 2018). The prospect of the inclusion of C-PTSD in the ICD–11 prompted the execution of several studies (e.g., Brewin et al., 2017; Hyland et al., 2017; Karatzias, Cloitre, et al., 2017; Karatzias et al., 2016; Karatzias, Shevlin, et al., 2017; Kazlauskas, Gegieckaite, Hyland, Zelviene, & Cloitre, 2018; Litvin, Kaminski, & Riggs, 2017; Powers et al., 2017; Thanos et al., 2017) that examined the validity of the C-PTSD diagnosis by looking at the latent class structure and factor structure of the ITQ. Three of the factors—reexperiencing, avoidance, and sense of threat—are associated with PTSD. Complex posttraumatic stress disorder encompasses these factors and three additional ones: affect dysregulation, negative self-concept, and disturbances in relationships. These additional three factors, which are indicative of C-PTSD, are regularly referred to in the literature as *disturbances in self-organization*.

Karatzias, Shevlin, et al. (2017) administered the ITQ (Cloitre et al., 2018) to 193 therapy clients of the National Health Service trauma center in Scotland. Their findings confirmed that the ITQ was able to distinguish PTSD from C-PTSD. Latent class analysis identified a class consisting of slightly more than 75% of the sample to have a high probability of meeting criteria for both PTSD and C-PTSD, whereas those in the remaining class (i.e., just under 25%) had a high probability of meeting criteria for PTSD but not for C-PTSD. Childhood trauma in particular was related to the first, the C-PTSD class. The ability of the ITQ to distinguish C-PTSD from PTSD also has been validated in investigations of clinical samples in a variety of countries, including ones conducted in Lithuania (Kazlauskas et al., 2018), Denmark (Hyland et al., 2017), and Israel (Gilbar et al., 2018). In a review of 10 studies assessing the validity of the C-PTSD construct as distinct from PTSD, Brewin et al. (2017) concluded that nine of them generated separate latent class profiles for PTSD and C-PTSD.

## CHARACTERISTICS OF FAMILIES OF ABUSED CHILDREN: THE CONTEXT OF MALTREATMENT

In the section Features and Consequences of Growing up in an Ineffective Family earlier in this chapter, I surveyed some of the areas of functioning that families of survivors of CTr often fail to foster. In this section, I examine the characteristics that commonly typify these families and how these qualities increase the risk of maltreatment among their offspring and compound the damage done by these abusive experiences. One piece of evidence for the contribution of family context to child abuse traumatization is that research identifies the same detrimental family environment pattern in survivors who were abused by perpetrators outside the family as those of survivors abused by family members (Gold, Hyman, & Andrés-Hyman, 2004; Ray, Jackson, & Townsley, 1991). In general, research findings indicate that the families of child abuse survivors, both in the form of sexual abuse and of physical abuse, were characterized by two or more of the following qualities (Fassler et al., 2005; Gold et al., 2004; Griffin & Amodeo, 2010; Mollerstrom, Patchner, & Milner, 1992; Yama, Tovey, Fogas, & Teegarden, 1992):

- a low level of cohesiveness, that is, a relative lack of a sense of togetherness, belonging, and family unity;

- a low level of emotional expressiveness, that is, inhibited display of or communication of affection and other feelings;

- a high level of interpersonal conflict, including frequent disagreements, possibly including verbal and even physical altercations; and

- an elevated level of control, that is, both explicit and, frequently, unspoken rules that constrain the behavioral freedom and decision-making ability of individual members, especially children.

Several studies have examined the relative contribution of abuse and family environment to psychological adjustment. Yama, Tovey, and Fogas (1993) compared the family of origin environments and levels of anxiety and depression of undergraduate women with and without a child sexual abuse history. Their results indicated that anxiety and depression were positively related to familial control and negatively related to cohesion and conflict. In addition, these three familial characteristics moderated the relationship between CSA and depression. In a finding analogous to that of Gold et al. (2004), Yama et al. (1993) found no difference between the family environment characteristics of participants with a history of intrafamilial abuse and those reporting extrafamilial abuse. Yama et al. (1993) concluded that

> results from this study demonstrate an association between childhood sexual abuse and later symptoms of anxiety and depression. This does not necessarily imply that the experience of abuse is the direct cause of later symptoms. It is more likely that there are processes that mediate this relationship; for example, some part of the child's environment may create a vulnerability which, in turn, increases the likelihood both of sexual abuse *and* [emphasis in the original] psychopathology. (p. 140)

Fassler, Amodeo, Griffin, Clay, and Ellis (2005) investigated the relative contribution of scores on an empirically derived measure of CSA severity and family environment to psychological difficulties in adulthood in a community sample of adult women. They found that severity was no more predictive than a dichotomous measure of presence versus absence of CSA. The combination of the presence of CSA and family conflict, expressiveness, and cohesion predicted all seven psychological adjustment outcomes assessed in the study. Standardized beta weights for these family environment variables were, on the whole, greater than those for CSA. Consequently, Fassler and colleagues concluded that further study of the contribution of particular characteristics of family environment to CSA outcomes is warranted. Moreover, they asserted that "a broader contextual approach which includes support systems outside of the immediate family may also aid in understanding the varied long-term outcomes for those who experience CSA" (p. 280).

Griffin and Amodeo (2010) identified strikingly similar patterns in a community sample of women with a history of childhood physical abuse (CPA). A measure of CPA severity was no more predictive of psychological outcomes in adulthood than the dichotomous presence or absence of CPA. As in the Fassler et al. (2005) investigation of CSA, family conflict, expressiveness, and cohesion appreciably improved the prediction of adult psychological adjustment beyond the presence of CPA alone. Griffin and Amodeo (2010) advised that "a broader contextual approach, perhaps including support systems outside of the immediate family, may also aid in understanding the varied long-term outcomes for those who experience CPA" (pp. 731–732).

The aforementioned studies (Fassler et al., 2005; Gold et al., 2004; Griffin & Amodeo, 2010; Mollerstrom et al., 1992; Ray et al., 1991; Yama et al., 1992, 1993) used subscales of the Family Environment Scale (Moos & Moos, 1986). In contrast, Hulsey, Sexton, and Nash (1992) administered the revised Family Functioning Scale (FFS-R; Bloom & Lipetz, 1987) to a primarily clinical sample of women, about half of whom endorsed a CSA history. Out of 15 FFS-R scales, 14 significantly contributed to a multivariate analysis of variance for abuse status. The authors concluded that the pattern of FFS-R subscale scores among participants reporting CSA indicated that their families tended to be authoritarian and were socially isolated from the larger community, and that its members lacked a sense of interpersonal connectedness.

What these studies consistently point to is that even when the abuse is by perpetrators outside the victim's family, the characteristics of the familial context make a substantial contribution to adverse psychological outcomes above and beyond that attributable to the abuse itself. Some investigators in this line of research have suggested that the interpersonal atmosphere in a victim's family may have an even greater impact on difficulties in psychological adjustment than is ascribable to the effects of the abuse per se (e.g., Hulsey et al., 1992; Rind, Tromovitch, & Bauserman, 1998). This position, however, is inconsistent with the CTT model, which posits that family environment increases the risk for the occurrence of child abuse, augments the likelihood that abuse will lead to traumatization, and fosters developmental deficits not directly attributable to the effects of abuse.

Moreover, the characteristics of the families in which child abuse survivors are reared have consistently been shown to regularly share certain qualities. They are authoritarian and controlling, marked by high levels of interpersonal conflict, low in systemic cohesiveness and interpersonal connectedness, and low in emotional expressiveness. If we consider the implications of these specific characteristics that are consistently found to be emblematic of the family environments of child abuse survivors, it is not difficult to deduce various ways in which children are affected by them.

**Vulnerability to Coercive Control and Abuse**

Being reared in a family context high in authoritarian control and low in cohesiveness and expressiveness is likely to appreciably increase the child's vulnerability to being targeted for abuse. Growing up in a family with low levels of cohesiveness and emotional expressiveness make it highly likely that children reared in such an atmosphere will experience intense unmet needs for affirmation and interpersonal connection. This sense of emotional and social deprivation in turn makes it probable that the children will be highly responsive to attention and affection when it is offered, especially from adults. Well-intentioned adults who recognize the child's emotional deprivation and are appropriately responsive to it can have a tremendously salutary influence on their sense of security, self-esteem, and overall psychological development. Predatory adults, on the other hand, are likely to be inclined to exploit the child's apparent neediness, using it as leverage to gain the child's confidence as a foundation for exerting control. This pattern of "grooming" a child for exploitation is well established in the professional literature on CSA. Perpetrators acknowledge that they frequently bombard their potential victims with attention and affection (Lanning, 2010) and seek to isolate them from other people (Olson, Daggs, Ellevold, & Rogers, 2007).

In addition, perpetrators use various tactics, sometimes physical but more commonly emotional, to exert coercive control over their prospective victims (Colton, Roberts, & Vanstone, 2010; J. Sullivan & Beech, 2004). Control can be easy to establish with children who grew up in relatively authoritarian and controlling family environments. In these circumstances, children often learn early and implicitly within the confines of their family that what sounds to others like a "yes" or "no" question has only one acceptable answer: either the "yes" or the "no" that the adult expects or insists on hearing. Such children have been taught, whether intentionally or unintentionally on the part of their parental figures, to be unquestioningly compliant. Furthermore, their parental figures have not only acted in ways that have failed to encourage independent thinking but have actively discouraged them from doing so. The twin forces of unquestioning obedience and marked unassertiveness render these children attractive and easy targets for adults and older children and adolescents who are seeking the opportunity to gain dominance over younger or otherwise less powerful victims.

## Vulnerability to Revictimization

A substantial and consistent body of research findings indicates that children who are sexually or physically maltreated are at much greater risk for repeated victimization later in life than individuals who were not exposed to abuse trauma in their youth. Often this observation has been framed as a quality of the abused children themselves, prompting the question, Why would someone who has been abused early in life continue to seek out maltreatment? The implicit assumption here is that the victim is in some way responsible for his or her own victimization or is even actively seeking it out. That perspective has bewildered researchers and clinical experts in psychological trauma precisely because it contradicts commonsense understanding of motivation, which is that human beings are oriented to maximize pleasure and minimize pain. Some individuals may be more prone than others to be subjected to forms of domination and violence, and may, in some circumstances, actively place themselves in situations in which the probability of this victimization occurring is markedly elevated, but the notion that they are actively and directly seeking to be mistreated and hurt is inconsistent with CTT theory.

CTT proposes that the same inclinations that made the child an attractive target to perpetrators of abusive behavior readily explain the phenomenon that has come to be called revictimization. The notion that survivors of childhood abuse later intentionally pursue their own victimization fails to recognize that (a) at least two participants are in an abusive encounter: a victim and a perpetrator; and (b) perpetrators do not select their victims randomly. Rather, perpetrators are actively on the alert for potential victims whom they perceive as readily manipulated, overpowered, and dominated. This is just as true when the intended object of exploitation is an adolescent or adult. Domestic violence offenders, criminal assailants, serial rapists—in general, people who are inclined to engage in coercive control and violence—tend to be habitually on the prowl for people whom they perceive will offer little resistance to attempts at domination and whom they can therefore easily control. This is why members of groups with limited social and political power, such as children, women, and ethnic minorities, are more likely to be targeted for coercive control than others. CTT suggests that by virtue of having grown up in a continuous atmosphere of deprivation of affection and demands for obedience, child abuse survivors have been primed (although not necessarily intentionally) to submit to coercive control. This inclination continues later in life and may be reinforced by victimization experiences in childhood.

## Increased Risk of Traumatization

As we have seen previously, a central empirical finding in research on psychological trauma is that not everyone exposed to a traumatic situation will be traumatized by it. Children who grow up in controlling, authoritarian, emotionally remote, and disconnected families are likely to possess less effective coping skills and to have less access to social support than those from more favorable family environments. When they do encounter traumatic events, therefore, they are likely to be a much greater at risk for traumatization. Alternately stated, such children are both more likely to encounter trauma and be more vulnerable to being appreciably and enduringly negatively affected by it than those from families that provide higher levels of attentiveness, emotional responsiveness, guidance, and support.

### Difficulty Tolerating and Benefiting From Trauma Processing Early in Treatment

The same weaknesses in coping ability that render survivors who grew up in deficient family contexts at higher risk for traumatization in response to traumatic events account for their difficulty in tolerating trauma-focused intervention procedures, especially when these procedures are attempted early in treatment. Having been reared in interpersonal environments that failed to adequately equip them with the coping resources or adaptive skills necessary for effective adult functioning leaves them highly susceptible to traumatic triggering and dissociative reactions when encouraged to revisit their traumatic history in therapy. For this reason, much of the course of CTT for survivors of CTr is devoted to remediating these gaps and warps in adjustment. Resiliency is bolstered by helping survivors of CTr to acquire the capacities to live a more effective and gratifying life in the present, including the acquisition of more productive and effective coping abilities. Once the survivor has made substantial progress toward this end, he or she is better equipped to confront past traumatic incidents and metabolize them rather than be just as overwhelmed by them as when those incidents originally occurred.

### Independent Contribution of Ineffective Family of Origin Context to Impaired Functioning

Implicit in the preceding section Difficulty Tolerating and Benefiting From Trauma Processing Early in Treatment is the notion supported in the research literature that rearing in an ineffective family environment leads to problems in adjustment over and above those attributable to abuse trauma. The role of a family is to prepare the child for the complicated demands of adult living by meeting the child's emotional needs and transmitting to the child the capacities for adaptive living. The inadequate family backgrounds of survivors of CTr lead them to arrive at adulthood with appreciable gaps in development, socialization, enculturation, and learning. CTT aims to remediate these areas of deficiency early on, forming a more resilient foundation from which to conduct constructive trauma processing subsequently.

In this chapter, we examined how the research on ACEs and the family of origin environments of abuse survivors can help to make the contribution of developmental deficits to their psychological impairment more visible. Drawing on these areas of investigation, we considered how the distinction between PTSD and CTr can be reconceptualized as one not merely of prolonged maltreatment but of a childhood marked by the combined presence of abuse trauma and developmental deprivation. We then considered how a particular type of origin family environment may increase their children's vulnerability to being targeted for maltreatment, being subjected to later revictimization, and increasing their likelihood of being traumatized by these events. We also explored how growing up in families such as these can promote problems beyond those attributable to abuse trauma. Chapter 4 delineates how the CTT model conceptually integrates the dual impact of child abuse and developmental deprivation to better understand and address the difficulties experienced by survivors of CTr.

# 4

# Integrating Figure and Ground

*A Major Shift in Perspective*

Building on the previous two chapters, we now consider how child abuse trauma and developmental deprivation in childhood interact to create a much more intricate pattern of difficulties than would be attributable to either of these factors in isolation. Recognition of the "ground" or "backdrop" of prolonged childhood trauma that is comprised of growing up in the type of ineffective family environment described in Chapter 3 parsimoniously explains a number of diverse components of the complex traumatization (CTr) process. The practical aspect of contextual trauma therapy (CTT) is most directly related to understanding that growing up in a deficient family environment promotes functional limitations beyond those directly attributable to the impact of the traumatic events themselves.

## A MODEL OF DUAL CAUSE AND EFFECT

CTT does not merely affirm that traumatic events and being reared in an ineffective family environment independently contribute to difficulties in functioning. It emphasizes that these two sources of psychological impairment are of fundamentally different qualities. It is this particular feature of CTT above all that distinguishes it from other trauma-related theories and treatments, and accounts for its particular applicability to survivors of complex trauma: The respective impacts of traumatic events and a deficient child-rearing environment are categorically different. Consequently, they frequently require

---

http://dx.doi.org/10.1037/0000176-005
*Contextual Trauma Therapy: Overcoming Traumatization and Reaching Full Potential,*
by S. N. Gold
Copyright © 2020 by the American Psychological Association. All rights reserved.

appreciably different treatment methods based on an understanding of their substantially different sources and characteristics.

Traumatization results in performance deficits. People traumatized by an instance of interpersonal violence for the first time in adulthood, for example, may retain the ability to be highly adept in social situations; however, they may nevertheless avoid social encounters because of trauma-related anxiety (see *Diagnostic and Statistical Manual of Mental Disorders*, fifth ed. [*DSM–5*]; American Psychiatric Association, 2013). They may have the capacity to interact effectively with others but do not exercise this competency out of fear-related avoidance. Therapeutic interventions, therefore, that resolve or neutralize the effects of having been exposed to traumatic events free up traumatized individuals to exhibit the functional capacities (in this example, social skills) that they already possess (see the discussion of performance deficits versus skill deficits later in this chapter).

In contrast, those who grow up in an ineffective family environment that does not provide the resources necessary for social learning, socialization, enculturation, and adequate psychological development are highly unlikely to arrive at adulthood adequately equipped to navigate the complexities of social situations. It is not that they have the ability to function in these circumstances but are blocked from functioning due to anxious avoidance or other trauma-related psychological difficulties. Rather, they have never acquired the necessary capacities to function in the social arena. These functional limitations, therefore, are appreciably different in type from those that are a consequence of encountering traumatic events. No amount of trauma-specific intervention will provide people who lack sufficient social facility to function effectively and appropriately in interpersonal encounters. What is needed to resolve this type of difficulty, which is a skills deficit, is the transmission of the ability to effectively navigate the social arena via strategies, such as modeling, instruction and explanation, role-playing, and interaction with the clinician in the course of the therapeutic relationship.

Another example may help further clarify the differential impact of CTr per se and inadequate acquisition of the capacities for adult living. Consider the case of an individual who had been operating adequately or even at a superior level at work before encountering a traumatic event and developing posttraumatic stress disorder (PTSD). Many of the symptoms of severe PTSD can interfere with occupational functioning in a variety of ways. Nightmares, flashbacks, and invasive thoughts about traumatic events can interfere with restful sleep, thus contributing to or augmenting insomnia and, in turn, leading to late arrival at work, difficulty staying focused during the day, and impaired work efficiency, in general. The same intrusive symptoms that interfere with sleep, when they occur during the day, are likely to interfere with concentration and work performance. Similarly, zoning out, amnesia, and other trauma-related dissociative symptoms are highly likely to disrupt efficiency and productivity. The affected individual may have performed in an exemplary fashion before the traumatic event. Subsequently, however, PTSD symptoms of chronic arousal, such as hypervigilance and irritability, can fuel interpersonal conflict and miscommunication on the job. In such a situation, the survivor had acquired the capacities to do well at work before the onset of traumatization, but that potential was hampered or even neutralized by the person's PTSD symptoms and created a performance deficit.

Although these same difficulties may impair the job performance of someone with complex posttraumatic disorder (C-PTSD; Herman, 1992b), additional factors are likely to hamper the person's ability to function adequately at work or even to be able to secure and maintain employment. Based on my extensive clinical experience, I have observed that the individual who grew up in an inadequate family environment and did not have positive role models or lacked sufficient parental input and guidance, or both, is less likely than other more fortunate prospective employees to be conversant with the norms and expectations encountered in the workplace. That person may not know how to dress appropriately for a job interview, for example. Basic social skills, such as smiling, shaking hands with the interviewer, and maintaining eye contact, may never have been imparted to them. If such an individual is successfully hired, he or she is more likely than others to lack the organizational skills, discipline, and sustained effort to approach the level of productivity expected by the employer. Although the presence of the symptoms of PTSD may further limit the individual's work performance, a basic source of his or her substandard functioning on the job is a number of fundamental skills deficits that are not directly attributable to the individual's traumatization.

These are examples of only two arenas of adult life (albeit extensive and essential ones) that can be impaired by limitations in socialization, enculturation, learning, and psychological development. Other aspects of adult living can be similarly constrained by having been reared in deficient circumstances. These aspects can and often do include areas such as sexual adjustment, management of personal finances, and the parenting of one's own children.

It is important to acknowledge, however, that just as an encounter with a traumatic event does not necessarily eventuate in PTSD or other forms of traumatization, growing up in a developmentally inadequate family system does not inevitably mean that a person from such a background will exhibit skill deficiencies across all areas of adjustment. For one thing, family environments can vary widely in the areas of developmental support in which they excel or are lacking. Some families may provide exceptional resources for academic and occupational success even though they are severely wanting in resources to foster comfort and proficiency in social and especially emotionally intimate situations. In others, the converse may be the case. Given the wide variety of strands of development and life skills that can contribute to productive and gratifying adult adaptation, the various permutations are theoretically infinite. In addition, it is certainly the case that some individuals who were reared in markedly unsatisfactory interpersonal environments have benefited immeasurably from the nurturing attention of a caring and responsive extended family member, teacher, coach, or mentor. Although these relationships are unlikely to entirely compensate for a severely substandard support system in their formative years, they can substantially mitigate the level and range of skills deficits that they would otherwise exhibit (Ludy-Dobson & Perry, 2010).

## BIDIRECTIONAL, CIRCULAR CAUSATION BETWEEN DIAGNOSTIC SYNDROMES AND FUNCTIONAL IMPAIRMENT

The harmful impact of inadequate and ineffective child-rearing associated with the adverse childhood experiences (ACEs; and other, similarly damaging factors, such as growing up in poverty or with community violence) on social and occupational functioning raises a pivotal theoretical issue regarding the way in which we commonly conceptualize psychological and psychiatric difficulties. Beginning with the third edition of the *Diagnostic and Statistical Manual of Mental Disorders* (third ed. [*DSM–III*]; American Psychiatric Association, 1980), rather than basing diagnoses on a general narrative description of the characteristics of each disorder, explicit criteria were prescribed for arriving at each diagnosis. Beyond the criteria specific to each syndrome, one criterion was assigned to a large proportion of diagnoses: that the difficulties composing these syndromes only constituted a diagnosable disorder if they appreciably interfered with academic, occupational, or social functioning.

Making a diagnostic criterion the statement that the features of these mental disorders cause impairment in social, occupational, academic, or self-care functioning carries a momentous theoretical implication. It suggests that, independently of the degree to which symptomatic manifestations deviate from the norm, what renders a syndrome pathological is not just the deviations from normative behaviors and experiences in and of themselves but their impact on functioning. The implicit assumption underlying this formulation is that it is the "symptoms" that are responsible for disruptions in adjustment (see Figure 4.1).

By proposing that many of the functional difficulties and limitations of survivors of complex trauma are due to the inadequate conditions in which they were reared, CTT opens up the possibility that causation can proceed in the opposite direction. Not only can symptoms interfere with effective functioning, but the problems in functioning resulting from growing up with inadequate resources for socialization, enculturation, social learning, and psychological development can foster the emergence of psychological symptoms. Insufficient or ineffective social, occupational, academic, or self-care capacities can and often promote disturbances, such as depression, anxiety, substance abuse, and other forms of distress, and desperate but misguided attempts to manage distress (see Figure 4.2).

**FIGURE 4.1. Symptoms as the Cause of Impairment**

**Psychological Symptoms** ⟶ **Functional Impairment**
(e.g., of anxiety, depression, substance use)      (e.g., of occupational, social, academic limitations)

**FIGURE 4.2. Impairment as the Cause of Symptoms**

**Functional Impairment** ⟶ **Psychological Symptoms**
(e.g., occupational, social (e.g., of anxiety, depression)
limitations)

 

Rather than suggesting that the causative relationship between psychiatric symptoms and adaptive functioning is the converse of that suggested by the *DSM*, CTT purports that in the case of C-PTSD, causation is bidirectional and circular (see Figure 4.3). The posttraumatic difficulties associated with the "experiences of threat" (i.e., the reexperiencing, avoidance, and sense of threat components of PTSD) that arise in response to traumatic events primarily constitute psychological symptoms. These psychological symptoms, in turn, lead to functional impairments in the form of performance deficits, such as the disruptive impact of the sense of threat on various areas of adaptation. The traumatized person has the ability to function in these situations but does not display those capacities because of the interference of threat-related experiences, such as anxiety. Gaps and warps in development that are attributable to experiences of deficiency in the interpersonal child-rearing environment consist of functional impairments (i.e., the affect dysregulation, negative self-concept, and disturbances in relationships components of C-PTSD; the disturbances in self-organization [DSO])—that is, skills deficits. These areas of ineffectiveness are likely to engender psychological disturbances (i.e., symptoms) often in the form of distress (e.g., anxiety, depression) and frantic efforts to counteract distress (e.g., substance abuse). Inadequate preparation to cope with and meet the demands of daily living are likely to fuel forms of distress and disturbed behavior. In general terms, this mode of causation calls for treatment approaches that target skills deficits. And as the *DSM* framework indicates, psychiatric symptoms are just as likely to interfere with forms of adaptive functioning. This mode of causation, in contrast, indicates the need for symptom-focused strategies that target performance deficits.

Consequently, differentiating traumatization from inadequate socialization, enculturation, learning, and psychological development is not just a conceptual or theoretical distinction. It is a highly practical distinction that informs treatment strategy. In general, trauma-related difficulties require interventions that reduce or eliminate factors that inhibit the execution of abilities that the

**FIGURE 4.3. Bidirectional Causation Between Symptoms and Impairment**

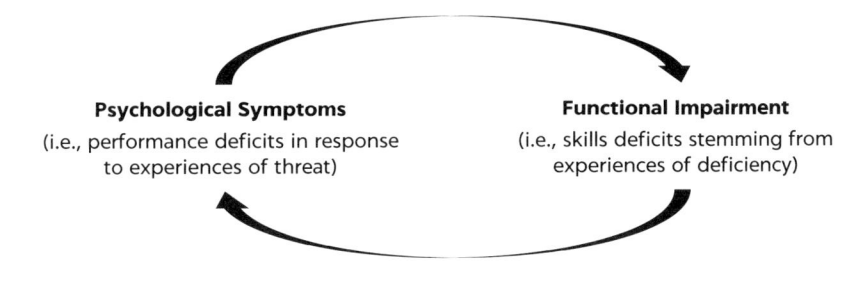

**Psychological Symptoms** ⇌ **Functional Impairment**
(i.e., performance deficits in response (i.e., skills deficits stemming from
to experiences of threat) experiences of deficiency)

affected person already possesses, that is, performance deficits. Conversely, problems attributable to limitations in socialization, enculturation, and psychological development stemming from having been reared in an ineffective familial context need to be addressed by methods that remediate these gaps and warps in functional capacities, that is, skills deficits (see Figure 4.3). A schematic depiction of the proposed pathway from childhood adversity to the dual and interacting consequences of psychological symptoms and functional impairment appears in Figure 4.4.

**FIGURE 4.4. Schematic Diagram: Contextual Trauma Therapy Model of Two-Pronged Causation of Complex Traumatization**

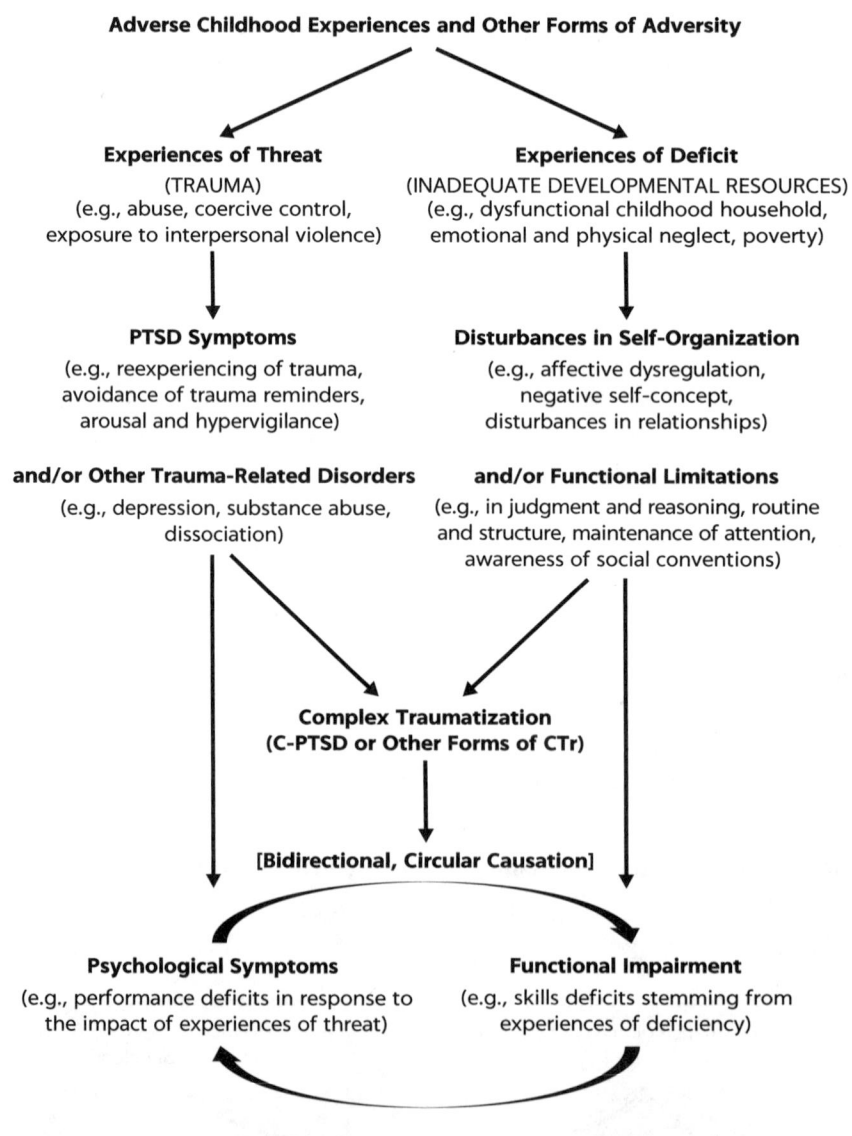

**Adverse Childhood Experiences and Other Forms of Adversity**

**Experiences of Threat**
(TRAUMA)
(e.g., abuse, coercive control, exposure to interpersonal violence)

↓

**PTSD Symptoms**
(e.g., reexperiencing of trauma, avoidance of trauma reminders, arousal and hypervigilance)

**and/or Other Trauma-Related Disorders**
(e.g., depression, substance abuse, dissociation)

**Experiences of Deficit**
(INADEQUATE DEVELOPMENTAL RESOURCES)
(e.g., dysfunctional childhood household, emotional and physical neglect, poverty)

↓

**Disturbances in Self-Organization**
(e.g., affective dysregulation, negative self-concept, disturbances in relationships)

**and/or Functional Limitations**
(e.g., in judgment and reasoning, routine and structure, maintenance of attention, awareness of social conventions)

**Complex Traumatization**
(C-PTSD or Other Forms of CTr)

↓

[Bidirectional, Circular Causation]

**Psychological Symptoms**
(e.g., performance deficits in response to the impact of experiences of threat)

**Functional Impairment**
(e.g., skills deficits stemming from experiences of deficiency)

C-PTSD = complex posttraumatic stress disorder; CTr = complex traumatization; PTSD = posttraumatic stress disorder.

It is this distinction, both a conceptual-etiological and practical-strategic one, that lies at the core of CTT. Although PTSD, as codified in the *DSM*, is often exclusively a function of traumatization, CTT—consistent with the definition in the 11th edition of the *International Classification of Diseases* (World Health Organization, 2018)—proposes that C-PTSD is frequently and perhaps almost always a result of traumatization and deficits in psychological development that prevent those individuals affected from adequately managing the requirements of adult functioning. The Adverse Childhood Experiences Study (Stevens, 2012) and especially Felitti's (2002) formulation of the ACEs study findings draw our attention to a crucial sphere of influence beyond that represented by either specific types of traumatic events (e.g., childhood sexual abuse, childhood physical abuse, childhood verbal or emotional abuse, exposure to domestic violence) or to other forms of childhood adversity not encompassed by the construct of trauma (e.g., growing up in a household in which a family member abused substances, attempted suicide, incarceration). As the quote by Felitti (2002) in Chapter 3 conveys (see, in particular, "a child does not grow up with an alcoholic parent or with domestic violence *in an otherwise supportive and well-functioning household*" [emphasis added] [Felitti, 2002, p. 361] in the section Adverse Childhood Experiences as Markers of an Ineffective Family Environment), the configuration of the results of the ACEs investigation (Felitti, 2002) points beyond the psychological consequences of the particular ACEs factors, either individually or in combination. It helps us to see, if we stand back and examine the gestalt created by the ACEs data, that the similarity in the types of psychological difficulties, health risk behaviors, and medical illnesses that would result from all of the 10 ACEs reveals a more extensive picture than that conveyed by the separate factors. From this broader, wide-ranging viewpoint, each ACE is not merely a cause of impairment but an indicator of a family system that is impaired in its ability to effectively meet the developmental needs of its offspring. What this perspective suggests, in conjunction with both empirical findings and clinical observation, is that the number of ACEs present in an individual's history is a gross measure of the degree to which his or her childhood household was unequipped to transmit adaptive living skills to the next generation.

The identification of distinct effects of those ACEs that consist of experiences of threat and those indicative of experiences of deprivation maps precisely onto the differentiation CTT makes between trauma-related difficulties and developmental gaps and warps. This two-pronged model of causation was originally based on clinical observation and has been supported over time by various sources of empirical evidence: the correspondence between particular family environment characteristics and profiles with child maltreatment (e.g., Gold, Hyman, & Andrés-Hyman, 2004; Ray, Jackson, & Townsley, 1991); the ACEs investigations (Stevens, 2012) culminating in Felitti's (2002) conclusion that the various ACEs factors are indicators of a broader atmosphere of household dysfunction; and the differential psychological impacts of experiences of threat and experiences of deprivation identified by McLaughlin, Sheridan, and Lambert (2014).

For those already knowledgeable about psychological trauma, a cursory glance at Figure 4.4 may leave the impression of two possible outcomes: PTSD in response to experiences of threat or C-PTSD in response to a combination of experiences of threat and experiences of deficit. However, discriminating the discrete psychological consequences of experiences of threat from those of experiences of deficit helps to delineate these two possibilities—the first two described in the following list—plus several other potential outcomes also listed:

1. PTSD: Having encountered experiences of threat but not experiences of deficit, meets criteria for PTSD but not for C-PTSD—In the absence of experiences of deficit, experiences of threat of sufficient magnitude might still culminate in the emergence of PTSD but not in C-PTSD. Consider, for example, someone reared in a well-functioning household characterized by few or no ACEs. Such an individual would be well positioned to arrive at adulthood having evolved the developmental capacities needed to function well. With a childhood history relatively free of experiences of deficit, the individual would not be likely to exhibit the DSO associated with C-PTSD. Moreover, the person's developmental attainment would likely include the capacity for comparatively resilient coping skills that would render them less vulnerable to traumatization than others from less fortunate backgrounds. However, in the face of traumatic circumstances of sufficiently severe proportions, the individual's coping skills may be overtaxed and compromised, thus resulting in PTSD.

2. C-PTSD: Having encountered both experiences of threat and experiences of deficit, meets criteria for C-PTSD—The preponderance of the research evidence indicates that C-PTSD emerges during childhood or adolescence and is a result of growing up in a household and surrounding community in which one was confronted with both experiences of threat and experiences of deficit (Briere & Rickards, 2007; Cloitre, Scarvalone, & Difede, 1997; Powers et al., 2017).

3. Trauma-related disorders (T-RD) other than PTSD: Having encountered experiences of threat, but not experiences of deficit, meets criteria for one or more T-RD but not for PTSD or C-PTSD—Extensive research evidence indicates that experiences of threat (i.e., traumatic events) can be related to a wide variety of disorders other than PTSD (Gold, 2004b; Luyten et al., 2017). Some of the most common of these trauma-related outcomes are depression (Maercker, Neimeyer, & Simiola, 2017), substance abuse (Najavits, 2015b), dissociative difficulties (Briere, 2006), and borderline and other personality disorders (Golier et al., 2003). Therefore, when these disorders have an onset in response to traumatic events and contain elements related to those events, they can legitimately be considered T-RD. When this is the case, recognition of the traumatic origins of the expressions of the disorder can be invaluable in formulating effective interventions for these syndromes.

4. Complex traumatization other than C-PTSD: Having encountered experiences of threat, meets criteria for one or more TR-D other than PTSD, and having a history of experiences of deficit, also meets criteria for DSO—Although not widely discussed to date in the literature, it has been recognized that just as individuals can exhibit disorders other than PTSD that are related to a history of trauma, there are forms of CTr (i.e., TR-D other than PTSD in combination with DSO) other than C-PTSD (Wamser-Nanney & Vandenberg, 2013). These situations would be exhibited by survivors of early repeated or ongoing trauma who do not meet full criteria for PTSD but to exhibit DSO, and who meet criteria for disorders other than PTSD that can be clinically identified as T-RD. Disorders of CTr, therefore, would encompass not only C-PTSD but also other clinical pictures related to a history of repeated or ongoing trauma that consist of the combined presence of one or more T-RD and the three components of DSO.

The latter finding broadens the implications of the CTT model considerably. The developmental limitations associated with having grown up in an environment characterized by experiences of deficit can be accompanied by a range of disorders other than PTSD. Consider, for example, the following case of an individual who described a history of childhood trauma in the form of extreme and ongoing verbal abuse that was related not to PTSD symptomatology but to major depression. Accompanying his moderate-to-severe depression were considerable developmental gaps and warps related to appreciable emotional neglect that formed the context in which his verbal abuse occurred.

**Case Example: Identifying and Treating Complex Traumatization**
Elliott, a White, Jewish man in his mid-40s, was referred to a trauma therapist with a CTT orientation by his psychiatrist, who conducted a thorough personal history that led her to recognize that Elliott's stultifying depression was primarily a response to the trauma of ongoing childhood verbal and emotional abuse, and emotional neglect. Throughout the initial assessment session, Elliott expressed in great detail all the ways in which he felt he had been a failure; he especially emphasized how inferior he was to his brother and two sisters. For one thing, he argued, they were all married and had children. Although he did not go into specifics on this point, he emphasized in general terms that their educational and career successes have been considerable, and that he was inferior to them in this respect. It was only in the last few minutes of the session that the therapist found out, someone accidentally, that Elliott was an accomplished professional who had graduated from a prestigious high school, college, and graduate school.

In the following meeting, close questioning by the clinician revealed that Elliott's siblings were in actuality not as academically or occupationally accomplished as he. His wildly inaccurate but sincere characterization of his educational and vocational background proved to be vivid examples of Elliott's strong tendency toward self-critical undervaluation of his accomplishments and abilities in a way that sharply contradicted the objective facts. As treatment progressed, it became evident that this perceptual tendency was clearly related to a history of intense, humiliating verbal and physical abuse by his moralistically Jewish father throughout his childhood and adolescence.

The CTT therapist was in full agreement, therefore, with the psychiatrist's conviction that Elliott's difficulties were an expression of his childhood trauma. The clinical picture was unquestionably one of major depression without any indication of coexisting PTSD. However, Elliott also clearly exhibited all three major forms of impairment associated with DSO: affective dysregulation, negative self-concept, and disturbances in relationships. He was easily overcome by depressed moods and a deep sense of discouragement. His entrance into therapy was precipitated when his chronic depression was exacerbated after he impulsively quit his position at a well-known medical center, partly because he believed he was not well liked or welcomed by his coworkers. He then berated himself for having left his job without first having secured another one. He saw himself, often in contradiction to the objective facts, as hopelessly inept and unlovable. Although he frequently went out with women he met on Internet dating sites, he rarely pursued them beyond a few dates. And, yet, he bemoaned the fact that he had not yet married or had children.

Elliott's CTT therapist initially relied on a highly structured program of behavioral activation to help him overcome his depression. Simultaneously, the therapist addressed cognitively Elliott's sense of hopelessness that his life could ever be decisively better, conviction of inferiority, assumption that he was doomed to forever be depressed, and self-perception of being unlovable. This was done partially by exploring the origins of these tendencies in his childhood verbal abuse and emotional neglect, and by helping him to challenge the accuracy of the ways in which his father had belittled him by having Elliott examine whether those attributions were verified or contradicted by the facts.

Simultaneously with these interventions, which targeted his trauma-related depression, the therapist helped Elliott to identify and remediate areas of developmental deficit stemming from the emotional neglect and the lack of structure and guidance that had characterized his childhood. In effect, Elliott was berated for his alleged shortcomings while not being provided with the resources that would help him to evolve the capacities to function more effectively. In therapy, he was taught to identify how to structure his days and exert the discipline to follow through on his goals and intentions. He was coached on how to move things forward in his dating life and how to determine whether he wished to transition from dating to an ongoing relationship, as well as how to manage this shift. His therapist assisted him in clarifying his career goals and strategizing how to find and apply for jobs that were more consistent with those goals.

As therapy progressed, it became clear to Elliott that he had established a pattern in childhood of reacting to the unpredictability in his household by making every effort to retreat into the monotony of a radically restricted lifestyle and by making life choices primarily on the basis of what he perceived as the path of least resistance. For almost 20 years, Elliott lived in the same apartment in the city in which he had grown up and allowed it to fall into a state of disarray and disrepair. He maintained friendships with those people still living in this hometown that he had first established in high school. Although he dated regularly, he would not allow these relationships to continue past the first few encounters, and he rarely, if ever, became sexually active with these women. Instead, he would engage in anonymous encounters with prostitutes as an outlet for his sexual needs.

Almost exactly 1 year after entering treatment, Elliott obtained work in a distant state. Rather than pursue his career in medicine, he obtained a position that was much more consistent with his values of promoting social welfare as an administrator in a community services agency that served low-income ethnic minority families. Appreciably less depressed and more optimistic than he had been a year earlier, his perceptions of the move to a new location and altered career path gradually shifted from constituting an intimidating "challenge" to composing an opportunity to establish a more gratifying lifestyle. He found it much easier than it had been previously to form new supportive relationships at work and in the community. Increasingly over time, he was able to step outside of his comfort zone and realize how the limitations he had placed on himself to maintain a sense of safety had imprisoned him in a stultifying life structure.

Having chosen a new career direction that was more consistent with his values and aspirations, he found himself regularly being praised and appreciated at work in a way that powerfully contradicted his self-critical bent. As his self-esteem grew in response, he no longer was drawn to rely on encounters with prostitutes to assuage his loneliness. Instead he was able to move from aimless, short-lived dating to more sustained, genuinely intimate relationships that were emotionally and sexually gratifying.

Although Elliott had previously been in treatment for many years with therapists who were not trauma oriented, the combination of addressing his long-standing depression in the context of his childhood trauma and identifying and remediating the developmental weaknesses related to his history of child neglect promoted much more extensive and stable reorientation to himself and others than he had previously been able to achieve. The verbal and physical abuse that had continued throughout his childhood and adolescence clearly were major sources of his chronic depression, which therefore constituted a TR-D. Simultaneously, however, Elliott just as obviously manifested a range of deficit-related developmental weaknesses manifested in the DSO difficulties he experienced in the areas of affect regulation, self-image, and interpersonal relationships. In addition, the bidirectional impact between his depressive and sexually addictive TR-D and his life-restricting DSO intensified and maintained both his depression and his constricted lifestyle. Decisive resolution of his long-standing depression, therefore, depended on a course of treatment that combined symptom-focused behavioral activation, cognitive processing of his childhood trauma and how it shaped his adult functioning, and developmental supports to strengthen his capacities to modulate emotion, provide a solid foundation for positive self-regard, and establish a more mature adult orientation to intimate relationships.

Elliott's course of therapy depicts how the success of treatment can depend on recognizing and being responsive to both the traumatization created by child maltreatment trauma and the developmental impairments resulting from a deficient family environment. He had been in therapy on and off for his depression for many years, but it was never explicitly connected to the physical and verbal and emotional abuse trauma he had been subjected to by his father. In the relative absence of emotional support and practical guidance, Elliott was unable to function effectively in intimate partner relationships, and despite his intelligence and academic ability, his career trajectory had been erratic and unsatisfying. By identifying and attending to both these factors, therapy was able to both resolve his trauma-related depression and bolster the functional capacities that had been insufficiently transmitted in his family of origin environment. Having completed coverage of the three main components of the CTT theoretical model—childhood abuse trauma, the familial interpersonal/developmental context, and the interaction between the two—we can now turn our attention to their implementation in beginning treatment.

# 5

# Initial Contact, Assessment, and Case Formulation

*Setting the Stage for Success*

We return in the next chapter to the practical issue of how to help complex trauma survivors overcome their performance- and skills-based trust limitations; there, we consider how to foster a productive, collaborative, therapeutic alliance. For now, it is crucial to understand that although identifying the potential origins of the two major areas of difficulty composing complex traumatization (CTr) can be extremely beneficial in conceptualizing an individual's situation, that does not mean that contextual trauma therapy (CTT) case formulation of a certain problem area is a simple either/or proposition. To understand the difficulties of a particular survivor of complex trauma, it is necessary for the practitioner to gather a detailed history that will empower them to identify the specific problems the individual has experienced and the unique intersecting combination of influences that created and perpetuate those problems. Accordingly, we now turn to how to apply contextual trauma theory to the psychological assessment of CTr so that we arrive at a sophisticated case conceptualization that forms the foundation of a treatment plan responsive to each individual's unique history and needs.

## INITIATING CONCEPTUALLY GUIDED TREATMENT

It is common in current practice to consider the overriding objective of a pretreatment psychological assessment to be this: to arrive at a diagnosis based on the assumption that doing so will dictate the treatment approach. In addition,

---

http://dx.doi.org/10.1037/0000176-006
*Contextual Trauma Therapy: Overcoming Traumatization and Reaching Full Potential*, by S. N. Gold
Copyright © 2020 by the American Psychological Association. All rights reserved.

in a case in which trauma is suspected to be a major factor responsible for psychological difficulties, a common inclination is to focus on exploration of a suspected traumatic event or series of events and determine whether the examinee exhibits difficulties that meet criteria for posttraumatic stress disorder (PTSD) or complex posttraumatic stress disorder (Herman, 1992b) in reaction to the identified incident or incidents (Garb, Lilienfeld, & Fowler, 2005; Schaffer & Rodolfa, 2016; Spores, 2013). This manner of proceeding makes sense if one assumes that the purpose of psychotherapy consists exclusively of applying specific interventions aimed at resolving a particular syndrome or group of coexisting syndromes.

The conceptual perspective of CTT is entirely inconsistent with such a procedure. Although structured diagnostic interviews and standardized tests can be helpful in arriving at or confirming the presence of complex posttraumatic stress disorder and its configuration and severity, doing so is not the culmination of the CTT assessment process but rather a jumping-off point. CTT explicitly recognizes that within the general territory of traumatization, especially of the potential proportions of CTr, each individual has a unique trauma history that extends well beyond the event or series of events that may have brought them to the attention of the helping professional. These individuals also have a particular developmental history that unfolded in a distinctive household embedded in a particular community that had a discrete set of cultural influences, which, in conjunction with their traumatic experiences, have generated a distinctive constellation of psychological problems, developmental deficits, and strengths (Gold, 2000, 2009; Gold & Ellis, 2017). This history is viewed within a CTT framework as often predating and contributing to the conditions that promoted maltreatment trauma. It also is understood from a contextual perspective to have had an impact in its own right independent of the consequences of trauma. It is therefore necessary to identify the interpersonal environment that preceded and accompanied the onset of explicit trauma, and that likely, in the case of CTr, independently contributed to the survivor's limitations in adaptive functioning.

Ultimately, the purpose of the initial assessment in CTT is to arrive at a case conceptualization that draws upon the areas covered in the first interview—chiefly personal history, history of traumatic experiences, resulting psychological difficulties (symptoms), areas of developmental weakness (manifested as areas of functional impairment), external resources, and personal strengths—to achieve a formulation that is employed to guide the direction and strategies of treatment. Applying CTT to a particular case requires, therefore, that the practitioner thoroughly explore each of these areas with the client and organize the client's account into a coherent conceptual formulation guided by the structure provided by the two-pronged, bidirectional causation posited by contextual trauma theory. The practitioner then uses the conceptualization arrived at to help identify (a) treatment goals and specific target areas to be addressed, (b) intervention approaches that appear to be most consistent with the client's needs and abilities at any given point in treatment, and (c) how the particular areas of strength and competency exhibited by the client can be leveraged to resolve psychological problems and remediate areas of developmental weakness.

To ground the treatment process in this type of case conceptualization, it is necessary at the outset to conduct a comprehensive assessment. As useful as such an evaluation is, it is essential to also keep in mind that the first interactions between practitioner and client can decisively set the tone of the therapeutic relationship and therefore of the rest of treatment. The CTT approach emphasizes the pivotal role of the quality of the treatment alliance in promoting therapeutic progress and positive treatment outcomes. Before discussing the intricacies of the assessment process, it is best to turn our attention to interactions that proceed and can set influential precedents for everything that follows.

**Starting at the Beginning: The Initial Contact**

The next chapter is devoted to extensive consideration of the powerful and essential function of the therapeutic relationship in working with trauma survivors. In relation to the current discussion, however, it is essential to recognize that the therapeutic alliance begins and its tenor starts to be shaped during the first interaction between professional and client. This initial contact does not occur at the first therapy session or even at outset of the pretreatment assessment. It begins even before the client arrives at the practitioner's office.

The first encounter, and therefore the initiation of the professional relationship, commonly occurs either over the phone or, increasingly frequently in recent years, via email. It is imperative for the professional to be cognizant of the impression that is conveyed not only by the content of communication but also by its tone. The same holds true if the client's first contact is with a receptionist or other member of the office staff; the client experiences office staff as a representative or proxy for the therapist. Staff, therefore, need to be thoroughly trained in how to interact with prospective clients in a trauma-informed manner. One of the fundamental tenets of trauma-informed practice is that one cannot accurately assume who is and is not a trauma survivor (L. S. Brown, 2008; Carello & Butler, 2014). Therefore, office staff who respond to initial phone calls need to be oriented to deal with all communications as if they are coming from someone with a background of trauma. Proceeding in this way not only increases the likelihood of establishing the foundation on which the client is more likely to build a sense of safety, security, and trust but also augments the probability that the client will appear at the first scheduled session and continue to attend sessions and actively and productively participate in treatment.

On the basis of unique trauma history and past interpersonal experiences, in general, especially within the family of origin environment, the trauma survivor's sense of that first encounter is colored by a corresponding set of fears, hopes, and expectations. One can anticipate that the hypervigilance that is a hallmark of traumatization will be operating during that interchange.

A sophisticated trauma clinician (or properly trained office staff member) will be keenly aware of and sensitive to the potential for these factors to color the survivor's perception of that preliminary encounter.

Many traumatized potential clients approach this encounter with considerable trepidation. A trauma-informed respondent will be especially mindful of the importance of placing concern for the client's welfare above business and financial considerations. Ideally, if it becomes apparent later in the discussion that the prospective client is not in a financial position to be able to afford the therapist's fees, even if there is provision for a sliding fee scale, the clinician should be prepared to offer referral to alternate, lower cost services. In addition, for someone who has been through a *traumatic experience*, defined as being controlled and taken advantage of, it can become an extremely sensitive issue to be careful to not overpower the client, even subtly or inadvertently, or to seem rushed or impatient. From the beginning, therefore, treating the survivor as a potential client who is considering retaining the clinician's services rather than as an impaired patient over whom the clinician presumes to have authority can make a decisive difference in the course that is set for the professional relationship and in the ultimate effectiveness of the assistance the clinician has to offer.

If it is an office staff member who receives clients' initial calls, they should limit the conversation to setting an initial appointment and conveying essential information about office policies and procedures, including fee-setting and billing practices. They should also make sure to inquire whether the client prefers to speak to the clinician before the first appointment. Doing so implicitly acknowledges that the client has a right to interview the therapist to obtain an initial sense of the therapist's interpersonal style and background and training, and the level of comfort the client experiences in the initial discussion with the practitioner. That inquiry also establishes a precedent for building into treatment an element that almost never is a regular fixture of the interpersonal environments in which child abuse survivors are reared: choice. From the outset of the therapy process and throughout its execution, being alert for opportunities to provide the survivor client with options, alternatives, and the invitation to express preferences serves as a powerful contrasting experience to past interactions imbued with coercive control.

Some prospective clients with a trauma history want the clinician to take the time to discuss some of their pressing concerns over the phone or address them in a response to an initial e-mail message. This may be particularly necessary if the client is trying to gauge whether the provider is conversant with the areas with which they are having difficulty, and how the clinician will respond to hearing about those problem areas. Especially if the communication is in the form of a phone call, some prospective clients feel uncomfortable revealing personal information during that first discussion and instead prefer to simply secure an appointment time and leave it at that. In my experience as a clinician and as a supervisor of doctoral trainees for nearly 30 years at the Nova Southeastern University Trauma Resolution & Integration Program, it is commonplace for traumatized clients to contact a therapist after a number of previous courses of treatment with practitioners who, in one way or another, demonstrated that they were insensitive to traumatization and were inadequately prepared to treat it. Generally speaking, therefore, the more the clinician can subtly communicate awareness of and sensitivity to a client's potential discomfort, the more likely it is that the clinician will establish a tentative basis for a sense of safety in the therapeutic alliance.

Before asking about delicate areas over the phone, the practitioner should make sure to inquire whether the client is calling from a place where they have privacy before inviting them to discuss any potentially sensitive or uncomfortable topics. These topics include asking about what they hope to get out of treatment and anything regarding the possible presence of a trauma history. Asking whether the client is in a private location gives that individual the option to walk to an area where they do have privacy or to call back from a place not within earshot of others.

When the client does indicate that they wish to discuss one of these delicate subjects, it is important for the practitioner to preface or phrase their inquiry in a way that makes it clear that, at this point, they are only seeking abbreviated, preliminary information rather than inviting an extended discussion. For example, the clinician might ask, "Can you give me an idea of what you hope to accomplish in treatment so that I can get a sense whether my expertise matches what you are seeking?" Similarly, in inquiring about the possible presence of a trauma history, the practitioner might query, "Do you have any ideas about what might be responsible for that difficulty [those difficulties], and, if so, is that a matter that you feel comfortable discussing now, or would you rather wait until our first meeting?" Between the two, finding out what the client is seeking from treatment is more important because it helps the clinician to determine whether their training and skills are a good match for the desired therapeutic objectives. If the client prefers not to go beyond scheduling a first appointment, either of these topics can certainly wait until the first face-to-face meeting to be addressed.

The general principle throughout this initial communication is for the clinician to convey to the client through their tone and behavior (rather than through explicitly stating so) that they are conversant with trauma-related issues and concerns, and are sensitive and responsive to them. Implicitly conveying these points via sensitivity and responsiveness is appreciably more effective and convincing than stating them directly. Doing so demonstrates to the client that the therapist is not only knowledgeable about the territory of trauma but also displays the types of trauma-relevant skills that make it likely that the clinician can be helpful to the client in facing and overcoming their difficulties.

In a similar vein, the therapist needs to be prepared to answer any questions the prospective client has about the therapist's philosophy and method of trauma treatment. Although it is not commonplace, particularly savvy psychotherapy consumers, especially those who have endured unsatisfactory previous treatment experiences, ask the practitioner questions along these lines. These consumers have a right to inquire about their prospective clinician's approach. The therapist who has thought through these matters sufficiently to clearly synopsize how they conduct therapy with trauma survivors is equipped with a formidable tool for building a foundation for the client's confidence.

Sometimes clients ask whether the practitioner is experienced in a particular treatment approach, such as eye-movement desensitization and reprocessing therapy or hypnotherapy. Usually when I am asked questions about approaches that I have training in and experience with, I avoid simply answering in the affirmative, because that answer is likely to be interpreted as an implicit agreement to provide that form of treatment. To prevent the client from assuming this is the case, I suggest that when we meet, we can discuss what the goals of treatment will be and then jointly determine how to best achieve those goals rather than prejudge how they will be accomplished.

**Case Example: The Therapeutic Impact of the Initial Client Contact**
A particular case example vividly illustrates the extensive impact on the course of therapy and treatment outcome that an initial contact can have.[1] Lorna, a White, Jewish woman in her late 40s with an especially horrific history of extensive and ongoing childhood abuse, called my office at the university where I direct the Trauma Resolution and Integration Program, the psychology training clinic that specializes in treating traumatized individuals. It is unusual for prospective clients to call me at that number, which is listed as an academic office. It therefore was clear to me when Lorna indicated that she was considering receiving treatment at our trauma clinic and wanted to ask me some questions about it that she had exercised considerable skill in identifying me the as the director of the clinic (this was before much information was readily available on the Internet) and securing my contact information. Her determination to speak to me directly could be seen as pushy and overbearing. Although this is a possibility that should be considered, the strength-based perspective of CTT raises the alternative that it is instead a sign of sophisticated abilities and determination to secure quality treatment—and subsequent evidence overwhelmingly indicated that this was the case.

During the course of the conversation, Lorna conveyed that, for many years, she had been in treatment for the effects of her traumatization with a number of therapists and had spent time in several residential treatment programs that specialize in this area. Lorna explained that she was currently seeing a clinician who had been helpful to her. However, this therapist had concluded that Lorna exhibited significant dissociative symptoms, an area in which her practitioner had not received much training. Her therapist had suggested that Lorna contact the clinic I direct and explained that as a facility specializing in trauma treatment, the clinicians regularly worked with clients with dissociative difficulties.

---

[1]For this case example, including the interview dialogue in Chapter 13 with Lorna, the client allowed the author to describe her case and use a transcript.

Lorna described a broad range of serious problems, including a history of nonsuicidal self-injury, extended periods of dissociative amnesia, agoraphobia that kept her housebound unless she was accompanied by a family member, daily panic attacks, and a period of about the previous 10 years during which she was unemployed and had avoided driving. Despite her account of these disabling difficulties, she convincingly conveyed that she was determined to overcome her problems. She also asked a series of thoughtful questions about our treatment philosophy and approach at the university-based trauma clinic.

As the discussion progressed, it was clear to me that she was evaluating the content and tenor of my responses while I was appraising hers. It became apparent that she was bright and had put a great deal of thought into the questions she asked me about our treatment program. Despite the severity of her difficulties and her level of impairment, she was extremely articulate and came across as entirely reasonable. I was especially impressed that she spoke about her current outpatient therapist in positive and respectful terms rather than seeming disturbed or rejected because that therapist had advised her to seek further treatment elsewhere.

Lorna did decide to enter therapy at the clinic. She was seen by one of the clinic's more skilled therapists, and in less than a year, most of the difficulties that prompted her to initially contact us were either significantly improved or entirely resolved. Although she still experienced problems that could benefit from further treatment, she decided that after having been in therapy for a decade before coming to this clinic, she would take a "break" and spend some time exploring life without being in treatment. By this time, she was driving extensively without any restrictions in the distance she traveled or the route she took. She also was employed full-time, exhibited an impressive level of ability and productivity on the job, and immensely enjoyed the work she was doing. She initially had reported that throughout the night, she would startle awake after sleeping for no more than 15 or 20 minutes at a time. These abruptly interrupted periods of sleep totaled no more than 2 to 3 hours a night. She marveled that she was now sleeping 6 hours straight on a regular basis.

After a couple of years, Lorna returned to treatment with us and addressed severe dissociative symptoms related to her complex trauma history. Because the program is a training clinic, therapists are generally not placed with us for more than 1 calendar year. She continued in treatment with the clinic for a number of years and was required to adapt to a new therapist at the start of each academic year. She was able to engage with each of her clinicians and steadily move forward in her treatment. Over time, she obtained a graduate degree and was not only fully employed but worked in an advanced professional capacity. Despite her previous intense agoraphobia that had kept her confined to her home for about a decade, Lorna had been invited to give professional presentations in several foreign countries and reveled in the opportunity to do so.

When her treatment at the clinic was complete, years after she had originally contacted me over the phone, I had the opportunity to meet with Lorna face to face and debrief with her about the course of her therapy with us.

(A transcribed excerpt from this debriefing interview is reproduced in Chapter 13.) Although all of her intervening treatment had been by the doctoral trainees who staff the clinic, she referenced the initial call in which she spoke with me as a key determinant of the course of her therapy. She attributed her confidence in the validity of our program and much of the progress she had made in the intervening years to the clarity of my responses to her questions, to my taking her inquiries seriously, and, above all, to her experience of my having treated her "as a human being."

For my part, that first contact had demonstrated to me that despite her multiple severe difficulties and restricted life structure at the time, Lorna was highly motivated to pursue treatment. She had the foresight and skill to find a way to reach and speak to me directly. She had prepared for our phone call with a series of carefully thought-out questions aimed at clarifying what our treatment philosophy and approach was so that she could make a careful assessment for herself whether it seemed reasonable to her. The determination, thoughtfulness, advance planning, and articulate communication all seemed to reflect substantial assets that would serve to support her progress in treatment. These impressions were borne out. Lorna entered therapy with the understanding that outcome depended largely on her willingness to take the risk of moving into unfamiliar territory, try new things, and follow through on her clinicians' directives and assignments between sessions. Consequently, she was able to markedly reduce or eliminate her trauma-related symptoms and radically improve her quality of life.

**Starting the Assessment**

The assessment process begins to establish the atmosphere in which treatment will unfold. If it concentrates initially, primarily, or exclusively on problems, this focus can foster negativity in clients and promote a sense of pessimism and hopelessness. The central function of psychotherapy is not to dwell on difficulties as an end in itself but to work toward their resolution. Clients with a history of complex trauma often enter therapy after a series of minimally helpful or counterproductive treatments and a long chain of personal problems and perceived failures. In addition, they frequently experience themselves as ineffective and helpless, and they therefore assume that treatment will only be successful, if at all, on the basis of the therapist's efforts.

Appreciably compounding these countertherapeutic factors is the remarkable frequency with which therapy clients have been told by other mental health practitioners across various disciplines—psychiatrists, psychologists, counselors, social workers, and case managers—that their "condition" is a "chronic" one. Although the term *chronic* means "long term," what is being conveyed by these professionals is that the diagnosis in question is permanent. Frequently, these clients have been warned that they will "always" struggle with their current symptoms and that the objective of treatment is to help them "learn to live with" or "manage" these difficulties rather than ameliorate or eliminate them. It is not uncommon as part of this discussion for the practitioner to admonish the client that strict adherence to their prescribed medication regimen is an (or *the*) indispensable component of effectively curtailing their symptoms and that failure to comply with taking their medication will result in symptom intensification and relapse.

Communications of this sort are deeply countertherapeutic. Practitioners who adopt and express such views are obviously not likely to see much value in seeking strategies for problem resolution beyond exhortations urging medication compliance. Worse yet, clients who place credence in these severely limited expectations of progress are almost certain to be convinced that exerting their own efforts to improve their mental status is pointless. Once the client has accepted this viewpoint, it is likely to radically hamper psychotherapeutic treatment because most forms of therapy rely on the client to implement procedures and follow directives imparted during sessions outside of the consulting room. These forms of discouragement by professionals are pervasive enough that it is incumbent on the trauma practitioner to be alert to indications that the client subscribes to them and to vigorously counter them.

**Case Example: Eschewing Change-Limiting Practices**
A particularly dramatic instance of this discouraging and counterproductive practice was described at length by Lorna, the woman in the previous case example. At the end of her treatment at our trauma clinic, she conveyed that she previously had been cautioned by professionals that the seriousness of her "condition" indicated that she would always struggle with severe psychological difficulties and that she was in danger of becoming psychotic if she did not remain in treatment indefinitely. She also indicated that she had been repeatedly warned by staff members at residential facilities that refusal to participate in psychopharmacological treatment would ensure that she would not only fail to improve but would hopelessly deteriorate over time. Lorna indicated to me that her own research suggested to her that medication was not necessary in her case. She explained that in addition to being convinced that psychiatric medications would be of little value to her, she found taking them intensely disturbing because she had been forcefully drugged to force her into submission in conjunction with the abuse she had experienced as a child. Consequently, despite these repeated reproaches by various mental health professionals, she was determined to not accept any medication as part of her recovery. At the conclusion of her therapy, Lorna reported with a considerable sense of triumph that she was especially proud to have proved these practitioners wrong. She had successfully overcome her many symptoms and had established an appreciably more sound level of functioning and gratifying lifestyle without relying at all on psychiatric medications.

**Case Example: Negative Prognostic Expectations and Their Refutation**
Similarly, William, a White, Jewish physician with PTSD that stemmed from an attempt on his life, had left his practice and gone on disability after his psychiatrist adamantly explained to him that there was no "cure" for his disorder. Consequently, he entered therapy and assumed that he would remain

on disability and would never return to the practice of medicine, and that the best he could hope for was help tolerating his symptoms of traumatization. Instances such as this can require considerable time and effort to convince the traumatized client that symptom resolution and significantly improved functioning are attainable. (Offering examples of other traumatized clients who have been able to overcome their difficulties can be immensely helpful in this regard.) Fortunately, in this instance, the psychotherapist was successful in persuading William that recovery and return to full professional functioning was possible. Within a year's time, William's trauma symptoms were resolved, and he was able to resume an active, full-time practice.

## ESTABLISHING AN ORIENTATION TOWARD SUCCESS

For all the reasons discussed previously, it is essential from the outset of the course of treatment (including the initial assessment) to orient the complex trauma survivor toward envisioning an appreciably more gratifying and productive future, and toward the understanding that the success of therapy is determined, in large part, by their efforts. This orientation is especially important because the aim of CTT-oriented therapy is to not only reduce and eliminate symptoms of PTSD and other co-occurring disorders but to improve the survivor's overall quality of life by remediating developmental deficits. Many survivors of CTr in childhood were incessantly assailed with criticisms and negative appraisals by caregivers, other authority figures such as teachers, and even bullying peers such that those assaults inculcated a deep sense of their own ineptitude and hopelessness that they and their situation could improve. Consequently, it is important for the trauma-oriented practitioner to actively monitor signs that the survivor holds such beliefs and respond by conveying that not only is change possible but that the survivor also can work toward symptom resolution and to establish an appreciably more effective and gratifying lifestyle.

After attending to initial "business" matters, such as reviewing paperwork completed by the client, briefly explaining important office policies and procedures, and reviewing the extent and limits of confidentiality, it is useful for the clinician to begin by asking, "If we are wildly successful here, how will your life be different when treatment is completed?" This question is carefully worded. The reference to being "wildly successful" is aimed at countering the apprehension and pessimism that clients often enter therapy with and encouraging them to set as high as possible their expectations of what they might accomplish in therapy.[2] Framing the question in terms of success represents an attempt to

---

[2]Some readers may find this level of optimism imprudent. I discuss this topic in greater detail in the following chapter on the therapeutic relationship. Suffice it to say here that a client's pessimism and disbelief that improvement is possible almost certainly will severely reduce the likelihood that they will make substantive efforts to follow through on therapeutic directives and work in a diligent, disciplined way toward improvement.

orient clients toward thinking along the lines of improving the quality of their lives rather than primarily in terms of reducing the intensity of or eliminating problems. Using the pronoun "we" is intended to convey that therapy is a joint effort. On one hand, the therapist alone is unable to accomplish changes for the client. On the other, the CTT practitioner is "walking" side by side with the client, providing encouragement, emotional support, understanding of the dual impact of trauma and developmental deprivation, and guidance in the form of interventions that the client frequently will be expected to carry out and follow through on between appointments, not just during session.

Based on my experience as a clinician and supervisor of clinical trainees at the Trauma Resolution & Integration Program, most survivors of CTr have a great deal of trouble envisioning what is possible to expect from psychological treatment. Undoubtedly, the greatest reason is that ultimately and ideally, CTT is aimed at is not merely resolving symptoms but also improving the quality of the client's life and equipping them to function in a way that is so foreign to their previous experience that it is difficult for them to imagine. From early in the process, therefore, is essential to survivors of CTr to think not just in terms of overcoming their difficulties but also along the lines of attaining a more productive, gratifying, and effective quality of daily living. Conveying this expectation is part and parcel of explaining that CTT takes into account and addresses both the impact of the trauma they lived through and remediation of the gaps in their functioning that are attributable to the emotional and practical support unavailable to them during their growing-up years.

As a means of attending to the formation of a collaborative working relationship from the beginning, I also explain that we will be working together to identify the goals of therapy, will agree on the sequence in which we will address those goals, will cooperatively decide what procedures to use to accomplish each of the treatment objectives, and will periodically and jointly evaluate treatment progress. These concrete behaviors constitute the core of what is meant by a *collaborative therapeutic relationship*, which consists not merely of a sense of joint endeavor but the fact of shared planning and execution of treatment. As is discussed in much greater detail in the next chapter, this perspective can seem entirely foreign to many survivors of CTr. Many have never had the experience of feeling that someone else has their best interests at heart, is on their side, will attentively listen to them, and will provide them with the assistance that they may have never realized is an indispensable requisite of attaining adult functioning.

## ASSESSING TRAUMATIZATION IN AN INTERPERSONAL/ DEVELOPMENTAL CONTEXT

To arrive at a conceptual formulation that provides an inclusive picture of the client's background, difficulties, and the probable causes of their problems as a means of guiding the initial stages of treatment, it is necessary to conduct a relatively broad-based assessment early in the therapy process. However, it is equally crucial to explicitly recognize that, almost inevitably, additional important information will emerge as treatment progresses and that, therefore, the initial conceptualization needs to be considered a preliminary one that is open to continual revision and refinement. Maintaining such a mind-set is a challenge, because, once we come to certain conclusions, it is difficult to remain open to taking in evidence that might contradict those suppositions and point to the need to revise them. Exercising this form of discipline despite the pull to rely on our prior assumptions, as difficult as it may be, is exactly the type of receptivity to new observations and perspectives that clinicians encourage in their clients. To fail to do so undermines treatment progress by demonstrating to clients that their clinicians encourage them to adhere to expectations but are unwilling to follow those expectations themselves.

For the CTT practitioner, the central aim of the initial assessment interview is to assemble a personal history of the traumatized client from which to arrive at a conceptual formulation that outlines (a) the major threat- and deficit-related experiences in the survivor's life, (b) how each of these types of adversity has contributed to difficulties in the form of symptoms and in the form of functional impairment, and (c) how these two primary forces have interacted to compound adverse impacts over time.

It is, however, more important to pace the gathering of information at a rate that is not overwhelming for the client. In general, attending to the quality of the therapeutic relationship and conducting oneself in a manner that forms the foundation for the client's formation of a sense of security, safety, trust, and connectedness with the therapist are the primary vital considerations. The amount and detail of information gathered and the rapidity with which it is collected ranks a distant second consideration. As useful as it may be to conduct a comprehensive evaluation at the outset, proceeding in a way that subverts the client's development of an experience of affiliation and collaboration with the therapist is much more critical in shaping the ultimate outcome of treatment, and even whether the client engages in the therapy process at all. It is essential to not lose sight of the personhood of the survivor client by single-mindedly firing off a series of predetermined questions in an effort to collect as much information as possible and as rapidly as possible.

Formulating a contextually grounded case conceptualization, therefore, requires that the practitioner conduct a detailed, conversational, open-ended interview that covers a range of topics that extend appreciably beyond the client's trauma history and symptom picture. These areas for exploration are listed next. They are followed by more specific subtopics to consider pursuing—a list of sample questions that can help elicit the information associated with each area. These questions, though, are merely suggestions. Rather than relying on a series of predetermined standard questions, it is usually more productive to allow the interview to be free flowing and individually tailored enough to investigate what appear to be the most pertinent areas in detail and what appraisal needs to be made as the interview process unfolds. An example of this style of assessment appears in the annotated transcript of an initial interview with a dissociative survivor of CTr (see Chapter 10).

Topics routinely explored include the following:

- family or community environment: exploration of the tone, characteristics, and norms of the household or family environment and larger surrounding community, including administration of the Adverse Childhood Experiences Questionnaire as part of the Adverse Childhood Experiences Study that appeared in the psychological research literature (Felitti et al., 1998; Stevens, 2012) and, to the extent that the survivor can tolerate it at the beginning of treatment, exploration of the details of any adverse childhood experiences that the client endorses;

- educational history: that includes academic performance and social adaptation in elementary, middle, and high school and college, and that pays special attention to fluctuations in functioning that may be related to experiences of threat and deprivation;

- history of addictive or compulsive patterns of behavior: that includes alcohol use, other substance use, nonsuicidal self-injury, sexually compulsive behavior, compulsive spending, compulsive gambling, and that pays special attention to when the behavior pattern began, what was happening in the person's life at the time that may have prompted initiation of the behavior, and how the frequency and intensity of the behavior may have waxed and waned over time;

- trauma history: identification of not only the traumatic experiences included in the Adverse Childhood Experiences Questionnaire but also traumatic events that have occurred since childhood and adolescence, such as criminal assaults, rape, intimate partner violence, combat and other military traumas, and natural disasters; standardized measures such as the Trauma History Questionnaire (Hooper, Stockton, Krupnick, & Green, 2011) or the Traumatic Events Questionnaire (Vrana & Lauterbach, 1994) can be helpful in this regard;

- employment history: that covers any military service and experiences in the military, types of jobs held, at what age the client was first employed, length of employment at each position, and reasons for the end of the position;

- relationship history: an overview of dating patterns and long-term relationships, how relationships began, the level of emotional and sexual intimacy and coercive control in each major relationship, and the circumstances leading to the end of each relationship;

- legal history: any arrests, the charges involved and the final disposition of charges; if incarcerated, inquiry into the client's adaptation to jail or prison and any traumatic experiences during incarceration and their impact; and

- client strengths: personal characteristics, life experiences, current resources, special skills, and noteworthy achievements that can be used in the service of attaining therapeutic goals.

Although it is useful to, at some point, touch on each of the areas listed relatively early in the treatment process, at least to ascertain if they require further exploration, it is usually neither required nor desirable to discuss each area in detail in the initial meeting. To avoid overlooking an area that might be particularly relevant, however, it is best to conduct an at least cursory investigation of each of these topics with the intention of returning at a later time to territory that seems to warrant further exploration. In most cases, the first four topics—family or community environment, educational history, history of addictive or compulsive patterns of behavior, and trauma history—and the last one, client strengths, are the ones most important to address in the initial assessment interview.

## INCLUDING THE PIVOTAL ROLE OF CLIENT STRENGTHS IN CONTEXTUAL TRAUMA THERAPY

Client strengths is an especially fruitful area to include in the assessment. It is an area that too often is overlooked or, if the clinician works in a setting where client strengths are required to be included in the intake report, is only given perfunctory attention. It is not unusual in these situations to see practitioners include items such as "The client is motivated for treatment, as evidenced by their attendance at the initial intake appointment" or "The client is sufficiently verbal to benefit from talk therapy." When commonplace, minimally noteworthy qualities like these are included in the report, it is easy to conclude that they are rote statements offered only because the facility the therapist is employed by requires the inclusion of client strengths.

This phenomenon is unsurprising when one considers that via required classes, such as psychopathology and diagnosis of mental disorders in academic training, the mental health professional devotes extensive time to coverage of the difficulties that can bring clients into therapy but often no or only minimal time to discussion of the assets that clients may possess. In the process, potentially critical information is lost. Progress in treatment often is attained by building on the positive qualities and competencies that clients exhibit. But, just as therapists are unlikely to recognize various psychological disorders if they have not been trained in diagnostic criteria and how they manifest, treaters are unlikely to be able to easily recognize the strengths clients possess if they are not trained in the skill of how to identify them. Such training is necessary because it is not unusual for survivors of CTr to have such an extensively negative self-image that they themselves may have a great deal of difficulty recognizing their own strong points. Elliott, discussed in Chapter 2, is a particularly good example of this tendency: After spending much of the initial interview stressing what he viewed as his many shortcomings and failures, it almost slipped out parenthetically at the end of the meeting that he was a physician.

In many instances, the alert psychotherapist will be much more likely to detect client strengths through careful observation and by reading between the lines. The case of Lorna that appears earlier in this chapter is an excellent example of the clinician's being attentive to identifying strengths—by understanding more than what Lorna had stated directly—that turned out to be powerful sources of treatment progress. Here is a case example of a client's skill that could have easily been overlooked but was able to be harnessed as one of the most potent sources of change in her treatment.

**Case Example: Recognizing and Using Client Strengths**
Dana, a White woman in her late 20s, was frequently, brutally, and sadistically molested by her stepfather for more than 10 years from early childhood into mid-adolescence. The abuse ended only when she left the household at age 16 to go live with her biological father. Haunted by severe posttraumatic symptoms, intense self-loathing, and extreme avoidance of close relationships, Dana sought out psychotherapy at the age of 23. Hearing about the viciously aggressive nature of the maltreatment to which Dana had been subjected, her therapist urged her to sue her stepfather and insisted that she would never be able to recover unless she "made things right" by obtaining "justice."

After several weeks of being pressured by her therapist, Dana contacted an attorney and filed a lawsuit. Soon afterward, it dawned on her that she had felt pressured by her clinician in much the same way that she had felt overpowered by her stepfather. She realized that she was not invested in legal action, but she was not about to back down by withdrawing the lawsuit. Instead, feeling that her therapist had proven himself untrustworthy by imposing his beliefs and wishes on her, she abruptly left treatment and vehemently vowed to herself that she would never again take the risk of going into therapy.

Dana continued to be plagued by severely disruptive manifestations of CTr for the next several years but adhered to her commitment to avoid psychological treatment. However, when she was informed by her attorney that a trial date had been set for the lawsuit, her anxious arousal skyrocketed, and her already disruptive flashbacks of sadistic assault intensified markedly. She still was determined to not retreat from legal action. As the designated trial date approached, her trauma-related distress became progressively elevated. Finding it unimaginable that she could face her stepfather in court without the support of therapy, she relented, made an appointment with a clinician, and promised herself that she would leave treatment as soon as the legal case was over.

Dana was barely able to convey this much in her first session with the new therapist before she abruptly fell silent with her face impassive as she stared blankly into space. With gentle encouragement from the therapist, Dana was able to reorient sufficiently to resume speaking. However, her voice was barely audible, and she continued to appear strikingly detached.

This pattern continued for the next two sessions. Dana would begin talking, audibly but extremely softly. After a few minutes, her voice tone would drop, and she would begin to mumble in a garbled, incomprehensible fashion as her eyes glazed over and she began to tremble. With soft and cautious prompting, her therapist was able to help Dana return her attention to the room but with an apparent lack of awareness that she was speaking barely above a whisper such that the therapist could not make out what she was saying.

This repeating pattern broke dramatically in the fourth session as Dana strode into the consulting room wearing business attire; her bearing and expression brimmed with confidence. Immediately on sitting down, she squarely met the therapist's gaze, and in a voice that was steady and strong, announced, "I just closed a million-dollar deal." The change in Dana's demeanor was extraordinary. Her relatively formal clothing conveyed to the therapist that this was the first time Dana had come directly to session from the office. In stark contrast to the terror she had exhibited in previous meetings, she appeared impressively calm and self-assured.

It immediately occurred to the therapist that Dana was exhibiting a powerfully resilient skill set that Dana could harness in the service of helping her make it through the trial. "I am not a businessperson," the therapist intoned. "There is very little that I know about that world. But one of the few aspects of the business profession I am familiar with is the creation of a business plan." The therapist then asked, "Would I be correct in assuming that you have considerable experience constructing business plans?" Dana replied, somewhat smugly, "I work up business plans all the time. I can practically design them in my sleep." The therapist said, "I realize that this is going to sound terribly strange. Please don't mistake what I am about to suggest as a sign of my ignorance. I fully understand how unconventional—if not bizarre—this idea may seem to you." She continued, "But with your level of expertise, I wonder if you wouldn't be able to construct a business plan that would guide you in making it through your court appearance."

Dana's eyebrows immediately shot up, registering intense skepticism mixed with more than a little derision. However, as the discussion continued, with the trial just a few weeks away and no obvious alternative strategy that was likely to be effective in such a brief time frame, Dana agreed to draw up and execute a business plan to arm her to comfortably manage facing her stepfather in the courtroom. By the time the trial had begun, Dana had attained a sufficient degree of calm to approach the situation with a surprising level of confidence. Ironically, when the day of the dreaded confrontation arrived, Dana's stepfather failed to appear, and the judge issued a summary judgment in her favor.

This vignette illustrating the power of identifying and making use of client strengths is admittedly an unusually dramatic one. It is, however, true. For the purposes of the present discussion, what this anecdote conveys is the considerable potential that can be tapped into when we step outside of an almost exclusive focus on our complexly traumatized clients' frailties and turn our focus in the direction of detecting and building on their assets. The therapist did not allow herself to get caught up in the illusion that the timid, fear-ridden, intimidated person that she encountered in the first three therapy visits composed the totality of Dana's behavioral repertoire. Rather, by being prepared to recognize, acknowledge, and make use of the resilient qualities that Dana had exhibited in the fourth session, the therapist had laid the foundation for a therapeutic outcome that was much more favorable than either she or Dana could have anticipated at the outset of treatment. Although, at the beginning, Dana's only aspiration for therapy was to make it through the legal trial, probably based on the impressive degree of success she was able to achieve in meeting that goal—one that far exceeded her expectations—she remained in treatment. As she continued in therapy, she was able to overcome her avoidance of emotional intimacy and establish an unprecedented capacity for experiencing interpersonal connection.

Although this vignette provides an example of the tremendous therapeutic value of being alert to detect the assets clients bring to the treatment endeavor, it also represents an instance of several other aspects of CTT to be covered in much greater detail in subsequent chapters. One salient one is creating and adapting interventions tailored to the individual client rather than exclusively drawing on existing, standard approaches. Another is encouraging the client to take charge of not only of carrying out the intervention but of collaboratively formulating it with the practitioner. And somewhat subtly but potently underlying this process and reinforcing forward movement is the clinician's implicit expression of confidence in the client's potential to successfully attain their treatment goals by tapping into their existing abilities. Moreover, throughout the session, the therapist is continually monitoring the client's wording, nonverbal behavior, and reactions to gauge how the client is receiving the therapist's communications and monitoring the ways in which those communications may need to be adjusted to instill hopefulness in the client and promote the client's sense of interpersonal connection.

In general, it is useful to keep in mind that the aim of treatment is to resolve problems; therefore, the most pressing area to clarify at the beginning of therapy is what the goals of treatment are. It is the goals that guide the focus of therapy. Other information gathered is in the service of the treatment objectives, something that is helpful to remember to avoid either prematurely and single-mindedly attempting to elicit a highly detailed account of traumatic events the client has experienced or being overly ambitious in attempting to comprehensively collect historical information.

## CONSTRUCTING A PROVISIONAL CASE FORMULATION

Constructing a serviceable CTT case formulation requires that the collected clinical data be organized in a way that provides a coherent depiction of the causal relationships among the client's trauma history, developmental (i.e., childhood household and community) background, present-day circumstances, and current psychological difficulties and functional limitations. The purpose of the formulation is not merely to explain the sources of the problems that led the survivor into therapy but to form the basis for a plan of treatment tailored to the client's particular objectives, resources, capabilities, and needs. Accordingly, it is useful to work backward from the client's stated treatment goals (supplemented by ones that the practitioner anticipates may be relevant). A contextually oriented conceptual formulation is designed to address the following six areas:

1. What experiences of threat are present in the client's history? At what point in the client's developmental history did each of those experiences occur? Do any of them appear to be related to the presenting problems or to the client's identified treatment goals? If so, are these experiences of threat manifested in current symptoms of PTSD or some other symptom picture that appears to be related to the client's trauma history, such as substance abuse, dissociation, depression, and so on? What are the specific manifestations of these syndromes?

2. What experiences of deficit are present in the client's history? Do any of them appear to be related to the presenting problems or to the client's identified treatment goals? If so, what areas of functional impairment are associated with those deficits? What skills deficits need to be addressed to remedy those areas of functional impairment?

3. Is there evidence of both deficit-related functional impairment and threat-related traumatization in the client's background? If so, in what ways, if any, do these forms of functional impairment and traumatization appear to have interacted to influence and exacerbate each other? In what ways have these interactions resulted in mutual influence and exacerbation of the client's skills and performance deficits?

4. How do the difficulties identified by the answers to the previous three questions correspond to or supplement the treatment goals expressed by the client?

5. How does the client's life trajectory appear to have been shaped by the experiences of deficit and experiences of threat and corresponding skills and performance deficits identified in response to the previous questions?

6. If the experiences of deficit and experiences of threat identified in the previous questions had never occurred, how would the client's life trajectory have been altered? In what ways would the client be different at this point in their life, and how would you expect their current life circumstances to be different than they are now?

The final question embraces the ultimate objective of CTT: to help the client become the person they would have been and the person they have the capacity to have been if they had grown up in more favorable circumstances. This is undeniably a lofty goal, and it certainly is a highly optimistic one in keeping with CTT's focus on client strengths. Despite its idealistic bent, this framing device serves several practical purposes. It helps the clinician avoid viewing the survivor of CTr exclusively or primarily in terms of their psychological deficiencies and difficulties. It draws the practitioner's attention to the client's personal assets and situational resources. And it helps direct treatment beyond an exclusive focus on problem reduction or elimination and toward assisting the client to establish a more gratifying and productive life structure.

## INCORPORATING THE THREE SPHERES OF CONTEXTUAL TRAUMA THERAPY

The function of pretreatment assessment is to inform and guide treatment. CTT advocates individualize assessment as a preparation for tailoring therapy to the specific characteristic of each particular CTr survivor. The general implementation of CTT, however, is guided by a conceptualization of therapy for survivors that is sufficiently generic to apply to each particular survivor. To address the intricacies of CTr, CTT approaches treatment by taking into account three major arenas, or spheres, of the therapeutic enterprise: relational sphere, conceptual sphere, and practical intervention sphere. Each is discussed in detail in subsequent chapters, but what follows here is a consideration of the nature of each of these spheres and how they interact. Although all three are intended to address the debilitating consequences of both experiences of threat (i.e., trauma) and experiences of deficit (i.e., failure by the family of origin to provide the conditions that foster adequate psychological development, socialization, and enculturation), they are distinct not only in the territory they target but also in their association with somewhat divergent and unique methodologies.

Beyond these differences, however, what CTT emphasizes is that what ties these three arenas together is that they are collaborative in nature. This approach is informed by the principle that survivors of CTr, by virtue of ubiquitous experiences of deficit throughout their formative years, have been deprived of the conditions that support adequate psychological development. Human development, in turn, is primarily the product of interactive, coordinated, collaborative, ongoing interchange with others.

Expressed in everyday language, children don't rear themselves, at least not successfully. Some survivors of CTr simply struggle through their formative years as best they can in the absence of the involvement of caring, responsive adults. Others do their best to, in effect, parent themselves in the absence of family members who are dedicated to and competent to provide for their developmental needs and foster their acquisition of the capacities needed for adult functioning. Still others with especially impaired families do their best to take care of themselves and, in many ways, do their best to parent their own parents. However, whatever their level of natural endowment, across all these situations, children do not reach chronological adulthood adequately socialized, enculturated, and developmentally equipped without the benefit of committed, capable parenting. Child development occurs in an interpersonal context, an intimate and intricate attuned interchange between parent and offspring. Therefore, to remediate gaps and warps in functioning resulting from experiences of deficit, each of these three major components of therapy is carried out as much as possible as a collaborative effort between survivor and therapist.

Although the three spheres of CTT address differing territories and are conceptually distinct, in practice, they often are implemented simultaneously and are interrelated, each informed by and influencing the others. The collaborative therapeutic alliance constituting the relational sphere shapes the way that joint conceptualization is carried out and how targets for and strategies of intervention are identified and accomplished. The conceptual sphere helps client and therapist understand how to make sense of and promote their evolving relationship and figure out what areas need to be addressed via intervention and in what order to maximize their effectiveness. And the interventions composing the practical intervention sphere are jointly constructed as a product of the collaborative therapeutic relationship and of the application of the principles of deductive reasoning that have evolved via conceptualization.

Much of what composes the practical sphere of CTT are methods that are commonly thought of as interventions, many of which are aimed at fostering changes in behavior. And certainly, in the conceptual sphere, helping clients examine and revise their cognitions is recognized as a form of intervention, too. However, in a real sense, the formation of a collaborative therapeutic alliance is itself an intervention that plays a major role in helping to resolve the patterns of emotion dysregulation, negative self-concept, and disturbances in relationship that are chief aspects of the disturbances in self-organization sector of CTr.

**Relational Sphere**

Although the therapeutic relationship is an essential contributor to treatment outcome in working with any population, it carries particular weight in working with survivors of CTr. For survivors reared in circumstances that did not provide the type of interpersonal experiences that promote acquisition of the capacities for productive and gratifying adult adjustment, a major function of the therapeutic alliance is to provide the relational characteristics that foster these aspects of development. This function of the treatment alliance renders it even more pivotal than in other populations. At the same time, particular and somewhat unique hurdles to the formation of a resilient therapeutic bond often presented by survivors of CTr need to be anticipated and surmounted. The establishment of a continually evolving and deepening collaborative working alliance that is both the medium through which change occurs and a means of remediating interpersonal deficits and difficulties requires a high degree of alertness and responsivity on the part of the clinician.

For complex trauma survivors who may not have ever previously experienced a relationship characterized by consistent, reliable attentiveness and concern, this is an alien experience that will take time to recognize and adapt to. After repeated experiences of threat and of deficit throughout and since their formative years, ongoing interaction with someone who is neither coercively controlling nor unreliably responsive also is an alien situation that will require time before the survivor accepts and feels comfortable with it. An essential aspect of the treatment is for the clinician to remain alert for, to discern, and to constructively respond to the relational challenges presented by complex trauma survivors and help remediate the interpersonal deficiencies that are the legacy of both having grown up in an relationally inadequate family environment and having been repeatedly subjected to episodes of abuse.

The practitioner who works with this population must be sensitized to these areas of relational difficulty and prepared to notice and effectively manage them as they arise. Among the many necessary and beneficial consequences of the formation of a collaborative therapeutic alliance for survivors of CTr is the acquisition of the capacity—often for the first time in their lives—to experience a tangible sense of connection to another person. This is a powerful and hard-won achievement that takes time and requires sustained effort and patience on the part of both client and practitioner. Once the ability to access the experience of interpersonal connection is established, it provides the survivor with an entire range of abilities supportive of effective adult functioning. These abilities include the capacity to discern who can and cannot be trusted; the banishment of a previously pervasive sense of isolation and alienation from others; *emotional object constancy*, the confidence that others continue to think about and care about them when they are not physically present, and the sense of reassurance that comes with this awareness; a level of self-trust and self-confidence that offers the ability to function independently of others; and the faculty of being able to enter into and maintain relationships marked by reciprocity, interdependence, and emotional intimacy. The gradual emergence and consolidation of these capacities obviously constitutes momentous attainments that counter the disturbances in self-organization components of CTr while fostering a level of trust and safety that creates a base from which to confront traumatic material with a greatly reduced risk of destabilization.

**Conceptual Sphere**

The spirit and principle of collaboration that typifies the relational sphere of CTT extends into the other two major arenas of treatment, the conceptual and practical intervention spheres. In the conceptual sphere, this approach dictates that although the process of conceptualization is a joint one, the client is the final arbiter of the conclusions that are arrived at. In general, because the survivor of complex trauma is unlikely to have grown up in a family environment in which rationality was consistently modeled, the therapist's role is to guide the process of deduction so that, over time, the client absorbs the underlying principles. However, the product of the conceptual process is considered the client's purview. This approach, therefore, requires that although the practitioner helps the client execute the deduction process based on the principles of reasoning and logic, they have to respect that determination of the outcome ultimately lies with the client.

Within the conceptual sphere, this same principle is applied to several objectives. Over time, it assists the survivor in formulating an understanding of how their individual and family history, and, in particular, the experiences of threat and experiences of deficit in their background in conjunction with their personal strengths and current life circumstances have shaped their life trajectory. This endeavor helps the survivor make sense of a chaotic and confusing past, provides sufficient distance to temper self-blame for self-perceived shortcomings and current difficulties, and offers cause for hope that problems can be overcome (rather than being an expression of the client's inherent flaws) and that, therefore, the future can be appreciably more gratifying. From this foundation, the client is helped to identify how they aspire to redirect their life trajectory and what treatment objectives they would need to achieve to support this repositioning. In addition, the same conceptual methodology is used to identify distorted and counterproductive beliefs, ascertain the sources of those ideas (including, but not limited to, experiences of threat and experiences of deficit), and revise them by reexamining them on the basis of logic and relevant evidence.

**Practical Intervention Sphere**

In response to the client's treatment goals and the conceptual formulation, a sequential series of procedures is designed to resolve threat-related psychological difficulties and remediate deficit-related restrictions in adaptive functioning. Some specific and somewhat unique intervention procedures have been constructed specifically for the CTT approach, although even these are based on already extant principles. For instance, the modulating dissociative dial technique delineated in Chapter 9 on dissociation that can also be applied to other potentially disruptive experiences is an extension of a general approach originally introduced by Milton Erickson (Rossi & Ryan, 1992, especially pp. 84–85). Similarly, the SCAN-R (which stands for select, cue, analyze, note, and revise; Gold, 2000; Gold & Seifer, 2002) technique for addressing addictive and compulsive behavior patterns discussed in Chapter 11 is an application of functional behavioral analysis as an intervention strategy. In many other areas, however, established interventions, such as the systematic practice of established relaxation techniques, behavioral activation to counter depression, and various forms of processing and exposure approaches to resolve traumatization, are incorporated in the course of CTT as they become relevant.

What distinguishes CTT from these other approaches is that practical interventions are explicitly woven into and directed by considerations emerging from the other two spheres of treatment, the therapeutic alliance and the conceptual framework. These conclusions inform decisions about practical interventions: targets selected for intervention, the order in which they are addressed, the intervention procedures to be used, and the modification of those intervention approaches in ways that will maximize their effectiveness for each individual client.

**Integration of the Spheres**

It would be inaccurate to frame any one of these three spheres as more central or decisive than the other two. All three of them are essential to planning, organizing, and carrying out effective treatment for CTr. However, CTT, unlike many other current treatment approaches, is driven primarily by conceptualization in the sense that it does not consist of a predetermined sequence of interventions that is applied to all clients. Therapeutic strategies are chosen and modified based on a joint understanding arrived at by practitioner and client about what is most suitable and most likely to be effective at any given point in treatment. CTT also does not presume that the same characteristics of the therapeutic relationship will be equally relevant to or prominent for all complex trauma survivor clients. In this respect, the conceptual formulation, jointly arrived at through collaboration between practitioner and client, is the guiding force in CTT. By organizing the specifics of each client's unique history, set of difficulties, strengths, and treatment goals into the framework of the contextual trauma model, the conceptual formulation acts as a blueprint for structuring the treatment alliance and the plan of intervention to be responsive to the individual's particular needs and characteristics.

The collaborative principle of CTT that guides all three spheres of treatment includes continually checking in with the client to obtain their agreement and consent regarding the aspects of treatment. Potential goals to be worked toward at any given time are explicitly discussed and chosen. When a focus of treatment is agreed on, it is initially the therapist's responsibility to ensure that the objective is followed through from session to session until either the client achieves it or until client and practitioner agree that it is best for the time being to shift and pursue another objective. Over the course of treatment, it is useful to encourage the client to increasingly share in this task to bolster their capacity to maintain a sense of continuity of experience and of accountability.

The single most important objective of the initial intake is to establish at least one mutually agreed on treatment goal by the end of the session. Doing so helps to ensure that from the beginning, therapy is oriented toward and organized around the attainment of measurable goals. Ideally, the client determines the initial focus of treatment. If they have difficulty formulating and articulating an initial objective, the practitioner can offer several options based on what has been discussed up to that point and ask the client which option seems to present the most pressing, attainable, and reasonable starting point.

In the same way that the conceptual sphere helps to shape the evolution of the collaborative therapeutic alliance and the particular intervention strategies to be used and in what sequence, each of the three spheres of CTT influences and informs the others. The following chapters explore the implementation of each of these three spheres. Following those individual discussions, we can then return to a more detailed consideration of how the three spheres impact and are integrated with each other into a coherent, individually tailored course of treatment.

# 6

# Forging a Collaborative Relationship

*Fostering Connection and Growth*

This chapter addresses the intricacies involved in establishing and maintaining the type of collaborative relationship with complex traumatization (CTr) survivors that functions as an essential catalyst of remedial psychological development and as a sufficiently safe interpersonal environment for productive trauma processing to occur. Treatment models that attribute CTr survivors' interpersonal difficulties exclusively to trauma may fail to prepare practitioners adequately to forge a solid collaborative alliance with them. Contextual trauma therapy (CTT) proposes that survivors' limitations in forming this type of relationship are not exclusively a performance deficit resulting from trauma but a skills deficit, too. Although forms of maltreatment may have compounded survivors' difficulty viewing others as predictably invested in their welfare, the original source of their lack of trust and belief in others, CTT suggests, is the failure of their family of origin to consistently treat them in a reasonably responsive manner.

First, I briefly review ways in which being reared in an ineffective family environment is likely to diminish the capacities for productive and gratifying interpersonal functioning. Then I describe the general interpersonal stance that CTT encourages clinicians to take to facilitate enhancement of survivors' interpersonal capacities. The bulk of the chapter is devoted to detailed exploration of major challenges posed by common characteristics of survivors stemming from experiences of threat and of deficit that need to be negotiated to build a collaborative therapeutic relationship. Therapists are likely to find this section of tremendous practical value. Key considerations related to

---

http://dx.doi.org/10.1037/0000176-007
*Contextual Trauma Therapy: Overcoming Traumatization and Reaching Full Potential*, by S. N. Gold
Copyright © 2020 by the American Psychological Association. All rights reserved.

issues of diversity are then discussed, followed by a brief section on the pivotal role of the relational sphere in CTT. The chapter concludes with consideration of the necessity for clinicians working with CTr to make self-care an essential aspect of their lifestyle.

By virtue of having been reared in an interpersonally distant, unsupportive, chaotic, or unpredictable family system, many survivors of CTr may never experience a reliably close, benevolent relationship during their formative years. As a consequence, the defining characteristics of a *collaborative therapeutic alliance*—working jointly toward a common goal with someone else, solely for their welfare, in the spirit of teamwork—are highly unlikely to be relational qualities that they have previously encountered. In the absence of previous experience of this sort, CTr survivors have no solid basis for viewing the therapist in these terms. In the terminology of attachment theory, they have no "working model" (Ainsworth, 1985) of a collaborative alliance. To forge such a relationship, therefore, both practitioner and survivor need to actively reach across this divide to cultivate the client's ability to envision, acquire proficiency in, and actively engage in collaborative interaction.

Growing up in a family characterized by pervasive conditions of deficit—ones that fail to provide (a) adequate emotional responsiveness and validation; (b) sufficient cognitive stimulation and transmission of knowledge and skills that constitute functional literacy (i.e., adaptive living skills in the broadest sense); and, above all, (c) the relational qualities that cultivate the capacity for the experience of connectedness with others—fosters limitations in adaptation and vulnerability to coercive control. These three areas of familial insufficiency form the experiential context that fosters the three components of disturbances in self-organization (DSO): impairments in affect modulation, in self-concept, and in interpersonal functioning. Within a CTT framework, therefore, DSO is a key aspect of the developmental gaps and warps that are the legacy of growing up in an ineffective family.

## CONTEXTUAL TRAUMA THERAPY'S RELATIONAL PHILOSOPHY FOR REMEDIATING DEVELOPMENTAL GAPS AND WARPS

Although, in various respects, CTr survivors may have developmental limitations as a result of the deficient interpersonal circumstances in which they were reared and the consequences of traumatization itself, CTT clinicians work to remediate these shortcomings by, as much as is practically possible, interacting with them as equal partners in the treatment process. For the clinician, maintaining a respectful relationship of this type is facilitated by continually attending to evidence of the client's evolving strengths as a guide for treating them as an equal partner as much as possible. This is a radically different approach from inner-child work (Abrams, 1990; Price, 1996) or reparenting (Del Casale, Munilla, Rovera de Del Casale, & Fullone, 1982). Maturation is fostered by an egalitarian form of interaction that encourages the survivor to rise to the occasion by aiming to function to the best of their ability at any given time rather than by revisiting past deprivations and upsets. Although there are undeniably instances when remediating developmental deficits and the processing of traumatic material may overlap, by approaching developmental remediation in this way, CTT offers a clear conceptual demarcation between the two. Trauma processing inherently entails revisiting and resolving the disruptive impact of past events; remediation focuses on enhancing current functioning with an eye toward potential.

Too often, whether explicitly or implicitly, mental health professionals and clients alike think of therapy as something that the practitioner "does" to the client (conveying, in effect, "*I* am treating *you*"). When the recipient of the clinician's ministrations does not actively cooperate in the intervention process or fails to benefit from it, they are likely to be perceived as obstinate, oppositional, or resistant. These attributions assume that the client is fully capable of productive engagement with the therapist but stubbornly refuses to exercise this ability. A key understanding in working with survivors of CTr is that by virtue of their deficit-related difficulties, they often enter into the treatment situation not fully able to engage cooperatively. This does not mean that they are not amenable to treatment but that their developmental/functional weaknesses need to be identified and ameliorated for them to become equipped to be effective partners in the change process.

Attentive, attuned interpersonal interaction is the medium through which human development occurs, not just at the level of behavior and experience but at the level of the structure and function of the brain (Siegel, 2012). It is largely through a deeply felt sense of connection with caring others that the capacities of self-organization—to regulate emotions, maintain a reliably solid sense of self-esteem, and participate in mutually gratifying relationships—evolve. Feeling a consistent sense of being cared about has an intensely calming influence that is internalized and translates into the ability to modulate strong affect and impulses.[1] In addition, an experiential connection with a caring other affirms one's worth in a way that becomes portable and fosters the ability to trust and accept the affectionate gestures of others and to reciprocate them with caring sentiments and actions.

This type of caring relationship gradually engenders the capacity for interpersonal connection. In its absence, CTr survivors often do not develop the "receptors" that allow for this palpable realm of experience to occur and be discernible. Survivors may even be unable to recognize overt behavioral evidence of others' benevolence toward them. These capacities are what ultimately are alluded to by the term *secure attachment*: not just the attainment of

---

[1] This observation helps illuminate a major contributor to the distress experienced by complex trauma survivors: the lack of an implicit ability to self-soothe because they had been deprived of a consistently and reliably responsive caretaker in childhood. This is why strategies such as the consistent practice of relaxation exercises (see Chapter 8) are needed to help complex trauma survivors get to the point at which self-soothing takes on an automatic quality. In this respect what is likely to be a performance deficit in PTSD is almost invariably a skills deficit in CTr.

a reasonable degree of comfort with intimacy but also the ability to experience it (Bentzen, 2015). Therefore, many survivors traverse childhood into adolescence and adulthood feeling intensely alone. Faced with these restrictions in the survivor's interpersonal capabilities, the practitioner must remain as experientially present, nonreactive, and productively engaged as possible in the face of a series of potential obstacles to forging a collaborative therapeutic relationship.

As was exemplified in the case of Chet in Chapter 3, because of their restricted psychological development stemming from experiences of deficit, survivors of CTr may slip into behaving in childlike ways and may even perceive themselves as children in adults' bodies. However, it is imperative for the clinician to remember that they are not children and that it is a grave and condescending countertherapeutic error to treat them as such (see footnote 3, which is cited in the Culturally Diverse Family Contexts section of this chapter). Doing so constitutes a misguided strategy for addressing developmental deficits that only reinforces the survivor's self-perception of ineptitude. Whether the tone of the therapist's behavior is punitive, exasperated, or subtly patronizing, such an approach is likely to reinforce the survivor's shame about their functional deficiencies and reinforce their sense of inadequacy.

Instead, the task of the trauma therapist working with CTr is to identify areas of developmental weakness along with the survivor and jointly formulate ways to remediate them. This task is accomplished not by going backward in an attempt to somehow redo what the client missed out on during childhood but to assist them to acquire competencies in the present and work toward a more gratifying and productive life now and in the future. Doing so requires building on the areas of strength and external resources identified in the initial assessment and being continually alert for talents and assets that have not been yet recognized or may have been obscured by the survivor's difficulties. It necessitates that the practitioner judiciously pace expectations, goals, and tasks aimed at expansion of developmental attainments at a point that is above the survivor's current level of functioning but close enough to be within their reach. In addition, both because of its reinforcement value and because survivors of CTr are instinctively oriented toward self-criticism rather than self-validation, noticing and reinforcing therapeutic progress are imperative.

*Collaboration* is a frequently used term that is not often closely examined. It is essential for the practitioner to thoroughly comprehend that the term *collaborative therapeutic alliance* has specific implications. Therapist and client coordinate their efforts (a) to work toward a common goal (*collaboration*) (b) for the sole welfare of one of them, the client (*therapeutic*), (c) in the spirit of and via engagement in teamwork (*alliance*).

This joint effort is the medium through which change occurs and a means of extending the client's developmental capacities for interpersonal relating. But creating this type of interaction with complex trauma survivors can be arduous because it is a form of relating that is likely in various ways to seem alien and unfathomable to them. Without a sophisticated understanding of the relational limitations that are likely to characterize the survivor of CTr, practitioners are at considerable risk for working at cross-purposes with the client and expending considerable time and effort that is unproductive or even potentially destructive.

## CHALLENGES TO THE FORMATION OF A COLLABORATIVE THERAPEUTIC ALLIANCE

Various obstacles to forming a collaborative therapeutic alliance are regularly encountered when working with survivors of CTr. One cannot reasonably presume that survivors will exhibit all of these interpersonal factors. However, being watchful to discern which of those factors may be present and being prepared to navigate through them can reduce impediments to forward movement and be a momentous source of improvement in and of itself. Enlisting the client in the process of recognizing these challenges and allying with the therapist to prevent the client from subverting treatment is an excellent example of how establishing a collaborative alliance is a central goal of therapy and the medium by which treatment goals are achieved. The process of cooperatively joining to combat obstacles to the establishment of the therapeutic alliance can be a powerful source of connection in and of itself.

### Distrust

Probably the most commonly encountered barrier to establishing a collaborative alliance among survivors of complex trauma is a considerable degree of distrust that is almost inevitably directed toward the therapist (Gobin & Freyd, 2014). In some instances, the indications of the survivor's distrust is overt and readily detectable. In others, it lingers and perhaps festers below the surface, and, at times, the fear of acknowledging that the practitioner is not trusted in itself invites attack and disparagement.

The distrust almost universally experienced by complex trauma survivors is often the legacy of traumatic events and the overall tenor of the survivor's family of origin environment. In an appreciable majority of instances in which traumatization occurs in response to an act of interpersonal violence, whether, for instance, in the form of child maltreatment, intimate partner violence, sexual violation, or criminal assault, a salient aspect of the destructive force of the incident is the experience of betrayal (Freyd, 1994). Acts of violence and coercive control are, after all, instances of the abuse of power. They convey to the victim that those in power are dangerous and cannot be trusted to restrain themselves from using their power to take advantage of others. For many survivors of such acts, the sense of betrayal generalizes to some degree well beyond the particular perpetrator(s) to people in general, fueling distrust of others and a pervasive experience of vulnerability and, frequently, of shame (Gobin & Freyd, 2014; Platt & Freyd, 2015). Their own sense of ineptitude and of being childlike may lead them to perceive practically everyone else as possessing more power than they do and therefore as posing a potential threat. In some cases, if they are parents, they may even feel intimidated by their own children.

**Trust and the Therapist**
It is naive to assume that somehow clinicians are held exempt from the pervasive distrust experienced by complex trauma survivors. After all, the therapist is, by definition, an authority on which the survivor relies for assistance. From the survivor's perspective, the practitioner, therefore, can potentially use their knowledge and skill to the survivor's detriment. Consequently, therapists need to be aware that they cannot, by any means, assume that the client will trust them. Rather, they need to expect that on some level, survivors may harbor a level of doubt and apprehension about the practitioner's motives and reliability (Bell, Robinson, Katona, Fett, & Shergill, 2018; Gobin & Freyd, 2014).

In addition to the distrust engendered by their history of experiences of threat and betrayal, complex trauma survivors are also prone to being mistrustful because of the general family atmosphere in which they were reared. If their own family did not consistently act in a way that demonstrated they cared about or for them, why would anyone else? Often the survivor has repeatedly endured relationships outside the family, both before and after leaving their childhood household, in which they placed their trust in an adult or peer only to again find themselves hurt, rejected, or betrayed. A long string of interpersonal disappointments often precedes entry into therapy and leaves the survivor with an abiding expectation that this encounter, too, will prove to be a disappointment. This conviction may be countered only by a sliver of desperate hope.

The experiences of deficit in the survivor's family of origin compound their mistrust of others because those experiences fail to meet the individual's emotional needs for love and protection and sometimes their physical needs for food, clean clothing, or medical care. Children growing up in circumstances such as these might conclude that if their own families have failed to take care of them, they have no reason to expect that they can rely on "strangers" outside the family. Sometimes ineffective families intensify the child's mistrust by telling them that they cannot trust people outside the family. The child may therefore conclude that as unreliable as their family has been, other people are even more untrustworthy. Similarly, some of these families warn the child that "no one out there will care about you" or tell the child things such as, "You think your teacher cares about you, but she doesn't really. She's just acting that way because she feels sorry for you." I've had several survivor clients report that as a child, they were told by family members, "You'd better not get too close to people because then they'll see how crazy you are and not want to have anything to do with you. We love you even though you're crazy. Strangers [that is, people outside the family] won't."

Experiences like these throughout the complex trauma survivor's formative years leave a deep and lasting conviction that people in general are untrustworthy and cannot be expected to care about them (Gobin & Freyd,

2014). Paradoxically, that effect not only leads to impairment of their capacity to trust but also may lead them to place their confidence in people they cannot rely on (Fertuck et al., 2016; Gobin, 2012). On the surface, this outcome seems baffling, but it becomes comprehensible when we consider that people are not born with the capacity to discern who is and is not trustworthy. And when one's confidence in others is repeatedly betrayed by the very people that society conveys one is supposed to find reliable—one's own family—one's ability to identify who can and cannot be trusted becomes even more muddled.

Clients recognize that trusting their therapist is an expected and requisite component of psychological treatment. Some may admit a lack of trust in the clinician and shamefully express that "I know I'm supposed to trust you. I'm doing this wrong." They may even have been told that by previous practitioners, the implication being that a lack of confidence in the therapist precludes progress in treatment. But trust does not emerge in response to exhortations. And practitioners' verbal encouragement that survivor clients trust them are misguided and can be more harmful than helpful. The client can take it to imply that anyone who says, "You can trust me" cannot be believed.

Therefore, as counterintuitive as it may seem, when complex trauma survivors express beliefs such as "I know I'm supposed to trust you," especially when they do so early in treatment, it is best to gently contradict this belief. Similarly, the client may say something along the lines of, "Oh, now that you said that [or, more rarely, 'done that'], I know I can trust you." A helpful response is along these lines:

> Trust is not something someone decides or chooses to do. It must be earned by the person to be trusted. And giving in to the temptation to trust someone on the basis of a single statement or behavior of theirs is not realistic. That determination cannot reasonably be made on the basis of such limited evidence.
>
> Now, you are right that trusting me will support your progress in therapy. It will be helpful to the therapy if you come to trust me. But it is not just up to you whether you trust me. It is up to me as well. Because, to have a sufficient basis for trusting me—or for trusting anyone—you need to collect evidence to determine whether I—or anyone else—deserve your trust. And so I will tell you how you can decide whether to trust me: *watch me.* Very carefully. Over time. And evaluate whether what I do indicates to you that I can be trusted. And *listen to what I say.* Very carefully to judge whether what I say makes sense to you and suggests to you that I am a trustworthy person who is invested in your welfare. And, in addition, you need to consider, as you watch what I do and listen to what I say over time, whether my behavior and my words match up. Is what I say to you consistent with what I do? And then, over time, continue to watch my behavior and listen to my statements, and see if they continue to make sense to you, are consistent over time, and continue to match with each other over time. If you conclude after some time that this is the case, that will be a basis to begin to trust me. But that doesn't mean you are done. Continue to watch me. Continue to listen to me. Continue to decide whether what you see and hear from me match up. And if you conclude that they do, then you have a basis to continue to trust me. The more that time goes by and you continue to decide I have been consistently acting and speaking in a reliable way, the greater the basis you will have for trusting me. And using the same method, you can assess

whether to trust other people as well. But, to some extent, learning whether you can trust someone is a process without end. Continue watching. Continue listening. Continue assessing. That doesn't mean you have to be continually mistrustful of others. It just means that you keep paying attention to the evidence. And the more favorable evidence that mounts up, the more confidence you can have that the person can be trusted.

A monologue such as this may seem excessively long. But if it helps the survivor acquire an understanding of and a yardstick for establishing trust, they will have acquired the basis for an invaluable skill in a span of a few minutes. It is an explanation that implicitly covers accruing a basis for trust *and* a basis not to trust. And people who are unclear about one side of this coin will almost inevitably be just as unclear about the other.

**The Therapist's Role in Fostering Trust**
Having encouraged the survivor to carefully observe and assess whether what the practitioner does and says over time warrants trust, it is obviously incumbent on the practitioner to conduct themselves in a trustworthy way. What this aspect of therapy requires of the clinician, therefore, is a commitment to monitoring themselves in as scrupulous and intentional a manner as possible. Although some therapists may have been oriented in their training toward continual self-observation, practitioners, if they have been trained to scrutinize behavior, verbalizations, and indicators of subjective experience at all, are much more likely to have been directed to closely examine them in the client than in themselves. But assisting individuals to become more adept at evaluating who is and is not worthy of trust requires a high degree of consistency and integrity from therapists who treat survivors of CTr.

This type of professional functioning necessitates a high degree of concentration. It entails doing one's best throughout each session to continually attend to what one can discern about the client's probable moment-to-moment experience, one's own overt behavior and subjective experience, and the interplay and mutual influence between the two. The practitioner attempts to operate in this manner for several purposes. One is to be as experientially present as possible, to provide the survivor with the experience of another's attentiveness and interest that was not a reliable feature of the environment of deficit in which the survivor was reared. Another is to be as responsive as possible to the nuances of the client's overt communication and inner experience. Yet another is to track the interaction between oneself and the client to assess whether one seems to be accurately understanding the client.

Exercising the commitment to operate out of integrity in all one's dealings with the client includes a willingness to, as much as possible, eschew defensiveness. Given the ineffective family environment that is associated with and promotes CTr, it is unlikely that the survivor received many admissions of missteps or apologies from others, especially from those in positions of authority. When the client takes the risk to point out what they see as a departure from reasonably expected behavior by the therapist, and the observation is a sound one, it is important for the clinician to acknowledge the lapse and apologize for it. This does not mean that the practitioner should validate accusations of transgressions whether or not they agree that they have occurred. To indiscriminately do so is as much of a deviation from behaving with integrity as refusing to admit a well-founded complaint of transgression. In some instances, therefore, the therapist may need to take time to consider whether the complaint is well founded by discussing it with the client to better understand it and the basis for it or through self-examination to as dispassionately as possible assess one's own behavior.

Earning the client's trust also entails regularly checking in with them about elements of the ongoing process of therapy. Proceeding in this way assures the client that their wishes and level of comfort are being considered and respected and is another expression of responsivity with which they are unlikely to have had much previous experience. Inquiries or statements such as the following make it clear to the client that, rather than unilaterally taking control, you truly are invested in carrying out treatment as a collaborative enterprise: "What do you want to work on next?" "Are you willing to start talking about _____?" "Do you have suggestions about how we might go about accomplishing _____?" "We can work toward accomplishing _____ in one of at least three ways, or a combination of them. Let's figure out together how to proceed."

**Case Example: Learning to Trust and Not to Trust**
Carol, an African American woman in her late 30s, reported that she and her brother and sisters were severely verbally, physically, and sexually abused throughout their childhood by their father. Her maltreatment and that of her siblings often occurred in the living room in the presence of each other and their mother, who did not protest and did nothing to stop it. Because they often witnessed each other's traumatization, they remembered the abuse in more detail than is usually the case. However, for 6 months before beginning outpatient treatment, Carol was in a residential facility that claimed to have expertise in trauma-related treatment. During her time there, the program's clinical director loudly berated her and insisted that there must be additional instances of childhood abuse that she did not remember because, otherwise, she would not be continuing to experience trauma-related symptoms. Periodically, he yelled at Carol, warning her that if she were unwilling to access additional memories of abuse during her time in the facility, those memories would all come flooding back at once, and she would suffer a severe psychotic breakdown.

Although this was a completely erroneous conviction on his part, because he was an authority figure, Carol placed a great deal of credence in what he was saying and mistrusted her own level of recollection. On entering outpatient treatment, therefore, she was terrified that the clinical director's prediction would come true and that she would become hopelessly psychotic. As a result, her outpatient therapist had to spend the first several months of treatment reassuring her that this was not the case and that the research literature strongly contradicted the assertions she had heard in residential treatment.

As therapy progressed, Carol confided in her outpatient practitioner that she had always had difficulty sustaining friendships and other close relationships. She had a serious substance abuse history and would periodically develop a friendship with a member of her 12-step group, but, inevitably, the person she chose to place her confidence in would take advantage of her and betray her. Married with three children, she expressed the awareness that her relationship with her husband had followed a similar pattern. Although she worked hard to cater to her husband's wishes, he often spent long periods away from the house, leaving her to be the sole caretaker of the children. Over time, she came to realize that he was repeatedly engaging in extramarital affairs while hardly bothering to hide that from her.

Discussion of this interpersonal pattern led Carol and her clinician to frame her repeated interpersonal disappointments as resulting from a proclivity on her part to consistently place her confidence in people who were unworthy of trust. Her therapist explained to her in much the same way as delineated in the earlier example monologue that a sound basis for trusting someone is to watch and listen to them closely over time and evaluate whether they are consistently reliable.

Toward the end of her second year of treatment, Carol began to express to her therapist that she was tired of the power imbalance and lack of reciprocity that had long characterized her marriage. She had tried to appeal to her husband to spend more time with her and made it known to him what she expected from him and their relationship. When it became clear to her that he was perfectly happy with the status quo and unwilling to reconsider the terms of their relationship, Carol, who throughout most of the marriage had been a homemaker without her own source of income, decided that she needed to prepare to establish sufficient emotional and financial independence to divorce her husband. She enrolled in technical school to learn a trade as a step toward becoming self-supporting. Several months into her educational program, she somewhat apologetically informed her therapist that because school and studying were taking up so much of her time and attention, she would have to leave treatment for the time being. The clinician assured Carol that she supported her decision; the purpose of therapy was to go out and live life, not to prioritize treatment over living.

About a year later, Carol called her outpatient practitioner and proudly and excitedly explained to her that she had been excelling in her training program. With just as much enthusiasm, she informed her therapist that for the first time in her life, she had assembled a caring, supportive, trustworthy circle of friends from among her fellow students. She elaborated that for the first few months of the program, she had sat back and observed the other students' behavior and listened carefully to what they had to say during and on breaks from class. On this basis, she arrived at conclusions about who did and did not warrant her trust. Thoughtfully and intentionally sizing up her classmates before proceeding to decide which to approach had paid off handsomely. For the first time in her life, Carol was able to establish a stable, reliable social network.

## Dependency

By virtue of having grown up in a family context that appreciably failed to meet their needs for emotional support, survivors of CTr, whether they express it overtly or do their best to hide it, can be expected to harbor intense unmet dependency needs. Those survivors who acknowledge their yearning for reliance on others often express profound feelings of shame in response to their own "neediness" (Dalenberg, 2000). Often their parents either explicitly or covertly conveyed an intolerance for and denigration of displays of dependency needs. Especially for those survivors who were reared in households in which this was the parental attitude, survivors often have an intense self-loathing in response to their own craving for responsiveness to their dependent desires.

At the same time, interpersonal violence traumas, such as sexual assault, especially when they occur in childhood, undoubtedly contribute to survivors' dependency (Hill, Gold, & Bornstein, 2001). It made a powerful impression on me to hear another trauma expert draw on almost exactly the same analogy—the desert analogy—that I had arrived at in trying to convey the experience of the survivor's experience of their dependent desires.

## The Desert Analogy

Imagine that you have spent your entire life in a desolate, dry, scorching desert. You are so unbearably fatigued from the burning sands and the sun radiating down that you are unable to hold yourself upright and walk. Instead, painfully, exceedingly slowly, you lay on your stomach and pull yourself forward, hand over hand, and drag yourself across and over the dunes. This state of affairs continues ceaselessly day after day. Every once in a while, you think you see an oasis in the distance only to find, as you get closer, that it was only a mirage.

As you are inching forward, you think you might see a dune on the far horizon that looks for all the world like a watercooler. Your heart leaps, but you do your best to not allow yourself to be misled by your ardent desire for relief from the parched dryness in your throat and the throbbing ache in your limbs. You've been mistaken too many times before and don't feel that you could bear getting your hopes up only to be fooled again. But as you draw closer, despite your wariness about allowing your intense wishes for relief to allow your perceptions to become distorted, you become increasingly certain that it is not in fact a mirage. It *is* a watercooler!

You finally reach it, grab a cone-shaped paper cup from the sleeve at its side, and feel the cold in the palm of your hand as the cone fills with clear, pure water. Your unbearable thirst is quenched, at least for the moment, although there turns out to be much less water in the cup than you originally thought. Now, what is the next thing that you do? Do you let the cup fall on the sweltering sand, drop back down on your abdomen, and continued to pull yourself forward? Certainly not! Every fiber of your being demands that you make every effort not to move an inch away from the watercooler. If you possessed a sturdy steel chain, you would wrap it around your waist and attach yourself to the watercooler. But for some maddening reason, each time you refill the cup and bring it to your lips, almost as soon as you feel moisture, you are perplexed when you look down and find the cup seems to have instantaneously emptied itself.

This is the plight in which the survivor of complex trauma with intensely painful unmet dependency needs finds themselves. After a lifetime of searing isolation and emotional deprivation, they enter the clinician's office and for the better part of an hour, perhaps longer, find themselves in the soothing presence of another person's undivided attention. The relief they experience in response to the therapist's attentiveness, concern, validation, and responsiveness, feels much like the cooling sensation of water trickling down the parched throat of the poor soul who has spent their entire life dragging their aching body through the desert.

For the complex trauma survivor suffering from the burden of accumulated ungratified dependent yearnings, the clinical setting can feel every bit as humiliating and frustrating as the wanderer in the desert who brings the cone-shaped cup to their lips, senses the tiniest bit of moisture, and discovers that the cup has immediately emptied itself. Painfully, the exceedingly dependent trauma survivor, having clawed their way to the practitioner and experienced soothing attentiveness, finds that between sessions, they are preoccupied with the moment of their next appointment when they will, once again, finally find themselves back in the therapist's office. But once there, their aching dependent need distracts them from resting their focus on being in the therapist's presence. Instead, they anxiously imagine the minutes slipping away like sand pouring through an hourglass until the time comes when they despairingly realize that time is up, and they are facing another long week of exile until their next appointment.

Although it compellingly appears as if being in the clinician's office is what quenches the thirst of their dependency, they remain unsatisfied because there is no bottom to their cup. In the absence of the capacity to experience a tangible sensation of connection with others, their time in the practitioner' presence is doomed to remain a frustrating and ultimately insufficiently gratifying tease. In the desert analogy, this diversion from the immediacy of what is transpiring in the consulting room corresponds to the interference of the leak in the bottom of their paper cup. And, so, they continue from week to week, thirsting after emotional relief that always seems just out of reach.

This frantic response to intensely dependent feelings generated by chronically unmet needs is completely understandable. However, it is counterproductive and creates barriers to therapeutic progress. The dependent client's preoccupation with the therapist powerfully diverts their attention from actively working toward accomplishing treatment goals. The distractedness created by the intense concern about time with the therapist slipping away paradoxically interferes with the client's focus on being with the therapist when they are together. And due to the, at best, tenuous and often almost completely absent ability to experience a palpable sense of connection with others, the belief that time with the therapist will be a source of relief from dependent yearnings proves to be frustratingly illusory. The following case example illustrates how extending contact with the practitioner promotes the opposite of the intended effect.

**Case Example: Unwittingly Feeding Dependency**
Alyssa, a lower middle-class, White woman in her mid-30s with a history of emotional neglect and childhood sexual molestation, sought therapy with a counselor who did not have any previous experience or training in working with trauma survivors. Based on Alyssa's repeated past experiences of abandonment by others in response to clingy behavior and an inability to recognize and respect appropriate interpersonal boundaries, she expressed the conviction to the counselor that he eventually would grow tired of her and terminate treatment. Although he assured her that he would never do that, she periodically would return to voicing her concern that she would be "too much for you."

Several months into treatment, Alyssa complained to her therapist that it was too difficult for her to tolerate waiting a full week to meet with him. In response to episodes of panic, she began making what she considered "emergency" phone calls to him. Eventually, she asked that they begin meeting biweekly, and the counselor agreed. As time went on, however, her distress elevated, and she requested that they move to a schedule of three meetings a week. Once again, believing that it was unbearable for her to see him less often and that more frequent meetings would help her become less anxious and allow her to progress in treatment, he acceded to her request. However, Alyssa's sense of dread only intensified, as did her between-session phone calls. After a year and a half of treatment, the counselor announced to Alyssa that he did not feel he could help her, and that he was terminating therapy. Within days, Alyssa made a serious suicide attempt and ended up being admitted to a psychiatric hospital.

**Resolution of Dependency**
How can the clinician help the survivor break this ongoing cycle that is sustained by the client's seeking relief from dependent feelings in ways that may seem reasonable on the surface but are ineffective and self-perpetuating? An essential means to accomplish breaking this cycle is to help the client understand why this strategy is doomed to fail and to explain that continuing to act on the belief that face-to-face contact with the therapist will assuage the distress of dependent feelings will, at best, prolong and more likely intensify them. Instead, a clear structure to treatment needs to be put into place to keep treatment focused on resolution of the client's difficulties. It is best to create this structure as soon as the practitioner becomes aware that the client is inclined to react to dependent longings in this way so that the message is conveyed dispassionately and clearly. Otherwise, therapist frustration and anger may mount if they allow the pattern to continue and escalate.

Having covered the rationale for maintaining a structure for treatment, it is best to convey to the client the elements of the structure that the clinician recommends. This discussion should include these points: the frequency of sessions, contact between sessions, and formation of a circle of support.

**Frequency of Sessions**

The ideal frequency of therapy sessions is once a week. The aim of therapy is to improve the survivor's quality of life. Accomplishing this aim requires more than meeting time with the therapist. It includes helping the client to develop the coping abilities and daily living capacities that the client would have ideally mastered in childhood and adolescence but did not fully absorb because they grew up with people who did not provide the resources that would enable them to do so. Becoming proficient in these areas, like any skill, requires practice, and this means that therapeutic progress rests not only on what happens during sessions but probably even more so on the client's willingness to follow through and put into practice in their daily life what is covered during meetings with the therapist. The more frequently therapy sessions occur, the more this frequency supports the misconception that time spent with the clinician is what reduces the client's distress and moves treatment forward. Meeting on a weekly basis is often enough to provide continuity but spaced out enough to give the client time to absorb and implement what is addressed in session.

**Between-Session Contact**

In the same vein, it is best to limit between-session contact to cancellation or rescheduling of appointments. Clients with intense feelings of dependency stemming from emotional neglect may find it exceedingly difficult to endure waiting for their next scheduled session. They are fully aware, however, that it is inappropriate to expect that their therapist will be available if they simply call them to "chat." What is sometimes considered acceptable, though, is to contact their therapist in an "emergency," as occurred in the preceding case vignette of Alyssa. When the client believes that such calls are allowed, the feelings of distress associated with yearning for contact with the clinician can escalate into panic. Paradoxically, therefore, when these "emergency" phone calls are viewed as permissible, they can actually fuel episodes of intense distress that may lead to destructive and impulsive behavior, such as nonsuicidal self-injury or even frankly suicidal gestures and attempts, that may be viewed as justifiable grounds for between-session contact. Conversely, when the practitioner conveys that between-session contact for reasons other than cancellations or rescheduling are not part of the structure of treatment, the likelihood of high-risk behaviors such as these occurring drops dramatically.

To set parameters on between-session contact, it is useful to make it clear to the client that (a) an emergency is a situation that is a threat to life or physical well-being and (b) such circumstances require an in-person response by calling 911 or going to the nearest hospital emergency room. Emergency situations cannot be responsibly addressed via discussion over the phone with the therapist. This approach encourages safety-maintaining behavior in the case of a genuinely emergent situation but simultaneously makes it explicit that contact with the therapist is not an effective or reasonable response to such circumstances.

Not all complex trauma survivors manifest dependency at a level of intensity that requires explicitly setting the structure delineated previously. Most are content with weekly sessions and do not engage in excessive or unwarranted between-session contact without such a discussion. But when survivor clients request to meet more than once a week from the beginning of treatment or otherwise convey that they expect a level of contact in excess of the norm for standard practice, then it is usually best to compassionately present at the outset of treatment the stipulations covered here.

### Active Encouragement to Form a Circle of Support

An important aspect of helping complex trauma survivors improve their functioning and alleviate unmet dependency needs is to actively encourage them to seek out and establish sources of interpersonal support outside of treatment. It is not unusual for survivor clients who are urged to work toward this objective to respond that they do not know anyone suitable to turn to for support. Ironically however, many of them, by virtue of a history of or current problems with substance abuse or other addictive behaviors, such as sexual compulsivity or compulsive spending, or codependency, participate in Alcoholics Anonymous or other 12-step meetings, which are grounded in the principle of fellowship. Others may participate in bible study groups or other organizations. And often on exploration, the therapist uncovers evidence of potential contacts in the survivor's life with people who may want a closer relationship with them or would be responsive to overtures for more contact but have not been approached by the survivor. Helping survivors gradually recognize the indicators that people are open to being more engaged with them and coaching them on how to approach these people can be a crucial step in treatment. In addition to the inherent value of forging greater social support, this strategy also helps the client recognize that people in their everyday lives other than the clinician can meet their interpersonal needs.

At times, survivors seeking social support ask for referrals to survivor self-help groups. I approach these resources with caution. My experience has been much in line with that of L. S. Brown (2008), who described a range of detrimental effects that self-help groups comprising CTr survivors can have, including pressure to disclose trauma without considering the potential negative consequences, other boundary violations, and even overtly abusive behavior. As useful as these resources can be when well administered, therefore, it is essential that therapist and survivor vet and monitor the norms and structure of any group in which the survivor is considering participating.

### Dissociative Disconnection

Dissociative difficulties, although they may not always rise to the level of a diagnosable disorder, are probably near-universal among CTr survivors. Several studies support the widely held view that dissociation is related to a history of trauma (e.g., Briere & Runtz, 1988; Chu et al., 1999; Dalenberg et al., 2012; P. T. Stein & Kendall, 2004). As discussed earlier in this chapter, however, CTT proposes that experiences of deficit also appreciably contribute to CTr survivors' vulnerability to dissociation. This proclivity is attributed by CTT to having grown up in a family that did not provide the level of emotional responsiveness and intimate interaction needed to develop the capacity for a tangible sense of connection to others.

The relevance of dissociation to the relational sphere (see introductory discussion of this and the two other spheres in Chapter 5) is that it reflects the existence of a barrier to a sense of interpersonal connection to the therapist and to people in general—an experiential disconnection between self and others. Chapter 9 of this volume addresses in detail how CTT conceptualizes dissociation and the types of interventions it uses to give the survivor control over dissociative reactions. In regard to its relevance to the formation of a collaborative treatment alliance, consider that the word *dissociation* literally means disconnection.[2] Within a CTT framework, the disconnectedness of dissociation encompasses dissociative symptoms, such as depersonalization and amnesia, and also the experiential disconnection or shutdown represented by phenomena such as *alexithymia* (limited awareness and ability to experience emotions; Grabe, Rainermann, Spitzer, Gänsicke, & Freyberger, 2000; Majohr et al., 2011), imperviousness to physical pain (*sensory shutdown*; Moormann, Bermond, & Albach, 2004), and the relative absence of an ability to experience interpersonal connectedness that corresponds to the construct of detachment in attachment theory (Barach, 1991; Liotti, 1992). Barach (1991) quoted Bowlby (1988) as explicitly stating that in the absence of the sustained presence of a responsive attachment figure, children become unresponsive to "the signals, arising from both inside and outside the person, that would activate their attachment behavior and that would enable them both to love and to experience being loved" (Barach, 1991, pp. 34–35). This is precisely the type of pattern seen in survivors of CTr. Whether in the therapist's office or in their daily interpersonal encounters, there is a glaring obliviousness to overtures of caring and indicators of potential emotional connection. CTT asserts that this relational pattern is not merely a function of pushing these overtures away or defending against recognizing them; rather, survivors of CTr have not adequately developed the receptive capacity to register their presence.

CTT emphasizes that for survivors of CTr, this form of interpersonal disconnection is not exclusively an intentionally mobilized defense mechanism that arose in response to experiences of threat. It is also attributed to the lack of

---

[2]I have written about this meaning of the word *dissociation* elsewhere (Gold & Seibel, 2009) as a tool for understanding what ties together the phenotypically diverse range of phenomena that are encompassed by it. A colleague of mine who is a well-known expert commented on how astute this comment was. For my part, I find it remarkable that this point has not been more widely recognized. It helps to demystify a realm of experience that too often has been portrayed as much more esoteric, elusive, and rare than it actually is.

development of the faculty of being able to feel an emotional connection to others that is the core of what the term *secure attachment* refers to. The interpersonal distrust and dependency that survivors of complex trauma often experience can act as barriers to the formation of this capacity for interpersonal connection, but their neutralization and resolution alone does not instill the capacity for connection. However, actively working with the client to help them reduce their distrust and dependency helps establish a foundation from which the ability to experience interpersonal connection can be forged.

The means by which the clinician can aid the complex trauma survivor in building the capability to experience interpersonal connection is by entering into that state with them. At first, because the capacity for this interpersonal experience is absent, the onus is on the therapist to provide the conditions under which it can develop. They must continually monitor the degree to which the client is experientially present in the consulting room. In the midst of wariness and distrust or the ache of dependent longing, the survivor's focus is elsewhere: on the sense of threat embodied by the clinician or on the dread that session time is dwindling and it will be another achingly lonely week before they see the therapist again. Without the ability to feel connected to someone else, the dependent urgency for a sense of contact with others is fated to remain ungratified.

Maintaining attention on the client sends out a signal for the client to tune into that eventually coalesces into the conduit for a sense of connectedness to others. But at the outset of treatment, the survivor, even though they may experience the discomfort of dependent longing, is relatively distant and perhaps even vacant, leaving the therapist with little to home in on. Nevertheless, if sustained over time, the determination to stay focused on the client, even during protracted silences and experiential absences, gradually pays off. As time passes, the alert practitioner comes to recognize more and more periods, fleeting at first but more sustained with time, when the client feels sufficiently safe (i.e., trusting) and soothed (i.e., no longer distracted by feelings of dependency) to be increasingly more attentive, responsive, and attuned, and therefore, present and interpersonally connected.

Although in the midst of acute dissociative episodes it may be fairly detectable that the client is not experientially present, to the degree that this is a more or less constant state, it is likely to be difficult for clinicians to discern, especially those with little experience working with dissociation. However, the more attentive the practitioner is to the survivor's moment-to-moment state, the more likely they are to be able to notice when the client is especially distant. This is important, because a dissociative state of mind does not necessarily correspond to obvious behavioral signs, such as a vacant stare, emotionless expression, robotic voice, marked immobility, or silence. Survivors with a proclivity to lapse into dissociative states can carry out conversations and complex behaviors without appreciably tracking what is occurring. They are unlikely to retain much of what has transpired during these periods; consequently, the therapist may assume that more progress is being made than is actually the case. This is one reason why clinicians need to assess therapeutic gains not just on the basis of in-session process but, to a greater extent, by noting outcomes over time.

At some point, the therapist is able to detect on an emotional and sensory level that the client is experientially present and attuned to the interpersonal interchange in a way they never seemed to be before. The survivor is now sufficiently engaged to be emitting a "signal" that is clearer and much easier to detect than previously was the case. They are "here" and engaged. If the therapist has been consistently monitoring the degree of the survivor's attunement all along and therefore is aware of this significant milestone, they will be strongly tempted to verbally acknowledge it to the client. For some survivors, this acknowledgment is reinforcing because it provides the feedback that "you're getting warmer." However, others may feel threatened and instinctively "back up." Although it is not an egregious error to misread whether the client is ready to admit to this new status, it is useful to make some attempt to assess whether the client will likely welcome or repel the affirmation of what is happening. If it remains unclear how the client is likely to react, the safest course is to probably not say anything about it or to inquire in indirect and general terms, such as by asking if they are aware of anything new and different in the quality of sessions.

Because a tenuous capacity for the palpable experience of interpersonal connection is a form of dissociation, the clinician can use the techniques for modulating dissociative symptoms presented in Chapter 9 to facilitate the development of a sense of bonding in the therapeutic relationship. It is best, however, to "work from both ends" by cultivating the survivor's capacity for connection via both the relationship sphere and the practical intervention sphere. Although there is some overlap, efforts in the relationship sphere primarily serve to build the survivor's interpersonal capacities. In contrast, deployment of techniques mainly addresses symptoms and practical aspects of functioning.

**Case Example: Cultivating the Capacity for Connectedness**
Janet, an exceptionally bright, White, female survivor of ongoing childhood sexual abuse by her older sister, emotional neglect by both of her parents, and severe verbal abuse by her father, and who began therapy in her early 40s, periodically became enraged at her therapist. When the clinician attempted to better understand Janet's viewpoint by asking questions aimed at clarification, Janet read these questions as veiled efforts to dispute the accuracy of her beliefs. In response, she grew rageful and either lapsed into silences in which she felt confused and paralyzed or yelled at her therapist for not understanding her and for "fucking with my reality" by questioning the validity of her perceptions.

At these times, Janet often accused the therapist of being either "just like my mother" or "just like my father." She described her mother as a vacuously optimistic woman who refused to acknowledge adversity and therefore refused to discern or validate the forms of maltreatment and distress that the client suffered at the hands of her older sister and father. In contrast, she depicted her father as an intellectualized and verbally facile narcissist who flew into rages and "squash[ed] me like a bug" with demeaning diatribes that elicited profoundly shameful feelings in her. Moreover, her older sister had structured her ongoing molestation of the client in a way that left Janet convinced that it was she who was responsible for sexual activity and led to the deeply humiliating perception that it was she who was the perpetrator.

Initially, the therapist was thrown off balance by these intense episodes of rage. She found that the more she tried to draw Janet out to better understand what was angering her, the more both Janet's and her own frustration and aggravation intensified.

A watershed moment in the treatment came when Janet attended an event in a distant state that she knew she would find intimidating. Her greatest concern was that the other people there would judge her critically. When she returned, Janet practically let herself fall into a seat in the therapist's office, let out a loud sigh, and sat in silence for several minutes. Finally, she said, "It's so good to be back in the one place where I feel safe." She then went on to relate that the event had indeed been anxiety provoking and intimidating for her but that she was sustained and comforted by the knowledge that one person on the planet, the therapist, knew her well and perceived her as a good person. What Janet was alluding to is a powerful example of what in developmental psychology is referred to as *emotional object constancy*, the ability to continue to maintain an image of an attachment figure in mind and sustain a sense of one's emotional bond to them even when that figure is not physically present.

Although this was a pivotal achievement on the way to a durable capacity for stable emotional connectedness, it was far from an end point. The periodic sense of being misunderstood and invalidated continued as did attendant bouts of rage. Forward movement depended on a continually evolving learning process for Janet and her therapist. The therapist learned to become more patient, restrained, and receptive to what the Janet had to say during these stormy interludes. And gradually, Janet was able to establish sufficient trust to risk the vulnerability of opening up more and revealing thoughts, feelings, and reactions that she had previously instinctively censored.

Bit by bit, Janet was able to identify that out of the fear and mistrust that had evolved in response to her family's pervasive empathic failures and invalidation, she instinctively and unwittingly avoided disclosing information that was essential to fully understand what she was trying to convey but that she anxiously anticipated would be used against her in an excruciatingly shaming manner. She was further able to express the recognition that her reflexive avoidance of self-disclosure out of terror that it would elicit the denigration and rejection of others ensured that she would end up feeling misunderstood and precluded opportunities for emotional intimacy, which compounded her sense of hopeless alienation from others. She realized, because of her early painful feelings in her childhood home, that although she craved closeness, she simultaneously viewed it as dangerous and anger provoking.

Becoming aware of this confluence of factors gradually allowed Janet to step outside of this pervasive and limiting pattern that had fed her difficulty with all three aspects of DSO: modulating her emotions, negative self-image, and problematic, confusing, and unfulfilling interpersonal relationships. Just as important, it enabled her to progressively risk opening up to her therapist more and to participate less fearfully in collaborative efforts at clarifying the communication between them. This new form of relating provided Janet with a platform from which to remediate her previously blocked potentials for social development, which, in turn, equipped her to enter into and sustain emotionally intimate friendships and romantic relationships, abilities that had neither been fostered nor modeled in her childhood household. As her previously unrecognized distancing behavior toward others diminished, she was astonished to discover that far from being ostracized, others were drawn to her. The treatment alliance therefore acted as what Janet described as a "laboratory" for developing and exploring these skills in an interpersonal atmosphere in which open communication and interpersonal connection no longer felt acutely dangerous.

**Disbelief**

We have already discussed how the entire therapeutic enterprise can be subverted by the types of discouraging proclamations frequently made to the survivor by mental health professionals. Although worded in various ways, these proclamations are, in essence, sweeping assertions that their psychological status is irremediable. They are therefore advised to "learn to live with them" or "learn how to manage them." When clients accept such statements as true, they have no incentive to make the sustained effort required to overcome their difficulties.

And although survivors' hopelessness that their level of adjustment and lives can appreciably improve is sometimes attributable to what they have heard from professionals—the very people whose job it is to help them overcome their difficulties—this is not always the case. It is also common for survivors to arrive at the conclusion themselves that change is impossible for two reasons. The first applies to individuals across the spectrum of traumatization, whether or not they are survivors of complex trauma: that it can be exceedingly difficult, when plagued by intrusive recollections of horrific circumstances, to imagine that one could overcome traumatization without somehow obliterating the memory of the traumatic event. This conviction that resolution is impossible as long as one can remember the traumatic situation is a crucial example of the importance of the conceptual distinction between trauma as event as traumatization as the adverse psychological consequences of that event. That someone who has been traumatized can, with proper intervention, get to the point of being able to think about the event without being triggered into traumatic reactions is a core premise of exposure-based interventions. These approaches are grounded in the principle that systematically and repeatedly confronting recollections of the traumatic event decondition the fight–

flight–freeze response (discussed in Chapter 2) to reminders of the event that maintains the symptoms of traumatization.

Among survivors of CTr is a second reason why they may find it unimaginable that they can make substantial gains in therapy. Growing up in an interpersonal context in which they felt unloved, unprotected, and belittled rendered them vulnerable to repeated instances of maltreatment and betrayal, experiences that seem to confirm the frequent negative appraisals they heard throughout their childhood. These setbacks leave them feeling irredeemably and irrevocably inept. These survivors have come to view the limitations imposed on them by CTr as who they are rather than a reflection of what has happened to them.

Fortunately, there are survivors of CTr who have not lost hope that they can attain resolution of their traumatization and significantly improve functioning, even if they have been cautioned by professionals that these aspirations are not realistic. The case vignette regarding Lorna in Chapter 5 is a vivid example of a survivor who was able to achieve radical changes in her functioning and quality of life. She was able to accomplish these changes because she was determined to do so and refused to place credence in discouraging claims that this transformation was impossible.

But many trauma survivors do not have faith that therapy will be substantially helpful to them. Sometimes they explicitly express this conviction to the therapist. In other instances, it seems so self-evident to them that they assume the clinician agrees, and it does not even occur to them to mention it. It is therefore necessary for the practitioner to be vigilant for indications that the survivor client subscribes to this belief. If it continues to go undetected and is not addressed, treatment can continue indefinitely while the entire time, the client's tacit assumption that progress cannot be made acts as a self-fulfilling prophecy.

The presence of this mind-set and corresponding inaction on the client's part raises a pivotal question for therapists whose assumption is that improvement in psychological adjustment is the core objective of treatment. That is, why would someone invest time and money in psychotherapy if they harbor the certainty that it will not eventuate in appreciable change? Due to the intensity of the emotional pain in which they are nearly constantly immersed, for some survivor clients, having an outlet for expressing their distress is in and of itself a source of relief, albeit a fleeting one. Having access to this means for obtaining even a transient reprieve from their anguish is adequately reinforcing to constitute sufficient cause to continue participating in treatment, sometimes indefinitely.

When the therapist surmises that this constellation of suppositions and corresponding behavior is being manifested by the survivor, it is necessary to identify and refute it. Doing so constitutes a necessary precondition for enlisting the client's persistent efforts to actively participate as an agent in their own progress in treatment. The clinical interchange that follows strikingly depicts the power of this principle.

**Case Example: Instilling Hope for Therapeutic Change**

Yolanda, a White woman in her late 30s, had been in both outpatient and residential treatment with several practitioners ever since her early teens. She grew up in a working-class household in which emotional neglect, childhood verbal abuse, and childhood physical abuse were a constant. From an early age, Yolanda became involved in a series of chaotic and coercive relationships with men appreciably older than she. She met criteria for complex posttraumatic stress disorder (C-PTSD; Herman, 1992a), alcohol and substance abuse, and borderline personality disorder. For most of her life, she relied on nonsuicidal cutting behavior and binging and purging in addition to excessive use of alcohol and other substances as a desperate means of trying to manage her considerable, almost constant emotional upset.

Approximately 3 months after starting treatment with a clinician trained in CTT, she began the session with a deep sigh, silently stared at the floor for several minutes, and then lifted her head and with tremendous sadness in her eyes directed her gaze at the therapist. With a mixture of slow-burning anger and resignation, she asked, "I'm never going to get better, am I?" What seemed to the therapist to be a protracted pause followed while she mentally scrambled to grasp at a response that would assure Yolanda that this was not true. It seemed to her that nothing she could say would be convincing to Yolanda. A possible solution occurred to her. It appeared highly unlikely that Yolanda would find anything that she had to say compelling. But perhaps there was an alternative.

"You know," the clinician began,

> most of the people I work with come from backgrounds very similar to yours and have very similar problems. And many of them, like yourself, have been in therapy for a long time in several settings and with several therapists. I've had the experience on several occasions of some of these clients at a certain point in treatment telling me this: "I've been experiencing something strange lately that I don't quite know how to put into words. If you had told me about this when I started working with you, it's not that I wouldn't have believed you. I wouldn't have had any idea what you were talking about. You might as well have been speaking a foreign language. I think perhaps what I've been experiencing is what other people mean when they use the word *content*.
>
> "But there's more. And I feel uncomfortable and more than a little foolish even thinking about saying it. I think that recently, every once in a while, I've gotten a brief glimpse of what other people mean when they talk about feeling *happy*."

When Yolanda's therapist finished this story, she gazed at Yolanda quietly, feeling more than a little pleased that she had hit on a response that she believed would be convincing. It therefore caught her off guard when Yolanda almost immediately began loudly yelling: "Why didn't anyone ever tell me this? I've been in treatment for so long in so many places. Why didn't anyone fucking tell me this?"

Subsequent to this session, Yolanda's outlook and behavior shifted markedly. She set herself the goal of relinquishing purging behavior and was successful. She committed herself to no longer engage in cutting and gradually was able to accomplish this goal. After several years on disability, she decided to enroll in a vocational training program to acquire a technical certificate that would make it possible for her to resume employment. Her progress did not take place in a consistent, unrelenting upward curve. As is nearly always the case, there were fits, starts, and setbacks. But instead of languishing in what had always been her status quo interspersed with periods of decline, she was decidedly moving forward because she now realized that her efforts to do so were likely to pay off.

An important principle is at work here, one that can be productively drawn on in various treatment situations. Providing the survivor with the detailed accounts of other similar clients' experiences and progress is highly likely to be much more compelling than assertions by the clinician. Recognizing that the client is convinced that resolution is impossible or that the distance they can move ahead is severely restricted and finding ways to disabuse them of that notion can make all the difference in the success of treatment.

**Undeserving**

One barrier to therapeutic change frequently encountered among survivors of CTr took me a long time to recognize. It is that CTr survivors often feel deeply underserving of good things in their lives. In response, when they encounter favorable occurrences, developments, and successes, they are severely shaken. Almost as soon as they detect that their situation is improving, they experience an intense pull to subvert it. In the absence of intervention, they almost always give into this inclination and scramble to undo any favorable circumstances or attainments that arise.

The extended period required to identify this constellation of emotional reactions and behavioral responses strikes me as a clear example of the perceptual and experiential gulf that sometimes exists between complex trauma survivors and clinicians from more fortunate backgrounds. The behavior of survivors when things go well is likely to be so foreign to practitioners from more favorable backgrounds that they are likely to have tremendous difficulty noticing, let alone understanding, what is occurring. In this regard, it can also be seen as an expression of the cross-cultural quality that working with survivors can take on. By virtue of the oppressive environment in which they were reared, survivors may subscribe to fundamental schemas that may be entirely foreign to therapists whose life circumstances have been more privileged. Being aware of such potential apperceptive disparities can help sensitize the therapist to be vigilant for their existence and potential disruptive influence.

What is particularly remarkable to me is that once I became aware of this phenomenon I was able, in retrospect, to detect its presence in previous cases. As a faculty member and clinical supervisor in a doctoral-level psychology training program, I periodically, with clients' written consent, audio- and video record my therapy sessions. After I came to recognize this pattern, I was astounded how often survivor clients on these recordings would use the phrase "I don't deserve \_\_\_\_\_." These three words could be followed by any number of endings: "I don't deserve to be happy"; "I don't deserve to live in a clean, well-organized home"; "I don't deserve to be loved"; "I don't deserve to eat"; "I don't deserve to live."

It is a common conception in psychology that an excessive sense of entitlement, such as that characterizing narcissistic personality disorder, is a clear sign of psychological maladjustment. It is also certainly widely acknowledged that low self-esteem is an indicator of psychological impairment. Negative self-image is one of the three identified characteristics of the C-PTSD DSO factor. But the dynamic we are discussing here extends beyond, and is distinct from, low self-esteem. It is, in effect, the converse of the narcissist's sense of entitlement: It is a powerful and fundamental sense of a lack of entitlement.

If one only attends to the behavior that is an expression of this sense of not being entitled, one is likely to mislabel it *self-sabotage*. But this term is misleading, suggesting that the survivor's behavior is motivated by a perverse drive toward self-destruction—that, somehow, they enjoy deprivation. Careful exploration of the feelings and intentions that provoke this pattern of behavior makes it clear that this is not the case. On the contrary, avoiding positive developments and working to dismantle them once they occur is actually directed by a desire to avoid catastrophic outcomes.

Repeatedly while growing up, the survivor desperately hoped in one situation after another that, in contrast to past experiences, the results of their efforts in the current circumstances would turn out to be positive. This time, the person they wanted to be friends with would reciprocate their interest. This time, a parent would recognize their achievement and praise them for it. This time, they would receive affection rather than being taken advantage of and exploited. And each and every time, it seemed, their hopes for things to be different were once again elevated only to eventually plummet and bring a cascading sense of disappointment, isolation, failure, and humiliation.

For some complex trauma survivors, once they left their childhood household and were on their own and felt more in control of their circumstances, hope that life could be different—that they could escape their misery and feel better about themselves and their lives—rose once again. But almost invariably it seemed that either because they misread the situation or because their deficient life skills interfered, they again concluded that their optimistic expectations were unfounded. With each instance, the consequent soul-crushing dejection grew more difficult to bear and instilled a greater sense of dread that wishing for their lives to improve would only inevitably lead to more cause for despair. Over time, after the repetition of such experiences, the appearance of the promise that things might get better and the hope that believing this might be warranted became a stimulus cue for discouragement and humiliation. In sidestepping favorable circumstances and outcomes, the survivor is not looking to hurt themselves through self-sabotage but, rather, is scrambling to avoid the shameful letdown of being "fooled again."

In conjunction with the maltreatment and verbal abuse that the complex trauma survivor experienced throughout their formative years, what seems like a cause-and-effect cycle of repeated hope and disappointment comes to take on the aura of confirmation that they do not deserve positive conditions in their life. With repeated experiences such as these, it is easy for them to conclude that God, fate, karma, or the physical laws of the universe have decreed that they be endlessly doomed to failure and misery. Given their life circumstances, is understandable how they have come to this conclusion. Obviously, however, this counterproductive cycle contradicts the central purpose of psychological treatment. The objective of therapy is to equip the client to live a more effective and more gratifying life. Therefore, as long as the fear of allowing improvement remains activated, therapeutic progress is thwarted.

The way out of this dilemma begins by identifying the client's fear and avoidance of progress by noticing what eluded me for so long: instances in which the client says, "I don't deserve \_\_\_\_\_"—something that would be to their benefit. What happened for a long time before this phrase caught my attention was that this statement was so far outside of my own perspective that it didn't register, as if it did not occur to me that those saying it literally meant it.

In other instances, one can detect the presence of this sentiment when the client expresses the intention to make a choice that dismantles an (often hard-won) and gratifying aspect of their life. They may, for instance, walk away from a small business they started that is generating a good income or leave a relationship that has been an important source of support. What especially raises a red flag about these decisions when they are driven by a sense of disentitlement is that the client is unable to provide a sound rationale for their intention.

Once the certainty of being undeserving and the corresponding behavioral sequence are identified, nonleading questioning (described in detail in the next chapter) often easily enables the survivor to explain the past experiences and current thoughts and feelings that lie behind it. As compelling as the conviction of being undeserving may be, this conviction does not usually preclude the intellectual understanding that it needs to be resisted for treatment to move forward. Proceeding with additional nonleading inquiries to help the client identify the circumstances, thoughts, and feelings that signal the activation of the pull to avoid or undo positive developments in their lives helps them be vigilant for and resist this urge. With repeated practice and each successful attempt to shun the temptation to give in to this impulse, its intensity is weakened, and it eventually extinguishes.

**Case Example: Extinguishing the Conviction of Being Undeserving**
Karen, a Latina woman in her early 40s, had grown up in a household with a hostile, overbearing, verbally abusive, and demanding mother who was painfully critical of her appearance and often complained that she was overweight. She described her father as emotionally bland and distant. She also reported having been sexually molested by several perpetrators throughout her childhood.

Karen had been in several serious romantic relationships with men throughout her twenties. Her most recent relationship had culminated in a marriage proposal. However, although her mother had frequently found fault with Karen for never having married, she convinced Karen that this man was not good enough for her. Doubting her own judgment and desperate for her mother's approval, Karen ended the engagement and had not dated since. She reported that she would have regretted her choice in any case, but it was particularly disturbing to her because she realized that she had tossed away the life she could have had with him. Her small apartment became increasingly cluttered as she developed a serious hoarding disorder that grew progressively worse over time. Her social life became increasingly barren. Although she had previously enjoyed throwing small dinner parties, because she was embarrassed about the condition her hoarding had created in her home, she stopped having friends over. Later, she stopped getting together with any of them and eventually ended all contact with them.

Karen seemed determined to move forward in therapy and improve the quality of her life. Over several months, she made substantial gains: She reduced her chronic level of anxiety, made small inroads into getting rid of unneeded possessions she had accumulated, improved the appearance of her home, and reached out to friends she had not been in touch with for some time. However, repeatedly after a few weeks of establishing these gains, she would suddenly retreat into her previous patterns of behavior and eliminate the progress she had worked so hard to achieve.

After several iterations of this sequence of events, as she and her therapist were trying to account for her repeatedly determined and successful efforts to overcome her difficulties that culminated in the loss of her gains, Karen was able to articulate some of what was driving this cycle. She explained that, at first, she felt good about what she was accomplishing. After a short while, however, she would begin to feel restless and then become increasingly nervous. As she became progressively more unsettled, she was plagued by the thought, "I don't deserve this."

Initially, she was unable to explain to her therapist what was behind this idea, but she insisted that it was more than just an obsessive thought; it was a deeply felt and anxiety-provoking conviction. As they continued discussing the matter, Karen reported that flashes of the climactic scene from what had always been one of her favorite films, *Carrie*, the original version starring Sissy Spacek that was based on the Stephen King novel, were running through her mind. Carrie, the title character, had been mistreated by her mother in much the same way that Karen had, and like Karen, throughout her school years had remained socially isolated and felt forever doomed to remain excluded from the "inner circle."

In the film, some of the other students in Carrie's class during her senior year of high school decided it would be funny to convince her that she was suddenly well liked and popular, and they treated her accordingly. The long-running "joke" culminated on prom night, when they elected Carrie prom queen. In a powerful moment of triumph, Carrie, wearing a white dress, was called to the stage, crowned with a tiara, draped with a sash, and given a bouquet of roses. At that moment, as everyone was smiling and applauding, one of the students pulled a rope attached to a bucket poised directly over the position on the stage where Carrie was standing. The bucket, filled with pig's blood, emptied, drenching Carrie in agonizing slow motion. Humiliated, Carrie saw in her mind's eye that everyone was mockingly laughing at her.

For Karen, this scenario forcefully evoked the emotions she anticipated being bombarded with whenever she allowed herself to believe that the wretchedness that seemed to have plagued her since childhood was finally coming to an end. Like other survivors of CTr, she framed this expected retribution as punishment for receiving what she did not deserve. Therapists often assume the corresponding behavior constitutes self-sabotage. But the aim is not self-harm; it is to avoid the harm that the survivor is convinced will befall them if they let their life improve. Detailed discussions with Karen and other survivor clients trace this apprehension back to the repeated experience of believing that there is reason for hope that things are getting better only to discover that they have been "fooled."

A common example of this cycle is the survivor who dreams of escaping the maltreatment and neglect of their childhood home, and then, in their late teens, marries someone and moves out only to discover that their spouse is verbally and physically violent toward them. From the vantage point of emotion is the compelling appearance that the plunge back into desolation and suffering was "caused" by their own hopefulness and the strivings to reach more favorable life circumstances. In retrospect, the disappointment and shame that they feel when they conclude that their aspirations were unfounded only compounds the anguish they were already experiencing.

By engaging in chain analysis with her therapist of the sequences composing this repeating scenario, Karen was able to slowly extricate herself from the emotion-based conviction that progress was dangerous. From this foundation, she was encouraged by her clinician to remain vigilant for instances when anxious anticipation accompanying the thought "I don't deserve \_\_\_\_" arose. She now was equipped to counter that previously deeply held feeling by examining the factual components of the situation she was facing that aroused this conviction and marshalling reasoning to reduce its intensity so that she could resist being held back by it. Little by little over time, she stopped dismantling therapeutic gains and was able to loosen the hold of the misperception of positive gains as indications of threat.

**Dimensions of Diversity**

A major objective of CTT is to assist CTr survivor clients in becoming conversant with the knowledge and abilities needed to navigate and function within the parameters and conventions of the predominant society. Various conditions may account for CTr survivors' difficulty negotiating the prevailing sociocultural milieu. One is being reared in an ineffective family of origin context that idiosyncratically deviates from mainstream norms in various ways. Another is growing up in a family characterized by one or more facets of cultural diversity. Yet another is that the client, by virtue of belonging to or identifying with a disenfranchised group, has restricted access to the predominant culture and is subjected to forms of discrimination and disparagement. Regardless of why the survivor is not fully acquainted with how to operate in keeping with the demands of the mainstream culture, the understanding with which the practitioner approaches helping them achieve this objective inevitably has a decisive impact on the quality of the collaborative alliance and consequently on the course of therapy.

**Idiosyncratically Deviant Family Contexts**
Being reared in an ineffective family environment that, because of its own particular idiosyncrasies and deficiencies, fails to model and transmit norms of the dominant culture to its offspring is tantamount to coming from an alien culture. The unique practices, beliefs, and values conveyed to the client by such a family background deviate in decisive ways from the dominant culture, which, in turn, can create an impediment to effectively adapting to social norms and expectations.

Familial deviations stemming from a lack of caring can be as or more detrimental than ones composing the parents' lack of practical knowledge and skills. As one survivor client expressed it, "People whose parents cared about them, as much as they really try, they can't imagine what it's like to have parents who don't care and how scary that is." It can be exceedingly difficult, perhaps ultimately beyond the realm of possibility, for someone who grew up with devoted parents to fully grasp what it is like to have had to do without this essential source of a sense of safety, well-being, and self-esteem. It may be nearly inevitable that being reared in such circumstances leads, on some level, to the feeling that one is not only unloved but forever and immutably unlovable and therefore inferior.

Beyond these effects, however, growing up in such an interpersonal atmosphere is also likely to be associated with a failure to acquire the proficiencies needed to effectively operate in the larger society. An individual reared in such circumstances may recognize at least some of the ways in which their social and cultural repertoire has been restricted by their family of origin environment. But identifying and remediating all their possible gaps in socialization and enculturation may be beyond the capacity of any individual without assistance from someone else who is more conversant in those norms.

**Culturally Diverse Family Contexts**
Another major dimension with similar consequences is the potential impact on families and their children of the disenfranchisement represented by dimensions of diversity. Entire sectors of society are effectively deprived of access to the types of societal knowledge and skills that more privileged subgroups take for granted and assume are within reach of anyone sufficiently motivated to master them. For members of the culturally diverse sectors of society, whether by virtue of gender, ethnicity, sexual orientation, economic status, (dis)ability status, work status or profession, or other dimensions of diversity, not only

the perception of others but their sense of identity are determined largely by the currently entrenched social context. And the same, often barely perceptible, "in the background" quality of context that tends to obscure its presence in other situations can render the societal context and its profound and ubiquitous promptings practically invisible and undetectable to those immersed in it.

An excellent example of this reality is documented in a CBS-TV *60 Minutes* segment about Strive (Hartman, 1999; see https://www.youtube.com/watch?v=fgm0iF6T9uQ), an apparently extremely successful program designed to help people from economically disadvantaged communities gain employment. The clients in the *60 Minutes* segment are primarily people of color. The bulk of the training depicted in the episode is not in concrete work proficiencies, such as clerical office skills or computer literacy. Rather, Strive is presented as primarily being devoted to providing instruction in interpersonally appropriate workplace behavior. These are competencies such as shaking hands in the manner predominant in the mainstream culture, looking someone in the eye while talking to them, smiling during interpersonal exchanges, and wearing the type of clothing expected in an office or other workplaces settings.[3]

Abilities such as these are ones in which members of more privileged subpopulations are usually immersed and which they therefore assimilate effortlessly and, to a large degree, assimilate even unwittingly from their surrounding social context. People who are reared in the predominant cultural context in which these types of conventions and social competencies are transmitted in an implicit, nearly automatic fashion are prone to view them as ones that are universally known, subscribed to, and mastered. They are therefore primed to disparage others who do not display the behaviors and attitudes that are expressions of these capacities, presupposing that individuals who fail to do so could choose to do otherwise but are being uncooperative, oppositional, or rebellious, or are indulging in maintaining "a bad attitude."

In parallel fashion, within mental health settings, behaviors that are considered socially inappropriate because they deviate from the norm may easily be assumed to be manifestations of psychological disorders. It may not occur to mental health professionals that one possible explanation for these departures from expected behavior is that the person who does not adhere to social conventions was denied opportunities to become familiar with them. Clearly, this type of deprivation-related impairment is fundamentally distinct from

---

[3] What is ironic, and more than a little disturbing, is that in the video, the staff of the Strive segment, also predominantly people of color, speak to the program clients in a demeaning and, at times, humiliating manner. It is conveyed in the segment that the staff were themselves former clients of the program who had themselves endured marginalization and indignities, such as unemployment, alcohol and drug addiction, homelessness, and incarceration. One cannot help but wonder if they rely on yelling and belittling their clients because this is the template for disciplining others that they themselves experienced growing up. This conjecture seems to be confirmed when the interviewer, Leslie Stahl, asked one of the staff, "Why so tough? . . . It's like an army drill sergeant. It breaks you down . . . ," and the staff member replies, "It's like my mother. My mother does that."

either traumatization or psychopathology. It is awareness of and responsivity to differentiation of the effects of these two categories of childhood adversity—experiences of deprivation and experiences of threat—that distinguish CTT from purely trauma-focused treatment by drawing attention to CTr survivors' need for skills-based strategies in addition to trauma processing.

**Sequestration and Microaggression**

It is certainly not coincidental that Strive's clientele overwhelmingly comprises ethnic minorities. What is commonly referred to as the "mainstream culture" is essentially equivalent to a White, cisgender male, heterosexual, economically stable, American-born, able-bodied, Christian culture. Those who fall outside any of these dimensions of diversity are highly likely to suffer from the experiences of deprivation represented by sequestration from mainstream knowledge and conventions, and therefore from access to desirable employment, housing, educational, and other opportunities.

In addition, they are likely to have been subjected to repeated experiences of threat in the form of microaggressions. Sue et al. (2007) defined *racial microaggression* as "brief and commonplace daily verbal, behavioral, and environmental indignities, whether intentional or unintentional, that communicate hostile, derogatory, or negative racial slights and insults to the target person or group" (p. 273). Although Sue and his coauthors were specifically addressing racial indignities, microaggressions can and regularly do occur to people of any disenfranchised group (e.g., Kattari, 2019; Sue, 2010). Emerging research studies provide empirical evidence supporting the debilitating psychological impact of microaggression (Forrest-Bank, Jenson, & Trecartin, 2015; Liao, Weng, & West, 2016; Swann, Minshew, Newcomb, & Mustanski, 2016). In the context of a family environment that fostered an intensely negative and self-depreciating sense of self, and a larger community that is likely to disparage differences, it is not uncommon for CTr survivors to be ambivalent toward or outright rejecting of their own intersecting diversity identifications. It is incumbent on the therapist, therefore, to more or less simultaneously help the client navigate the predominant culture while they support the client's exploration and embrace of the components of their diverse identifications.

The CTT practitioner needs to recognize that conducting therapy with CTr survivors invariably entails issues of diversity, if only because of the idiosyncratic subculture of the client's ineffective family of origin and the social alienation that comes with survivor status itself. Being a CTr survivor is an alien status when living in society in which the validity of trauma is often questioned and its impact is widely misunderstood. Commonplace questions such as, "If you really were abused, why didn't you tell anyone sooner?" and "That happened so long ago, why can't you just get past it?" are demoralizing and invalidating.

Given these varied dimensions of diversity, the clinician must be invested in being educated by each particular survivor about their identifications and the unique, intersecting difficulties and assets associated with those identifications. Productively helping survivors become more familiar with and adept at navigating the mainstream culture requires that the therapist be clear about the distinction between what is "prevalent" and what is "superior." The reason to promote client proficiency with mainstream societal practices and perspectives is not because they are in any way better than others, but because "fluency" in the predominant culture, like being conversant in a country's primary language, offers access to opportunities that can improve the quality of life. Conversely, exclusion from these opportunities by virtue of minority status is a major aspect of what terms such as *marginalized* and *disenfranchised* signify.

Moreover, therapists need to familiarize themselves and explicitly encourage clients with diverse identifications to educate themselves about their experience as members of those subcultures. Microaggression and experiences of disapproval and disparagement by the larger society have likely interfered with the survivor's ability to embrace these aspects of their identity fully and unambiguously. These critical appraisals by the larger culture easily dovetail with negative feedback received during their formative years that fuel self-critical attitudes and self-rejection.

When the practitioner is locked into assuming that their own learned customs and norms are the "proper" or "preferable" ones, this assumption in itself is likely to be experienced by the client as microaggression. Recognizing that many complex trauma survivors did not grow up with or had limited access to the capacities needed to navigate the dominant culture can go a long way toward preventing countertherapeutic misunderstandings and unintended slights.

## THE NECESSITY OF THERAPIST SELF-CARE

Trauma work, especially involvement in the partnership represented by a collaborative treatment relationship, is not an undertaking that can be carried out in an emotionally disengaged manner. The strains of trauma work, consequently, can and often do take an appreciable emotional toll on practitioners, especially those who specialize in trauma and whose caseloads therefore consist of a substantial proportion of survivors. In this respect, it is not only the survivor who can pose challenges to the formation and maintenance of a collaborative relationship. It is the practitioner's responsibility not only to themselves but also to the client to manage the strains of trauma-focused treatment by ensuring that they are consistently attending to their own needs by maintaining a rewarding personal life. My own conviction is that accomplishing this objective requires both taking time alone and sustaining supportive and experientially connected relationships.

A long-standing line of research documents that trauma-related practice can be stressful for service providers in a number of ways. Figley (2002) introduced the term *compassion fatigue* to refer to a particular form of burnout that can occur in trauma work due to emotional depletion related to "the costs of caring, empathy, and emotional investment" (p. 1433). The designation *secondary traumatic stress symptoms* (STSS), although lacking a clear consensus definition (Sprang, Ford, Kerig, & Bride, 2019), is generally construed as a constellation of symptoms that parallel or approximate those of posttraumatic stress disorder (PTSD) and is provoked in practitioners by hearing accounts of trauma from the clients they serve. Pearlman and Saakvitne (1995), who used the term *vicarious traumatization*, noted that the effects on therapists of hearing about clients' traumatic experiences are prone to build over time. *Burnout*, a construct that predates compassion fatigue and STSS by almost 2 decades, refers to emotional exhaustion resulting from the conditions under which a professional functions (Freudenberger, 1977) but that can occur in response to a wide range of influences not exclusively associated with trauma work.

Butler, Carello, and Maguin (2017) studied burnout and STSS in a sample of 195 social work trainees. Although more than half of those students were working in nonclinical settings, the entire sample reported exposure to traumatic material during their placements. Although the mean level of burnout was low, most of the students exhibited some level of STSS. However, engagement in self-care was associated with lower levels of STSS. An unanticipated finding was that students indicated that trauma-related coursework was even more stress-inducing than field work with trauma survivors.

Providers with adverse childhood experiences in their own backgrounds appear to be especially vulnerable to burnout and STSS, but self-care practices were associated with reduced degrees of these outcomes in this group, too (La Mott & Martin, 2019). Vio, Vivanco, and Morales (2009) assessed the effectiveness of a five-session, cognitive, behaviorally oriented self-care workshop on 21 clinical psychologists who had been found to score above the cutoff on a measure of STSS. Nine of the 21 were available to participate in the workshop. Those who took the workshop significantly increased their self-care behaviors and reduced their STSS. Conversely, the 12 who did not participate did not change in their level of self-care, and their STSS level increased.

Danieli (2005) outlined three steps in self-care for trauma professionals: (a) develop awareness of signs of distress; (b) learn to identify and be able to express these reactions, and remember that, like all emotional responses, they will subside; and (c) "heal and grow" (p. 664). The heal and grow component includes aspects of self-care, such as consulting with other professionals, forming a network of colleagues to discuss trauma-related professional activities, and engaging in activities that offer avenues for stress reduction, such as creative and expressive pursuits.

It may be that CTT is structured in a way that reduces the intensity of the stress produced in therapists by secondary trauma exposure. As is the case with other phase-oriented approaches to treatment for traumatization, the majority of the course of therapy is devoted to Phase 1 stabilization work rather than to Phase 2 trauma processing. The client's mastery of coping skills, reduction in crises, and improvement in the present-day quality of life in Phase 1 tends to mitigate the impact of traumatic material when it is more extensively and directly addressed in Phase 2. These factors, in conjunction with titration of trauma work by processing traumatic material a little at a time and in a fashion that each particular CTr survivor can best tolerate, tend to reduce the accompanying distress in a way that is likely to make this phase of treatment appreciably less taxing for both survivor and clinician than it would otherwise be.

Nevertheless, both preventative self-care and steps to address flare-ups in vicarious traumatization or STSS are requisite components of conducting trauma-focused treatment. L. S. Brown (2008), among others, flatly stated that

> VT [vicarious traumatization] is not a passing experience; if a psychotherapist stays engaged in work with trauma survivors, then VT becomes another component of self. This is not necessarily a bad thing; in fact, when VT is acknowledged, embraced, and integrated into a psychotherapist's sense of self rather than denied and disowned, it becomes a source of resilience and an inner place from which a psychotherapist can join empathically with trauma survivors in ever more profound ways. (p. 251)

In CTT, the ultimate objective is not just to help the CTr survivor resolve the sequelae of their traumatic experiences but to equip them to radically improve the effectiveness and quality of their daily lives. A substantial component of this approach to living is self-care: getting enough sleep, eating well, exercising, maintaining a stimulating social life, and making time for recreational activities and downtime. To a large extent, therefore, our obligation as therapists to our survivor clients is to practice what we preach for their sake so that we can approximate a reasonable level of professional functioning. It is also important for therapists to practice what we preach for our own sake so that our engagement in trauma practice does not lead to compromising the quality of our extraprofessional lives.

## THE CENTRALITY OF THE RELATIONAL SPHERE IN CONTEXTUAL TRAUMA THERAPY

Herman's (1992b) original formulation of C-PTSD suggested that what causally differentiated it from PTSD was repeated encounters with traumatic events as opposed to a single or circumscribed traumatic incident. CTT does not dispute this perspective but builds on it by suggesting that what potentiates both the likelihood of repeatedly encountering traumatic events and the emergence of DSO is a childhood atmosphere of pervasive developmental deprivation. According to the CTT conceptual model and consistent with the tenets of developmental psychology, the converse of DSO—the ability to regulate emotion and impulses, a stable positive sense of self, and the capacity to enter into and maintain mutually gratifying relationships—are all the product of favorable interpersonal experiences, the most impactful of which is the quality of ongoing parent–child interaction.

It is, therefore, the DSO component of CTr that makes the role of the characteristics of the collaborative therapeutic alliance so centrally influential in CTT. Just as weaknesses in the parent–child relationship are the essential source of DSO, the evolution of a resilient, cooperative partnership between survivor and therapist is the most imperative contributor to resolving DSO.

To effectively treat CTr, therefore, practitioners need to be much more than technicians. They must hone a level of interpersonal sensitivity, receptivity, responsiveness, and finesse that is indispensable in working with CTr. To a greater extent than in working with other types of problems, the quality of the therapeutic alliance is likely to be the prime determinant of successful treatment outcome.

The cultural assumptions predominant in the United States, and to a considerable but perhaps somewhat lesser extent in other Westernized countries, is that people are "self-made." We like to think that we construct our own sense of self and freely choose its various components—our self-concept, values, beliefs, life goals, social affiliations, and so on. It may be reassuring to believe that the most intimate thing about us—our core sense of identity—is self-constructed, especially for those of us who feel good about who we are. But sober, objective consideration of the matter (and much of the research literature in developmental psychology) contradicts this potentially comforting illusion.

My own thinking about this issue has been intensely shaped by the perspective of Harry Stack Sullivan (1953; Gold & Bacigalupe, 1998), the mid-20th century psychiatrist for whom psychological development and dissociation were key elements of understanding human behavior. H. S. Sullivan (1953) titled his theory of personality *interpersonal psychiatry*. As part of an intricate conception of personality development, he argued that our sense of self is constructed from reflected appraisals, both verbal and nonverbal and often subliminally apprehended reactions that others have to us. The most powerful and enduring reflected appraisals are those that emanate from the people we are closest to, especially during our formative years.

What H. S. Sullivan's (1953) construct of reflected appraisals implies is that just as we derive an image of what we look like from what is reflected to us by physical mirrors, our image of who we are coalesces from the overt and subtle feedback we receive from those we are closest to growing up. The destructive force of the negative appraisals generated by experiences of deficit (frequently acting in conjunction with experiences of threat) almost inevitably results in an extremely distorted self-image that is encapsulated in the "negative self-concept" constituent of DSO. If children who grow up in relatively benign or favorable interpersonal environments are surrounded by mirrors from which they derive a more-or-less accurate sense of self, those who are reared in inadequate, neglectful, and abusive circumstances are encircled by distorted fun-house mirrors that convey to them a misshapen, disfigured, deleterious, and intensely inaccurate image of who they are.

Ultimately, therefore, the function of the relational sphere of CTT is to furnish the survivor of CTr with an interpersonal setting that implicitly contradicts the distorted, harmful, and inaccurate self-image that they were inculcated with as a child and that has sustained ever since. In addition, as survivor clients sometimes recognize and explicitly state, the collaborative therapeutic alliance evolves into a safe space, a "laboratory" for investigating and experimenting with new forms of interpersonal interaction that are more productive and certainly more comfortable than those originally learned. These novel approaches to relationships can then be tested out in situations external to the consulting room.

In actuality, none of the three spheres of CTT operates independently of the other two. Conceptually, being alert for opportunities to assist the client in applying evidence and reason to assessing the accuracy of their beliefs about themselves is a reasonable adjunctive strategy for correcting a distorted self-image. Practical interventions can help, too. Survivors who are certain that their maltreatment was warranted can be encouraged to visit a local park or playground that children frequent so that they can identify the qualities that identify a child as being deserving of abuse. It is always surprising to me that survivors agree to carry out this experiment and unfailingly follow through with it. And just as inevitably, they return to the next session with the solid recognition that although they saw some unruly or bratty children, not one of those children merited maltreatment. By implication, neither did the client.

These examples illustrate that conceptual and practical intervention spheres can and do enter into the reexamination of the survivor's self-concept and the revision of their approach to interpersonal relationships. In actual practice, the three spheres of CTT are inexorably intertwined. The rubric of spheres is primarily a conceptual device to help practitioners identify the constituent components of CTT, how they differ from each other, and how they each compose a relatively unique contribution to treatment outcome. Nevertheless, it should be clear that more than the other two spheres, the relational sphere is the driving force behind empowering the survivor client to revise their negative self-concept, to enhance their ability to participate in mutually gratifying and sustainable relationships, and, above all, to be able to interact with the clinician in a way that is supportive of productive and lasting gains in therapy.

# 7

# Collaborative Conceptualization
*Jointly Constructing Cognitive Understanding*

Having examined the role of the relational sphere in contextual trauma therapy (CTT), we turn to the function of the conceptual sphere. First, we consider the core procedure for implementing *collaborative conceptualization*. The primary function of this approach is to bolster the survivor's reasoning abilities by guiding them through the process of cognitively scrutinizing types of issues in a way that empowers them to arrive at their own conclusions. We explore the rationale for proceeding in this way and then delineate the particulars of the procedure itself.

Next, we explore major areas of application of collaborative conceptualization. These areas include case conceptualization as an ongoing endeavor that helps the client make sense of their chaotic history and its impact on their present functioning, and, based on the case conceptualization, the collaborative construction of strategies to overcome their psychological difficulties. In addition, as the clinician identifies cognitive distortions engendered by both the client's traumatic experiences and having been reared in an ineffective family context, they use the same procedure of walking the survivor through the critical thinking process of jointly examining these beliefs while keeping the survivor in charge of the outcome. Regardless of the immediate purpose for using the procedure, its aim is simultaneously to promote the development of logical reasoning and decision-making capacities that have been adversely affected by experiences of deficit and experiences of threat.

---

http://dx.doi.org/10.1037/0000176-008
*Contextual Trauma Therapy: Overcoming Traumatization and Reaching Full Potential,*
by S. N. Gold
Copyright © 2020 by the American Psychological Association. All rights reserved.

## THE COMBINED NEGATIVE IMPACT OF DEPRIVATION AND THREAT ON SOUND REASONING

The complex traumatization (CTr) survivor has, by definition, lived through a confusing, demoralizing childhood and adolescence permeated by experiences of deficit and experiences of threat. Each of these influences acts to compromise the CTr survivor's reasoning ability. In examining the role of establishing a collaborative therapeutic alliance in the relational sphere of CTT in Chapter 6 we have seen how the conditions that characterize an ineffective family of origin context fail to foster the development of the relational capacity to experience a felt sense of connection with others. In parallel fashion, the same familial qualities—low levels of encouragement of autonomy and intellectual achievement, a relative lack of a sense of interpersonal cohesion and emotional expressiveness, and elevated levels of interpersonal conflict and control (Gold, Hyman, & Andrés-Hyman, 2004)—work against the evolution of the conceptual capacity for independent, critical thinking. Consequently, facilitating cognitive development is the central aim of the conceptual sphere.

The developmentally deficient interpersonal/developmental contexts that foster CTr are steeped in irrationality. Adults in ineffective family environments often act in ways that are unfathomable, because they are capricious, erratic, and unpredictable. The impact of such an atmosphere is especially powerful on children whose welfare and safety depend on the adults with whom they live. Children are driven to make sense of their surroundings and to please and appease the adults to whom they instinctively look for protection, guidance, and nurturance (Barlow & Freyd, 2009; Freyd, 1994). When those adults who are responsible for providing for the children's well-being appear to be inadequately meeting their emotional or sometimes even basic physical needs, the children are inclined to blame themselves for their own deprivation, surmising that they are unlovable and unworthy of care. This effect is reflected in the studies that have identified negative self-concept as one of the components of disturbances in self-organization stemming from experiences of deficit (Alessandri & Lewis, 1996; Bennett, Sullivan, & Lewis, 2010; Chan, Brownridge, Yan, Fong, & Tiwari, 2011; Kealy, Rice, Ogrodniczuk, & Spidel, 2018).

As discussed in Chapter 3, formative years marked by deprivation and trauma unfavorably impact brain development in multiple ways. In connection with their work on forms of impairment associated with experiences of deficit, McLaughlin, Sheridan, and Nelson (2017) reviewed extensive evidence that early developmental deprivation is related to restricted cognitive development, including limitations in implicit learning, language abilities, and executive functioning. Beyond the experiential learning processes that interfere with the development of sound reasoning and facilitate the adoption of counterproductive beliefs, research has been revealing with increasing intricacy how being reared in such an environment negatively impacts development on a neurophysiological level (Carrion & Wong, 2012; Perry, Pollard, Blakley, Baker,

& Vigilante, 1995). Experiences of deficit correspond with understimulation of the areas of the brain responsible for higher order cognitive processes, decision making, and the tempering of emotions and impulses (Carrion, Garrett, Menon, Weems, & Reiss, 2008; Carrion & Wong, 2012).

Experiences of threat promote sensitization of the areas of the brain that activate affect and impulses (Ganzel, Kim, Gilmore, Tottenham, & Temple, 2013). In general, child maltreatment is associated with reduced brain volume (De Bellis et al., 1999), restricted elaboration of brain structures associated with emotion and impulse regulation (Barch, Belden, Tillman, Whalen, & Luby, 2018; van Harmelen et al., 2010), and stunted development of the prefrontal cortex (De Bellis et al., 2002), the area of the brain involved in thinking ahead, planning, and decision making. In addition, child abuse and childhood neglect have been found to be related to reduced volume of the corpus callosum (Teicher et al., 2004), the bundle of nerve fibers that connect the two hemispheres of the brain, thereby facilitating integration of emotion- and logic-based learning. Teicher and colleagues (2004) found that in boys, neglect was related to smaller corpus callosum volume than either physical or sexual abuse. In addition, experiences of threat in the form of abuse trauma compound these effects by continuing to haunt the survivor, triggering the arousal and shutdown components of the fight–flight–freeze response, which, in turn, disrupts the ability to think things through in a calm, dispassionate manner.

## PRINCIPLES OF THE COLLABORATIVE CONCEPTUALIZATION PROCESS IN CONTEXTUAL TRAUMA THERAPY

The combined impact of the forces previously delineated make it imperative that treatment for complex trauma survivors helps stimulate and strengthen cognitive processing. Experiences of deficit constitute a failure to adequately transmit the elements supporting effective cognitive functioning. Experiences of threat disrupt cognition and intensify reactivity. Overall, the dual influences of child abuse (experiences of threat) and child neglect (experiences of deficit) converge in the direction of intensifying impulsivity while restricting cognitive capacities, such as thinking ahead and considering the consequences of behavior that otherwise could be invoked to restrain impetuous behavior. Therapy that does not address the conceptual arena or that is merely directed at the content of thought rather than also at enhancing cognitive processing capacities inadequately equips the survivor to more effectively manage the demands of daily living in the adult world. Equipping the survivor of CTr to more productively engage in sober assessment of situations, exercise sound judgment, think ahead and consider the consequences of their actions, arrive at sensible decisions, and balance out emotions and impulses with reason is the central objective of the collaborative conceptualization component of CTT.

This orientation entails patience and discipline on the part of the CTT practitioner because it requires relinquishing the temptation to steer the client toward a particular conclusion. Instead, the focus is on assisting the survivor to systematically apply sound reasoning to whatever issue is being examined in any particular instance so that they are equipped to come to their own conclusions. The freedom to do so is exactly what is likely to have been stifled, whether unintentionally or purposefully, in their childhood interpersonal environment. Repeatedly exercising the principles of logical deduction supports the development of those cognitive capacities that were restricted by a childhood steeped in experiences adversity.

**The Client Is the Content Expert**

A collaborative orientation helps the therapist maintain the humility fostered by the recognition that the client is the only one with access to most of the data from which the conceptual formulation is constructed. Only the client can know the details of their personal history, what they think, what they feel, what they experience, why they do what they do, and what their aspirations are. Obviously, this knowledge is not always accessible to the client. Others may make conjectures about it, some of which are likely to seem compelling. But these suppositions are just that: unverified conjectures that, if shared with the client, may derail them and obscure retrieval of the knowledge that has not yet come into focus. What, then, is the legitimate role of the clinician in the conceptual enterprise?

**The Practitioner's Primary Role Is to Operate as a Process Guide**

The survivor is the only one who is privy to the content from which the conceptualization is constructed. However, as a result of having grown up with extensive deprivation and threat, they often have not mastered the ability to process information effectively. Moreover, in all likelihood, they were treated in a way in their family of origin that has instilled deep doubt in their own judgment. The therapist's appropriate role, therefore, is to assist the survivor in bolstering their capacity to exercise sound reasoning.

The core methodology for executing this task is not novel. It is Socratic interviewing, a form of intervention central to many variations of cognitive behavior therapy. As Clark and Egan (2015) discussed at length, the Socratic method, although widely associated with cognitive behavior therapy, is not always identified as a core component in its diverse variants and has rarely been systematically defined. In theory, the purpose of Socratic interviewing is to help the client come to their own conclusions. In practice, however, it can be difficult for the practitioner to resist presupposing the existence of a "correct" answer and framing questions designed to lead the client to that response. Particularly when working with CTr survivors within a CTT framework, it is imperative that the therapist not give in to this temptation. On the whole, helping the client absorb the principles of sound reasoning is substantially more important than the particular conclusion they reach. The rightful role of the clinician is to guide the client in applying the principles of sound reasoning to the material provided by the client's efforts to formulate a conclusion to a particular matter.

In carrying out this procedure, the therapist must keep in mind that they do not know the answer that ultimately will be obtained. Only the client has the information that will lead to the conclusion, even though, at the outset of the process, they are unaware of what it will be. The therapist composes questions devised to help the client construct a greater understanding, not to maneuver the client in any particular direction.

**The Football Field Analogy: Two Distinct but Complementary Vantage Points**

I frequently offer the following analogy about the collaborative conceptualization process to my survivor clients. Its purpose is to dispel the misperception that somehow, as a clinician, I have a superior ability to discern "the truth." However, the analogy serves equally as a reminder to myself about the limitations of my own understanding. It goes as follows.

Imagine that client and therapist are both in a football stadium. The clinician is perched up in the stands at a height and distance that affords an extensive, panoramic vantage point from which to observe the playing field. From this location, the practitioner has a wide-angle, almost bird's-eye view. This perspective might fool the therapist into thinking that from up in the stands they can observe everything and can do so from a position of "objectivity" that can at least roughly be equated with "accuracy."

But they would be wrong. Although from high in the stands, the observer can take in a broad scope of information, their distance from the playing field severely limits the type of information to which they have access. (The term "Monday morning quarterback" captures this fallacious attitude well.)

In this analogy, the client is down on the field, one of the players situated in the midst of the action and vigorously participating in it. In this position, the survivor is privy to immediate, intense, and vital information that the practitioner cannot discern from such a distance. Only the client has the potential to come into contact with the visceral data of what it is like to be in the middle of the game, blocking, tackling, and attempting to weave through the opposing line and advance toward the goal post.

The therapist has no way of knowing this realm, and believing otherwise is at best misguided and at worst arrogant and counterproductive. It is useful for the practitioner to engage their imagination to track as empathically as possible what the survivor's experience might be like. But even a clinician who has lived through their own experiences of deprivation and traumatization, a decided advantage in appreciating the survivor's viewpoint, is not in a position to be certain what their client's idiosyncratic childhood experience was like or how it is impacting them currently.

In many areas of conceptual exploration in therapy, it is subjective data that are the most relevant. It is imperative, therefore, that the clinician be able to appreciate the limitations in the information that they can ascertain: direct knowledge only available to the client. Only the survivor has the potential to discern what they feel, what they think, and what their past experiences have been. Only the client can know their subjective world. Everyone has some degree of limitation in awareness of their own thoughts, feelings, and recollection of their personal history. The role of the clinician is not to surmise what the survivor is experiencing and share these suppositions but, rather, to help the survivor approach, examine, and articulate experiential territory that may have previously eluded their awareness and assist them in processing it from the relatively objective vantage point of logical reasoning.

Certainly, the twin forces of deprivation and traumatization can act to hinder the survivor's retrieval of this information. But it is imperative to keep in mind that the person themselves is the only one who has the potential to access data such as these, which consist of their firsthand, lived experience. As obvious as this point may be to some, it is all too easy to forget it, especially for therapists extensively trained in interpretive modes of treatment. To some extent, practitioners have historically seen it as squarely within their jurisdiction to explain or "interpret" to the client various aspects of their "inner" world: why they do what they do, what they are feeling, what they are thinking, the connection between their current functioning and their history, and so on. In some therapeutic orientations, the ability to make such interpretations, what I would argue amount to "explaining the client to the client," is viewed as a cornerstone of their expertise and function.

Too often, interpretation is aligned with the presumption that the clinician can deduce what the client's experience is better than the client themselves. A stance such as this implicitly serves to undermine the survivor's confidence in their ability to accurately be aware of their own experience and trust their own perceptions and conclusions. The well-known psychoanalyst Winnicott (1971) seems to have been expressing a similar sentiment when he wrote,

> It appals [sic] me to think of how much deep change I have prevented or delayed in patients *in a certain classification* [italics in original] category[1] [footnote added] by my personal need to interpret. If we can only wait, the patient arrives at understanding creatively and with immense joy. . . . The principle is that it is the patient and only the patient who has the answers. (pp. 86–87)

The implication of the football field analogy is that each participant in the therapeutic enterprise is working with a limited set of data. From the distance of their position up in the stands, the clinician has the distance to wonder relatively dispassionately about a particular issue at hand and ask a series of questions about it. The client can respond by assessing their reactions to those inquiries from the immediacy of the playing field. The practitioner's attitude needs to be one of curiosity untainted by investment in any particular outcome. The immediate aim is to help the survivor gain more clarity about the

---

[1] It is not entirely clear to me what Winnicott (1971) means by this italicized phrase, but it appears in the context of the surrounding material that he is referring to clients with an appreciably limited capacity for interpersonal connection and places them within the same general territory of those addressed here.

matter at hand, not by steering them in a particular direction but by following their responses wherever they lead. The inquiry is conducted in the spirit of curiosity in which each answer points to a subsequent clarifying question. I refer to this procedure as *following the thread* provided by the client, knowing that they do not know in advance where that thread will lead. The following synopsis of a session captures the spirit of "following the thread."

**Case Example: The Hidden Presence of Deprivation**
Daphne, a White woman in her early 40s, presented for treatment with an unambiguous history of overt trauma and classic symptoms of posttraumatic stress disorder (PTSD). She entered psychotherapy in response to a life-threatening rollover automobile accident that left her with flashbacks, nightmares, intense avoidance of driving beyond the boundaries of her immediate neighborhood that later generalized to considerable hesitancy to leave the house, and chronically elevated anxiety. She also reported that she had been sexually molested by a brother several years older than she on an ongoing basis starting in early childhood. This experience seemed to account for avoidance not only of sexual activity but also of almost any form of physical contact, such as being hugged when greeted by another adult, and a substantial hesitancy to attend social events.

As therapy progressed, many of Daphne's PTSD symptoms appreciably reduced in intensity. Some became less constant and more episodic, occurring only in response to identifiable triggers. Others trauma-related difficulties dropped out altogether. Her general level of anxiety declined markedly, and she was able to leave the house to engage in social situations and began to actively seek them out and enjoy them. She even was able to resume driving, which allowed her to more frequently visit her parents and extended family, whom she clearly loved and with whom she enjoyed spending time. However, her discomfort at being touched, even by family members, remained as strong as ever, as did sexual avoidance that was a source of appreciable tension in her marriage.

Daphne's behavior patterns conveyed the impression of someone extremely considerate and caring who nevertheless was profoundly physically inhibited and behaviorally constricted. She also was religiously observant and seemed to subscribe to strongly conservative views and values regarding sexuality. Her therapist therefore was completely caught off guard that Daphne not only expressed that she was willing to address her sexual avoidance, but in doing so, revealed what she referred to as a history of "promiscuousness." Initially, her clinician assumed that her "promiscuity" was exclusively a result of her early sexual traumatization, but as she questioned Daphne about this period in her life, which began in her early teens, another dimension of her background unfolded.

As Daphne somewhat shamefully described her sexual activity from her early adolescence into her early adulthood, what emerged was not a litany of numerous casual encounters. Instead, she provided a chronicle of serially monogamous relationships with a number of men, occasionally close in age to her but in the vast majority of instances considerably older. In the course of responding to exploratory inquiries by her therapist, it became clear that, at the time, Daphne had perceived these interactions not primarily as sexual encounters but as romantic relationships. As the therapist's inquiry proceeded, they appeared in actuality to have been instances of her being taken advantage of sexually by most of these men. In the course of describing these relationships, Daphne seemed to increasingly become cognizant that her intense yearning to be loved had rendered her vulnerable to being exploited by them. Despite her growing recognition as the discussion continued that this was the case, she persisted in condemning herself for what she continued to perceive as promiscuity. She expressed the conviction that she had acted in an immoral manner and that she therefore did not deserve (see Chapter 6 for a discussion of this belief) to experience pleasure either in the form of sexual gratification or of the emotional comfort provided by physical touch.

Her therapist asked Daphne how she accounted for her intense need to be loved during this period of her life. In response, Daphne described a pattern of deprivation throughout her growing-up years that contradicted the therapist's previous supposition, based on Daphne's devotion to her family and frequent visits to see them, that her history of experiences of threat had been unaccompanied by substantial experiences of deficit. Instead, Daphne indicated that she did not remember ever receiving physical affection from either of her parents, although she asserted that this was by no means the case for either her two older siblings or her younger sister whom she perceived as having been especially intensely doted on. She conveyed that as the oldest daughter in the family, she was expected to act as a surrogate parent to her younger sister while her mother and father were away from the house to work at the bakery they owned. Furthermore, at age 12, she was charged with joining her parents in staffing the business, and she worked there throughout her teens until she moved out on her own, an arrangement she was resigned to but deeply resented. Her period of so-called promiscuity began shortly after the onset of her work at the bakery. Without any prompting from her therapist, she was able to recognize that her compulsive search for love was prompted by her despair at feeling unloved and exploited financially by her own family.

The practitioner was unaware of the extensive experiences of deficit in Daphne's background—a salient context of her traumatization—until this juncture in treatment. Despite that substantial progress in the reduction of Daphne's trauma-related difficulties had been made, once her childhood history of deprivation had been uncovered, it shifted Daphne's and her therapist's perspective on all that had been dealt with previously in therapy. This revelation had not come to light during previous, systematic and direct exploration of Daphne's history. It arose in response to following the thread that started by exploring what accounted for her self-assessment of her sexual behavior in adolescence and young adulthood as promiscuousness. Once this pivotal feature of her family background came to the fore, it provided a much clearer understanding of the interrelated influences in Daphne's early years that contributed to her persistent negative self-image and interpersonal difficulties. This understanding, in turn, opened up entire additional territories for exploration, suggested new strategies for intervention, and, above all, provided the therapist with a much more multidimensional picture of Daphne as a person. The productive impact of this expansion in the scope and consequently the effectiveness of treatment was rendered much more likely by application of a therapeutic model that recognized the critical impact not only of overt trauma but also of the context of Daphne's traumatization, a family environment characterized by excessive control and minimal nurturance and affection.[2]

The discovery of the emotional and developmental impoverishment that typified Daphne's familial environment was an invaluable and pivotal moment in the course of her treatment. There was, however, no a priori supposition by the therapist that this information was lurking in the background. It would have been highly unlikely to have occurred other than by following the thread initiated by Daphne in characterizing her past sexual behavior as promiscuousness. The therapist did not know and in actuality could not have known about the existence of this material in advance. It is not unusual that the dramatic quality of events such as child sexual abuse can be so compelling that it overshadows and blinds therapists to the impact of the underlying family context that may have accompanied or even facilitated them. Once her family context was identified, the CTT model helped the practitioner to recognize its relevance and importance over and above the explicit trauma that Daphne had experienced.

## DELINEATION OF THE PROCEDURE OF "FOLLOWING THE THREAD"

The instance of following the thread depicted in the previous section was initiated when Daphne referred to herself as having been promiscuous in her late teens and early to mid-twenties. Beyond the self-critical attitude encompassed by this term, Daphne's therapist found this self-description of Daphne's past behavior notable because it was markedly at variance with her view of Daphne. It was this apparent contradiction that led the clinician to initiate this sequence of following the thread. The objective was not to dispute or refute Daphne's use of the term *promiscuousness* but to obtain clarification: What was Daphne's past pattern of behavior that she was designating as promiscuousness? The tone of the clinician's inquiry in this procedure (and the experiential stance that the clinician attempts to adopt and maintain) is one of open-minded curiosity.

---

[2]Daphne's situation illustrates a key but sometimes overlooked point about the context of childhood traumatization: by virtue of differential treatment, siblings may grow up in the same household but in radically different family environments. Another vivid example of this principle can be found in the transcript of the initial intake session presented in Chapter 10.

Although some of the provider's questions might seek to identify the reasons for the client's behavior, beliefs, feelings, and so on, it is preferable to avoid using the word *why*. Survivors are prone to hearing inquiries incorporating this term as critical and challenging. Instead, it is safer to phrase questions aimed at ascertaining reasons or motives in ways that eschew the word *why*. For example, one might ask, "What do you think accounts for that?" "Do you any thoughts about the reason(s) for that?" or "Can you think of any way of explaining that?"

As the clinician proceeds through an instance of following the thread, it is important to listen carefully for the words the client uses and to ask oneself if one is reasonably certain about the meaning being ascribed to them. Asking Daphne how she was applying the term *promiscuousness* to herself and her past behavior was the entry point into the entire course of inquiry. The resulting line of investigation revealed extensive information about her history, her perception of her family of origin and of her relationships with men, and her understanding of the connection between these areas and her current-day discomfort with and avoidance of physical contact with others. Absent this information, it might easily be assumed that her avoidance was directly and simply an expression of distress stemming from her childhood molestation by her older brother. Instead, Daphne revealed that she viewed her avoidance as a form of repentant self-denial of a form of pleasure and comfort of which she considered herself undeserving. This outcome underscores the value of putting the client in charge of the content of conceptual investigation and assuming a one-down stance of ignorance. The greater the degree to which the practitioner recognizes that they are ignorant and do not and cannot know the client's experiential world without being told, the more genuinely they will convey this attitude. Getting in the habit of assuming this posture—as opposed to slipping into an attempt to talk the survivor out of their position—conveys that the therapist is aligning with the client to improve joint comprehension of the matter being discussed. Examples of inquiries framed from this perspective are

"I'm not sure I'm following. Can you help me understand better?"

"You were there. I was not. Can you describe that situation in more detail so that I can get a clearer idea of what exactly occurred and what that was like for you?"

"When you use that word, what do you mean by that?"

In Daphne's situation, continuing to follow the thread in the next session might be initiated by asking, "You told me last time that you believe you don't deserve sexual activity or other forms of physical contact because of your past behavior. I'm not at all sure I see the connection. Can you say some more about it?"

The CTT approach advocates resisting yes/no inquiries as much as possible and instead framing questions in as open-ended a manner as possible that does not presuppose any particular response. Take a relatively concrete example of assessing for the presence of PTSD once the client has identified an event that meets the Criterion A (see discussion of this criterion in Chapter 2) definition of *trauma* in the *Diagnostic and Statistical Manual of Mental Disorders* (fifth ed. [*DSM–5*]; American Psychiatric Association, 2013). The clinician can ask a series of questions such as

"What was that like for you while it was going on?"
"Was there anything noteworthy you experienced right afterward?"

[If so:]

"How long did that go on for?"
"Did it change at all over time?"
"If there were any ways that other people would have had any idea what you were experiencing without your telling them, what would they be?"

If PTSD is present, these types of questions are likely to elicit indicators corresponding to various diagnostic criteria: intrusive trauma-related experiences, avoidance behavior, alterations in cognition and mood, and alterations in arousal and reactivity. When the survivor spontaneously identifies these reactions without being presented with an oral checklist corresponding to the diagnostic criteria, both client and practitioner can be more confident that the information produced is accurate. The same principle holds with just about any inquiries regarding the survivor's past or present experience: If the response is independently produced by them, not only is it more likely to be valid, but it is more helpful to the client because, in most cases, it is not an exclusively cognitive answer. It is the result of an internal search for subjective experiences that are viscerally and not just intellectually convincing, and therefore much more likely to contribute to substantive and enduring change.

## TWO MAJOR AREAS OF APPLICATION OF COLLABORATIVE CONCEPTUALIZATION

The principles of the conceptual formulation are used to achieve various ends. They are used to construct a framework for formulating treatment goals; for helping the client make sense of their chaotic and painful past, and ensuing life trajectory; for assisting the client to arrive at sound decisions and reach valid conclusions while modeling the mechanisms for doing so; and for aiding the client in identifying and revising erroneous beliefs.

### Collaboratively Constructing a Case Conceptualization

The purpose of a CTT-oriented case conceptualization is to arrive at a comprehensive understanding of the survivor client's life trajectory, including, but far from limited to, their current psychological problems. It has the dual purpose of guiding treatment and helping the survivor attain perspective on their difficulties by identifying the experiences of threat and other factors that contributed to those difficulties. One of the crucial assets of recognizing the adverse impact of traumatic experiences on psychological adjustment is that when clients come to comprehend the extent to which their difficulties are attributable to trauma, it helps them to see that their problems are not a reflection on them but rather a reflection of what happened to them. This distinctly less stigmatizing formulation helps to reduce self-blame and direct the attention of client and therapist to where the causation of their difficulties actually lies. As the source of the client's impairment is identified as stemming from past experiences of deficit and threat, the resulting problems are demystified, and reasonable strategies for neutralizing them can be constructed and implemented. At the same time, a major source of self-denigration has been identified and is now open to being defused.

The more subtle, less widely recognized effects of experiences of deficit, when properly understood by the client, are similarly destigmatizing. Understanding the nature of the deprivation the survivor underwent and how that has restricted their development, socialization and enculturation allows them to discern that many of their functional limitations are not a reflection on them; they are a reflection of what was not provided to them. It is often the case that the survivor is not fully aware of the ways in which they have been deprived. They may have grown up in a family that was relatively isolated from the larger community, and that may have even actively dissuaded or outright forbidden them to make friends or visit other families' homes (Hulsey, Sexton, & Nash, 1992). These factors can effectively prevent the survivor from observing how different their upbringing is from others in the community. They therefore may be largely unaware of how their background deviates from the surrounding mainstream culture and consequently blind their own deprivation and the stunting of their functional capacities.

Construction of a continually evolving collaborative case conceptualization is one of the major tasks within the conceptual sphere of CTT. Its purpose is to yield an increasingly integrated formulation of how the survivor's personal history, family and social history, traumatic experiences, experiences of deprivation, current psychological problems, current functional limitations, functional resources, and personal strengths are interrelated. It serves not only to direct treatment but to provide the survivor with coherent understanding of how their past and present circumstances have shaped their current level and pattern of adjustment.

As therapy moves forward beyond its initial phases, the clinician increasingly encourages the survivor's input and collaborative participation in revising and refining the case conceptualization. At the outset of treatment, the clinician carries out an initial, tentative conceptual formulation that provides a direction for the earliest phases of therapy. Even at this stage, however, the clinician elicits, as much as possible, the client's input and perspective, and incorporates them into the conceptual formulation. As treatment proceeds, the practitioner progressively cedes more and more of the direction of the conceptualization process to the client so that it evolves into a joint endeavor in which the survivor increasingly is taking the lead. From the outset, the practitioner encourages the client to identify what they would like to accomplish in therapy rather than the practitioner's primarily establishing goals of treatment based on diagnostic considerations.

The overriding purpose of CTT is to reduce or eliminate the symptoms that compose the diagnosis and to equip the client to establish a quality of life and life trajectory that is considerably more productive and gratifying than has previously been the case for them. (A particularly good illustration of this broad-based orientation is the case of Lorna presented in Chapter 5.) In cases of CTr, although experiences of threat are primarily related to symptoms such as those associated with PTSD, depression, or substance abuse, experiences of deficit largely lead to more general impairment in broad areas of living, such as occupational or social functioning. Enlisting the client as early as possible, preferably in the first session, to envision the type of life they would hope to lead through the gains made in treatment aims to convey from the outset that it is possible to expect more from therapy than symptom relief. It also begins to help to establish that although the clinician may have expertise in how to solve problems and reach goals, it is the client's prerogative to determine the goals of therapy.

Once the initial phase of treatment is underway, case conceptualization transitions to become increasingly a joint enterprise. It helps to guide treatment by successively identifying areas to target for resolution and improvement, and by suggesting causal factors that might help inform strategies for achieving these treatment goals. It also serves to provide the survivor with a progressively more detailed and coherent picture aimed at helping them to make sense of the confusing, often chaotic muddle of circumstances and experiences that have shaped their life trajectory up until the present.

**Revising Distorted Beliefs**

A second function of the conceptual sphere is the identification and reexamination of distorted, counterproductive general conceptual schemas and particular beliefs ascribed to by the CTr survivor. Some of these schemas and beliefs are a vestige of the disruptive, confusing impact of various traumatic events. Often prominent among these cognitive distortions are intensely self-denigrating and frequently self-rejecting self-statements that are directly traceable to what verbally abusive caretakers repeatedly told the survivor about themselves.

Others are reflections of experiences of deficit, which can be subdivided into two distinctly different types. One is erroneous self-denigrating conclusions the survivor has arrived at in response to emotional neglect (e.g., "I am not loved because I am not loveable"). The other comprises areas of ignorance about social conventions and practical matters that are attributable primarily to the failure of the survivor's family of origin and larger social environment to adequately transmit the knowledge and skills needed for adaptive adult functioning. This lack of knowledge and skills can lead the survivor to denigrate themselves for seeming incapable of doing what others appear to accomplish with ease and to experience intense shame when others become aware of, and perhaps make fun of, their ignorance.

Most cognitive distortions can be effectively addressed with the same Socratic, following the thread methodology applied to collaborative case conceptualization. However, this last source of distortions—lack of information about social conventions and practical matters—calls for a different form of intervention.

## TWO DOMAINS OF UNDERSTANDING: FACILITATING DEDUCTION VERSUS PROVIDING INFORMATION

In the preceding chapter, we discussed the necessity of establishing as respectful and egalitarian a therapeutic alliance as possible when helping CTr survivors remediate the developmental deficits that they are left with as a result of having grown up in an ineffective family context. A respectful stance in the conceptual sphere entails making a distinction between arenas of cognitive deficit to handle them differentially. The essential question is, What domains of understanding can someone reasonably be expected to be able to arrive at on the basis of logical examination, and what domains, because they are not subject to logical deduction, must be transmitted or explained by someone else? Fairly clear-cut examples of these two domains, respectively, are identifying and making sense of one's own subjective experience versus becoming aware of socially determined standards of appropriate behavior.

It is important that the therapist not impose their understanding on the client; there are areas in which the clinician properly takes on the role of providing answers rather than guiding the client in arriving at their own conclusions. However, it is equally crucial to recognize that this approach is not effectively applied in a rigid way regardless of the topic at hand. These are matters in the realm of general, consensually agreed on knowledge rather than of subjective experience. They consist of practical information or social conventions not deducible by logic. What follows are general guidelines on distinguishing between these two areas.

### Practical Information and Learning How to Learn

There are often many areas about which the survivor client's family of origin failed to impart knowledge and skills essential to establish and maintain adequate adult functioning. These are generally points of fact that people are unlikely to know without being told and abilities that people usually are taught, either explicitly through overt instruction or implicitly via modes of transmission, such as modeling.

In the age of the Internet and online search engines that make it easy to call up information, and readily available videos that demonstrate how to execute various tasks, it is easier for people who have not been exposed to certain classes of information and skills to educate themselves about them. For clients who may have been deprived of exposure to many areas of practical daily living skills, a benefit of alerting them to the availability of this much of this material on the Internet is that it empowers them with the ability to educate themselves. It also spares the survivor the from acknowledging ignorance about subjects that may be embarrassing to reveal.

Even with ready availability of resources such as the Internet (access to which presumes computer literacy), some survivors, especially those with limited formal education, may need assistance in learning how to use information resources. A key aspect of this process especially relevant to using the Internet as a resource is developing the skills to critically assess the source and validity of the information offered. Recognizing when what appears to be a news article, for example, is really an advertisement aimed at selling merchandise or services or when the source of what appears to be objective information has an agenda that may make the content of what is being conveyed suspect are vital skills that entail being able to recognize and critically evaluate subtleties. Discerning subtleties such as these may entail viewing and critically discussing Internet entries or printed material; walking the client through procedures they may be unfamiliar with, such as how to create a monthly budget; or helping the client think through important decisions, such as whether it is advisable to make a major purchase or how to address a major medical issue.

In the area of skills acquisition as opposed to concrete information, the Internet or printed materials are likely to be of limited value. Certain people may be able to acquire some skills from watching Internet-based or other instructional videos, but for many, this is not an effective way to learn. In these cases, client and therapist may need to identify avenues through which in-person transmission of these capacities is available.

**Social Conventions**

Although social and cultural customs may take on the appearance of being entirely reasonable or even inevitable, they are almost always the product of chance circumstances that ceased to be relevant long ago. This is a point that may be readily grasped by someone who has traveled extensively and been confronted with radically different behavioral expectations in different countries and different cultures or who has lived long enough to witness extensive changes in conventions of conduct in their own culture. For example, in many Western industrialized countries in the mid-20th century, what was considered proper office attire was markedly different than it is today. Women wore dresses, stockings, and high-heel shoes. Men were expected to wear suits and ties on a daily basis. It was not unusual for high school students to dress similarly.

Similarly, in many parts of the United States, it is presumed that when you meet someone for the first time, you shake hands with them ("Handshake," n.d.). This is such an automatic behavior for many people that it is difficult for them to imagine greeting in any other way someone they are introduced to.

In other countries, though, it is customary to kiss the other person on the cheek (Moss, 2017). Not to do so would be considered just as rude as failing to shake someone's hand when introduced to someone in the United States. And in still other countries where kissing the other person on the cheek is common, kissing both cheeks is expected polite behavior, and kissing one cheek only would be considered a slight.

The *60 Minutes* television segment on the Strive program (Hartman, 1999), discussed in Chapter 6, depicts how disenfranchised groups may be unfamiliar with or unaccustomed to practicing some of even the most basic practices of the larger dominant culture. Other social customs, such as the culturally prescribed manner of arranging flatware in a table setting, are more elusive in that they are less universally known. Regardless of how widespread they are, it is not be unusual for survivors of CTr to be unaware of certain common social conventions that they may not have engaged in or that were not transmitted in their families of origin, a consequence of having been reared in an atmosphere marked by experiences of deficit.

Lack of awareness of these socially prescribed practices, whether they pertain to the workplace, social situations, or academic settings, poses an impediment to social adaptation and social acceptance. As illustrated by the *60 Minutes* Strive segment (Hartman, 1999), these conventions, although they may seem trivial to some, can have real pragmatic costs to those who are unaware of them or insufficiently conversant in them. There is a considerable risk that others will view the failure to subscribe to these behaviors as indicators of rudeness, offensiveness, hostility, callousness, or indifference, perceptions that can interfere with the attainment or maintenance of job opportunities, social connections, or academic success. The bottom line is that because social custom is rarely logically deducible, this is one area that clinicians may need to explicitly impart.

As discussed in Chapter 6, when clinicians are conveying social conventions, they need to be mindful that the reason for doing so is to equip the survivor with the capacity to effectively navigate the dominant culture so they can access resources, such as employment and social relationships. Maintaining awareness that the rationale for imparting these conventions is a practical one can help the provider avoid unintentionally conveying that the mainstream culture is in any way superior to others. Orienting clients to the dominant culture needs to be balanced with helping them explore their diverse identifications. Doing so assists the survivor in examining how to navigate the dominant culture while embracing and integrating aspects of their unique intercultural identity.

## INTERSECTION OF THE RELATIONAL, CONCEPTUAL, AND PRACTICAL INTERVENTION SPHERES

Although the division of CTT into the relational, conceptual, and practical intervention spheres yields helpful pedagogical categories, it is vital to appreciate that, in practice, these functions continually intersect and inform each other. Guiding the survivor through the application of principles of judgment and reasoning to a particular issue is simultaneously a relational endeavor as well as a conceptual one. By helping the client arrive at their own conclusions rather than attempting to lead them to a particular response, the therapist acts in a way that furthers the objectives of the relational sphere of CTT. Proceeding in this manner is consistent with gaining the survivor's trust. It promotes their ability to exercise their autonomy rather than dependently relying on the clinician for advice or to make decisions for them. The intense focus fostered by jointly proceeding through the reasoning process helps the client resist dissociative fogginess and supports a sense of interpersonal connection. Aiding the survivor to come to their own conclusions includes helping them to explore and embrace their intimate knowledge of their unique cultural background. And the act of collaboratively engaging in the reasoning process implicitly conveys the belief that improvement in their situation is possible and that they deserve a better quality of life.

It is self-evident that guiding the survivor through the reasoning process is both a conceptual enterprise and a practical intervention aimed at helping to remediate cognitive deficits. In a similar fashion, the practical intervention sphere is executed in a way that ensures that treatment objectives and methods are continually jointly discussed, planned, modified, and agreed on. One pivotal objective of the collaboratively executed reasoning process is empowering the survivor to decide what the goals of treatment will be. How to achieve those goals is also subjected to the collaborative process of jointly choosing and constructing practical interventions with which the client is comfortable and that they believe will be effective in meeting their particular needs and preferences. Throughout the therapeutic process, therefore, the CTT practitioner is constantly providing the survivor with choices, offering options of intervention approaches, and encouraging the client to suggest modifications to the intervention strategies suggested by the therapist. For someone who by virtue of experiences of threat and experiences of deprivation has been deprived of options and choices, this way of proceeding is in itself a therapeutic mechanism. It helps construct a collaborative therapeutic alliance that instills a sense of safety, trust, autonomy, and connection.

The remaining chapters in this volume, 8 through 13, delineate strategies for achieving various treatment goals via the practical sphere. Although the relational, conceptual, and practical spheres have been presented here in sequential order, in actuality, they are implemented more or less simultaneously. Attending to the establishment of a collaborative relationship and the joint construction of a shared conceptual understanding increase the likelihood that the client will actively engage in and thereby benefit from the interventions that compose the practical sphere. Conversely, facilitating the client's involvement in the practical sphere, if executed in a way that attends to the other two spheres, can be a substantial means of facilitating the strength of the collaborative relationship and the client's sense of safety in interacting with the therapist. Increasing the survivor's overall sense of safety and security is the focus of Chapter 8.

# 8

# Establishing a Sense of Safety and Contentment

*Overcoming Chronic Dysphoria*

Complex traumatization (CTr) survivors invariably suffer from forms of distress that often include anxiety, anger, and depression. This chapter discusses in detail intervention strategies for helping the survivor learn to reduce and hopefully eventually eliminate these varied forms of distress. First, I consider a general approach for helping the CTr survivor temper their relatively constant experience of anxiety. A case example illustrates how essentially the same approach to anxiety reduction can be applied to bouts of anger. Then I explore a general approach to assisting the survivor in overcoming depression.

It is a defining feature of posttraumatic disorders that even when the trauma is in the past and the survivor is no longer in harm's way, a feeling of not being safe persists. This phenomenon is related to the subjective experience when the fight–flight–freeze response (introduced in Chapter 1) is triggered or remains continually active following encounters with traumatic events involving a sense looming danger, fearfulness, and hopelessness. This frequently pervasive sense of threat is so emblematic of posttraumatic distress that until the most recent version of the *Diagnostic and Statistical Manual of Mental Disorders* (fifth ed. [*DSM–5*]; American Psychiatric Association, 2013), posttraumatic stress disorder was categorized as an anxiety disorder. In the *DSM–5*, it is relegated to a separate section titled "Trauma- and Stress-Related Disorders."

This reclassification reflects a growing recognition that acute, prolonged, and traumatic stress can lead to a wide range of forms of distress other than or extending well beyond anxiety per se. In addition to or instead of anxiety, distress itself can manifest as depression, dissociation, anger, guilt, or shame.

---

http://dx.doi.org/10.1037/0000176-009
*Contextual Trauma Therapy: Overcoming Traumatization and Reaching Full Potential*,
by S. N. Gold
Copyright © 2020 by the American Psychological Association. All rights reserved.

Accordingly, I use the term *dysphoria* as a means of referring to the entire range of unpleasant affects and experiences that are commonly observed expressions of traumatic distress. If trauma processing is attempted before providing the CTr survivor with tools to diminish or manage these forms of dysphoria, they can intensify dramatically on confronting traumatic material and thus subvert the goal of trauma resolution.

It is generally agreed that individuals with CTr must first be safe and feel safe before confrontation of their traumatic experiences can be undertaken as an effective approach to resolving their trauma-related symptomatology (Gold & Brown, 1997; Gomez-Perales, 2015; Herman, 1992b). "Being safe" means that treatment strategies requiring processing of past traumatic experiences are contraindicated when the person is still in danger. For example, it makes no sense to engage in trauma processing with someone who is currently in a relationship in which intimate partner violence occurs. The priority in such a situation is to provide the client with strategies and tools that can be used to increase their safety.

In addition to the dysphoric impact of traumatic experiences themselves, CTr survivors' capacity to feel safe is likely to be limited by childhood experiences of deficit. Inadequate emotional support and interpersonal connection during their formative years leave many CTr survivors without a substantial capacity for self-soothing. In this respect, the relational sphere of contextual trauma therapy (CTT) can help to moderate dysphoria and a lack of a sense of safety by providing a consistent, predictable, trustworthy, supportive interpersonal connection. However, for most CTr survivors, it takes a while to develop the capacity to experience a level of connection that is sufficiently palpable to sustain them when they are not in the therapist's physical presence.

For these reasons, among the various treatment goals within the practical intervention sphere, distress reduction is often, but not always, the first priority. For instance, if the survivor is experiencing such intense or disruptive dissociation, or is so compromised by ensnarement in addictive or compulsive behavior patterns that it would preclude their being attentive enough to benefit from distress reduction strategies, then those difficulties may need to be addressed first. These considerations provide just one example why it is imperative that treatment assessment, planning, and execution be a collaborative process. Client and practitioner need to explore and decide together what course of action makes the most sense at any given time.

For most CTr survivors, however, distress reduction is likely to be the first practical objective to be tackled. A reduction in overall distress not only better equips the client to eventually effectively navigate and benefit from trauma processing, but it is likely to foster a number of other benefits. A range of difficulties that are secondary to distress—insomnia, difficulty concentrating, a proclivity to worry, hypervigilance, an exaggerated startle response, nightmares, flashbacks, physiological and emotional arousal in response to trauma-related cues—can be expected to ameliorate once there is an appreciable and stable reduction in baseline distress. To the degree that they are reactions to and attempts to contain distress, vulnerability to experiencing dissociative episodes and relying on addictive and compulsive behaviors lessen once a diminution in distress is achieved.

In addition, it is not unusual among complex trauma survivors that depression is the main form of dysphoria experienced. After years or decades of having been burdened by elevated distress, depression can arise from the conviction that relief will never come. Therefore, when depression is a major component of CTr, it is not unusual for it to partially or even completely remit once there is an appreciable reduction in distress in the form of anxiety, anger, guilt, shame, or some combination of them. When distress reduction is more salient and has been addressed but does not result in a substantial improvement in depression, then depression is directly targeted. In cases of CTr in which depression is the predominant form of dysphoria, it clearly needs to be the focus of intervention.

## REDUCING BASELINE DISTRESS

This section covers the standard approach in CTT to assisting the CTr survivor to acquire the capacity to lower their continually elevated experience of distress. First, I describe the essential role of providing the client with a thorough understanding of the rationale behind this intervention. Then I present the various steps in actually carrying out this procedure. A crucial aspect of the procedure is to tailor the distress reduction technique that will be used by identifying one that is clearly effective for the particular individual.

### Providing the Rationale

Clients, understandably, are much more likely to follow through in carrying out therapeutic tasks if they are clear about the reasons for them. To increase compliance with distress reduction strategies, therefore, the therapist needs to take the time to thoroughly convey the rationale for their use. This explanation is that in response to a dangerous situation, the fight–flight–freeze response is set off to mobilize the body in a way that increases the likelihood of responding in a way that increases the likelihood of survival. The response consists of an automatic and dramatic shift in physiological reactivity. In circumstances in which either fighting off an attacker or fleeing from the threat is possible, reactivity rises sharply, such as increased heart and respiration rates. If the freeze component of the response is engaged, physiological reactivity may plummet or may consist of a combination of increased reactivity and muscular immobility.

In some instances, once the danger has passed, the response subsides and leaves no lasting effect. In others, the response is sensitized in reaction to the traumatic event so that it either remains activated after the traumatic episode is over or is suddenly and dramatically set off when cues related to the traumatic situation are encountered later. The triggering of the fight–flight–freeze response is subjectively experienced as distress, which can take common forms such as anxiety, anger, or dissociative shutdown. Because this is the action of a reflex, it is as much a physiological or somatic reaction as a psychological one. Therefore, desensitizing the now overreactive response requires a strategy that is effective not only at the psychological (subjective) level but also on the physiological or somatic level.

In emphasizing that the distress component of traumatization is at least as much physiological as psychological, the stage is set to explain that the consistent, repeated use of distress reduction techniques is required to bring one's distress level down and have it stay down. Surely, countless therapists have taught their clients distress reduction techniques and encouraged them to practice regularly between sessions with little or no responsiveness from the client. It is essential to take as much time as necessary to explain the rationale behind this approach to ensure that the client practices regularly. Without a clear understanding of the underlying principles and expected outcome, the client is unlikely to have sufficient motivation to follow through outside of the therapy office. This explanation is especially important in working with survivors of CTr, because their repeated encounters with experiences of threat and of deficit and related distress date back to childhood; thus, their lifelong anguish can make it particularly difficult to imagine that their distress level can be reduced and stay lowered.

In explaining the implications of the physiological nature of fight–flight–freeze response for reducing its reactivity to trauma-related cues and recollections, it is useful draw on the analogy of working out. The central point is that desired changes in the body and its functioning occur with repetition. Most people have had enough experience with physical exercise that they are well aware that although it is probably more beneficial to work out once every few months than not at all, this pattern of physical exercise cannot be expected to result in substantial noticeable changes in resting heart rate (in the case of aerobic exercise) or muscle mass (in response to weight training). These achievements require consistent exercise, preferably several times a week, sustained over a period of months at the least. It may take an appreciable portion of a session to carefully explain the relationship of the fight–flight–freeze response to subjective distress and other manifestations of traumatization, the physiological nature of this underlying mechanism, and the principle of repetition over time that can lead to successful reduction in reactivity to trauma-related cues, and to ensure that the client understands these points. Once accomplished, the therapist can proceed to the intervention itself.

## Using the Subjective Units of Distress Scale

Although some survivors of CTr may only experience spikes in distress in response to trauma-related cues, in my clinical experience, most report chronically elevated distress that peaks even higher when they encounter such reminders. To assess a client's level of distress and establish an initial baseline against which to evaluate changes in distress in various situations and in response to interventions designed to reduce distress, it is helpful to use the Subjective Units of Distress Scale (SUDS; Wolpe, 1958) in the initial intake session. The client is asked to rate their level of distress on a numeric scale ranging from 0 (*completely calm, no distress whatsoever*) to 10 (*the highest level of distress ever experienced*), or, preferably, ranging from 0 (*completely calm, no distress whatsoever*) to 100 (*the most distress you have ever experienced*). The second numeric range allows for much finer gradations in measurement and so can be extremely useful in evaluating the impact of interventions meant to lower distress level over time. Although people often specifically associate distress with anxiety, the SUDS is equally applicable to other forms of dysphoria: anger, shame, dissociation, and so on.

A minority of survivors may protest that they cannot assign a number to their level of distress out of concern that they may be "wrong." Sometimes it is possible to convince them that because the scale is intended as a means of measuring their judgment about their own subjective experience, it is impossible for them to be wrong. If they persist in maintaining that they are unable to use a numeric scale, one can resort to simply having them indicate whether their level of distress is higher, lower, or that same after using a technique for lowering their distress. In most instances, however, even if the survivor initially proceeds in this manner, they can eventually be persuaded to use numerical ratings, which provides much more detailed feedback to client and practitioner.

It has been my experience that on a 0-to-10 SUDS, most survivors of complex trauma identify their usual level of distress as being at least 7, if not higher. Usually it is best to obtain several SUDS readings keyed to various circumstances, starting with (after having explained the scale to the client) "At this moment, as we sit here, what number are you at between 0 and 10?" One reason for starting with that prompt is that it is easier to accurately assess one's level of distress in the present rather than retrospectively. This question then provides an anchor point for the others, such as whether the rating for right now is higher or lower than the level where the client was on average or most of the time during the preceding week. The client can then assign a rating to the previous week and be asked if, during that week, their level of distress was at a typical level, and, if not, how they would rate their typical level of distress.

It can be useful to ask them what the SUDS rating would be if they were in exceptionally low stress circumstances without responsibilities or demands, such as a day when they did not have to go to work and could do whatever they liked. I have consistently found that in response to this question, complex trauma survivors, counterintuitively, almost always respond with a rating of 5 (as opposed to 0 or close to it). If it is explained to them at this point that most people who did not live through the types of extraordinarily debilitating circumstances they have are, under ordinary conditions, at a 2 or below on the scale, they are astounded. It is beyond their imagining that anyone, under any conditions, reaches a level of distress below the scale midpoint of 5. One survivor of extensive childhood abuse and deprivation, on being told this, replied, "Do you mean to tell me that people out there who didn't grow up the way as me are experiencing the same thing I did when I shot up heroin?" His extraordinarily high level of baseline distress was, of course, precisely the reason he was addicted to heroin. When someone suffers a constant state of intense distress, they are inclined to do anything they can, independent of the cost, to provide even a few moments of relief. (This topic, reliance on addictive and compulsive behaviors to relieve distress, is addressed in detail in Chapter 11.)

**Identifying a Suitable Distress Reduction Procedure**

It is not usual for people to wonder which stress reduction technique works best. What the rationale described earlier implies is that the particular distress reduction technique used is of far less consequence than regularly practicing whatever method is adopted, preferably at least twice if not three times a day. This is a central aspect of the rationale, but one that is easy to overlook. The temptation is to use a distress reduction exercise when distress peaks or spikes, and this approach is perfectly permissible to obtain a measure of immediate relief. However, if the technique is used only in response to a discrete elevation in distress, that is all that is likely to be achieved. The level of distress returns to baseline, the chronically elevated level at which the person is most of the time and at which their distress was before it momentarily spiked even higher. The ultimate goal of the procedure extends beyond momentary relief: the achievement of a reduction in baseline distress. This objective requires that the distress reduction technique be practiced on a regular basis and not just in response to momentary increases in discomfort.

After taking enough time to explain the relationship between the fight–flight–freeze response, traumatization, and distress, the practitioner can begin to introduce methods for stress reduction. Before doing so, they need to make sure to ask the client what their SUDS level is at that moment. This information provides a level of comparison from which to judge the effectiveness of the stress reduction method the practitioner is teaching.

Practitioners cannot assume that the same approach works for everyone. Some methods do not work at all for certain people, whereas other techniques may be highly effective. Therefore, in CTT, the practitioner, based on their assessment of the client, starts by teaching an approach that seems likely to be most suitable for that individual. Just before teaching each method, the therapist obtains the client's SUDS level and then again asks their SUDS level after the client has executed each method. On identification of a method that results in at least a two or three SUDS point drop, it is probably best for the practitioner to stop there and encourage the client to use that method.

Methods can be grouped into different categories, and in considering which technique is most likely to be a good match for a client, the category usually is a more pertinent guide than a specific procedure that falls within it. For example, breathing techniques are effective for many people because they directly impact physiological arousal. But, obviously, for those with respiratory disorders, these methods may not be feasible. In addition, some survivors associate the sound of breathing with past experiences of sexual assault, rendering breathing-based approaches disturbing rather than a source of relief.

One breathing technique that is relatively easy to learn and is effective in reducing distress is diaphragmatic breathing (Ma et al., 2017). In this procedure, the person is instructed to take a deep breath, expand the abdomen, and then slowly exhale as much air as possible from the lungs so that the abdomen contracts. Some people find it helpful initially to place one hand on their chest and the other on the abdomen, with the objective of breathing so that the chest moves up and down as little as possible, whereas the abdomen expands and contracts in a controlled manner. Ma and colleagues found that in comparison with a control condition, diaphragmatic breathing practiced in 20 sessions over 8 weeks not only resulted in a decrease in distress but also was associated with an increase in sustained attention.

Imaginal approaches draw on the client's ability to call up perceptions and sensations in their mind that, because the individual associates them with feeling calm and soothed, have the effect of lowering their stress level. But not everyone has the capacity for forming and maintaining relatively stable and clear mental imagery. Imagery methods, therefore, are unlikely to be effective for those to whom this ability does not come naturally.

For those who do have fairly easy access to mental imagery, a particularly useful approach routinely used in eye-movement desensitization and reprocessing therapy (Shapiro, 2017) is safe place imagery. In this procedure, the client selects the images used for distress reduction by identifying a place where they would feel safer than any other place they can think of. They are then asked, in turn, to describe what they would see, hear, feel (touch and temperature), and smell if they were there. The clinician writes down their descriptors, and when they are done, asks them to imagine they are actually there; the clinician reads back to them the various sights, sounds, sensations, and scents they would experience there. When the client indicates that they have brought the image of that place into focus as clearly as they can (which usually only takes a few moments because they have just described the place and had their description read back to them), they are asked what their SUDS level is.

Another technique, deep muscle relaxation (DMR; Ferguson, Marquis, & Taylor, 1977), works well for most people in that it can produce an intense experience of stress relief. However, a full DMR protocol can take anywhere from 20 to 40 minutes or more when one is first learning it. Although the time needed to proceed through the procedure is likely to shorten with repetition, the time-consuming nature of DMR makes it unlikely that people will practice it regularly. For some people who are dedicated enough and have the time to devote to it, it can be effective, and after a few rounds of practice, they can summon the relaxation response relatively quickly and easily. However, for some people, this is unlikely to be the case.

Hypnotic approaches also have the potential to be helpful. The literature on hypnosis indicates wide individual variations in hypnotizability, and evidence shows that hypnotizability is higher in traumatized individuals than in others (Bryant, Guthrie, & Moulds, 2001; Moene, Spinhoven, Hoogduin, Sandyck, & Roelofs, 2001; Spiegel, Hunt, & Dondershine, 1988; Terhune & Cardeña, 2015). Some survivors, however, because they mistakenly have surmised from depictions in the popular media that hypnosis involves relinquishment of control, may be at best wary and at worst outright unwilling to avail themselves of this option. In any event, the ethical and effective use of hypnotic approaches requires specialized training (Walling & Baker, 1996).

If hypnosis is used for distress reduction, it is imperative that it be taught to the client in the form of self-hypnosis. If hypnotic induction by the clinician is the only means by which the survivor can experience a reduction in distress, this means that the effect is only be attainable in the therapist's presence. This approach limits the usefulness of the method and may foster dependency on the practitioner. From its first introduction, the therapist needs to explain that in-session hypnotic induction is being used as a means to teach the client how to elicit the hypnotic state in themselves and use it as a means to reduce their distress on their own. Otherwise, the client is likely to assume that they can only achieve a hypnotic response and a related reduction in distress if the clinician performs the induction.

Regardless of the type of distress reduction technique used, it should be one that is under the client's direction so that they can make use of and practice it outside of the consulting room and away from the therapist's presence. The client needs to practice the procedure on a regular basis, and this is not possible if the approach relies on techniques, such as guided imagery or hypnotic methods, that are conducted solely by the clinician. Even audio recordings of these methods are not ideal, because they require that the client draw on an external source and a key aspect of distress reduction procedures is that they are fully portable. Although current technology, such as smart phones and earbuds, may be carried with one and is available wherever one goes, an important objective of distress reduction for survivors is that they have the sense of efficacy and safety that comes with knowing that the technique is under their control, readily accessible, and can be executed whether or not particular equipment is at hand and operational.

One possible exception for those who, at the outset of treatment, are too dissociative or distractible to maintain sufficient focus to effectively use a self-directed distress reduction procedure is listening to music. Even in this case, the client should choose the music on the basis of what they find soothing and not on what the therapist assumes will be calming to them. And the goal should not only be to lower distress but to practice developing a greater capacity to focus by making an effort to stay attentive to and immersed in the music (using earbuds or headphones). Although evidence shows that music can be effective as a stress reduction tool (Miller & Spence, 2013; Stanton, 1984), it should be treated as a short-term alternative to a method that does not rely on externals, such as the availability of a device for playing music. Listening to music is only a means of reducing distress until the client has established the ability to focus better. Once that has been accomplished, the other types of techniques discussed here can be used. In this way, distress reduction can be practiced using methods that are under the full control of the client—ones that do not rely on external stimuli, props, or instrumentation.

The reason for grouping distress reduction techniques into categories is that if one approach in a category is ineffective for a particular client, it is unlikely that a variant from the same category (e.g., imagery) will work. When teaching a technique, assess its effectiveness by having the client report their SUDS level before and after using it in session. At a minimum, an effective approach elicits at least a 1-point drop on a 10-point SUDS, but the greater the drop, the more likely it will be effective. If a particular distress reduction intervention does not result in a reduction in SUDS level of at least 1 point, and ideally more than 1 point, move on to a technique from another category.

**Monitoring and Reinforcing Practice of the Distress Reduction Technique**

Once the client understands the relationship between the fight–flight–freeze response and trauma-related distress, and has learned to assess their level of distress using SUDS, and a distress reduction method that works for them has been identified, the challenge is to find ways to secure compliance in the consistent, repeated practice of the exercise. Practice is monitored and reinforced by instructing the client to log their SUDS level on their smartphone, if they own one, or in a small memo book or on a piece of paper. They are asked to practice the technique and write down the SUDS ratings before and after practicing the distress reduction technique: during their routine on awakening, sometime in the middle of the day, and during their bedtime routine.

Clients are instructed to carry out the exercise sitting in a comfortable chair in a place where they will not be disturbed. I have found that they rarely ask how much time they should devote to each instance of practicing the technique. It is probably best not to address the issue, therefore, unless they bring it up. If they press for an answer, it would be that once there is a noticeable drop in their SUDS level, but they sense that there is not likely to be a further reduction unless they spend a substantial additional amount of time doing the exercise, they can stop.

Each session after that until the client reaches a baseline of at least 4—if not lower—the practitioner needs to remember, preferably at the outset of the meeting, to ask to see the client's log of SUDS levels before and after each instance of practice, and discuss it with the client. For one thing, the client's knowing that there is an expectation to bring the log into each session and discuss it increases the likelihood that they will follow through on practicing the distress reduction technique. Certainly, entering numbers on the log merely to create the illusion of follow-through is a possibility, but it is difficult to convincingly maintain this impression knowing there will be pointed discussion of the data on the log in each session. Review of its contents helps illuminate various implications of the SUDS ratings for both client and practitioner, and level of adherence to the agreed on level of practice is only one of them. It is necessary to examine whether the client is experiencing a drop in SUDS level most of the time after having practiced the distress reduction technique. If not the case, new methods, most likely ones in categories not used previously, need to be found that work better for that particular individual.

Scanning down the "before" columns provides an assessment of whether the SUDS level is dropping over time. It is unrealistic to expect a noticeable drop within a 1- or 2-week period. To evaluate this dimension, it is usually necessary to graph the data obtained over a period of weeks or months. In the short run, there is likely to be variability from day to day. Over longer spans of time, however, trends are much easier to detect. Even in the case of Tim, presented later in this chapter, a client who achieved unusually rapid resolution of his distress, it would have taken graphing data from at least three or four 2-week practice record sheets (see Figure 4 in Gold, 2000, p. 142) to fully capture the trajectory of his progress.

Comparing SUDS "before" ratings across rows can reveal trends regarding typical levels of distress at various times of day. Frequently, SUDS levels are consistently higher either on awakening, at midday, or at bedtime. Those clients with greater elevations on awakening are likely to experience distress that is primarily related to anticipating negative experiences later in the day. Higher stress at midday is most often found among clients who are employed and encounter the most stressors at work. SUDS levels that are highest at bedtime may signal that the client is apprehensive about difficulty obtaining adequate sleep or is having nightmares.

Although daily practice three times a day is optimal, with some clients, it is unrealistic to request that degree of consistency from the beginning. For those who are unemployed and do not leave the house much, have a great deal of time on their hands at the outset of treatment, and are likely to be in need of the distress reduction more than most, it may be entirely reasonable to ask that they regularly practice all three times per day. For others with a busier schedule who may be prone to experience the exercise as more of a burden than a relief at first, carrying out the exercise and documenting the SUDS ratings before and after twice a day, usually on awakening and just before bedtime, is more realistic. And for others, who are especially overwhelmed and functionally compromised, starting out with once a day may be acceptable, although the expectation is that times per day will increase as they get used to the procedure and its benefits.

I find it interesting how often survivors of CTr hand over their ratings (often without having to be asked) at the outset of a session and say, "You're going to be disappointed in me" because they have missed two or three possible practice times out of 14 or 21 for the week. This statement, which one hears from some survivors in various circumstances, reflects past experiences of deficit consisting of frequently being told by a parent or other authority figure that they are a disappointment, an experience that leads to a chronic conviction of "never being enough." This is a wonderful example of a situation that calls for a convergence of the practical and relationship spheres of CTT by conveying that perfection is not required or expected, and that although aspiring to complete adherence is even more effective, a "hit rate" of approximately 80% to 85% adherence is completely fine. In this way, the current level of compliance is reinforced, as is the implied desire to increase it, and simultaneously constitutes a response that contradicts their interpersonal expectations of criticism and negative self-appraisal.

For many survivors whose experiences of deficit included a lack of household structure and routine, increasingly consistent use of the practice record sheet (see Figure 4 in Gold, 2000, p. 142) fosters the establishment of new skills, an altered self-image, and a greater familiarity and comfort with self-discipline. Beyond reducing baseline distress, regularly remembering to do the exercise and log the corresponding SUDS ratings offer additional and more subtle and implicit but equally robust benefits. They help the survivor learn how to maintain a routine that provides structure to their day, develop productive habits that become second nature rather than feel oppressive, and establish a greater sense of competency and accomplishment that begins to positively transform their self-concept.

### Case Example: Successful Application of Distress Reduction for Trauma-Related Anger

Tim, an unemployed, White, heterosexual man in his late 20s, had grown up with constant verbal and physical abuse by his father, who also sexually molested him in his early adolescence for a time. Tim's central complaint was his inability to control his anger, which seemed to be constantly bubbling beneath the surface. He reported that he frequently lost his temper and ragefully yelled at others out of impatience almost daily, got into fistfights with strangers at least once a month, and, most disturbing to him, started verbal altercations with his girlfriend that he realized would eventually lead her to break up with him.

Although he understood intellectually that his anger stemmed from his father's unrelenting maltreatment of him, this awareness did not help him restrain himself from lashing out at others. His intense desire to stop attacking others was offset by recurrent entreaties by well-meaning but misguided family members to reconcile with his father with whom he had entirely cut off contact. For 10 years, he had smoked marijuana daily in an attempt to obliterate his painful memories of abuse and sooth his simmering rage. However, although he was a valued employee with meticulous performance on the job, his excessive reliance on marijuana resulted in frequent lateness and absences from work, which had led to his being fired 1 month before he entered therapy. Impressively, in the intervening period, he had eliminated his marijuana use by going cold turkey within days of losing his job. This degree of determination proved to be a tremendous asset in treatment in that it galvanized a fervent level of dedication to consistently practicing distress reduction and keeping a log of his SUDS levels.

Despite his commitment to overcoming his rage, at the outset of therapy, Tim was worried that he could not overcome his problem controlling his anger. However, his investment in doing whatever he could to put an end to his numerous lapses into aggressive behavior was a powerful motivator. From the beginning, he conscientiously executed the distress reduction technique he had learned from his therapist and logged his SUDS ratings before and after each practice session three times a day. Consequently, his progress in overcoming his angry outbursts was unusually rapid and complete.

Two weeks after initiating application of the distress reduction procedure, he told his therapist that he was astounded that he had made it through the entire week without lashing out at anyone. A couple of weeks later, he reported that he was amazed to discover that he had not felt appreciably angry the entire week. About another 2 weeks afterward, he came in with the following (paraphrased and slightly sanitized) account:

> You know, as someone who was constantly just one short step away from losing it, until I first came to see you, I was the King of Road Rage. And I got to tell you, there's one fortunate son of a bitch out there who needs to thank his lucky stars that he's alive today. That stupid bastard for sure won the lottery. I'm sitting at a red light the other day minding my own business, and for some reason, this damn idiot gets out of his car in the lane to the left of me, comes over to my driver's side window, and starts screaming at me, cursing a blue streak. Now, if this imbecile had pulled this stunt just a couple of months earlier, I would have been out of my car and pounding his brainless skull into the asphalt before he knew what hit him. I was completely blown away. Not by this nitwit, but by my own reaction. I just wasn't interested. Didn't even turn to look at him. Not an ounce of irritation. I just didn't care.

Tim's progress in overcoming his anger was much more accelerated than that of most survivors of CTr for whom the same degree of improvement would have occurred gradually over several months. In a sense, it appeared that he used the very anger that brought him to therapy as an asset. It fueled his resolve not to allow his painful past to shape his future. But given the intensity and constant disruptions fomented by his rage, even if it had taken much longer, what he accomplished still would have been momentous. It certainly unquestionably changed the trajectory of his life. He ended up marrying his fiancé, they had three children, and in a commitment to be everything to them that his own father had failed to be to him, he dedicated himself to being an exemplary parent.

## RELIEVING IMMEDIATE SPIKES IN DISTRESS

Although the use of distress reduction techniques can be effective in relieving short-term spikes in distress, their regular daily use is intended to reduce baseline distress. With consistent repetition, these exercises become second nature and increasingly effective. Some clients have reported that, eventually, these approaches become conditioned to distress so that without even consciously initiating them, they find that, for example, there is a shift in their breathing or they are engaging in safe place imagery spontaneously in response to stressful circumstances. However, in the early stages of mastering a distress reduction exercise, the level of focused attention required to effectively execute the technique may preclude its effective use in response to sudden elevations in distress.

In this regard, it seems to me that the ubiquitous trend of using the terms *relaxation, meditation*, and *mindfulness* interchangeably promotes unnecessary confusion. *Relaxation* techniques are intended to reduce distress. As illustrated in Tim's case, the distress may take the form of anger or other types of dysphoric arousal. *Meditation* spans a variety practices and objectives. *Mindfulness* meditation is a practice specifically aimed at fostering the ability to sustain focal attention on the present moment. It is a much more demanding enterprise than the rehearsal of a relaxation technique. Although it eventually can instill a sense of calm and increased freedom from distress, this is a by-product of the ability to sustain focused attention that can take a while to master and usually is achieved only after an extended period of restlessness and frustration during mindfulness meditation practice.

Until clients become proficient enough with practice of a distress reduction exercise to achieve a substantial drop in dysphoria even in the midst of a spike, another method is likely to be much quicker, easier, and more effective in providing immediate relief. In session, help the client generate a list of things they find enjoyable. (This is not an inventory of things that relax or soothe them but one of things they enjoy.) For instance, they may list options such as reading, calling a friend, taking a walk, going to the gym, watching television, going online, or taking a drive. As they come up with items, have them keyboard them into their smartphone or write them down on a small piece of paper or index card, something they can easily carry with them. Suggest that when they are suddenly triggered or extremely distraught (and therefore may not have the presence of mind at that moment to remember the activities on the list), they simply pull out the list, look for an item on it that they can readily engage in at the moment, and do it. The pleasure they derive from the activity and the distraction from what is bothering them is likely to be more accessible and provide a greater level of relief than a technique that requires them to practice to become proficient. Once they have mastered a distress reduction exercise, they may choose to make use of that instead, but, again, the main purpose of those exercises in CTT is to reduce baseline distress through regular, not only as-needed, practice.

## OVERCOMING DEPRESSION

For many survivors, depression is a secondary reaction to lifelong distress and the despair that arises from the conviction that it will never end. For a good number of survivors, therefore, once they see that their distress is lifting, the resulting depression remits along with it. However, for some, depression is a more prominent ongoing response to the combined impact of experiences of deficit and experiences of threat than distress, which needs to be addressed separately from and, in some cases, before or instead of distress. The case of

Elliott in Chapter 4 nicely illustrates CTr's consisting primarily of trauma-related depression accompanied by the triad of disturbances in self-organization impairments.

Although various forms of cognitive intervention are closely associated with the treatment of depression in the literature (Beck, Rush, Shaw, & Emery, 1979; Segal, Williams, & Teasdale, 2013; Zettle, 2007), it may not be well suited for most complex trauma survivors. Above all, their depression is likely to be so severe and their cognitive abilities so compromised that they are unlikely to benefit from this approach. In addition, often the depression experienced by this population is largely a function of two primary sources, both related to the negative self-concept component of disturbances in self-organization. First, no matter what other adverse experiences characterized their formative years, verbal abuse is probably the most common and pervasive type of maltreatment associated with CTr in which depression is a central feature. Constant put-downs and humiliation throughout childhood almost invariably engender intense self-criticism and hopelessness.

Second, experiences of deprivation make it highly likely that the survivor's life trajectory has been marked by repeated disappointments and perceived failures in functioning. Sometimes this is the case in one arena, such as social adjustment. In other instances, it is the case across the board, encompassing social, academic and occupational adaptation. Looking back on what seems an endless track record of disappointment and failure seems to many survivors to comprise an irrefutable confirmation of all the demeaning appraisals they heard growing up.

The power of long-standing verbal abuse combined with a history of difficulty in life adjustment constitutes a powerful prescription for depression that is not easily negated cognitively. Furthermore, poor modeling of logical reasoning and judgment leaves many survivors of CTr ill equipped early in therapy to refute the belittling feedback and history of disappointments that have seemed a central feature of their lives as far back as they can remember. In addition, survivors, partly as a response to depression itself and partly as a function of poor parental modeling, often have fallen into a lifestyle that actively promotes depression. They may rarely leave the house; have either minimal social interaction or interpersonal relationships in which they are treated disrespectfully, manipulatively, or outright abusively; live in an atmosphere of physical chaos and disarray; and maintain a lifestyle that fails to support adequate nutrition, sleep, and exercise.

Especially early in therapy, therefore, the primary strategies that are likely to help survivors surmount long-standing depression are behavioral ones, particularly ones that help survivors establish a more productive and gratifying lifestyle. In the absence of role models and templates of such an orientation to daily living, the process of transition to a pattern of behavior antithetical to depression requires a gradual process of education and implementation. This is a territory in which understanding the effects of growing up in a developmental context permeated by deprivation of emotional support and pragmatic knowledge is immeasurably helpful. As one survivor client succinctly expressed it, "You cannot know what you haven't been taught."

A detailed interview exploring the client's activities the previous day, starting with the time they woke up and following through until the time they went to bed and fell asleep, is an efficient way to systematically assess behaviors that promote depression and ones that guard against depression. It is best to walk through a particular day, because inquiry about a "typical" day is less likely to yield accurate information. It is prone to evoke the client's assumptions about how they spend their time rather than an account of their actual behavior.

Start by asking what time they woke up (i.e., opened their eyes) and then probe about when they got out of bed. For survivors who are severely depressed, there may be a lag, sometimes several hours, between these two events. Then trace through the day to identify how they spent their time. As you do, keep points of information such as the following in mind: Did they shower or bathe? Get dressed? Leave the house at all? Engage in any interactions with other people? What does their living space look like? Is it cluttered? Disorganized? When was the last time they picked up or cleaned? Are the window treatments open during the day or left closed? At what times did they eat, and what did they eat? What productive activities did they engage in? Enjoyable activities? Did they get any exercise? If they are currently unemployed and able to work, did they engage in any job search-related activities? If so, what were they? If they are prescribed psychiatric medication, did they take it? Was it taken at the prescribed times of day and at the prescribed dosages? Do they have a usual bedtime routine? If so, what is it, and did they follow it last night? What time did they get in bed? Once they did get in bed, were they lying quietly? Reading? Watching television? Surfing the Internet? At what time did they fall asleep?

An interview such as this can reveal a number of habitual behavior patterns that foster depression. Once identified, therapist and client jointly determine which of them to target initially for modification and understand that changes in behavior are planned out in negotiated increments. For example, if the client is waking up at around 2 p.m. and going to bed around 4 a.m., approaching a reversal of day and night, an earlier bedtime and wake-up time are called for. But it is not reasonable, desirable, or likely to be effective to change these times by several hours in one or two nights. Instead, it might be negotiated that each day of the coming week, the client will either be in bed a half hour earlier or set an alarm to wake up 15 minutes earlier. Similarly, if they lie in bed for 1 hour and 15 minutes on awakening, it might be agreed on that they will stay in bed no more than an hour each morning after waking up. Similar agreements can be made regarding other aspects of their daily routine. If, for instance, they are not leaving the house at all most days, it might be established that in the coming week, they will leave the house to check the mail each day. Once this is achieved, it might be negotiated that they will go outside to take a 5- or 10-minute walk each day.

To help the client remember these short-term goals and provide them with a means to track their progress, they are asked to create a daily activity log, a weeklong calendar on which to log their activity regarding the agreed on behaviors to be modified. The days of the coming week are indicated along the top and the targeted activities are entered as row headings on the left-hand margin. Each day, as each activity is supposed to occur, the client logs in the appropriate space the time when they did it; if they didn't do it at all, they leave that space blank or draw a line through it. Once the client is consistently meeting the agreed on goal for an item, the target for that goal is either extended (e.g., waking up another 15 or 30 minutes earlier) or, if the end goal is achieved, the item is dropped, perhaps to be replaced with a new target behavior. The daily activity log procedure does not merely gradually shape behavior that reduces and eventually eliminates depression, but it also teaches the survivor elements of adaptive daily living that they may have been previously unaware and how to maintain them. The examples given here are admittedly extreme but far from unusual among survivors of CTr with severe depression. The procedure is one that can lead to radical changes in the client's daily lifestyle that provide a foundation for much more extensive gains in social and occupational adjustment.

Arriving at a point at which baseline distress is down and chronic depression has been overcome is obviously a major turning point in treatment. With substantial progress toward these accomplishments, the client is much closer to being able to benefit rather than be overwhelmed by exposure-based and other trauma-processing methods. However, many survivors of CTr continue to manifest considerable dissociative difficulties subsequent to the appreciable reduction of distress and depression.

A widespread assumption is that dissociation is exclusively and always a defense, and that it therefore is a reaction to some other form of dysphoria. But dissociation, the freeze component of the fight–flight–freeze response, can continue to be triggered by trauma-related cues even after other forms of dysphoria have been substantially diminished. We therefore next turn our attention to helping survivors learn to modulate, and in many cases, eventually extinguish, dissociative reactions.

# 9

# Learning to Modulate Dissociation

*Expanding Focus and Awareness*

Dissociative symptoms can be extremely distressing to those who are susceptible to them. Moreover, in practical terms, they intrude on daily effectiveness by interfering with the capacities to sustain focal attention; to identify subjective experiences, such as emotions and sensations; and to feel bonded with other people. Helping complex traumatization (CTr) survivors acquire the capacity to modulate, disrupt, and perhaps eventually extinguish dissociative reactions altogether, therefore, provides them with a valuable tool for increasing their functionality.

Research (Luoni, Agosti, Crugnola, Rossi, & Termine, 2018; Powers et al., 2017; Zucker, Spinazzola, Blaustein, & van der Kolk, 2006) and clinical observation (van der Hart, Nijenhuis, & Steele, 2005) strongly indicate that dissociation is especially prominent in complex posttraumatic stress disorder (Herman, 1992b), and one would assume, by extension, also in all forms of what I refer to here as CTr. Consistent with a strong association between dissociation and complex trauma, in a study of dissociation among individuals with posttraumatic stress disorder (PTSD), D. J. Stein et al. (2013) concluded that

> dissociation among respondents with PTSD is associated with childhood onset, exposure to prior traumatic events (and especially to a high number [five] of prior traumatic events), and childhood adversities. When considered in conjunction with the finding that dissociation is not related to trauma type, this implies that early age of exposure and repeated exposure are more critical than the content of exposure in promoting dissociative symptoms among people with PTSD. (p. 309)

---

http://dx.doi.org/10.1037/0000176-010
*Contextual Trauma Therapy: Overcoming Traumatization and Reaching Full Potential,* by S. N. Gold
Copyright © 2020 by the American Psychological Association. All rights reserved.

These findings are also consistent with the contention of contextual trauma therapy (CTT) that CTr is specifically associated with repeated trauma in childhood. In addition, although type of trauma was not associated with dissociation, D. J. Stein et al. (2013) reported that out of 12 childhood adversities assessed, the four that were significantly related to dissociation among study participants with PTSD were parental mental illness, parental substance disorder, family violence, and parental divorce. With the exception of parental divorce, the other three factors represent parental maladjustment.

A relative dearth of training about psychological trauma generally exists in the training of helping professionals, and there is substantially less on an exceedingly common conglomeration of responses to trauma: dissociative reactions. Many clinicians have minimal familiarity with the topic let alone substantive knowledge of how to treat dissociation. The situation has not been helped by a general skepticism about the existence of dissociation that has been fueled by detractors (Baldock & Leichner, 1995; Dell, 1988; Lynn et al., 2014) who tend to especially focus on the most severe and extreme of its manifestations, dissociative identity disorder (DID; e.g., Merskey, 1994). These critics seem to have ignored the extensive empirical evidence supporting the validity of dissociation, in general, and DID, in particular (Dorahy et al., 2014; Gleaves, May, & Cardeña, 2001), and that it is related to severe traumatization (Dalenberg et al., 2012).

Dissociation is much more commonplace than has been generally recognized. The prevalence of dissociative disorders of any kind in the general population appears to be approximately 10% (Ross, 1991; Ross, Joshi, & Currie, 1990), and dissociation is especially prevalent among survivors of CTr (Brand, Lanius, Vermetten, Loewenstein, & Spiegel, 2012; Brand, Myrick, et al., 2012; van der Kolk, Roth, Pelcovitz, Sunday, & Spinazzola, 2005; van Dijke, Ford, Frank, & van der Hart, 2015). Working effectively with this population, therefore, requires a thorough familiarity with the various manifestations comprising the five-symptom typology of dissociation devised by Steinberg (1995) and how to help clients effectively respond to dissociative experiences and episodes.

## VARIETIES OF PROBLEMATIC DISSOCIATIVE EXPERIENCES

One of the most frequently encountered forms of dissociation in CTr and in PTSD is amnesia that is not associated with an organic cause, such as a blow to the head. Many trauma survivors have incomplete recall of traumatic events, which has been a defining feature of PTSD since its appearance in the third edition of the *Diagnostic and Statistical Manual of Mental Disorders* (American Psychiatric Association, 1980). Adverse childhood experiences have been found to be associated with impairment in the ability to recall childhood events generally (D. W. Brown et al., 2007). Reported histories of child abuse have been found to be related to recent gaps in memory (Şar, Alioglu, Akyuz, & Karabulut, 2014). In a factor analysis of two measures of dissociation, Dell (2013) found that dissociative amnesia loaded onto three factors: "gaps in remote memory," "lapses of recent memory and skills," and "discovering dissociated actions" (p. 29; e.g., finding items in one's possession that one has no recollection of having purchased, "coming to" in various circumstances [p. 30, Table 1]).

Another relatively common type of dissociative experience in trauma survivors is depersonalization. On the whole, *depersonalization* experiences consist of feeling unreal (Simeon & Abugel, 2006) and can be either episodic or chronic. The person experiencing depersonalization may feel that they are markedly removed from their own subjective experiences, such as their feelings, thoughts, and bodily sensations. As a result, they may feel as if they are not fully alive, as if they are a zombie going through the motions of life without a sense of agency. They may feel so detached from themselves that they feel as if they are outside of their body. Depersonalization has been found to be related to adverse childhood experiences, most prominently to emotional abuse and emotional neglect (Thomson & Jaque, 2018). However, it is also known to be triggered by drug use (Simeon, Kozin, Segal, & Lerch, 2009).

One particularly puzzling phenomenon sometimes reported in conjunction with depersonalization is *disembodiment* in which a person intensely experiences themselves as disconnected from their body (Tanaka, 2018). In some instances of especially severe dissociation, disembodiment can take the form of out-of-body experiences in which one sees things not through one's eyes but from a point outside of the body and often from above, and, in some instances, also feel as if one is located outside one's body. This type of experience can occur during a traumatic event (referred to as *peritraumatic dissociation*), episodically, or chronically. I have worked with several severely dissociative survivors who indicated that they only discovered during treatment, when they began to experience being "in" their body and seeing through their eyes, that doing so was possible let alone the norm. It was so different from their usual mode of experience that some of them initially found it extremely uncomfortable.

An analogous form of dissociation that some experts believe always accompanies depersonalization is *derealization* in which a person feels as if their surroundings or other people are not real (Simeon, 2014). Some individuals in a state of derealization insist that they recognize that a person's appearance and voice are those of a friend or loved one but that they do not feel convinced that it really is that person. They may similarly express that their surroundings have a familiar appearance but do not seem fully real. Rather, they may describe them, for example, as feeling like a movie set, a dream, or surrealistic painting.

Yet another type of dissociative experience is *identity confusion*, which has been found to be prominent among individuals with borderline personality disorder and those with DID (Laddis, Dell, & Korzekwa, 2017). However, identity confusion is distinct from the sense of changing identity that is the defining characteristic of DID. Rather than a shifting sense of who one is, identity confusion is uncertainty about who one is—the absence of a clear sense of self. Sometimes this lack of clarity is experienced as a sense of conflict or inconsistency about one's beliefs, likes and dislikes, or aspirations.

*Identity alteration* is the experience of feeling as if one is shifting between different senses of identity that is the hallmark of DID (formerly known as multiple personality disorder). The central characteristics of DID are the experience of at least two distinct senses of identity accompanied by amnestic experiences (American Psychiatric Association, 2013). As Herman (1992b) recommended for complex posttraumatic stress disorder, DID treatment is phase oriented and involves engagement with the client's identity states (Brand, Loewenstein, & Spiegel, 2014). A widely recognized perspective for treating the DID can be found in the treatment guidelines of the International Society for the Study of Trauma and Dissociation (2011). Laddis et al. (2017) reported that although both borderline and DID participants in their study scored high on identity confusion, only those with DID generated high scores on identity alteration. In a study of a sample of college students, Şar et al. (2017) found that although self-reports of this phenomenon were associated with all forms of childhood trauma, identity alteration assessed by clinicians was specifically related to childhood sexual abuse.

Although in popular media, identity alteration is depicted as externally observable changes in vocal and behavioral mannerisms, episodes of "overt switching" observable by others are relatively rare in individuals with DID, who exert considerable effort to conceal shifts in their sense of self (Kluft, 2005). Their various senses of identity are more likely to manifest internally in the form of hearing voices, both of adults and children, that are experienced as speaking directly to or about the person themselves or talking or arguing with each other, and that first emerge before age 18 (Dorahy, Shannon, et al., 2009). This is often a source of confusion to helping professionals, who assume that hearing voices is symptomatic of schizophrenia rather than DID. However, research findings indicate that this and other first-rank Schneiderian symptoms (e.g., auditory hallucinations, delusional thinking) traditionally associated with schizophrenia are more common in DID (Dorahy, Shannon, et al., 2009; Kluft, 1987).

## DISSOCIATION AS EXPERIENTIAL DISTANCE AND DISCONNECTION

What is it that memory problems, a sense of being unreal or one's surroundings being unreal, uncertainty about one's identity, and the experience of shifting between identity states share? I would argue that one can answer this question in several related ways. One pertains to the literal meaning of the term *dissociation*, which means not associated with or, more plainly stated, disconnected from. Dissociation can consist of a relative lack of experiential connection to (attention to, awareness of) oneself, one's surroundings, or other people. As Barach (1991) noted, a sense of disconnection from other people expresses itself as a form of dissociation that Bowlby (1980) referred to as *detachment*. If a person is not firmly connected to their present experience, they are unlikely to clearly remember it later (i.e., amnesia). If they are not solidly connected to their own subjective (i.e., proprioceptive, sensory, perceptual, cognitive, or emotional) experience, then they are vulnerable to feeling unreal (i.e., depersonalization). If they lack a distinct connection to their surroundings, those surroundings are likely to similarly seem foreign or unreal (i.e., derealization). The more removed an individual is from their own feelings and therefore their preferences, the more prone they are to be confused about their sense of self (i.e., identity confusion). And in the absence of a strong, consistent, and enduring sense of who they are, they are susceptible to experiencing a sense of sliding or shifting between various senses of identity (i.e., identity alteration). In terms of identity alteration, although DID is commonly thought of as the existence of a variety of senses of self, it is simultaneously a manifestation of the absence of a well-defined, consistent, enduring sense of self.

The various modes of dissociation indicate a relative lack of focus that creates an experiential gap between oneself and the dimensions of experience: of self, others, environmental surroundings, interpersonal interaction. The forms of dissociative experience have been proposed to fall along a continuum and frequently are visually depicted as being ordered left to right, from normal dissociative experience (i.e., absorption) to depersonalization/derealization, amnesia, and identity confusion/identity alteration (Brand & Frewen, 2017). Although these are qualitatively different manifestations of dissociation, their order along a continuum suggests that they can be conceptualized as forming a spectrum of increasing experiential disconnection that corresponds to progressively intense levels of experiential distance.

Although, conceptually, the substrate of dissociation can be thought of as disconnection or distance, subjectively, it corresponds to what is referred to in everyday terminology as spaciness or zoning out. Being removed, detached, or distant from one or several dimensions of experience translates into a foggy, indistinct, or, at the extreme, even absent or blank quality of experience. This understanding of dissociation implies that counteracting unwanted episodes of dissociation entails strengthening the capacities for maintaining focus, attention, and awareness.

## A CONTEXTUAL CONCEPTUALIZATION OF DISSOCIATION

An extensive, solidly established body of empirical literature supports the proposition that problematic dissociation is related to a history of trauma (Dalenberg et al., 2012). However, substantial evidence shows that dissociation is related to experiences of deficit. Both Ogawa, Sroufe, Weinfield, Carlson, and Egeland (1997) and Dutra, Bureau, Holmes, Lyubchik, and Lyons-Ruth (2009) found that maternal unresponsiveness in infancy was related to pathological dissociation in early adulthood. The link between a weakened capacity for interpersonal attachment and a proclivity for dissociation suggests that, as proposed by Barach (1991) and Liotti (1992), growing up in an interpersonal environment that fails to provide sufficient resources for the formation of secure attachment can contribute to the likelihood that an individual will be vulnerable to dissociative reactivity.

Drawing on empirical findings, a number of authors have proposed that most forms of dissociation are related to developmental processes in childhood that extend beyond attachment (E. A. Carlson, Yates, & Sroufe, 2009; Putnam, 1997). Dutra et al. (2009) framed dissociation as an interpersonal developmental process. Mann and Sanders (1994) found that inconsistent and rejecting parenting were associated with elevated levels of dissociation. Similarly, Modestin, Lötscher, and Erni (2002) reported that low levels of parental bonding were related to dissociative experiences in a nonclinical sample of young adults. Other studies have identified a generally impaired childhood family environment (Nash, Hulsey, Sexton, Harralson, & Lambert, 1993), a chaotic family environment (Paley, 1988), and maternal neglect (Draijer & Langeland, 1999) as being related to dissociation.

E. A. Carlson et al. (2009) asserted that "pathological dissociation may reflect an absence of the normative decline in dissociative processes across development and/or an increase in individual (idiosyncratic) dissociation" (p. 40). Ogawa et al. (1997) opined that dissociation may be more normative early in life and gradually may be more indicative of psychopathology with age. From a contextual perspective, this is an important proposition: CTT views dissociation as a normal, salient phenomenon early in development that becomes progressively less prominent as development proceeds. What is problematic, according to CTT theory, is not so much the presence of dissociation as the relative absence of a facility for sustained, focused attention (i.e., mindfulness). With maturation, mindfulness tempers dissociative reactivity and increasingly eclipses it.

According to CTT theory, the mechanisms underlying dissociation that arise in response to trauma and those that result from developmental deprivation are appreciably different and promote somewhat different forms of dissociative reactivity. Trauma-related dissociation is seen as corresponding to the freeze component of the fight–flight–freeze response. In PTSD, as opposed to CTr, these reactions are likely to take the form of zoning out into a state of diminished present-day awareness, flashbacks in which the vivid perceptual and sensory components of past trauma override current experience to a greater or lesser degree, or periods of depersonalization/derealization. All of these dissociative experiences certainly can and often do occur to survivors of CTr, but they also are more vulnerable to the more extreme varieties of dissociation: amnesia for present-day events, identity confusion, and identity alteration.

Consistent with CTT theory, what this suggests is that dissociation, especially its more severe forms, such as identity confusion, identity alteration, and dissociative amnesia, is a response to a combination of experiences of threat and experiences of deficit. In keeping with this proposition, Brand and Frewen (2017) noted that "most of the DDs [dissociative disorders] can be considered childhood trauma disorders" (p. 222). In contrast to the dissociative experiences commonly occurring in PTSD, identity confusion and alteration appear to have their onset early in the lifespan (Goff & Simms, 1993). Various studies have found that 70% to upward of 90% of individuals with DID reported a history of childhood physical abuse, sexual abuse, or both (Ellason, Ross, & Fuchs, 1996; Ross & Ness, 2010; Şar, Yargiç, & Tutkun, 1996).

Siegel (2012) noted that "interactions with the environment, especially relationships with other people, directly shape the development of the brain's structure and function" (p. xii). Consider the implications of this observation in light of the literal meaning of dissociation: disconnection. The degree, quality, and consistency of interpersonal interaction experienced by the developing child, especially relationships with parents and other attachment figures, determines to what degree the child will have the capacity for experiencing connectedness to others. This is the essence of what Bowlby (1977) meant by the term *attachment*: "the propensity of human beings to make strong affectional bonds to particular others" (p. 201). At the same time, the more consistently attentive, responsive, and nurturing these interactions are, the greater the level of neuropsychological stimulation of the sensorium to promote brain development via neuronal interconnections (Siegel, 2012). The availability of salutary interpersonal interactions with others fosters connection to perceptual and cognitive processes that moderate awareness of both subjective (i.e., self) experience and the surrounding environment.

The stimulation provided by consistently safe, nurturing and responsive interpersonal interactions promotes the capacity for and experience of connectedness not only to others but also to one's own inner experience (Laible, 2007; Meins, 2003; Sakagami & Suganuma, 2001) and awareness of external surroundings. To the degree that this developmental resource is lacking, there is a proclivity, to use vernacular terms, to space out, zone out, or, at the extreme, go blank. This realm of unfocused experience corresponds to a sense of distance, or disconnectedness, from self, others, and environment. It is not difficult to deduce how the various exotic-appearing dimensions of pathological dissociation emerge from this experiential underpinning. Other experiences of disconnection, unawareness, and distance, such as *alexithymia* (i.e., difficulty identifying the presence of and distinguishing and articulating feelings; Mason, Tyson, Jones, & Potts, 2005; Modestin et al., 2002; Serrano-Sevillano, González-Ordi, Corbí-Gran, & Vallejo-Pareja, 2017) and *anesthesia* (i.e., an insensitivity to pain; Moormann, Bermond, & Albach, 2004), also have been construed as dissociative manifestations. It is noteworthy that Mason et al. (2005) found a small but significant relationship in their sample of undergraduate students between alexithymia and participant reports of a history of a lack of maternal care.

CTT proposes that dissociative experiences are universal; represent states of consciousness rooted in processes of attention and awareness; can be both maladaptive and adaptive, depending on the circumstances and their function; and are related to psychological development. Although the notion that dissociation is related to development resurfaced in the late 20th century with recognition of its relationship to attachment theory (Barach, 1991; Briere, Runtz, Eadie, Bigras, & Godbout, 2018; Kong, Kang, Oh, & Kim, 2018; Liotti, 1992), it dates back to French psychologist Pierre Janet and other "dissociationists" (Cotsell, 2005, pp. 20–49). The zoned-out state of consciousness that CTT suggests lies at the core of dissociative experience is in effect the opposite of presentification. In dissociative states, the person's relative diminution of awareness equates experientially to a sense of not being fully present.

It appears obvious why this hazy state of consciousness would be difficult to move beyond for someone growing up and being maltreated in various ways. Experiences of threat implicitly evoke the survival and safety needs that in dire circumstances trigger the fight–flight–freeze response. Experiences of deficit in the form of a relative lack of emotional responsivity, consistency, and nurturance by caretakers fail to adequately provide the medium through which a sense of connection to other people, subjective experience, and one's surroundings, and therefore the capacity for sustained, focused attention, develops (Siegel, 2012).

The "normal" level of psychological development manifested by the majority of people, however, is characterized by a much more tenuous degree of awareness, attentiveness, and connectedness to others, subjective experience, and the environmental surround than is generally acknowledged (Gold, 2004a). Consider the following quotes by cognitive psychologists Segal, Williams, and Teasdale (2002), who distinguished *doing mode*, which corresponds to everyday "normal" functioning, from and mindfulness-based *being mode*:

- In doing mode, the mind often travels forward to the future or back to the past, and the experience is one of not actually being "here" in the present much of the time. . . . (p. 73)

- Because doing is often propelled by automatic, well-worn routines, it can easily crowd out other ways of being with one's experience. . . . We can learn to switch out of automatic pilot by bringing our awareness to the present moment. (p. 77)

- Whereas doing mode involves thinking *about* the present, the future, and the past, relating to each of these through a veil of concepts, being mode is characterized by direct, immediate, intimate experience of the present. (p. 73)

What they are describing as doing mode is a ubiquitous, normal state or degree of dissociation that people in general are rarely cognizant of and that may only become apparent via the radically more aware, focused, and attentive experience of mindfulness. The rise in popularity of mindfulness meditation and other mindfulness-related practices, and the emergence of mindfulness-based forms of psychotherapy, such as dialectical behavior therapy (DBT; Linehan, 2015), acceptance and commitment therapy (Hayes, Strosahl, & Wilson, 2012), and mindfulness-based stress reduction (Kabat-Zinn, 2003), can be seen as confirmation of how pervasive normal dissociative disconnection is. "Core Mindfulness" is the title of the first module taught in DBT skills training groups (Linehan, 2015). Mindfulness in DBT is used as an antidote to a habitually poorly focused and undiscerning dissociative state of consciousness and its numerous adverse consequences.

Dissociative experiences, when volitional, have adaptive (i.e., productive and functional) and maladaptive applications. They allow individuals to detach from their surroundings to reduce the impact of everyday stressors and to create the conditions to productively redirect their attention away from potentially distracting internal, external, and interpersonal stimuli when, for example, they are reading. The goal of CTT treatment for dissociation, therefore, is not to eliminate it entirely but to teach complex trauma survivors how to modulate it so that dissociating becomes a choice that can be directed toward adaptive uses rather than an unbidden and unwanted intrusion.

CTT views dissociation as being related to development in that its predominance wanes as the capacities for connectedness, awareness, and sustained attention are expanded. It becomes less prominent with development not because the capacity to dissociate is lost, but because it is eclipsed by the increasing ability to stay attentively focused and experientially present. Redirecting attention away from the circumstances of the present moment remains an option. Dissociation becomes problematic when it occurs outside of the person's volition and control, and thereby interferes with adaptive functioning. Interference with adaptive functioning can occur because trauma-related cues trigger the freeze component of the fight–flight–freeze response due to a developmental deficit-related weakness in the ability to maintain focused attention, connectedness, and awareness, or, especially in the case of CTr, a combination of these two factors (i.e., the freeze component of the fight–flight–freeze response and developmental deficit-related weakness).

The implication of this conceptual formulation of dissociation is that to the degree that problematic dissociative experiences are threat related, an effective intervention strategy is to teach the trauma survivor how to counteract its emergence, or, once it arises, reduce its intensity. In contrast, to the extent that it is deficit based (i.e., an expression of inadequate development), it is best to help the survivor of CTr to remediate their relatively fragile capacity to focus and sustain attention. As in other problematic areas, a manifestation of CTr may be similar in appearance, but the mechanisms underlying it may differ depending on whether it is trauma related, deficit related, or both. Being able to deduce the origins of the difficulty help to clarify how to best resolve it. This is the essential point of CTT: Recognizing that some of the difficulties experienced by CTr survivors are deprivation-related skills deficits rather than trauma-related performance deficits helps guide the formulation of effective intervention strategies.

## STRATEGIES FOR MODULATING AND EXTINGUISHING DISSOCIATIVE REACTIONS

The CTT approach to helping survivors of CTr resolve dissociation-related difficulties, as is the case with nearly every treatment objective, varies considerably from one individual to the next. In general terms, however, there usually are three stages to CTT-oriented intervention for dissociation. The first is to help the survivor learn how to reduce the intensity of disruptive dissociative reactions, typically through the use of grounding techniques. The second is to train the survivor how to modulate the intensity of problematic dissociative episodes through a procedure referred to in CTT as the dissociative dial. The third stage builds on the grounding and dissociative dial interventions to extinguish automatic, unwanted, intrusive dissociative reactions by repeatedly disrupting them.

Two principles that apply across all the goals worked toward in the practical intervention sphere are particularly important to emphasize when working to ameliorate the difficulties created by involuntarily triggered episodes of dissociation. The first is that the practitioner's role is not to reduce, eliminate, or resolve a problem but, rather, to equip the survivor with the tools to do so themselves. Having been deprived of guidance that would promote the acquisition of knowledge and skills in their formative years, it is particularly important for survivors of CTr to experience agency and mastery of competencies throughout treatment. These abilities are then available for them to use when the inevitable problems of life arise subsequent to termination of treatment. Debriefings with clients well after they completed CTT have confirmed that they continued to apply and appreciably expand on the competencies they learned during therapy long after it is completed, which fostered further progress and growth (e.g., the case of Cassandra in Gold et al., 2001).

A second principle that guides the practical intervention sphere is supporting the client's right to exercise choice. Dissociation, even when it emerges involuntarily and creates disruptions, is familiar to survivors and often (rightfully in many circumstances) experienced and perceived as a source of protection. It is therefore especially important when assisting the survivor in learning how to modulate their dissociative reactions to emphasize that the practitioner is not attempting to take away their dissociative ability. Instead, the practitioner is empowering them to have more choice whether to dissociate or, in any given instance, exercise a greater capacity to mindfully remain present.

### Grounding to Reduce Dissociative Intensity

Grounding techniques are a widely used strategy for reducing the intensity of a dissociative reaction once it has already been triggered or in an attempt to fend off a dissociative episode when the survivor senses one is about to occur. An introduction to the use of grounding techniques is best initiated in session when the client reports that they are experiencing dissociation at that moment. This strategy allows for the application of grounding techniques in a situation in which it is actually needed and in the presence of and with the support and guidance of the therapist. Just as important, when client and practitioner explore the application of grounding techniques jointly, they can collaboratively identify which grounding approaches work especially well for that particular individual.

The essence of grounding techniques is deceptively simple. The client directs their attention to stimuli that help to keep them aware and present (i.e., "grounded"). I discuss here targets for directing attention and offer generalizations about which of them seems to be more powerful and effective for most people. However, expect wide individual differences in which modalities are experienced as most effective. It is therefore essential to explore with each particular client what works best for them rather than assume that the order in which I present the targets for focused attention is the optimal one for everyone.

Before discussing grounding per se, it is best to start by considering ways to detect when a client is dissociating. People can and do engage in complex behaviors and carry out entire conversations in a dissociative state. In most instances, therefore, indicators that a client is dissociating in session are not particularly obvious and certainly not as dramatic as portrayed in films, theatrical productions, and television shows. There may be a repeated delay in responses to questions, a subtly vacant facial expression, or simply a sense that the client is "not fully there." One potential indicator is that their behavior may mirror the experiential withdrawal that characterizes disconnection. They may not maintain eye contact. Their head may be bowed. They may pull their arms inward toward their body; at the extreme, they may appear to hug themselves. They may pull their legs off the ground onto the furniture on which they are sitting. If they do speak, their voice may have an unmodulated, monotone quality to it. Although the practitioner will only see all of these external signs to an obvious degree in some unusually intense instances of dissociation, being alert for some level of these behaviors can help in learning to detect when a client is drifting away.

If the practitioner suspects that a client is experiencing a level of dissociation, it is best, especially if the topic has not been breached previously, to gently inquire to determine if there is some level of detachment. Questions such as "Can you see me?" "Are you having trouble hearing me?" or "Do you feel as if you are drifting away?"—when asked in as nonthreatening a tone as possible—help the client to acknowledge that they are experiencing some difficulty staying focused. The reason to approach these inquiries carefully is that many survivors are primed to believe that the practitioner will be angry at them for "not paying attention." One of the catch-22s of growing up with experiences of threat is that it is not uncommon for survivors to have been berated as children when the natural tendency to respond to danger dissociatively evoked the anger of caretakers because the children were "not paying attention." To avoid eliciting the survivor's misperception that the practitioner is displeased with them for being inattentive, it is crucial to approach inquiries about dissociation in as nonthreatening a way as possible.

Especially when the client appears to be in an intensely dissociative state, probably the most effective approach to orient them to the present is movement. Standing up, motioning with one's hand, and softly saying something like, "Come with me," is usually enough to elicit responsiveness. One can then leave the therapy office with the client. The point is to get them walking because just moving and having to navigate in space without bumping into things can help reorient them. What I routinely do is walk with them out into the hallway outside my office suite and staying by their side as we walk. I say something like, "Notice the alternating pressure on each foot as you walk." Timing the words to the pace at which we walk, I say, "Feel your right foot touch the ground. . . . Now your left foot. . . . Right. . . . Left . . . ," and so on. We walk down the hall in this manner, turn around, and do the same thing on the return until we reach the door of the office suite. Usually, on a 10-point scale, clients' level of dissociation drops at least 3 to 4 points.

This approach is only necessary if the client is so dissociated that their awareness of their surroundings is extremely minimal. In most cases, the sense of touch alone rather than gross motor movement helps a client who is having difficulty staying focused and present. If they are seated, suggesting that they place their feet flat on the floor and feel the resulting pressure on the bottom of their feet can help reorient them. Bringing their attention to the sensation of pressure of the furniture on which they are seated and that is holding them up also can help. If a greater level of stimulation is needed, rubbing their hands together or reaching up and touching their face can be a more potent way to orient themselves.

Given that many people with problematic dissociation have a history of sexual violation, it is inadvisable for the clinician to touch the survivor in an attempt to reorient them because doing so can be triggering and seriously disrupt a sense of safety with and trust in the therapist. It also contradicts the CTT principle that intervention is aimed at helping the client learn tools to resolve difficulties for themselves. By learning techniques to do so, they not only are empowered to resolve the problem they are experiencing at the moment but also are equipped to effectively address similar difficulties that are likely to arise outside of therapy.

Touch is an effective avenue for grounding for many, but not all, clients. Some people have more success counteracting dissociative experiencing by attending to other sensory modalities. For many, the auditory channel is appreciably more grounding than touch. No matter where people are, we are almost never surrounded by absolute silence. We regularly and automatically tune out subtle extraneous background noises, such as the sounds of the air conditioning or heating system, traffic sounds, voices in an adjoining room, or the rustling of leaves. This is an example of normal, adaptive dissociation. We screen out these noises because they are usually irrelevant to whatever we are attending to at the moment and can therefore be distracting. Focusing on these sounds can feel as if we are suddenly turning on an audio track that had been muted. For some individuals, this instantaneous shift in experience carries a powerful sense of tuning into the present moment.

Although most people seem to find either the tactile or auditory channels the most powerful in counteracting dissociative spaciness, for some people, attending to the visual perceptual channel can be an aid to grounding. Noticing whatever is in their visual field and silently labeling it, often with descriptors such as the color or other characteristics of what they see, can help them stay present. For example, they may look around and say to themselves that they see "gray industrial carpeting, beige armchair, bright red throw pillow," and so on.

The preceding forms of grounding are in response to feeling disconnected from one's surroundings and result in a level of disorientation to place. Grounding skills also can be applied to disorientation for time. Consulting cues about the date, time, and one's own age can help offset entry into a traumatic flashback or a period of dissociative identity alteration to a sense of self at a much earlier age. At a time when many people have smartphones, just remembering to look at the calendar, time, or photos on the phone can serve this function. It can be helpful to engage in self-talk that reinforces awareness of one's temporal location, such as, "It is 2019; what I was beginning to experience happened back in 1997," or "These are pictures of my children; I am not a child; I have children of my own."

Unlike relaxation exercises, these grounding exercises to promote connection and orientation to place and time in the external environment do not need to be practiced regularly. Once the survivor has learned them in session, they usually have no trouble using them outside of therapy as needed when they notice that they are entering into a dissociative state. Obviously, the earlier in the process they catch themselves zoning out or slipping away, the more effective grounding is likely to be in counteracting a dissociative reaction.

Once the survivor has mastered grounding to place-orienting external stimuli and identity- and time-orienting cues, and their overall tendency to slip into unwanted dissociative states has been noticeably attenuated, they can attempt grounding to sensory stimuli. This technique is not aimed at counteracting particular episodes of dissociation. Rather, it is a strategy to help survivors of prolonged traumatization with an appreciable degree of dissociative anesthesia to begin to cultivate a greater awareness of sensory experience.

Often survivors are chronically disconnected to some degree from sensory experience, emotional awareness, or both. This lack of awareness of sensory or emotional experience (i.e., anesthesia and alexithymia, respectively) tends to be relatively constant. The objective of grounding to sensory stimuli, therefore, is to help the survivor who is relatively numb to bodily sensations and emotions to establish a foundation for awareness of these realms of experience. Both of these domains involve experiential connection to "inner" subjective experience as opposed to "outer" orientation in place and time to the external environment.

Inner bodily sensations are the building blocks of emotions. People know they are sad, for example, because they notice sensations such as a tightness in the throat, heaviness around the eyes, or slumping of the shoulders. The practitioner therefore can help increase the survivor's awareness of bodily sensations by drawing their attention to the sensations that accompany breathing. These sensations are more difficult to detect than the tactile, auditory, or visual stimuli that are initially the focus of grounding techniques. They consist of considerably more subtle impressions, such as those of air passing through the nostrils or down the windpipe, the chest rising and falling, and the abdomen expanding and contracting. Rather than simply suggesting paying attention to the sensations of breathing, it is best to suggest in session that the survivor take a deep breath and then talk them through noticing these experiences as they slowly inhale and exhale:

> Very slowly, take a deep breath, and as you do, notice the feeling of air passing through your nostrils, down the back of your throat, and into your windpipe. As you breathe out, notice your belly and then your chest contracting. Good. Now, as you take another slow, deep breath, notice your chest rising and your belly expanding. . . .

Readers familiar with mindfulness practices will recognize this grounding technique as a core component of mindfulness meditation. Its purpose here, however, is not to attempt to remain attentive to the sensations of breathing over extended periods, as in mindfulness meditation, but, rather, to assist the survivor in cultivating a greater facility for cognizance of bodily sensations. It is useful for survivors to practice this grounding technique one or several times daily until they are able to quickly establish awareness of bodily sensations. They can accomplish establishing this awareness by monitoring their sensation while repeatedly focusing on taking a few slow, deep breaths over a period of less than a minute.

Once the survivor has become adept at attending to the subjective sensations accompanying breathing, they can then progress to another exercise commonly used in conjunction with mindfulness meditation: the body scan. The purpose is not to do a meditative exercise, a form of relaxation, or to resist falling into discrete episodes of dissociation but, rather, to help the survivor develop recognition of visceral sensations that compose the constituents of emotional awareness. Having learned to recognize subtle bodily sensations by attending to breathing, this next step is designed to increase awareness of the even more subtle subjective experiences that are a bridge to being more aware of emotions.

Forms of body scan exercises are easily accessed online. I recommend teaching survivors the structured, systematic technique of slowly moving their attention from the top of their head, through various levels of the body, as if in cross sections, down to the soles of their feet. Initially. the practitioner can teach this technique by slowly talking the client through these different levels of the body. For instance, the therapist might say,

> Make sure you are sitting in a comfortable position. You can reposition yourself at any point during this exercise if you need to make adjustments to maintain your comfort. If you like and if you believe it will help you to focus, you can close your eyes. But if you are more at ease keeping your eyes open, that is fine, too. Now, gently bring your attention to the top of your head. Once you have done that, you might ask yourself, How did I locate where the top of my head is without looking in a mirror or using my hands to feel it? The answer probably won't be in words but in sensations that tell you where the top of your head is. Notice those sensations and take a little time to see if you can slowly bring them more into focus. Good. Now, gently bring your attention downward as if you are lowering a large ring down over your head to the level of your brow and see what sensations you notice there. . . .

From there, you can continue gradually downward through the body in sections, ending with the soles of the feet. Progressing slowly gives the client the time to unhurriedly bring the sensations corresponding to each level of the body into focus. This process can easily take the greater part of a session. However, once this orientation to body scanning is completed, survivors can then devote 5 minutes or less practicing it daily at home to become more adept at noticing the visceral sensations that will equip them to grow more attuned to emotional reactions.

**Modulating Dissociative Intensity Using the Dissociative Dial**

A somewhat more intricate intervention that I have come to refer to as the *dissociative dial*, is a method of teaching survivors of CTr to modulate their level of dissociation. The technique is based on principles and interventions introduced by Milton Erikson (Rossi & Ryan, 1992, especially pp. 84–85). The essence of the approach is derived from the observation that it is much easier for an individual to increase than reduce the intensity of disturbing experiences, such as anxiety, depression, dissociation, or even physical pain. However, once someone has successfully intensified a problematic experience, it is much easier to then diminish it. In this way, one has in effect located the dimmer switch that can alter the intensity of the experience in either direction. However, this modulation of experiential intensity in either direction is much easier to accomplish if it is not attempted in a direct, conscious fashion. The approach can be considered a quasihypnotic one because the effect is produced outside of conscious intentionality. This is important because the technique does not involve having the client purposely alter the intensity of their experience. Instead, the response is subtly implied.

The type of dissociative phenomenon to which the dissociative dial technique can be applied varies widely. It can be simple zoning out, depersonalization, derealization, sensory analgesia, or alexithymia. In some instances of rapidly alternating switching between senses of self, it can be used to reduce the speed and intensity of identity alteration. It also can be applied to unwanted experiences other than dissociation, including anxiety and physical pain. Here, though, I focus on dissociation. Because dissociation and hypnosis are closely associated experiences (Cleveland, Korman, & Gold, 2015; Frischholz, Lipman, Braun, & Sachs, 1992; Kluft, 2012), this quasihypnotic approach is especially well suited to modulating dissociative experiences. I have found the technique to be effective in some instances as a form of inducing hypnosis itself.

The procedure begins by having the client rate their degree of dissociation[1] on a scale from 1 (*no dissociation*) to 100 (*maximal dissociation*). However, I usually leave it to the client to decide what the meanings of the two extremes of the

---

[1]Although some clients are familiar with the term *dissociation*, not all are. Regardless of the term adopted, by the time the procedure is used, the client will have identified a particular form of dissociative experience (e.g., depersonalization) or general realm of experience (e.g., dissociative spaciness) that corresponds to dissociation.

scale are because, in some instances, it makes more sense to them if the poles are reversed. For example, if they are working to reverse dissociative anesthesia, they may use 0 to indicate no sensation whatsoever and 100 to signify full sensory awareness. The practitioner then shows the client a picture of the 100-point scale arranged along a semicircle to depict a dial with an arrow or indicator (see Figure 9.1) and asks what their current level of dissociation is between 0 and 100. The client is then asked to picture the dial in their head with the indicator pointing to the number that corresponds to their current level of dissociation.

The next step is important: The therapist asks the client to picture the indicator slowly moving one notch in the direction of a greater level of dissociation. Two points are absolutely essential here. First, do not ask the client to move the indicator. Request that they watch it move. The idea is for them to passively observe the indicator move and *not* to intentionally move it. The second key point is to ask them to watch the indicator move in the direction that represents more dissociation.

Here is an approximation of what the therapist says during the procedure. In this case, the client has reported that their current level of dissociation is a 43 and that the higher the number, the greater the level of dissociation:

> Picture the dial I just showed you in your head with the indicator pointing to 43. Got it? Good! Now, watch the indicator slowly moving to the right and let me know when it's pointing at 44. . . . [Client indicates the arrow is at 44.] Good! Now, let's wait a minute . . . [pause at least 10 to 15 seconds]. Great! Now, watch the indicator slowly move farther to the right and let me know when it's pointing at 45. . . .

The procedure continues in this manner; the practitioner pauses at each number and continues progressively in the direction of greater dissociation. It is possible that at some point, the client's level of dissociative spaciness may become so intense that they begin to lose touch with the practitioner and are no longer able to hear or perhaps even see the practitioner. It is therefore important to observe the client closely to monitor as best as the therapist can whether the client seems to be growing so foggy that they are at risk for no longer being responsive. If the therapist senses that the client is approaching this point, move one notch in the direction of less dissociation, pause, and then back one notch toward greater dissociation. From there, move directions back and forth, and progressively move more in the direction of less dissociation.

**FIGURE 9.1. The Dissociative Dial**

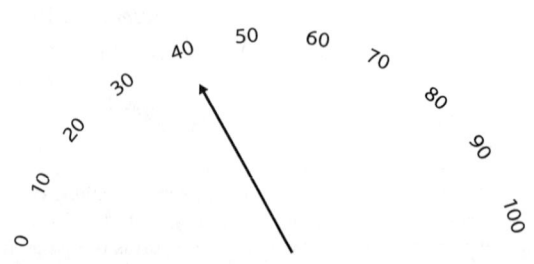

Consider the example of a client who has decided that higher numbers signify greater levels of dissociation. They start at a 43 on a 100-point scale, then watch the indicator move one point at a time as in preceding example (i.e., the approximation of what the therapist says during the procedure) until they reach 73. At this point, the practitioner senses the client is dissociated enough that they are beginning to lose touch with the practitioner, so the therapist checks in and confirms that this is the case. The practitioner then suggests that the client watch the indicator move one notch to the left to 72 (in the direction of less dissociation), then back to the right to 73, left to 72, left to 71, right to 72, left to 71, left to 70, right to 71. The therapist slowly has the client picture the indicator move more to the left than to the right, going back and forth until they are appreciably below the starting point of 42 and perhaps now at 34. Then the therapist can test the limits by asking the client to watch the indicator and see how far to the left it moves before it stops. Perhaps it moves even farther to the left, to 29.

It is important to move back and forth rather than to give in to the temptation to immediately move toward lowering the intensity of dissociation. The purpose of the intervention is not just to achieve a reduction in dissociation but for the client to become adept at moving in both directions so that they can replicate the effect on their own without the therapist's assistance once the session is over. The therapist should plan for the procedure in advance to begin it early in the session and devote most of the session to the (somewhat laborious) process of slowly increasing the level of dissociation, moving back and forth, and then slowing decreasing the level of dissociation.

By end of the session, the client should have mastered the ability to modulate in both directions on their own. The practitioner can then ask that the survivor spend a few minutes once a day practicing picturing the dial and watching the arrow move in the direction of reducing the intensity of their dissociation. Now that they have spent an entire session practicing moving in both directions, the therapist can explain to the client that they no longer have to first increase their level of dissociation to be able to move in the direction of decreasing it. If the client feels more comfortable or confident doing that, they can, but they are likely to find it is no longer necessary to intensify it to know how to reduce it.

This single training session provides the survivor with a tremendously powerful resource. Because clients can experience dissociation as a comforting refuge from distress, I make a point of emphasizing that nothing has been taken away. They can still dissociate or increase their level of dissociation if they choose to. But they now have the option to reduce their level of dissociation so that it does not interfere with their daily functioning and know that they can choose to increase it again if they wish.

### Repeatedly Disrupting Dissociative Reactions to Extinguish Them

The survivor has now been provided with two helpful resources that allow them to manage their level of dissociation rather than be at the mercy of its automatic appearance outside of their intention or control. However, a practical problem remains. What if, as is often the case, dissociation arises and overwhelms their awareness before they even notice what is occurring, and overrides the opportunity to intervene? They are likely to first become aware of the dissociative episode when it is already subsiding.

A final step is required, therefore, to empower the survivor to notice the emergence of an instance of dissociation and to work toward disrupting dissociative reactions repeatedly until they are extinguished. To accomplish this outcome, the survivor is encouraged to be vigilant for the inception of dissociative reactions and to notice what happens just before the dissociative response begins. Often when they are just beginning to practice being vigilant, the opportunity to catch themselves at the onset of the dissociative reaction slips by them, and the episode progresses to becoming full blown.

However, they still may be able to mentally revisit and reconstruct what led up to and triggered the incident, especially with some (nonleading) guidance and coaching from the practitioner. Let's say, for instance, that the dissociative incident was an episode of amnesia. It might be easier to start at the end of the episode by asking, "What is the first thing you remember after the period of amnesia ended? And after that? And after that?" The survivor's ability to identify answers to these questions is likely to help increase their level of confidence so that they can then answer questions such as, "What is the last thing you can remember before you 'went blank'? And what happened before that? And before that? What were you feeling at the time? Thinking?"

In this way, the survivor can isolate the cues or triggers that consistently set off instances of dissociation. At times, the trigger is an external event, such as a sudden, unanticipated loud noise or someone touching them without warning. In other instances, the dissociation is proceeded by a subjective experience, such as the sensation of their heart pounding or a feeling of dizziness. Whether the trigger or cue for the initiation of a dissociative episode is external, subjective and "internal," or both, it is important not to jump to conclusions that the trigger in one instance is always the only cue that sets off dissociation. The client needs to examine a good number of dissociative episodes and see if they can identify a trigger. Eventually, they may come to conclude that a class of stimuli consistently set off dissociative reactions, such as being caught off guard or feeling penned in. The more reliably they can identify possible cues for dissociative episodes, the better prepared they will be to notice those triggers when they occur so that they can be ready to invoke grounding methods, modulation of the dissociative experience via use of the dissociative dial, or, in some instances, anxiety reduction exercises.

There is a tendency to assume that dissociation is always preceded by anxiety. I have worked with clients whose previous therapists attempted for protracted periods—to no avail—to help them reduce their dissociative responding more or less exclusively by focusing on anxiety reduction. Dissociation is often a conditioned response, but it can be conditioned to a wide number of cues, many of which are not anxiety related.

Beyond being able to identify the triggers of dissociation, survivors can even extend the process to learn to at least partially undo a recent amnestic incident. The therapist can facilitate this process by asking, "What is the last thing you remember before the onset of the amnesia? Good. What happened just after that? Just after that?" And at the other end of the episode: "What is the first thing you remember after you came out of the amnestic episode? Great. And what happened just before that?" Clients are often surprised how often they can answer these questions, which indicates that what occurred during an amnestic episode (as long as it is not organically based) is not forever lost to them. This procedure, in turn, forms a basis for retrieving recollections of recent events for which they were previously amnestic, if they choose to.

Armed with relaxation techniques, grounding strategies, and the dissociative dial, and being alert to external and subjective triggers of dissociation, the survivor can now set about practicing vigilance to be cognizant as early in the process as possible when a dissociative reaction (whether it takes the form of amnesia, depersonalization, or some other mode of dissociation) begins. The earlier in the process they catch it, the more likely they are able to disrupt the emergence of dissociation and prevent it from escalating into a full-blown episode. However, I explain to survivor clients that, at first, they may find that they are only aware of a dissociative episode as they are coming out of it.

With continued vigilance, they are likely to detect dissociation before it fully develops, but too late in its emergence to stop it from continuing, Eventually, they will be able to catch it early enough to intervene with relaxation, grounding, or dial-assisted modulation but not soon enough to keep the episode from proceeding. But with time and dedication, they will come to a point where they are able to recognize the presence of their dissociative triggers and intervene in time to prevent the dissociative reaction from occurring. With repeated disruption of dissociative episodes, they will begin to occur with less and less frequency and with less and less intensity, and move toward extinction.

# 10

# Identifying Complex Dissociation

*Annotated Transcript of an Initial Assessment Interview*

The transcript presented in this chapter provides an example of a pretreatment assessment interview with a man who, several months earlier, had contacted the university-based trauma clinic that I direct because he was seeking treatment. Unfortunately, a lag of several months occurred between his initial phone contact with the clinic and this meeting—not an uncommon occurrence, given that the demand for services consistently results in a substantial waiting list. I conducted the interview, which was video recorded, behind a one-way mirror with the clinic's doctoral trainee staff observing.

The transcript, in which variables have been changed to protect client privacy, exemplifies a contextual trauma therapy approach to conducting an initial assessment interview with a prospective client suspected to suffer from complex traumatization. Because, in this instance, the client believed several of his more prominent difficulties were dissociative in nature, his descriptions of them provided useful examples of how these phenomena manifest in daily life and were phrased in nontechnical, experiential language. Rather than consisting of a series of predetermined queries, the interview unfolded spontaneously, thereby allowing the client to take the lead in determining the direction and content. Among other advantages, a spontaneous approach puts the onus on the client to describe their dissociative experiences in their own words rather than merely respond to a series of yes/no questions. The degree to which this particular client's account of his experiences conformed to dissociation reflected a crucial element in evaluating the validity of his suspicion. Along the way, experiences of threat and experience of deficit were revealed.

---

http://dx.doi.org/10.1037/0000176-011
*Contextual Trauma Therapy: Overcoming Traumatization and Reaching Full Potential*, by S. N. Gold
Copyright © 2020 by the American Psychological Association. All rights reserved.

The transcript conveys a conversational and informal tone that helps to ensure the client's comfort and to avoid the distancing conveyed by a rigidly professional stance. The flow of discussion, however, is goal directed. The initial questions are predominantly fairly broad, open-ended ones, and are phrased in as nonleading a way as possible. The focus is on the client's concerns, how they are related to the client's present and past life circumstances, and the changes that he would like to put into effect. As the transcript illustrates, he and I are working together and engaging in a joint effort aimed at providing both of us with an increasingly clear understanding of his experiences and treatment objectives. The intention is to avoid having the interchange take the form of an interview that approximates interrogation but, instead, to facilitate a collaborative discussion.

## THE ASSESSMENT INTERVIEW

**THERAPIST:** So, how long ago did you first contact the clinic?

**CLIENT:** Oh, early fall.

**THERAPIST:** Oh, right. I'm sorry for the wait.

> **AUTHOR'S COMMENT:** I conducted the interview in early January.

**CLIENT:** Yeah, I was told that there was going to be a wait.

**THERAPIST:** Yeah. So, back when you contacted us, what prompted you to call at that time?

> **AUTHOR'S COMMENT:** The focus from the beginning is on the client's objective in seeking treatment. The phrase "at that time" acknowledges that because of the lag between the initial phone call and this interview, the client's concerns and situation may have changed.

**CLIENT:** Actually, I had, uh, read this book. [*Pulls a copy of* The Stranger in the Mirror [Steinberg & Schnall, 2000] *out of his backpack.*]

**THERAPIST:** Ah, okay. How did you come across that?

**CLIENT:** I had figured out that I was dissociating a while ago, maybe like 5 years ago. And so I had just been researching here and there when I had time to figure out how this works, and I had just

*Identifying Complex Dissociation* 205

CLIENT: happened to come across I think it was on Amazon. I was looking at some other book on dissociation, and it popped up.

THERAPIST: So, you put "dissociation" in the search [engine]?

CLIENT: I think I might have been searching for a specific book, but then, you know, it always gives you suggestions, and so I was looking through those. . . .

THERAPIST: Mm-hmm. . . .

CLIENT: And this came up, and I said, "Oh, wow, this is all about dissociation. I have to get this." So, I read it and I took the little mini-quizzes in here, and I said, "Oh, I'm scoring very high. I need to have someone help me with this."

THERAPIST: What did you think of the book?

**AUTHOR'S COMMENT:** This question, conversational in tone (as opposed to, e.g., "How did that make you feel?"), gives him an opportunity to further discuss his experience of reading a book that reinforced his suspicion that what he was experiencing was dissociation.

CLIENT: I thought it was really good.

THERAPIST: Yeah?

CLIENT: It's in language that you can understand. It gives you examples of like the normal, the moderate, and the severe, so it gives you a good understanding of it, and it made me a little less afraid, which I think was a big deal.

THERAPIST: That's great! So, what first brought this to your attention 5 years ago?

CLIENT: Just . . . just being so fuzzy and knowing that I like constantly disconnected, just emotionally shut off, like empty.

**AUTHOR'S COMMENT:** Although momentarily, this client describes several "classic symptoms" of dissociation, albeit in his own experiential language, he starts out with the phrase "just being so fuzzy." Rather than pointing to the dissociative phenomena that are prevalent in the professional literature—amnesia, depersonalization, derealization, identity confusion, or identity alteration—he leads with the identification of the fairly generic and experiential quality of a "fuzzy" state of awareness.

**THERAPIST:** Okay. . . .

**CLIENT:** And just going through the motions. And then, sometimes I would just be really sad [*voice chokes a bit*], depressed, and I realized I couldn't make up my mind about things. Why am I not making my mind up? It's like sometimes I like this and other times I don't like that, and I'm back and forth, and sort of all over the place.

> **AUTHOR'S COMMENT:** This is a clear description of identity confusion. He is not indicating that he experiences distinct senses of identity; that would constitute identity alteration. Instead, he is indicating that he is extremely uncertain about a key aspect of identity: what he likes and does not like. In the same way that fuzziness or spaciness can be considered the fundamental experience at the root of other dissociative phenomenon, identity confusion is in effect a substrate underlying identity alteration. We tend to think of identity alteration and the syndrome most closely associated with dissociative identity disorder as being about having several senses of self. But what the less extreme, more essential experience of identity confusion helps to bring into focus is that a key aspect of what is at play in identity alteration is the lack of an enduring sense of self.

**THERAPIST:** Okay, um. . . . So, you know this is one of the things that we specialize in, is dissociation. But there's a lot of mental health professionals who know very little about dissociation. How did you even come across the word and connect that up with what you were experiencing?

**CLIENT:** I was at a bookstore. And I was thinking, "Okay, I have to figure out what's going on with me, why I'm so fuzzy headed and I have a hard time remembering things, like big chunks of my past at least. I don't remember most of my childhood. I'm thinking, okay, this is not normal." I mean, I have a brother and a sister and friends, and my wife and her family, they can sit around and talk about stuff that happened during their childhoods and remember just about everything, and I remember very little.

> **AUTHOR'S COMMENT:** Here, he transitions to explicitly indicating the presence of amnesia. More specifically, he is describing a form of amnesia commonly encountered among survivors of multiple severe childhood traumas, major gaps in his recollection of his personal history, especially in childhood.

**THERAPIST:** So, your sister and brother remember a lot more than you do?

**CLIENT:** Yes. And it was weird. We had a family weekend, and they were talking about all these memories and all these things that happened, and I'm sitting there going, "Are you sure I was there because I have little recollection, or none."

**THERAPIST:** This was recently or 5 years ago?

**CLIENT:** No, it was a while ago. The 5 years ago, I was in a bookstore, and I was trying to figure out. I happened to go in the psychology section, and then I found *Dissociative Children: Bridging the Inner and Outer Worlds* [Shirar, 1996]. I think that was about 5 years ago or so from what I can piece together. And it struck me: I saw a lot of that in there. I'm thinking, I don't know why I have trauma responses, because I don't really remember anything terribly traumatic. I mean, yeah, I got bullied at school and I sort of didn't get a lot of attention at home. So, I don't know if it was just loneliness or what. I don't know if it was fear of rejection, but I don't remember like any huge traumatic event, right? So, I don't know. But I did see a lot of myself in those kids. "My god, okay. Dissociation. Yeah, that's what's happening." So I . . . I've known it for a while.

> **AUTHOR'S COMMENT:** Bullying certainly is a form of trauma. However, as we learn later in this transcript, this client had many other experiences of threat and deficit in his childhood and adolescence. What is interesting and not entirely unusual is that he himself has difficulty discerning or perhaps acknowledging the presence and extent of adversity in his formative years. Probably a main reason is that for the most part, there was no (in his words) "huge traumatic event." What was present in his background was an ongoing atmosphere characterized as much by deprivation (primarily emotional neglect but some degree of material deprivation, too) as by trauma per se. The entire context of his formative years was permeated by deprivation.

**THERAPIST:** And then when you read, *The Stranger in the Mirror* it was like, yeah, this really. . . .

**CLIENT:** Holy crap!

> **AUTHOR'S COMMENT:** His language here is one of many indicators that he feels at ease and is not experiencing the exchange as overly stifling or excessively professional.

THERAPIST: [*Laughs*]

CLIENT: Yeah, really, it was like, "Oh, my god, that's me! Whoa! I'm not the only one that's doing this weird stuff!"

THERAPIST: What things stood out for you the most when you read through that book?

CLIENT: Just relating to it.

THERAPIST: Mm-hmm.

CLIENT: So much. I think it was, I scored severe on everything except for derealization, which was moderate. And, so, I was like, wow [*points, as if to different subareas of dissociation covered in the quizzes*], that's me, that's me, that's me.

THERAPIST: So, you scored high on depersonalization, which means there are times. . . . well, tell me what you experience that would fall under "depersonalization."

**AUTHOR'S COMMENT:** I begin to define depersonalization, but then catch myself and ask him what he experiences that he believes constitutes depersonalization.

CLIENT: Sometimes I just don't feel like my body's real. Sometimes I just don't feel like I'm connected. I talk about my body as almost like it's a separate thing from me. I talk about "my body." I don't talk about "me."

THERAPIST: Mm-hmm.

CLIENT: I even talk about myself in the third person. Everything is so . . . distanced.

THERAPIST: When you're talking to other people or when you're thinking?

CLIENT: When I'm thinking. I'm always saying, you, you, you, like it's someone else talking to me. I've had times when I've noticed when I'm talking about myself to other people, I slip into "We." I'm like, no I'm one person, it's "me." [*Chuckles nervously*] I don't know, it's like a complete disconnection.

**AUTHOR'S COMMENT:** The client is beginning to enter the territory of conveying what at least approximates identity alteration, shifting between several senses of self. But it is not yet clear that his predominant experience of his identity is one of alteration between senses of self or a lack of certainty about his own identity. From a contextual trauma therapy perspective, this is as much a developmental issue as one of diagnosis. The overriding concern is not establishing whether he has alternate senses of identity but that he lacks a well-defined sense of self that is fairly continuous and consistent over time, and even more important, how disconnected he is from his own experience. This alone could account for why he thinks in terms of "you" when thinking to himself.

A lot of ground has been covered, and a markedly relaxed tone has been established in this initial meeting, all in a span of fewer than 6 minutes. For the next few minutes, I explore with him what his level of recall was for his childhood. It seemed spotty, but when he starts talking about the bullying he had mentioned earlier, some interesting events and observations come to the fore. He explains to me that, by sixth grade, the bullying got so bad that even though he had always loved learning, he wanted to stop going to school.

CLIENT: Kids were picking on me. Some of the teachers saw it, didn't care. They let it happen. They were like, "Whatever."

**AUTHOR'S COMMENT:** The client not only suffered from being bullied but also was disturbed by the perception that the adults around him in positions of authority, who could have put a stop to the bullying, saw what was happening but were not invested enough to intervene. Bullying is an experience of threat. That the failure of adults who had the power to support and defend him declined to do so is an experience of deficit, the context within which the trauma of bullying is embedded. They are two sides of a single coin. Although the bullying left him with a chronic sense of looming danger, the failure of adults to protect him "taught" him that he could not trust others to care about and protect him, that is, that he is all alone and cannot rely on others. Consider how this "lesson" would affect his orientation toward relationships later in life, and how both sides of the coin would interfere with his social development.

THERAPIST: So, especially that the teachers were seeing what was going on, and they didn't do anything.

CLIENT: Some of them, yeah. And the kids knew which teachers they would get in trouble with and which ones didn't care, and they timed it. Like they were looking out on the side of the building during recess: "Okay, this teacher's coming. We've got to stop now."

**THERAPIST:** Wow.

**CLIENT:** And, so, there were a couple of times when they circled around me and were making fun of me, and kicking me, and. . . .

**THERAPIST:** Gee. So, it wasn't just verbal bullying. It was physical assault, too.

**CLIENT:** A little bit, yeah. Mostly verbal. Mostly just making fun and constantly picking on me, and having the fun of rejecting me and making sure I wasn't accepted by anyone.

**THERAPIST:** Were there specific things that they picked on you about?

> **AUTHOR'S COMMENT:** It is important to word this type of inquiry in a way that cannot be taken to suggest that he was in any way responsible for his victimization (as in, "Why were they bullying you?").

**CLIENT:** Um, I don't know. I remember one time—I had one older brother and one younger sister—and my older brother and I were almost the same height. I was growing a little faster than he was. And my parents were trying to hand out clothes. And, so, they'd give me his clothes, and I'm like, "They're already too small." So, there were times when I had pants that were too short. And they were like, "Oh, where's the flood? Ha, ha, ha." So, I remember . . . I remember that instance. And I remember I would always tell myself, "They're kids. They're going through a phase. Whatever. They'll grow out of it."

> **AUTHOR'S COMMENT:** There is a convergence here of deficit adversity: a degree of physical neglect in the form of not having reasonably well-fitting clothes, and threat adversity—being bullied because of the weird appearance created by ill-fitting clothing. In addition, he introduces a theme he is about to flesh out more fully: a pattern of coping with others' attacks and neglect of his needs by trying to rationalize or even justify their behavior. As the transcript reveals soon, this orientation seems to have its roots in a childhood household context in which he saw himself as, and may have been, more mature and "adultlike" than his parents were.

**THERAPIST:** As a kid, you said this to yourself?

**CLIENT:** Yeah, so I'm like, was I even a child as a child, or did I have an adult mentality? I'm not even sure, but I remember, I don't know, just trying to understand people and sort of seeing their perspective and being able to, I guess, talk my way out of being upset.

> **AUTHOR'S COMMENT:** Note how these experiences set the stage for identity confusion. Am I a child or am I an adult? Are my parents adults or are they children? Am I inferior or superior to others? Am I deficient or exceptionally mature? What he is describing is a pseudomature stance assumed in a desperate attempt to cope with untenable circumstances but unsupported by the actual capacities—capacities that emerge from the reliable support of others—for mature functioning.

THERAPIST: Mm-hmm. Can you think of other examples when you were a kid where it seems like you were somewhat more adult than you would expect of a kid that age? Like at home?

CLIENT: Yeah, with my parents, I could tell they were stressed about money. And, so I would, I made sure I didn't act up or anything. And I sort of downplayed everything, and I didn't really ask for anything, like I know kids are always used to asking for toys. "Can I get this and this and this?" I think I asked one time. One time, like, "Can I get a cassette player for Christmas?" That's what I wanted. And I didn't ask again, not one time. I didn't want to upset them. [*Suddenly restrains himself from weeping*]

THERAPIST: [*Points*] There's ... there's some tissues there. So, do you remember what happened when you asked?

CLIENT: [*Speaks in a soft voice, still trying to hold back tears*] I think they were a little bit surprised.

THERAPIST: Uh-huh.

CLIENT: 'Cause I didn't really ask for anything. And, uh, I got the present, but I was like, "Oh, my god. Wow."

THERAPIST: What was that like, that you got it?

CLIENT: [*Weeps*] I was kind of surprised, because I wasn't used to getting things. I was just, um, I was really happy. I took it, and I was playing with it. And we, um, we had to go to church or something. And when we came back, I was playing with it all day.

> **AUTHOR'S COMMENT:** Later in the interview is a more detailed discussion of the atmosphere in the client's family of origin. He makes a vague reference to his parents' relationship being problematic and his siblings' thinking that their parents are "nuts."

**THERAPIST:** What was it about your parents' relationship?

**CLIENT:** My mother's like a laid-back woman, and she's nice, but my dad pushes her around, so it's . . . he's . . . everything's about him. I happened to come across the definition of *narcissist*. I'm like, "Oh, my god, that's my father. [*Speaks in a softly sarcastic tone*] Great. Lovely." He's just a bully. If people don't do what he wants when he wants, he'll, like attack you, and he's like a pit bull. When he starts, he just doesn't stop.

**THERAPIST:** Mm-hmm.

**CLIENT:** And just people figure that out pretty quickly about him, and so then he gets his way, and then he runs around, "See? I'm right. I'm right all the time." It's like, just get over yourself. Life isn't just about you. It's about other people, too. You know, people you interact with. And he verbally abuses my mother. Then she'll snap. And then they get into huge fights, and then it's just. . . . My sister [name deleted], she's 3 years younger than me, and we've talked about this a fair amount, and she felt it, too. She couldn't wait to get out of the house. She would disappear all the time just to get away. So, it was just like a pressure to have this façade of the perfect family. And we'd go out, and my dad would be bragging about, oh, look at my beautiful kids, you know. They're good looking, and they're smart, and they're so wonderful. And we would get home, and he would favor my older brother. And the rest of us were just like [*shrugs his shoulders and tilts his head*], "Yeah."

**THERAPIST:** When your folks would fight, did it ever get physical?

**CLIENT:** They would look like they were about to get physical, and they would have this crazy look in their eyes.

**THERAPIST:** Both of them?

**CLIENT:** Yeah. And they would both, it was like they had just enough restraint not to get physical. I remember one time my dad was throwing things at my mother in their bedroom.

**THERAPIST:** Were you present?

**CLIENT:** Yeah.

**THERAPIST:** You were there in the room?

**CLIENT:** I was in the doorway. I was like, 'What is going on?'.

**THERAPIST:** You weren't just hearing it; you were seeing it?

**CLIENT:** Yeah. That's how I know he was throwing things.

**THERAPIST:** And how old would you have been then?

CLIENT: [*Pauses*] I'm not sure. I think that might have been [*pauses*] junior high or high school?

THERAPIST: What do you remember about what you were feeling as this was going on?

CLIENT: My parents are crazy, and I don't understand this. This is nuts. Why are they behaving like this? It makes no sense. They don't need to be doing this.

THERAPIST: Hmm. So those are all thoughts. Do you remember what you were feeling?

CLIENT: [*Falls silent. No response.*]

**AUTHOR'S COMMENT:** He unquestionably demonstrates himself to be bright and articulate, and insightful in many respects. But when asked about feelings, he falls silent. This disparity is a possible sign of *alexithymia*, the difficulty recognizing and verbalizing emotions that is often an expression of dissociation. Recall his account of his difficulty maintaining a stable conviction about what he likes and does not like. Preferences and desires, a key facet of a stable sense of identity, are grounded in an awareness of emotions. If you do not know what you feel, it is difficult if not impossible to form an enduring sense of what you want.

THERAPIST: Would you say that's about the most extreme situation you can remember, or were there others that were that extreme or more extreme?

CLIENT: The screaming. The screaming at the top of their lungs and accusing, that happened a bunch of times. That was typical. You had to like walk on eggshells to try to keep that to a minimum. I mean, that's what you think as a kid. I don't know how much control a child really has over parents fighting like that. You try to as a kid, but they're adults, they're going to behave like they're going to behave. But as a kid, you don't really get that.

**AUTHOR'S COMMENT:** This passage brings us back to his attempt to cope by assuming a stance of maturity that was beyond his age and beyond his developmental capacity. It is like attempting to construct a building without the presence of a foundation. It is inevitable that the structure will be weak and vulnerable to collapse, unable to sustain itself.

**THERAPIST:** Right. So, what would you try to do to. . . .

**CLIENT:** Just lay low. Lay low. Try not to cause any problems. Try not to argue or anything. If I could have just melted into a wall and disappear, I would have. I kind of tried to do that.

> **AUTHOR'S COMMENT:** His attempts to maintain as much peace in the household as possible came at the cost of maintaining his own invisibility and treating his own desires as less important than the preferences of those around him. Combined with a lack of parental attention, this pattern is a powerful precursor to a practically inescapably fragile and indistinct sense of self and of identity confusion. In this respect, dissociation is at least as much a function of his ineffective childhood family context as of the trauma of the ongoing altercations between his parents. He apparently was not consistently attended to or was not encouraged to express himself and what he wanted.

**THERAPIST:** Mm-hmm. I imagine when they had that look in their eyes, they were coming at each other, that you really had no way of knowing, Is it going to get physical at any moment?

**CLIENT:** No, because it looked like it could have every single time.

**THERAPIST:** But as far as you remember, it never did?

**CLIENT:** Right.

**THERAPIST:** But you were thinking, "Oh, this could be the time that they go over the edge"?

**CLIENT:** Yeah, just when you see that look in someone's eyes and they're like snapping, you just don't know how far they're going to go. And they would direct it at us sometimes.

**THERAPIST:** Do you remember what that was like for you?

**CLIENT:** [*Pauses, then no response. Looks noticeably vacant.*]

**THERAPIST:** [*Makes a point to directly engage eye contact while speaking quietly and gently so as not to increase his anxiety*] . . . When they would go for you?

**CLIENT:** I got a little scared, but it's that disconnection thing where I didn't . . . I didn't freak out. I was able to still look at them, and I'm looking at them like, "You are just absolutely out of your mind." Right? And just having a hard time even comprehending that someone could get that far.

*Identifying Complex Dissociation* 215

> **AUTHOR'S COMMENT:** His description implies the presence of a reciprocal relationship between his parents' impulsivity and emotional disinhibition and his own emotional shutdown. The more volatile they were, the more he felt a need to restrain himself to avoid contributing to the chaotic environment in the household.

THERAPIST: What about times when they were charging. Both of them. Both of them? Either one of them would charge at you? Or at your brother and sister?

CLIENT: *I* was more concerned about if they were going to hurt them than me. I don't know. I guess there was fear. But I don't. . . .

THERAPIST: Uh huh. And when you saw one of them charging at your brother or sister, what was that like?

CLIENT: I don't know. Uh. . . . I mean I sort of know of it, but I . . . I've shut all the emotions attached with it off. [*Sounds weepy*] It's like part of me doesn't want to think about it, right?

THERAPIST: Uh huh. So now that you do, you know, think about it a little bit because I brought it up, are you aware of feeling anything?

CLIENT: Just that it's wrong. Like this should not be happening.

THERAPIST: Mm-hmm.

> **AUTHOR'S COMMENT:** His response is typical of people with a dissociative orientation. Although they may behave in a way that indicates the presence of emotion (in this case, weeping), they may seem (and actually be) remarkably unaware of what they are feeling and therefore unable to put it into words. When I asked what he was feeling, he responded with a thought: "That it's wrong."

CLIENT: [*Still sounds weepy*] It's totally unnecessary. I was . . . I can't make sense of it. It's senseless.

> **AUTHOR'S COMMENT:** I have in effect tested the limits to get a sense of what his capacity is to experience feelings and put them into words. It seems fairly clear, at least as it pertains to the particularly upsetting incidents we were discussing, that he is both threatened by and unable to

> directly experience his emotional reaction to these extremely disturbing childhood events of rage between his parents. This type of dual presentation, such as showing behavioral signs of distress but appearing unaware of accompanying feelings, is emblematic of dissociative responding. At this point, it seems best not to push the issue, so I turn to the quality of his memory.

**THERAPIST:** So, let me get back to a question I asked you before. Is there a point in your life after which your memory gets better? [As in] I can remember from this point on, say, pretty much.

**CLIENT:** It's fairly fragmented. I've just been in such a daze like the whole time.

**THERAPIST:** So even now would you say your memory is fragmented and spotty? For now, the recent past. . . .

**CLIENT:** Not as fragmented as the far past. But, yes, there's certain things where it takes me, and I try not to remember, and. . . .

> **AUTHOR'S COMMENT:** His saying "try not to remember" could be taken to mean that he was intentionally attempting to avoid thinking about these things. My reading of what he intended to say based on speaking directly with him during the interview is "try to remember," but he misspeaks—perhaps a kind of Freudian slip.

**THERAPIST:** Are there times when it's the afternoon, and you have a lot of trouble remembering, "What was I doing this morning?"

**CLIENT:** Yeah, it depends. Some days, I'm a little more clear. Some days, I'm more tired and foggy headed, and sort of out of it. I'm on a special diet, and that seems to be helping me get more and more clear. It's the ketogenic diet, so it's the healthy fats and the natural proteins, and low-to-no carbs, and I do better on that. I notice if I have sugar or anything like that, I can actually start to get anxious just from having sugar, and I have no idea know why. I have no idea why, but I'm avoiding that. But sometimes I sabotage myself, and have it anyway. And why do I sabotage myself when I know I feel better not having it? And I know I sabotage myself a lot in a lot of things, like I'll start something and I never finish it. I don't know why.

> **AUTHOR'S COMMENT:** I was concerned by the self-accusatory tone of the term *self-sabotage*. As discussed in Chapter 6, behavior in survivors of complex traumatization that may appear to be self-sabotaging on the surface often has different aims. To explore this area without sidetracking into an intellectual discussion about the matter, while avoiding implicitly validating the term he has used to frame the behavior, I simply reply:

THERAPIST: Okay, so I'm going to use your wording, although I may not agree that we're really talking about sabotage.

CLIENT: Okay.

THERAPIST: But what are some other things, behaviors that you would consider sabotage?

CLIENT: I have intentions of doing things for other people. Like if I'm going to send someone a package, and then I just never do it. And then of course there's guilt that I didn't do it, and it's just like, "Shut up, brain, just shut up, just stop."

THERAPIST: Have you ever intentionally caused yourself physical pain?

CLIENT: No, but I've been suicidal. Although you could, I guess, take me eating certain stuff, because sometimes I get physical pain, and I do it anyway. So, in that way, yeah, I do hurt myself.

> **AUTHOR'S COMMENT:** What he means is that even though certain foods disagree with him, he eats them anyway and considers this as an intentional effort to cause himself physical discomfort.

THERAPIST: What about cutting yourself, burning yourself? [*Client shakes head to indicate "no."*] No? When you say suicidal, can you explain that some more?

CLIENT: In high school and part of college, I just was so miserable I didn't want to live.

THERAPIST: It sounds like this was over a long time. Not, "I want to kill myself right now," but a constant. . . .

CLIENT: Like every day, "I don't want to be here anymore," but somehow making it through anyway.

THERAPIST: How close did you get? Did you ever attempt suicide?

218   *Contextual Trauma Therapy*

**CLIENT:** No. I got close one time. And there were lots of times where I was driving, I was like, "You know, I could just floor it and crash into something, and just kill myself." Lots of thoughts like that.

**THERAPIST:** Did you ever like speed up and then, "Well, maybe not," or. . . .

**CLIENT:** No. But at one point in high school, I was in the kitchen, and my family was out, so I was by myself. And I felt so [*chokes up*] drawn to the drawer with the knives in it. And I started walking over. And, yeah. I was like, "You know what, everything happens for a reason. I must be here for a reason." So, I [*chokes back tears*] didn't do it. But it was very surreal. It was almost like I was doing it, and I had to work really hard to stop myself, because it was like I really wanted to do it, but it wasn't me.

> **AUTHOR'S COMMENT:** What he is describing here could reflect the presence of dissociation in that there is an experience of being on *automatic pilot*, being drawn to act without feeling in control or having a sense of intentionality, and of *being of two minds*, simultaneously fighting the pull toward suicidal action.

**THERAPIST:** Mm-hmm. So that was one of those situations where your body was moving, but you didn't feel . . .

**CLIENT:** Yeah.

**THERAPIST:** [*Continues*] . . . connected to the behavior. Was that the time you mentioned before when you came close to killing yourself, or was that another time?

**CLIENT:** No, that was the one.

**THERAPIST:** And how did you stop?

**CLIENT:** I don't know. I just kind of, I guess, came to.

**THERAPIST:** [*Nods*]

**CLIENT:** And it was sort of like, "Wait a second. Time out. What am I doing here? Whoa!"

**THERAPIST:** So, when you say, "Came to," do you mean up to that point you were blank? Or do you mean that was the point at which

*Identifying Complex Dissociation* 219

you felt you went from automatic pilot to feeling more in the driver's seat of your behavior.

**CLIENT:** I wasn't blank. It's like part of me knew what was going on and wanted it. And then I sort of came to, like "Wait. No. It [*sic*] doesn't want this. This is a permanent decision, and hold on." So, yeah. I would say that's what it was like.

> **AUTHOR'S COMMENT:** This, then, is a dramatic example of something he discussed earlier in the session: an "indecisiveness" about what he likes or wants. From here, we go on to discuss the financial and other stressors in his childhood household. This line of inquiry leads back to the period when the client had been bullied in school. Eventually, he told his father. The client's description of his father earlier in the interview made the father sound largely inattentive to the client, but it was clear that at least in this instance, the client had his father's attention. So, in an attempt to clarify how this situation might have differed from others, I ask:

**THERAPIST:** When he started questioning you about it, what was his tone? What did he sound like when he was asking you?

**CLIENT:** I know it took a lot for him to register, because he was just trying to leave in the morning and it was like, "Wait a second. That's not like my son. Hold on." And I remember, he . . . he was listening, and I think he got like really angry. I remember him saying, I don't know if it was right away, but I remember him going over to the school and yelling at the principal.

**THERAPIST:** What was that like for you?

**CLIENT:** It was kind of, um, kind of mixed, because I was like, okay, maybe . . . maybe I can get out of the situation, maybe the kids will stop, like I was sort of hoping, but at the same time, I don't like it when people yell. So even though my dad's mad, he had every right to yell, I was just sort of like, I hope this isn't going to cause any problems for him, or I didn't know what was going to happen. I sort of was just hoping the kids were just going to stop without having to say anything. So I felt like I was at the breaking point, and so that I had to say something. So, it was, I don't know.

> **AUTHOR'S COMMENT:** It is certainly interesting that he expresses the hope that "this isn't going to cause any problems *for him* [his father]." This seems to be an expression of the parentified attitude he established early in life. Here, he has been suffering mightily, his father is finally noticing and taking a supportive stance toward him, and his predominant concern is whether doing so will be detrimental to his father.

THERAPIST: Were you there when he was yelling at the principal?

CLIENT: [*Speaks in a tone suggesting he is not at all certain*] I think so. I sort of try to see, like what's my memory versus what I've been told, you know? Because it's. . . .

THERAPIST: Uh huh. It's hard.

CLIENT: But um, I remember sitting outside the principal's office. I'm not sure why. I'm not sure if that's that incidence or something else. I don't know.

> **AUTHOR'S COMMENT:** What is being conveyed here is typically dissociative. The recollection of what happened is not entirely obliterated, but important aspects of it are foggy, and he is therefore uncertain about them. This was clearly a significant episode in his life, and yet his memory of it is sufficiently cloudy that he is not sure whether he was present or merely heard about it. This may indicate that the event was so emotionally laden, that is, that he was so terrified of the consequences of his father's behavior, that he responded to the situation dissociatively and therefore was later unable to recall it with relative clarity.
>
> Although dissociation is frequently viewed as rare and exotic, such instances of dissociative experiencing are sufficiently commonplace among people that, in general, they may not seem entirely foreign. Many of us have had the experience of not being sure whether we witnessed an event or only were told about it. The difference is in the frequency and intensity of these experiences, including in situations with enough personal relevance and sufficiently beyond an early age that we would expect to have a better defined recollection.

THERAPIST: When you told him, he registered, he started really paying attention, and then around that time or soon after, he started really getting angry, is that right?

> **AUTHOR'S COMMENT:** Rather than diving into a series of faulty assumptions, I want to make sure that I understand him correctly.

CLIENT: Yeah.

THERAPIST: Were you concerned at all that he was angry at you?

CLIENT: I don't know. I have had a feeling like, "Why didn't you say something sooner?" and that type of thing.

THERAPIST: That maybe he said that to you?

CLIENT: Yeah.

THERAPIST: So maybe you were worried that he was angry that you hadn't said something sooner?

CLIENT: Possibly.

THERAPIST: It's really not clear?

CLIENT: No, that's the thing. It's like, I don't know, I remember being so nervous about finally telling him that I don't know if I registered much after that. I think I was just kind of relieved to get it off my chest.

> **AUTHOR'S COMMENT:** This situation, for both practical and emotional reasons, gives every indication of having been a momentous event for him. His parents switched him to another school, where the bullying stopped. Any yet, as important as the event seems to have been, his memory for it is extremely vague. He makes a point of saying that when he told him his father he was being bullied, his father's anger was scary for him. He found the idea that his father yelled at the principal especially unsettling. And, yet, he cannot remember, although he would have been at least 10 years old at the time, whether he actually witnessed his father yelling at the principal or just heard about it. Although he is able to recall being outside the principal's office, he can't place whether this was when his father was yelling at the principal or another incidence.
>
> What is especially of interest in this interchange is that when I imply more than once that perhaps he was afraid of his father's anger because he believed his father was angry at him, he does not latch onto and go along with this idea. He responds that "possibly" this was the case, but his tone of voice suggests that he was not at all certain that this was his experience. Therefore, although he seems to be dissociative generally

> and his memory for this incident is foggy, he does not react in a way that indicates he is highly suggestible. He is uncertain but is able to maintain his experience of uncertainty rather than allow himself to be swayed by my conjectures. This assumption that dissociative individuals are highly suggestible contradicts the commonly held but erroneous conception that dissociative individuals' memories can be easily distorted. Research findings refute the equation of dissociation with suggestibility (Dalenberg et al., 2012; Dienes et al., 2009; Kluemper & Dalenberg, 2014). In any case, the way that he handled the situation when the bullying resumed in middle school is striking, a marked change from his behavior when he was younger. He transitions markedly from trying to explain away their behavior to embracing his own anger about the way he was being treated.

CLIENT: I got really pissed off at the end of seventh grade, and I was like, you know what, screw everyone. I'm a good person. I don't deserve this. They're just a bunch of assholes. And they're taking it out on me, and it's not my fault that they're miserable pricks. It's not my fault.

THERAPIST: And you came to all of that on your own?

CLIENT: I was just pissed. And I didn't have anything happen over the summer, I kind of just dreamt it out. And then when I came back in eighth grade, there was one incident in the lunch line where they tried to pick on me for peeing my pants in second grade. And I just threw it back at them, and they were kind of like, "Oh. . . ."

THERAPIST: How did you do that?

CLIENT: Um, I don't know. They were like, "Oh, yeah, we were throwing erasers and stuff." And I was like, "Really? You were playing in my pee? That's disgusting guys. Way to go!"

THERAPIST: [*Laughs with conspiratorial delight at the client's ability to rally and stand up for himself*]

CLIENT: Yeah, so I was like, "You guys are disgusting. Are you sure you want to be telling people this . . ."

THERAPIST: [*Laughs again, breaking in*] And that ended it?

CLIENT: [*Continues*] ". . . in public?" 'Cause it was in the lunch line, like other people were hearing, I'm like, "No!" Because I had just had it. "I'm a good person. You guys are just bullying assholes." Like there's no reason, they went out of their way.

> **AUTHOR'S COMMENT:** This is what he is thinking to himself to frame the situation and bolster his confidence that it was they and not he who should feel ashamed.

**THERAPIST:** I'm thinking that would have been very unusual behavior for you before then. Is that right?

**CLIENT:** Right.

**THERAPIST:** And you came to this conclusion on your own. "I don't deserve this. This isn't okay. This has to stop."

**CLIENT:** I guess my patience wore out, because I had been telling myself for years, "They're going to grow out of it. They'll figure it out." They didn't. So that's when I was like, it's been years, seriously [*laughs to himself*]. If you're not stopping, you're never gonna stop, and I don't deserve it, so screw you.

**THERAPIST:** What was that like?

**CLIENT:** When it started, I was a little bit nervous, but I was so mad at that point that I was like, "Bam! That's it. I've had it."

**THERAPIST:** And when you saw, over time, when you saw that they backed off, after that, what was that like?

**CLIENT:** I don't know. I kind of, I was so mad, I kind of expected it. You know?

**THERAPIST:** So, it never occurred to you? . . .

**CLIENT:** . . . I was like, I'm not going to take their shit, I don't care who it is, I don't care where, when. I was just done.

**THERAPIST:** Were you present? Were you really present for that?

> **AUTHOR'S COMMENT:** This may sound like a strange way of speaking, but he unquestionably understands what I am conveying here.

**CLIENT:** I was pretty present. I was really fired up. I was definitely paying attention more.

**THERAPIST:** In general, when you get—would it be fair for me to assume that there are times now when you get fired up?

CLIENT: Mm-hmm.

THERAPIST: Are you usually pretty present when you get fired up?

CLIENT: Yes. Because it usually takes a while, to, I guess, to break through the fog and whatever, and then I get fed up and I'm like, "Oh, my god, I can't take it anymore!" And, yeah, I. . . . [*Voice trails off.*]

> **AUTHOR'S COMMENT:** What he is implying here is that a prominent aspect of dissociative responding for him is that the "fog" has the impact of maintaining an experiential distance from his feelings.

THERAPIST: Can you think of other circumstances that help you break through the fog, where you're more present than usual?

CLIENT: When I have to explain something to someone, it makes me focus and concentrate, figure out my thoughts and lay out the approach in my head, and give it to them in an orderly way, and I have to pay attention to make sure that they're really understanding it, so it's that connection.

> **AUTHOR'S COMMENT:** This is an insightful observation that, independently of the proclivity to dissociate, is a prominent mechanism that operates to make the therapeutic situation helpful. One can mull over a difficulty endlessly in one's own mind and not get far in clarifying or resolving it. But when we are in a position to describe it to someone else to make it comprehensible to that person, we are prompted to think about it and articulate it in a way that can make it more well defined and understandable to ourselves. The sharpened awareness is not necessarily derived from the input of the other person but from the need to express our experience in a way that will make sense to the listener. This is a major contributor to the effectiveness of allowing the process of conceptualization to remain largely under the client's direction.
>
> Later in the interview, I ask:

THERAPIST: How did you do in high school academically?

CLIENT: Very well, and I don't know how, because I don't remember most of what I learned.

THERAPIST: Do you remember taking tests and thinking you didn't know anything and being surprised at the grades you got?

> **AUTHOR'S COMMENT:** This is a phenomenon I have heard described by other dissociative clients.

CLIENT: Yes. There are times when I was like, "Okay, God, if you're up there, I don't know this, I don't remember. I know I studied this information all night, but I don't remember it." And I was just going with what sounded familiar, what sort of made sense, trying to make sense from the question. I was in advanced classes. I don't know how I made it through. I mean, I think I came out ninth in my class.

THERAPIST: Out of how many?

CLIENT: Ninety something. And there were some real brainiacs in my class.

THERAPIST: [*Laughs*]

CLIENT: They're working for the government now. I don't, I just, I don't know. I couldn't even remember. I would walk in the door with the textbook and my notes, saying, "Okay, just hang in there for 45 minutes," because that's how bad my memory was. I just couldn't remember.

THERAPIST: And yet, somehow. . . .

CLIENT: And somehow, I came out with all As and Bs. There were some times where like, I know biology, but that was probably—that and sometimes algebra were like really, really hard for me. Just the memorizing, I couldn't keep up with memorizing. And I was so foggy-headed, I couldn't think through algebra problems. I did a little better, I think, in chemistry. Biology, they were like, "Maybe you should go down to the regular class," and I was like, "No, that's not an option!" [*Laughs*] "No!"

THERAPIST: What was that about?

CLIENT: Well, I think it was a matter of pride but also family expectation.

THERAPIST: Both parents?

CLIENT: Yeah, but my dad was always the one that was the driving force behind everything. And he had to have his bragging rights and all that.

226  *Contextual Trauma Therapy*

> **AUTHOR'S COMMENT:** Toward the end of the interview, after covering more of his history, I ask about elements of the client's current life situation. As we approach the end of our allotted time together, I explore what he has been experiencing in the way of dissociation and distress while the session was unfolding.

**THERAPIST:** On a scale of 0 to 10, with 10 being the most anxious you've ever felt and 0 being completely calm, where on that scale would you say you are right at this moment?

**CLIENT:** I'm very calm. I'd say, 2 or 3, maybe.

**THERAPIST:** Over the past week for the most part, where would you say you've been on that scale most of the time?

**CLIENT:** Most of the time? I don't know. Anxious and calm. Well, most of the time I'm calm because I'm just kind of shut off.

**THERAPIST:** Mm-hmm.

**CLIENT:** There are times where I've been trying to tap into my feelings, like "What am I feeling?" And there are times where I've felt terror. Which shocked me. Just absolutely, just terrified, and I don't know of what.

> **AUTHOR'S COMMENT:** This statement speaks to the power and effectiveness that dissociation can have in insulating a survivor from extreme distress. It is not unusual for survivors of complex trauma to come to the astounding realization that they have lived their lives in a constant state of terror but were almost completely unaware of it because it was contained behind a dissociative barrier.

**THERAPIST:** Mm-hmm. Where would you say the number is then?

**CLIENT:** Ten.

**THERAPIST:** Um, so this week most of the time. . . .

**CLIENT:** This week mostly calm, mostly, um, 2 or 3.

**THERAPIST:** Would you say that was, that this week was a typical week, in that most of the time, in general, you were at a 2 or a 3?

**CLIENT:** Most of the time, yeah. And then some sort of emotion will sort of breakthrough, and I'm trying to . . . to pay attention, just sort of tell myself it's okay to feel even if it's unpleasant. It's normal to feel. I need to feel. I'm a not robot, I'm a human being. It's part of being human. So, I'm trying to talk myself through that and [*pauses*] I don't know. It would be nice if I had a sense of who I am.

> **AUTHOR'S COMMENT:** Both the sense of being like a robot, a sign of depersonalization, and the lack of clarity about who he is, identity confusion, are indicators of a dissociative orientation.

THERAPIST: Mm-hmm. Do you ever find that you're thinking about things that you don't want to be thinking about and you just can't stop?

CLIENT: [*Nods, indicating "yes"*]

THERAPIST: And what sort of things are you usually thinking about then?

CLIENT: God, anything. My brain's always, always going. And I'm always looking at things from different perspectives. It's like I have this perspective, and I have that perspective, and they're all like looking at the same thing, and I hear all these different perspectives. There're [*sic*] times when I'm paralyzed because I can't agree with myself on what I want to do or eat or look like.

THERAPIST: So, it's more like hearing the perspectives than thinking from different perspectives?

CLIENT: I'm not sure. I . . . I'm not sure. It's . . . I . . . it's like one part of me will like the smell of cigarette smoke, but another part of me hates it. I don't understand how I can have such a variance on something that's either you like it or don't. Usually you don't flip back and forth on it. Sometimes I can look at myself in the mirror and be like, "Yeah, this is me." Look again and, "Oh, this is just so wrong." This doesn't, like, "No, I should get a haircut, or. . . ." I've done all these different things throughout the years, like a goatee, beard, trying to find what feels like me and I haven't. . . . I don't know, I mean, I would think, you know, dying your hair should be fun, not trying to find yourself. But for me, it's like trying to find who I am.

> **AUTHOR'S COMMENT:** This preceding passage is a coherent description of identity confusion. This is someone who does not have an enduring sense of self and so, at times, looks in the mirror and does

> not recognize himself or experiences the conviction that what is being reflected back to him is not an accurate image of what he looks like. He is not saying he should get a haircut; rather, he is saying he doesn't look like that. He skips over some words in speaking. If spelling it out, he would have said, "This doesn't look like me. I [should] have shorter hair." The way he expresses this is important because it is the way some people with this disorder would express a disconnect or incongruence between what they are seeing and their self-image, including their idea about how they actually look.

**THERAPIST:** Along those lines, do you ever have trouble deciding what to wear? Do you own clothes that are really different styles and. . . .

> **AUTHOR'S COMMENT:** This experience is common enough among highly dissociative individuals that it is an item on the Dissociative Experiences Scale (Bernstein & Putnam, 1986; E. B. Carlson & Putnam, 1993), a measure of dissociation that has been widely used in research studies on dissociation.

**CLIENT:** There's times where I've come back home from buying clothes, and a couple of days later, I try on something and I'm like, "These pants don't even fit. What frame of mind was I in when I bought something that's the wrong size? I don't . . . I don't get it." For a while, I was just so foggy headed I was like, "Am I shrinking my clothes in the dryer? Like what's going on?"

**THERAPIST:** Does it ever seem like any of these perspectives are giving you orders like, "Do this"?

> **AUTHOR'S COMMENT:** Here, I am looking to assess whether what he is describing is limited to identity confusion or whether it reaches the extent of identity alteration.

**CLIENT:** Yeah, they're like monitoring everything I do. Everything I do, I say, I think, my emotions. "Don't be too exaggerated, don't do this, don't do that." It's just like, I don't know, I think I get overloaded. Maybe that's why I zone out, I don't know.

> **AUTHOR'S COMMENT:** Within a contextual framework, it would be conjectured that this statement is an expression of a habit of self-monitoring that began in childhood as a means of navigating the chaotic family environment in which he lived. The experience of "them" monitoring his behavior, of a sense of self-identities that feel separate from his, might, at least in part, have their origins in this pattern of coping with a highly stressful interpersonal childhood environment.

THERAPIST: Mm-hmm. As far as not being able to shut things off in your head, do you ever find yourself thinking about unpleasant events and not being able to shut that off?

CLIENT: Oh, yeah.

THERAPIST: What events?

CLIENT: I used to like relive when I got bullied, um, rejection. Also things that could happen. I was like, "Oh, my god, I'd be horrified if that happened," and that would go and go and go, and I'm thinking, "Okay, it didn't happen. Relax."

> **AUTHOR'S COMMENT:** Here, he is confirming the presence of the intrusion component of posttraumatic stress disorder.

THERAPIST: So, you're saying "used to." Does that not happen anymore?

CLIENT: Not as much. It still does happen.

THERAPIST: Like what? I'm thinking about events that happened in the past that are unpleasant.

CLIENT: Well, I used to, stuff at school, um, and then....

THERAPIST: The bullying?

CLIENT: The bullying, but also, "Oh, my god, why can't you remember things?" and just beating myself up on this stuff that I couldn't do. It's like I have this part that likes to pick on myself, and then I have this other part that gets really mad.

> **AUTHOR'S COMMENT:** This is the first time he explicitly refers to a "part," possibly suggesting the presence of coexisting and competing senses of self, but this is a term used by people who aren't especially dissociative, too, so this is just a conjecture.

**THERAPIST:** If 0 is totally present and 10 is the most dissociated you've ever been, what number would you say you've been at for most of this discussion today?

**CLIENT:** Ten, the most dissociated, and 0. . . .?

**THERAPIST:** Right.

**CLIENT:** Um, present thinkingwise or present emotionally or fully like, like acting?

> **AUTHOR'S COMMENT:** He seems to be indicating here a divide between thinking and feeling. He can be aware and feel present in one arena while simultaneously being unaware in the other arena.

**THERAPIST:** Across the board.

**CLIENT:** Um, maybe 5. Right in the middle.

**THERAPIST:** And emotionally, in particular?

**CLIENT:** Emotionally, 7 or 8. Like, "No, I'm not going to cry. Just shut it down so I don't [*voice quivers a bit*] break down."

> **AUTHOR'S COMMENT:** Here again, we encounter evidence of a split emotionally between experience and behavior. To the outside observer, he has been on the brink of tears several times during the session, but he rates his level of emotional unawareness during the session as high. This is a key point for clinicians to be cognizant of and remember. One cannot assume from outward manifestations of an emotion that the highly dissociative survivor is registering the emotion.

**THERAPIST:** You have any questions for me?

**CLIENT:** No. I'm just trying to process everything.

**THERAPIST:** Okay. We'll get you a therapist as soon as we can. Has anyone spoken to you about our [dialectical behavior therapy] groups?

**CLIENT:** A little bit. They said it was kind of like a classroom where you learn techniques.

**THERAPIST:** Coping skills. Which from what you're saying . . .

**CLIENT:** [*Breaks in*] . . . I desperately need?

THERAPIST: [*Continues*] . . . you kind of had to figure that all out pretty much on your own. Would that be fair to say?

> **AUTHOR'S COMMENT:** Here, I am looking to temper a possible tone of self-recrimination that might be implied by his phrasing that more effective coping skills are something that he "desperately needs."

CLIENT: Yeah. I learned how to shut down. [*Voice quivers*] That was it.

> **AUTHOR'S COMMENT:** In other words, he had to rely on dissociation as a major, and possibly primary, mode of coping. When teaching survivors how to modulate their dissociative reactivity, this is one of the reasons to emphasize that the objective is to provide the flexibility that comes with reducing their level of dissociation rather than eliminating or "taking away" the capacity to dissociate.

THERAPIST: Mm-hmm. So, it sounds like that would be something that would be really useful for you.

CLIENT: Yeah, as long as I remember to employ them.

THERAPIST: Right. Okay.

CLIENT: Yeah.

THERAPIST: It was really good meeting you.

CLIENT: I'm looking forward to getting some help on this. Thank you.

> **AUTHOR'S COMMENT:** What I failed to do in this initial session that would have been preferable was to ask him toward the end about his vision of what he would like his life to be like in response to treatment. Even if he were unable to summon and articulate a detailed response to this question, it would hopefully prompt him to begin thinking along these lines. The aim is to avoid framing treatment merely as the reduction or elimination of symptoms, but, instead, as picturing and moving toward the life the client would have had if he had been reared in more favorable circumstances.

# 11

# Relinquishing Addictions and Compulsions

*Acquiring Adaptive Coping Abilities*

It is common for trauma survivors generally and survivors of complex traumatization (CTr) especially to rely on addictive and compulsive behaviors (ACBs) as a means of trying to cope with forms of distress. Early childhood trauma has been found to be related to alcohol and drug addiction (Enoch, 2011). Moreover, Sharkansky, Brief, Peirce, Meehan, and Mannix (1999) found that patients diagnosed with posttraumatic stress disorder were more likely than those without the diagnosis to increase their level of substance abuse in response to unpleasant emotions, interpersonal conflict, and physical discomfort.

In this chapter, I delineate how contextual trauma theory can be applied to understanding the mechanisms that drive ACB. I then describe an approach to intervention for addictions and compulsions consistent with a contextual perspective. This approach is interwoven with case examples to illustrate how the intervention is implemented.

## A CONTEXTUAL UNDERSTANDING OF TRAUMA-RELATED ADDICTIVE AND COMPULSIVE BEHAVIORS

At one time, it was assumed that addiction was a process that occurred only in the form of physiological dependence on a substance, such as alcohol or drugs. Increasingly over the past 2 decades, it has come to be generally

http://dx.doi.org/10.1037/0000176-012
*Contextual Trauma Therapy: Overcoming Traumatization and Reaching Full Potential*, by S. N. Gold
Copyright © 2020 by the American Psychological Association. All rights reserved.

accepted that this is not the case. A wide range of behaviors beyond the use of substances can take on an ACB pattern, as acknowledged in the fifth edition of the *Diagnostic and Statistical Manual of Mental Disorders* (American Psychiatric Association, 2013) that includes a behavioral addiction diagnostic subcategory (Kardefelt-Winther et al., 2017). In line with this supposition, following a review of the neurobiology of ACBs, Grant, Schreiber, and Harvanko (2012) concluded that "although different drugs and behaviors can manifest differently in terms of clinical symptoms, research has suggested that substance and behavioral expressions of addiction appear to share a common neurobiology" (p. 132).

In a study of trauma and substance abuse, Delker and Freyd (2014) found that abuse trauma by caregivers particularly in childhood was associated with the use of substances to cope, difficulty recognizing risk, and self-destructiveness. (In regard to self-destructiveness, compare with the construct of "don't deserve" discussed in Chapter 6.) Contextual trauma therapy considers these factors, especially using addictive behaviors as a means of managing distress in the absence of more adaptive coping skills, to be the source of the extensive variety of addictive and compulsive patterns that survivors frequently manifest. The threat-related source of CTr engenders an elevated level of distress that usually is fairly constant. The deficit-related component practically guarantees that the survivor will not have learned productive coping strategies. Between the two, it is almost inevitable that the survivor will rely on the immediate, powerful relief that ACBs can provide as a means of managing distress.

The ACBs that survivors of CTr commonly exhibit include alcohol and drug abuse (P. J. Brown, Recupero, & Stout, 1995; Ouimette, Kimerling, Shaw, & Moos, 2000; Rosenkranz, Muller, & Henderson, 2014), compulsive sexual behavior (Smith et al., 2014), compulsive gambling (Grubbs, Chapman, Milner, Gutierrez, & Bradley, 2018), Internet addiction (Hsieh et al., 2016), and compulsive eating behavior (Imperatori et al., 2016). In addition, survivors of CTr often engage in behaviors with self-destructive but tension-reducing properties, such as nonsuicidal self-injury, and eating-disordered behaviors, such as food restriction and binging. As with any group, when survivors of CTr have progressed in an ACB to the point that it is so out of control as to be life threatening or otherwise a source of serious danger to them, a specialized intensive residential treatment program is called for.

However, in many instances, CTr is associated with not one but a number of such behavior patterns (Carnes & Delmonico, 1996). At the Nova Southeastern University Trauma Resolution & Integration Program, we have often observed that when one such ACB appears to the survivor to be seriously progressing to the point of being decisively out of their control, they are likely to switch on reliance on another. For instance, if a survivor who has been depending on alcohol begins to worry about the negative consequences of their problem drinking, they may instead begin to engage in nonsuicidal self-injury. If that pattern of behavior starts to escalate to the point that the survivor becomes concerned about the potential negative medical consequences of their self-injury, they may turn to sexually compulsive behavior as a means to stress reduction. It is not unusual for a survivor to engage in several of these ACBs simultaneously.

In addition to the tension-reducing or coping functions of ACBs, evidence shows that these patterns of behavior are related to dissociative states. Dissociation has been found to be related to sexual compulsivity (Chaney & Burns-Wortham, 2014), Internet addiction (Caretti & Craparo, 2009), alcohol dependence (Evren, Şar, & Dalbudak, 2008), nonsuicidal self-injury (Evren et al., 2008), and various ACBs in adolescents (Di Nicola et al., 2017). What remains unclear is whether ACBs promote dissociative states, or if dissociation represents a proclivity to engage in ACBs. In an effort to address this question, Penta (2000) compared a group of hospitalized patients with addictive disorders and a control sample without a history of addiction. The addictive sample was significantly higher in dissociation, and their level of dissociation did not significantly drop 1 year into remission.

Regardless of whether dissociation fosters ACBs, is intensified by these behavior patterns, or is not causally related to them, it does seem to impede resolution of ACBs. Somer (2003), for example, found that dissociation was negatively related to abstinence from substances among a sample of patients in treatment for drug addiction. He concluded that treatment outcome is hindered when trauma-related dissociation is inadequately resolved.

## SCAN-R: A CONTEXTUAL TRAUMA THERAPY STRATEGY FOR RESOLVING ADDICTIVE AND COMPULSIVE BEHAVIOR PATTERNS

Due to the evidence that ACBs are aimed at distress reduction because of the complex trauma survivor's ineffective coping skills and that dissociation compromises treatment for ACBs, contextual trauma therapy usually only targets these behaviors once appreciable progress has been made in helping the survivor reduce their levels of distress and dissociation. Clinically, we have encountered extensive evidence that ACBs generally are initiated and carried out in a foggy, dissociative state of consciousness; a subjective sense of operating on automatic pilot; and a tendency to experience amnesia for the details of the ACB episode (Gold & Seifer, 2002).

The contextual trauma therapy approach to treating these patterns of behavior is informed by these observations and is referred to by the acronym SCAN-R (Gold & Seifer, 2002), which stands for select, cue, analyze, note, and revise. In large part, SCAN-R is the application of functional behavioral analysis as an intervention, although it embraces other elements, too. The procedure is an excellent example of a collaborative approach to intervention.

### Introducing the SCAN-R Procedure

Once an addictive or compulsive pattern has been identified and the client has expressed a desire to relinquish it, they are asked to delineate their reasons for wanting to stop engaging in the behavior. The clinician encourages them to enumerate as many incentives for relinquishing the compulsion as they can. The clinician then introduces the procedure by presenting the following introduction (note that the exact wording can vary; the crucial elements are contained in the content):

> You've told me you want to stop doing this, or at least to stop doing it in a manner that is outside of your control rather than a matter of choice. At some point, you may find that you can engage in the behavior in a way that is no longer detrimental to you. We're not assuming at the outset that the objective is necessarily complete abstinence as long as it is no longer harmful to you. [*Note.* If the behavior involves explicit self-harm, such as nonsuicidal self-injury, food restriction, or purging, the goal of moderation rather than relinquishment does not apply.]
>
> In any case, the method we will use to help you address the behavior does not require that you stop doing it. [In most instances, it will be the case that:] You have already tried to give up the behavior entirely many times, and that has not worked. So, we're going to approach this differently. I'm not going to ask you to try to stop engaging in the behavior. All I ask of you is this: Each time you do carry out the behavior, be prepared the next time we meet to tell me—as early in the session as possible—that you did so and be willing to answer any questions I have for you about what transpired. Are you willing to agree to that?

I have not encountered a survivor who declined to participate in this procedure. For many people who have previously been told that a commitment to lifelong abstinence is a prerequisite of recovery, it is often a relief to hear that abstinence is not be demanded of them. An essential aspect of this approach is for the therapist to maintain a nonjudgmental stance. Shame frequently is a major factor in maintaining ACBs. I have often heard survivors who relapse say, "I know you are going to be disappointed in me." Promises to themselves and others to stop engaging in the behavior or to moderate it in some way are repeatedly made and repeatedly broken. To the extent that the addiction is a means of trying to diminish distress, self-recrimination and tension created by failing to keep these promises almost guarantees that the survivor will again engage in the behavior to escape from the resulting shame.

The survivor is not oblivious to the costs of the behavior or its potential dangers. As tempting as it is to address these risks, to do so is likely to be counterproductive. They are already taking themselves to task for failing to resist the pull of ACBs. Criticism imposed by others, especially their therapist, is likely to be experienced as confirmation of their self-perceived badness, therefore increasing their distress and exacerbating their temptation to act on the ACB.

### Beginning SCAN-R: Selecting an Instance of an Addictive and Compulsive Behavior

Once the survivor has struck an agreement with the therapist that they will report any instances of ACB, it is likely that at least one, if not several, "lapses" will have occurred by the following session. The *S* in the SCAN-R acronym stands for "select," which refers to the selection of a particular incident of ACB, is essential to the success of the procedure. It is futile to ask the client about what usually or routinely happens. Much of the point of SCAN-R is that the client does not know what usually occurs. The automaticity of compulsive behavior, which often, at least among survivors of CTr, is preceded by or engenders a degree of dissociation, obscures much of what transpires either leading up to or during episodes of ACB. Client and practitioner therefore must collaboratively identify a particular incident to examine, preferably the most recent incident but, if at all possible, one from the week preceding the session.

### Identifying Cues That Trigger Addictive and Compulsive Behavior Episodes

After selecting an instance of ACB, examination of the incident begins with the gathering of information that might help clarify the elements that prompted the incident. It is best that the practitioner start by asking the survivor when, before engaging in the ACB, it first occurred to them to do so. From this jumping-off point, the practitioner and client trace through the thoughts, feelings, behaviors, and circumstances that transpired until the point at which the client carried out the ACB. Almost invariably, as long as the addiction is active, once the thought to act occurs, it leads to the behavior. Sometimes the progression from thought to action is instantaneous, but sometimes a considerable lag transpires between contemplation and action. When a lag occurs, the information gathered about the incident contradicts the survivor's previous assumption that the behavior is characterized by impulsivity.

### Case Example: Compulsive but Not Impulsive

A heterosexual, male, African American complex trauma survivor in his mid-30s entered treatment specifically to establish the ability to refrain from compulsively procuring prostitutes. He expressed a great deal of disturbance about the impulsivity that he felt drove this behavior. After his therapist secured an agreement from him to adhere to the parameters of the SCAN-R procedure, the client began the next session, which was on a Tuesday, by announcing that he had once again visited a prostitute that week. As is routine in SCAN-R, the practitioner asked him when it first occurred to him to contact a prostitute that week.

The client was able to identify in detail when the first thought about it. It was the previous Thursday night, when he was at a bar having drinks with friends. He reported that he began to feel bored and resolved that he would make a phone call to schedule a meeting with a prostitute as soon as he left the bar. However, when he departed, it occurred to him that one of his favorite television shows aired from 10:00 p.m. to 11:00 p.m., so he decided he would wait until the program was over at 11:00 p.m. to make the call. At 11:00 p.m., realizing that it was a Thursday night and he had to be at work the next morning, he decided not to call. Over the next few days, he made a series of similar decisions to postpone making contact. Ultimately, he made the call and met with a prostitute on Monday night, 4 days after he had originally contemplated doing so. This lag alone helped him to recognize that the "compulsion" to visit prostitutes was not as uncontrollable as he had previously believed.

**Sampling Multiple Instances**

In carrying out the SCAN-R procedure, it is tempting to jump to conclusions. Experience shows, however, that obtaining multiple data points by examining a number of instances of an ACB leads to more accurate, nuanced, and clinically useful conclusions. The objective of the SCAN-R procedure is not to merely garner insight into what drives the behavior but, above all, to provide leverage to stop engaging in the behavior, or to reduce it to a level that is no longer detrimental.

**Case Example: Clarifying the Nature of the Cue**

Deanna, a White woman in her early 40s, sought out treatment for a pattern of compulsive Internet use. She usually had no trouble keeping her time online within reasonable limits. However, at times, she was aware that she felt an urgency to go online, message a random stranger, and engage them in conversation for as long as she could keep them involved. This pattern went on for a protracted period until the early morning hours, when she would finally shut down her computer and go to sleep. In addition to the unreasonable amount of time she spent online and the loss of sleep it caused, she was disturbed that when she woke up the following morning, she had only a dim recollection of the online conversations that had continued until just a couple of hours earlier.

In the session following the one in which the practitioner had introduced the SCAN-R procedure to her, the clinician asked Deanna to identify the most recent time she had experienced a bout of compulsive Internet use. She indicated that it had occurred just the night before and that she had not gone to bed until sometime after 5:00 a.m., even though she needed to wake up and get ready for work that day at 7:30 a.m. When asked when it first occurred to her to go online, she was able to recall that the previous afternoon, she was sitting at her desk at work and felt exceptionally restless and bored. She remembered looking up at the wall clock, noticing that it was almost 4:00 p.m., and feeling as if making it through the next hour until she could leave work and get home would be unbearable. She immediately exclaimed, "That's it! It's boredom that sets it off!" Her therapist, however, encouraged her to reserve judgment until they could examine additional instances of compulsive Internet use.

The following session, Deanna acknowledged that she had spent the better part of two nights that week on the Internet in what, from her description, sounded like an intense dissociative fog. The first of the two incidents had occurred the night after the last session. The most recent one had occurred two nights before the current session. Because it was more recent and she was therefore likely to be able to recall more of it and the circumstances leading up to it, she and her therapist agreed to examine the most recent episode. This time, when asked to identify when she first started thinking about going online in that instance, she remembered that just before it had occurred to her to surf the Net, she had experienced a profound, almost intolerably painful bout of loneliness. Almost as soon as she said this, she burst into tears.

In an account initially punctuated by sobs, Deanna related a series of painful memories of her childhood. She explained that she was an only child and that both of her parents were severely alcoholic. Frequently in the midst of their drinking, they would become ensnared in vicious verbal altercations. Deanna experienced their rageful clashes as so excruciating that she would race out of the house, even in the midst of winter, when it was bitterly cold with snow piled up outside, without stopping to put on a coat. Rather than go back inside to warm up and have to hear her parents screaming at each other, she preferred to remain outside in the freezing weather. She insisted, however, that even worse than the blistering cold was the ache she had experienced of feeling emotionally abandoned, cut off, and alone.

The emotional intensity that permeated these recollections was in stark contrast to Deanna's previous, dryly intellectual formulation that it was boredom that triggered her compulsive online conversations. In addition, there was a clear thematic link between the feelings surrounding her painful childhood memories and the anonymous contacts that filled her hours online. The childhood recollections and the intense emotions associated with them reflected a powerful convergence of experiences of threat (her parents' violent altercations) and experiences of deficit (the neglect Deanna suffered because of her parents' alcohol abuse and preoccupation with their ongoing interpersonal conflict) that had intensely compromised Deanna's sense of self-esteem, safety, and interpersonal functioning. She came to recognize her compulsive Internet activity as a futile and misguided attempt to simultaneously manage and suppress awareness of these painful experiences while trying to obtain the sense of interpersonal connection denied to her throughout her childhood. Treatment, therefore, was redirected to process Deanna's disturbing childhood experiences and actively assist her to remediate her impaired self-image and limited capacity for a sense of connection with others.

In Deanna's case, the intensity of her emotional reaction and the flood of memories that accompanied it helped to quickly bring into focus the forces behind her ACB. In other instances, it may take a client many sessions of reviewing various episodes of ACB to extract and clarify the factors propelling it. The effectiveness of the SCAN-R procedure depends on patiently accumulating enough data to form the basis for sound, reliable conclusions that are informed as much by emotional evidence as by logic.

The characteristics that consistently trigger instances of ACB can vary widely from one individual to another. Even if the practitioner believes they have identified the mechanism that leads to initiation of the behavior, it would be of little use to share this with the survivor. The same principle holds here as that discussed in Chapter 7 on conceptualization. A clever clinician may easily be able to come up with convincing explanations, but even if their conclusions are accurate, they are unlikely to do much good if the survivor is deprived of the opportunity to reach their own inferences that are shaped by their immediate emotional reactions and experiences. The case of Deanna provides a compelling example of this principle. An astute clinician might have deduced from Deanna's Internet surfing, which consisted of engaging in one-time interactions with strangers, that her behavior was driven by loneliness. But if Deanna were told that rather than coming to this conclusion on her own, she would have been unlikely to have the immediate experience of the painful sense of isolation and emotional abandonment that had permeated her childhood, the force behind her ACB, and a motivation to stop relying on it. Although the intensity of her emotional reaction and power of the flood of memories that prompted her realization were more dramatic than most, they illustrate that a therapeutic recognition requires more than a dry intellectual formula offered by someone else.

**Analyzing Episodes of Addictive and Compulsive Behavior**

For Deanna, simply attending to the cues that trigger episodes of her online ACB helped to reveal what was motivating and shaping her it. In most situations, however, this is not the way that SCAN-R progresses. It is usually necessary to explore over a number of treatment sessions the sequence of thoughts, feelings, behaviors, and circumstances that compose one instance of a pattern of ACB after another. The therapist's role is limited to asking the client to provide detail regarding how the particular instance of ACB being discussed in that particular discussion unfolded. Beginning with establishing when the client first thought to carry out a particular episode of ACB, the practitioner then tracks the sequence of events, thoughts, feelings, and behaviors that transpired in sequence until the client carried the ACB out. The aim is to identify the cue that led to the client's thinking about engaging in the ACB and identify the intervening elements that resulted in acting on that thought. Often the trigger for thinking about acting on the ACB and the impetus for carrying it out differ. Again, the understanding is that it is premature to generalize from a single instance that the same precise cue sets the ACB in motion every time. With repeated examination of various episodes of ACB across sessions, enough data accumulate to establish a sufficient foundation of evidence from which the client arrives at solid inferences about what is operating during instances of ACB. To illustrate the complexity that patterns of ACB can take on and the intricate implications they can have, consider the following example.

**Case Example: Behavioral Analysis of an Addictive and Compulsive Behavior**

Emilio, a Latinx man in his early 60s who identifies as heterosexual, had been molested by several men during his childhood and reported engaging in a number of sexually compulsive behaviors. One of these behaviors, as initially described by him, consisted of going to the back of pornographic bookstores, making contact with another man, and engaging in sex with him. The back of pornographic bookstores typically contain private booths with doors that can be locked from the inside. In the booths, one can pay to watch a few minutes of pornographic videos at a time on a screen. Often, men go into these booths together and anonymously participate in sexual encounters.

As Emilio described various instances of this ACB over time as they occurred, several aspects of it came to light that contradicted his initial depiction. It eventually became apparent that every time he entered a bookstore to carry out this ACB sequence, the first thing he invariably did as soon as he walked in the door was to make an urgent dash to the restroom. Although it had never registered for him before that this was an invariant aspect of this ACB pattern, he came to realize that the reason he rushed to the restroom was that once he entered the store, he immediately experienced an intense need to defecate.

After emerging from the restroom, Emilio would make his way to the back room of the store. What he was able to identify during the SCAN-R procedure that he had not noticed previously was that entire walk to the back of the store was agonizing. On questioning, he realized that he felt awkward and embarrassed from the time he left the restroom until he arrived at a booth in the back the store. He was able to articulate that as he made his way to the back room, he was certain that everyone else in store was glaring at him and thinking to themselves how "goofy" he looked and what a "loser" he was.

In reviewing instances of this ACB pattern over a number of sessions, Emilio came to realize that he participated in three different sequences of behavior on different occasions once he entered a booth. In some instances, he would repeatedly pay for a few minutes at a time of a pornographic video, masturbate, and leave. On other occasions, when another man would push open the door to his booth, he would allow them to perform oral sex on him. When that occurred, however, he would inevitably come a point at which he would push the man away, rush out of the booth, and leave the store. In other instances when another man would try to push open the door to the booth, Emilio would forcibly keep the door shut to prevent the other man from entering. After the man gave up and went away, Emilio would leave the store.

**Noting Inconsistencies Between Previous Assumptions and Actual Circumstances**

A major aspect of the effectiveness of the SCAN-R procedure is that it calls the survivor's attention to aspects of the ACB of which they were not previously aware. In a considerable number of instances, the failure to notice what may seem to the outside observer to be obvious features of the ACB seems to be attributable to the presence of a state of moderate-to-extreme dissociation that either leads up to or is set off by the initiation of the ACB sequence.

Often with repetition, inconsistencies between the survivor's previous understanding of what was occurring and the accounts they provide in session become apparent to them without the therapist's pointing them out. In the rare instances in which the survivor seems to remain oblivious to these features after many repetitions, it may be helpful for the clinician to gently question them about the inconsistencies. For example, if, after several iterations of the sequence in the pornographic bookstore described by Emilio, he still did not seem to register the significance of the need to defecate as soon as he arrived, the clinician might have called this significance to his attention: "It seems like quite a coincidence that this occurs every time you go to one of these stores. How might you account for that?" However, the impact and effectiveness are likely to be greater if the practitioner waits for the client to come to recognize incongruities on their own.

**Case Example: Noting Anomalies and Revising Understanding**
Following repeated recitations over time of the pattern of ACB at pornographic bookstores, Emilio came to a number of conclusions on his own. He recognized that the reason for the urge to defecate was that arriving at the store and anticipating a sexual encounter with another man was terrifying to him (as it had been during child sexual abuse events he had experienced). The need to defecate was a bodily reaction to that fear. However, he had not noticed the remarkable consistency with which the urgency to defecate occurred each time he entered a pornographic bookstore. Rather, he had assumed that he was going there because he enjoyed what he was doing.

Similarly, the realization of how self-conscious and humiliated he felt as he proceeded to the back of the store had eluded him until he discussed specific instances of the ACB sequence in session. He eventually was able to identify that the constellation of feelings and thoughts he experienced during this segment of the sequence replicated how he felt as a boy in response to being molested. He had the conviction that other people knew what was happening to him and that they ridiculed and despised him for it.

As Emilio repeatedly discussed the events at the bookstore, the culmination of the sequence and its significance became increasingly clear to him. He had believed that his trips to the bookstore always ended in sexual contact with another man. He came to see that on those occasions when he did allow another man into the booth, they performed fellatio on him—what the sexual abuse he had experienced as a child had consisted of. He never touched those men or initiated sexual contact with them. It was only during the execution of SCAN-R that he realized that when sexual encounters in the booth did occur, he did not have an erection, nor did he experience sexual pleasure. Instead, what he was feeling was mounting terror that paralleled what he had felt during instances of child sexual abuse. It was when the terror rose to a level that he could no longer bear that he would push the other man away and rush out of the store. Although on the surface, the pattern appeared sexual, clearly carnal desire was not what was driving the behavior.

Moreover, he came to understand the significance of the two other scenarios: when he watched videos in the booth, masturbated, and left, and when he pushed against the door of the booth so no one could get in. In both situations, he concluded, he was proving to himself that he could enter into what he perceived as a dangerous situation and keep himself safe. Even when he allowed someone to enter the booth and had sexual contact with him, what Emilio was repeatedly demonstrating was that he could overpower them, stop what they were doing, and get away.

**Appreciating the Effects of SCAN-R**

The case example of Emilio illustrates how divergent the reality of ACBs can be from the survivor's unexamined assumptions about them. In many instances, this discrepancy seems to be attributable to an appreciable degree of dissociative amnesia and automaticity during the execution of these behaviors. Probably one factor that maintains this dissociation is that even when ACBs involve interaction with other people, they remain encapsulated in the individual's inner experience, which the individual almost never discusses with others.

These experiences are autistic—not in the sense of the diagnostic spectrum of autism but in the literal sense of the prefix *aut-* (i.e., auto): They are self-referential and unimpacted by an objective or consensual perspective. This is the reason for the initial agreement that is the foundation for the SCAN-R method. In agreeing to discuss instances of ACB sequences with the practitioner, the survivor permits the conditions to take place that are likely to break through the dissociative lack of awareness characteristic of these behaviors. Each time the survivor repeats an ACB sequence, they know on some level that they will later find themselves back in the clinician's office reporting what has transpired. In addition to the cognitive awareness fostered by revisiting the sequences of behaviors and viewing them from a more objective viewpoint, the simple act of discussing them with another person—making them interpersonal rather than strictly intrapersonal (and, in this sense, "autistic")—helps to shatter the dissociative bubble of unawareness in which they previously persisted.

Ultimately, ACBs are relinquished in response to the SCAN-R procedure because once they are seen for what they truly are, they no longer exert the pull on the survivor that they once did. For survivor clients who undergo SCAN-R not as a stand-alone treatment for ACBs but as one component of contextual trauma therapy, directly addressing ACBs may have been preceded by extended phases of work on reduction of baseline dysphoria and establishment of the ability to modulate dissociation. These capacities provide a solid foundation for overcoming ACB patterns via SCAN-R. Due to appreciable reductions in the intensity and frequency of dysphoria and dissociation, the pull of ACBs has already reduced by the time they are targeted in treatment.

The first of the three phases of CTT aims at equipping the CTr survivor to reduce their baseline level of dysphoria, modulate the inclination to be triggered into dissociative reactions, establish less vulnerability to engage in ACBs, form a relatively resilient bond with their therapist and individuals in their daily life, and logically conceptualize their experience. Once a reasonable degree of stability has been achieved in these areas, the quality of the survivor's present-day existence will have improved appreciably. Their daily life will be considerably more functional and gratifying than when they entered treatment, and their coping skills will be markedly more effective. Thus armed, it is now much more likely that they can enter the second phase of treatment—the processing of past traumatic experiences—in a way that will be productive rather than destabilizing. The next chapter provides a detailed discussion of how to customize Phase 2 trauma processing to optimize the likelihood that it will proceed relatively smoothly and lead to trauma resolution.

# 12

# Resolving Trauma

*Exorcising the Destabilizing Past*

Having covered a wide range of topics on the contextual treatment of complex traumatization (CTr), we now arrive at the subject matter that many assume lies at the heart of trauma treatment: addressing traumatic events and, in doing so, working toward resolution of their enduring negative psychological impact. That this topic appears toward the end of this book should not be taken as an indication that trauma-focused intervention can only be approached toward the latter phases of treatment. Remember, the topics covered in each of the five previous chapters do not necessarily appear in the order in which they are addressed in treatment. That sequence can vary appreciably from one client to another, depending primarily on which therapeutic objectives are most pressing and relevant at any given point in treatment. In complex trauma therapy (CTT), treatment is structured on the basis of a conceptual understanding of the particular client, their history, and current circumstances and difficulties, not on a predetermined sequence or prescribed set of interventions.

Because it is conceptually guided, CTT often incorporates interventions from other treatment approaches to achieve various ends. In this chapter, forms of therapy or components of them specifically designed for Phase 2 trauma processing are briefly described (see also the discussion on phases of treatment in the section The Necessity of Therapist Self-Care in Chapter 6). What appears here are only brief overviews that in no way substitute for carefully reviewing the respective treatment manuals for the forms of therapy before attempting to implement them. The phases of therapy are the general

---

http://dx.doi.org/10.1037/0000176-013
*Contextual Trauma Therapy: Overcoming Traumatization and Reaching Full Potential,*
by S. N. Gold
Copyright © 2020 by the American Psychological Association. All rights reserved.

structure of therapy—three extensive periods of treatment—as opposed to the particular interventions used within each phase. The order in which goals are addressed within each phase and the particular interventions used to achieve those goals vary from person to person based on their individual needs, priorities, characteristics, and proclivities. Even the phases of therapy as not strictly sequential, a point that is discussed in Chapter 13.

The capacity to face and to productively process traumatic experiences that, by definition, were beyond the survivor's capacity to handle when they originally occurred, requires more than the passage of time. In addition, it is not the severity of traumatic experiences or number of incidents alone that dictates whether they are overwhelming. The client's coping capacity is a key determinant. For survivors of CTr, the experiences of deficit that were an integral aspect of their upbringing practically guarantee that their ability to manage the extraordinary stress related to trauma will be compromised. For resolution strategies based on repeatedly revisiting traumatic incidents to be productive rather than detrimental, the survivor must possess the resiliency, stress tolerance, and coping skills to endure confronting the specifics of the events so that they can move toward being desensitized to, rather than overwhelmed by, them. This exacerbation, in turn, can lead to relapse into reliance on addictive, compulsive, and self-injurious patterns of behavior, precipitous premature termination of treatment, or long-standing avoidance of returning to therapy either with the same or a new practitioner.

When and how to most productively approach and initiate the processing of traumatic experiences can vary radically from one individual to another. These determinations are guided by the ongoing collaborative assessment process between client and practitioner. In cases of posttraumatic stress disorder (PTSD), as opposed those of CTr, I have seen individuals in their seventies and eighties with severe symptomatology related to a life-threatening automobile accident or natural disaster rapidly recover from their traumatization in response to exposure-based treatment that was initiated as early as the first session of therapy. Conversely, I have also witnessed people in their early 20s with CTr histories radically decompensate in response to being urged to continue in poorly timed exposure-based treatment in a way that they find reminiscent of their childhood abuse (Gold & Brown, 1997). The case examples of Jeanette in Chapter 1 and Valerie in Chapter 2 illuminate the harm that can be done when a history of trauma and the presence of traumatization are simplistically equated with PTSD, in particular, and when trauma-focused exposure is poorly timed or inappropriately applied.

The processing of traumatic material is not confined to exposure techniques directed at the traumatic event itself but can take a variety of forms. This point is important for two reasons. First, some modes of trauma processing carry little or no risk of setting off adverse reactions in survivors of CTr, even at the outset of treatment. These methods allow various trauma-related psychological difficulties to be addressed without extensive confrontation with and experiential immersion in the traumatic event itself.

Second, depending on the purpose of trauma processing, trauma-focused exposure may not be the most relevant or effective way to achieve a particular treatment objective. Each form of trauma processing has a distinct purpose. This reason illustrates why within the practical Intervention sphere of CTT, practitioners are encouraged to familiarize themselves with a broad range of intervention techniques. Doing so provides the clinician with the flexibility to choose among them and to adapt the treatment approach applied to any given problem to the specifics of the situation and to the individual client's characteristics and proclivities.

In distinguishing among methods of trauma processing, we can group them into three categories listed in order of increasing potential to be destabilizing: (a) cognition-centered, (b) cue-centered, and (c) event-centered. *Cognition-centered processing* approaches are various methods of examining traumatic events and traumatization through a conceptual lens. The purpose of these strategies is to enable survivors to examine the traumatic event and erroneous beliefs derived from it in a rational manner that tempers the intense trauma-related emotions and resulting distortions they can foster. *Cue-centered processing*, like event-centered processing, is exposure based; however, rather than focusing on the traumatic incidents themselves, it targets reminders of past trauma that the client encounters in the present and that elicit PTSD symptoms. *Event-centered processing* is the form of intervention that is most commonly thought of as indispensable to trauma treatment. It consists of exposure-based intervention methods that are intended to promote confrontation with, and desensitization of, vivid, intrusive images, emotions, and sensations associated with the traumatic event. The distinguishing features of each form of trauma processing are discussed in detail in this chapter and are summarized in Table 12.1.

## COGNITION-CENTERED TRAUMA PROCESSING

If managed carefully and executed appropriately, and not conducted in an overly intrusive manner, most forms of cognition-centered trauma processing carry minimal risk of triggering adverse effects, even among survivors of CTr, a relatively vulnerable group. One can usually use this strategy with those survivors in the earliest phases of therapy without undue concern that it will be destabilizing. The key is to empower the client to take the lead and proceed at their own pace in examining traumatic events or trauma-related beliefs from the emotional distance of a cognitive perspective.

### Cognitively Exploring Possible Links Between Present Difficulties and Past Trauma

This form of cognitive processing is aimed at discerning the origins of a difficulty that is targeted for resolution in therapy. Sometimes the origin is traceable to traumatic events. Sometimes use of this procedure can identify other causes unrelated or indirectly related to past traumatic experiences. In either

TABLE 12.1. Forms of Trauma Processing

| Form of processing | Object of processing | Mode of processing | Goal of processing | Typical methods of implementation |
| --- | --- | --- | --- | --- |
| Cognition-centered | The survivor's perceptions and understanding of the traumatic event or distorted beliefs stemming from the traumatic event | Rational analysis based on relevant evidence and logical deduction | To construct a more accurate understanding of the traumatic event or to refute distorted beliefs related to it | Cognitive processing therapy, Socratic questioning, chain analysis, "following the thread" |
| Cue-centered | External reminders of the traumatic event, including situations, people or classes of people, and places and objects associated with the event | Repeated, often graded, exposure to trauma-related reminders (cues) | To extinguish emotional or physiological arousal in response to and avoidance of present-day reminders of the traumatic event | Imaginal exposure, in vivo exposure |
| Event-centered | Thinking about the traumatic event and the images, sensations, and emotions associated with it | Repeated exposure (via overt expression or mental imagery) to the traumatic event or to salient aspects of it | To extinguish arousing, intrusive, and avoidant reactions to thinking about the traumatic event | Prolonged exposure, eye-movement desensitization and reprocessing, traumatic incident reduction, counting method |

instance, identifying a possible historical cause of a difficulty is not predicated on the assumption that addressing the cause is called for to resolve the problem. The purpose of this form of cognitive processing is twofold: It can help the client recognize the reason they are struggling with a particular matter so that self-blame does not compound the problem, or it may help point to a solution. At times, the problem can be strategically addressed independently of its historical origins. In other instances, knowing the source of the difficulty is invaluable in helping to construct a plan of action to resolve the problem.

In the case example of Jeanette (see Chapter 1), for instance, carefully assessing the onset of her difficulties (immediately following her grandmother's death) and their basis (loss of an important supportive figure in her life) would have helped bring into focus that despite her history of trauma, Jeanette's symptoms were depressive ones much more directly related to experiences of deficit (which her grandmother served to buffer and mitigate) than of traumatization related to experiences of threat. It is important that this form of trauma processing be anchored in the present by using the current problem as a starting point without assuming that the cause will necessarily be traced back to trauma. Client and practitioner then work together to "follow the thread" of evidence pertaining to the difficulty and see where it leads, while shunning preconceptions as much as possible. They identify the problem area and explore it without any presupposition of the causal or maintaining factors associated with it. If investigation of the problem by following the thread leads the client–practitioner team back to traumatic material, so be it. If it leads in another direction, that is fine, too. Rather than assume that all the survivor's problems are trauma related, therapist and client simply logically follow the relevant data and see where they leads them.

A contextually based understanding of CTr makes it explicit that not all resultant difficulties are trauma related. Instead, many are consequences of experiences of deficit and resulting developmental, socialization, and enculturation-related difficulties. Still other problems may have antecedents that are neither deficit nor threat related. Staying close to the clinical data and seeing where they lead is a much more reliable and effective way to proceed than assuming that either historical trauma or childhood deprivation are the only possible source of a particular problem and single-mindedly embarking on a fishing expedition to find evidence supportive of that assumption. The following vignette is an example of how application of this approach indicated that traumatic incidents were the original cause of the problem being examined.

### Case Example: Cognitively Identifying the Connection Between Past Trauma and Present Difficulties

Gladys, a White woman in her early 40s, was physically abused throughout her childhood by a rageful, unpredictable father while her mother stood by impassively and did nothing, even when she was in the same room when her husband became violent toward their daughter. Her father's beatings were far from the only adversity that Gladys experienced growing up. He also frequently would come into her room at night and sexually molest her. In addition, her mother did her best to prevent Gladys from making friends so that she could retain Gladys at home as much as possible as her companion. Although she did not protect Gladys from her husband's fits of rage, she seemed to quietly despise him and prefer her daughter's company to his. Nevertheless, Gladys's mother was just as cold and distant as her father and left Gladys feeling isolated and lonely while simultaneously depriving her of access to the larger world outside her family home except during the school day. The combination of violent and terrifying abuse in her childhood household, growing up in an emotionally sterile environment, and relative exclusion from contact with the larger community left Gladys with complex posttraumatic stress disorder (C-PTSD; Herman, 1992b) intermingled with severe dissociative pathology.

Despite the extreme experiences of threat and deficit in her background and the resulting intensity of her difficulties, Gladys steadily made progress in treatment with a CTT-oriented practitioner. Even before this course of treatment, she had maintained steady employment at a large multinational company for many years and functioned well at work. Soon after the course of CTT treatment began, she extricated herself from a psychologically and physically abusive husband who treated her in sexually demeaning ways. She made it through a stressful and protracted divorce and eventually met and married a much more suitable and supportive man with whom she formed a blended family.

At a certain point in treatment, Gladys began to express a disturbing self-perception that she tended to be a "surface person" who never thought about things "too deeply." Her therapist, who had known Gladys to be intelligent and introspective, found this self-appraisal surprising. In treatment, they had held many discussions that exhibited Gladys's ability to think about and discuss matters in a reflective and insightful manner. She was able to note that the college she had attended highly valued logical analysis of the material being taught and the ability to cogently express a line of reasoning. She admitted that this was a capacity that she felt competent at in that setting and for which she had been praised by her professors.

On further discussion, Gladys was able to identify that more recently, she often experienced discomfort with following her own train of thought and interests. She was able to recognize that she felt this discomfort most strongly in the presence of her current husband. On further reflection, she identified that she was fearful that if she focused on what concerned her rather than what her husband wanted to talk about, he would become angry at her and she would be "punished." She then was able to recognize that her determination not to express herself dated back to a constant pattern of interaction with her father. He had consistently referred to the severe beatings he had inflicted on her as "punishment," even though they rarely were related to transgressions on her part. In response to avoid his physically assaults, she had been exceedingly careful to eschew any behavior that was even remotely likely to engender anger in him. She further made the connection that in her dealings with her husband, she had been resisting speaking up due to a pervasive fear that if she displeased him, he would get angry and "punish" her. "Just simply the fact of him being angry is almost paralyzing to me. . . . I feel like a child and that he's right and I'm wrong. . . . ," Gladys said. "I often feel very disconnected from him. This is kind of a new thing. I feel disconnected, I feel unloved, I feel really alone. . . . It chips away at our bond because I don't feel safe."

It was clear to her that her tendency to continually restrict her own behavior and even her train of thought harkened back to the way she had learned to act around her father in a vain hope of avoiding beatings. It also seemed apparent to her and her therapist that revisiting her traumatic experiences with her father did not appear to be the most effective or direct route for resolving her present-day difficulties. She easily became panicky and overcome by a dissociative fog when she thought about his maltreatment of her, and her reflexive fear of anger seemed to now have taken on a life of its own. She had, in effect, developed a phobia of anger, and addressing that fear itself struck both Gladys and her therapist as a more sensible and likely more effective strategy than exposure to the traumatic events that created her fear. They therefore set up a regimen of imaginal exposure that did not target the physical abuse by her father but, rather, Gladys's fear and extreme avoidance of her husband's, other people's, and even her own anger.

As in the case of Gladys, the intervention at which a client and therapist ultimately arrive often directly targets the current problem behavior rather than seeks resolution by somehow addressing historical events or circumstances that first created the difficulty. With Gladys, the objective was to clarify or identify the origins of a powerful tendency to limit her consideration of most matters to a superficial level. Following the thread of her cognitions led, in turn, to the realization that she was capable of examining issues on a deeper level—she had done so in college—but instinctively chose not to. What, then, accounted for her not routinely exercising this ability? Continued investigation led to the awareness that she was holding back intellectually to preclude what she perceived as a high probability that failure to do so would create conflict with her husband. She then was able to identify that this strategy was motivated by fear that her husband would get angry at her if she expressed herself, which was associated in her mind with being *punished*. That term quickly sparked the realization that she was afraid of anger because it was associated in her mind with ongoing, severe physical abuse inflicted on her by her father throughout her childhood, which he had framed as punishment.

Cognitively following the thread helped to reveal to Gladys that the origins of the current problematic pattern of behavior lay with certain aspects of her childhood trauma. There was no way of knowing in advance that this was where the thread would lead. It might just as well have led to factors associated with experiences of deficit in childhood or current patterns in her marriage, or in some other direction. However, by bringing into focus the connection between her current behavior and traumatic experiences in childhood, this analysis provided a cognitive foundation for distinguishing the past from the present. That awareness alone would have been insufficient to extinguish the association of thinking on a deeper level and the expression of her opinions with evoking anger and maltreatment from others, but it did make it clear to her that the difficulty was not of her own making. She and her therapist could then work together to formulate a plan of action to sever the connections that had formed long ago. In this instance, graded exposure to contemporary situations that set off her fear of anger, first via imaginal exposure and then in vivo exposure, seemed to both Gladys and her therapist to unquestionably constitute a more direct and sensible solution than processing the traumatic origins of the difficulty.

Gladys was not at all triggered or distressed discussing her current-day difficulties. She was able to spontaneously relate them to her experiences of intense physical abuse by her father without becoming unduly anxious or disoriented. It was useful for her to have the cognitive perspective provided by the understanding that it was not her husband's anger itself that made her anxious but rather that it acted as a potent reminder of the catastrophic consequences of her father's anger. Directing exposure to a graded hierarchy of present-day, anger-related situations that set off her fear seemed to make much more sense than detouring to the original childhood experiences with her father that were the source of her phobia of other people's anger. Although this was a form of trauma processing, what composed the focus of processing was contemporary problematic situations rather than the direct confrontation of the traumatic events themselves. Reducing her fear of anger emboldened her such that she supplemented individual CTT with participation in a women's empowerment group led by a trauma-informed therapist.

### Identifying and Processing Trauma-Related Cognitive Distortions

A form of cognitive processing that is more directly trauma focused is the identification and disputation of distorted beliefs the survivor holds about themselves in response to traumatic events. Many of these erroneous convictions are variations on self-blame. A woman who was 5 years old when her 40-year-old stepfather molested her may irrationally hold herself accountable and assert beliefs, such as "I must have acted seductively toward him. Why else would he have approached me sexually?" or "I should have done something to stop it." A man who was repeatedly beaten by his mother with extension cords and wooden boards throughout his childhood may insist that "she wouldn't have treated me that way unless I deserved it. I guess I was just a bad kid." Commonly, practically inevitably, someone who was frequently verbally abused by being criticized, cursed at, and belittled may come to believe what they were repeatedly told about themselves, even—as is typically the case—when what they were told was groundless.

Several cognitively based strategies are used to challenge such trauma-related irrational beliefs. One of the simplest and often most effective ones is not to dispute the survivor's assertion but instead ask them to logically defend it. If, for example, they insist that, as a child, they should have done something to stop abuse by an adult, asking them how they would have gone about stopping the abuse is usually inevitably met with an extended silence. I cannot think of an instance in which a survivor who subscribed to the belief that they "should have done something" had ever seriously thought this claim through. A brief period of sober reflection reveals that even now, in hindsight as an adult, they cannot think of a way that, as a child, they could have effectively eluded abuse.

A young child typically has no way to stop an adolescent or adult from overpowering them. Often the belief that they could have done so is motivated by the wish that they somehow could have prevented or stopped the horror they experienced. On an emotional level, they would rather blame themselves than acknowledge that they were helpless and could not do anything to elude the traumatic incident. As disturbing as self-blame is, it is frequently perceived as preferable to facing the limits of their control over external circumstances, and therefore the implication that they are not immune to encountering traumatic events beyond their control again in the future. The price of believing they could have done something to prevent the trauma from happening, however, is guilt and self-loathing.

Essentially the same approach can be used to address similar unreasonable beliefs, such as the conviction in response to childhood physical abuse that "I must have deserved to be beaten." Asking what they did to deserve beatings is again likely to be met with silence or with responses that they find difficult to defend. The same general principle holds here. The survivor would rather believe that there was some obscured aspect of justification to how they were treated than to come to terms with the acknowledgment that they were treated unfairly and likely could have done nothing to stop the abuse.

Self-denigrating beliefs among survivors of complex childhood traumatization can also often be traced to the disparagement they repeatedly heard from a verbally abusive parent, other adult, or older sibling. These are most often self-perceptions, such as "I'm so stupid. I'll never amount to anything," "I can't let anyone get close to me. Then they'll see how crazy I am." or "I'm hideous looking. No one will ever love me." On hearing such pronouncements, an experienced trauma therapist often has the intuitive sense that they are verbal formulas that did not originate with the survivor. They are someone else's words that the survivor now believes and ceaselessly repeats to themselves, and frequently are oft-repeated putdowns by a parent. Somewhat less frequently, they may have been reiterated by an older sibling or, later in life, by a spouse or other romantic partner. Simply inquiring of the survivor, "Did you ever hear anyone else say that about you?" will often elicit an immediate response acknowledging that they heard it said of them "all the time" by someone close to them. That simple recognition, however, is usually insufficient in and of itself to cause the survivor to doubt the belief's validity. They became convinced long ago of its veracity.

Although these recurrent pronouncements usually are unsupported by evidence or logic, the survivor experiences them as compellingly true. The simple repetition of these attacks over time, often for most or all of the survivor's formative years, and the humiliation and shame that these attacks evoke, gives them an emotional power that lends a sense of accuracy to them. They place credence in what they have been told about themselves at least in part because people tend to perceive the emotional intensity evoked by a particular belief as evidence that it is true. Helping the survivor see how baseless these internalized pronouncements are, therefore, often takes considerably more time and effort than distortions consisting of self-blame for their own maltreatment.

One approach is to suggest that the survivor keep two running lists, usually on a single page with three columns. The first column has the date. In the second column is the list for enumerating evidence the client encounters that confirms the negative belief about themselves. The third column is a list of instances that contradict those negative beliefs. It is best to recommend that each day, usually in the evening, the survivor review the day and assess whether there was evidence for and against the self-critical belief that is being targeted.

Once this procedure is implemented, it is important to remind the client to bring the list to each subsequent session until they have become convinced that the self-critical belief is groundless. Although this process may take a few weeks, inevitably, they find that although they have clung to the belief for a long time, the overwhelming preponderance of the evidence refutes its validity. To ensure that the client continues to follow through with the list, it is imperative that the practitioner ask to see it at the outset of each session, which markedly augments the client's likelihood of continuing the procedure. If the therapist finds out on asking to see the list that the client has stopped working on it before coming to a conclusion about the belief, they need to urge the client to resume working on it. The value of this method is that the accumulation of relevant evidence is entirely under the auspices of the client, and therefore the conclusion reached will be a stable one that will be difficult for the client to negate.

**Using a Cognitive-Centered Approach to Process Traumatic Incidents**

Although, in general, cognitive strategies for processing trauma-related material are less likely to carry the risk of destabilization than exposure-based methods, cognitive processing of traumatic incidents themselves can still sometimes be overwhelming for survivors of CTr. In several respects, this approach lies in an intermediate territory between other cognitive processing techniques and exposure because it requires the survivor to focus on and discuss traumatic events themselves. Nevertheless, cognition-centered processing of traumatic events is not as potentially destabilizing as event-centered exposure techniques in that the survivor examines the trauma from the distance provided by an intellectual perspective that does not require discussing the event in great experiential detail. The point of event-centered exposure, in contrast, is to confront as directly as possible the disturbing emotions and sensations that accompanied the traumatic event.

**Case Example: Cognitive Processing of a Traumatic Incident**

Donnie, a White male who grew up in the Midwest, was in his mid-30s when he began therapy. Although his immediate reason for seeking treatment was a serious addiction to painkillers, he was aware that his reliance on drugs began in response to the emotional anguish created by a brutal rape in his mid-teens. Donnie reported that he had always felt distant from and unloved and unprotected by his family. From childhood onward, he had felt socially awkward and had difficulty making friends. He therefore was elated when, in his first year of high school, Edward, a senior, took him under his wing. They began hanging out together, and gradually Donnie met Edward's circle of friends and was regularly invited to join them when they got together. Usually, they would all get together in the finished basement of Donnie's house and sit around, drink beer, and talk. On occasion, after a few beers, they would begin engaging in horseplay and wrestle with each other. For several months, things continued in this fashion.

For the first time in his life, Donnie finally felt a sense of acceptance and belonging he had always longed for but had never experienced. He saw Edward not just as a friend but as an older brother and mentor around whom he felt safe, protected, and valued. Over time, this perception began to give way to a vague sense that Edward, because he was older, more worldly, and more popular than Donnie, enjoyed a feeling of superiority over him and in subtle, initially hardly noticeable, ways took advantage of him and made fun of him when his other friends were around. In general, Donnie did his best not to pay much attention to these suspicions. He told himself that he was being paranoid because he was not used to acceptance. Perhaps, he thought, it could be chalked up to his inexperience socially; maybe he just did not realize that this was a kind of competitive aura through which guys related to each other, like the wrestling that their get-togethers almost always culminated in.

One Friday afternoon, just as he had done many Friday afternoons before, Donnie went over to Edward's house after school. It was one of the occasions when it was just the two of them hanging out, drinking beer, and talking. After a few beers, Edward began horsing around and wrestling with Donnie. It was nothing unusual—just a routine that they had shared many times before. But as the wrestling continued, Edward seemed to be more forceful than usual, and Donnie grew uncomfortable and apprehensive. In a flash, Edward had him down on the floor and was tugging Donnie's pants down. In a mixture of confusion and panic, Donnie began violently struggling. Before he could fully register what was happening, Edward was anally raping him.

Donnie woke up the following morning in his own room and unable to remember how he had gotten home. Perhaps he should have been angry, but all he felt was a burning sense of shame. He avoided Edward for the rest of the year, and was relieved to hear that Edward had left for college early and enrolled in summer semester classes.

Years later, in treatment for his opioid addiction, Donnie had difficulty giving his therapist any more details beyond blurting out that he had always had trouble making friends, and that when he did begin hanging out with other guys in high school, one of them had raped him. Donnie's discomfort with the matter was apparent to the therapist, so she made a point not to probe any further. Instead, she nonverbally showed sufficient interest and concern to make it clear to Donnie that she would be open to hearing more when and if he wanted to discuss the matter further. The immediate focus of treatment was helping Donnie overcome his abuse of painkillers. Poking around in a sensitive area that Donnie clearly did not want to elaborate on would only make it harder for him to stop using drugs or, worse, might lead him to intensify his drug use or prematurely terminate treatment.

When Donnie felt secure in his abstinence from opioids, was doing better at work, and was no longer socially isolating himself, he decided he was tired of carrying around the specifics the rape to himself. The worst part, he told his clinician, was that it was his own fault. Why didn't he get out of there before Edward attacked him? The therapist was attentive, but said little—just enough to signal to Donnie that she was listening and to convey in her tone of voice and expression that she could resonate with what he was experiencing. It was clear to her that he had never told anyone about this incident before. He needed time and space to sort things out without interference.

A couple of sessions later, a profusion of his jumbled thoughts and emotions about the rape tumbled out, as if the door of an overstuffed closet had sprung open. Did he somehow want the rape to happen? That did not make sense to him. It was unquestionably the worst moment of his life. But he had seen all the signs. For a long time, he felt a sense of discomfort around Edward, but he had ignored those feelings. That afternoon, when Edward had begun wrestling with Donnie and started to become so aggressive, why did he stay put like a sitting duck and allow himself to be raped? Was he so afraid of being friendless again that he was willing to pay the price of being assaulted to continue to be included by Edward and his friends?

When Donnie seemed ready, his therapist asked if he felt up to describing what had led up to the rape. He nodded his assent, and she asked him to walk her through what happened from the time he and Edward left school that day. She left the level of detail up to him. When he got to the moment when Edward began to shove him down to the floor and he realized that Edward was no longer horsing around, Donnie suddenly fell silent. He had a slightly puzzled expression on his face, his head was down, and his eyes darted around. The clinician said nothing. She could see he was piecing something together and needed time to let things come into focus. Eventually Donnie lifted his head and looked at her. The tension and shameful expression that was there a few minutes ago was gone. "I didn't know," he said softly, almost in a whisper. "I had no idea what was coming. There was no way to know. By the time I knew what was happening, it was too late."

Although Donnie was thinking and talking about his rape trauma, he was doing so in a primarily intellectual way rather than discussing the moment-to-moment experiential details of the assault itself. He was trying to figure out why he had not gotten himself away from Edward before the rape occurred. Like many, probably most, sexual assault survivors, he had never told anyone what had happened in much detail. Close to 15 years had elapsed between the rape and telling his therapist about it. Her single question about the events leading up to the assault turned out to be all Donnie needed to answer his own question. He had viewed the incident from a position of hindsight, knowing how it ended. Until he discussed what had happened out loud to someone else, it had not occurred to him that at the time it was happening, he had no idea where things were headed. He had no reason at the time, he realized, to suspect that he was about to be sexually assaulted.

It might seem to some that, in effect, Donnie's therapist did next to nothing here and that it was simply fortunate that Donnie decided to open up and came to the conclusion that he did. As obvious as Donnie's realization might seem, it would not have been helpful if his therapist had simply told him that he had no way of knowing what was coming. She was wise to step back instead and let him sort it out. If she had done otherwise, rather than being reassured, he might well have construed her explanation as an attempt to let him off the hook. He is likely to have seen it not as an explanation but as an excuse for his failure to take action and an attempt to explain that away.

By allowing him the space to figure things out on his own, the clinician ensured that Donnie's deduction was infused with an air of being indisputable. It was fortunate that he arrived at a resolution so quickly. The rapidity with which he was able to settle the matter was certainly unusual. In most instances, it would have taken more than a single session to realize what Donnie did about the situation. But trying to rush things in the hope of providing him with relief by offering a conclusion to him, no matter how well founded, would have robbed him of the certainty he felt by finding the answer himself to the question that had troubled him for so long.

**Cognitively Identifying Current Reverberations of Trauma's Impact**

Another instance in which trauma processing is likely to be beneficial, even once PTSD symptoms have subsided, is when client and therapist deduce that persisting difficulties are related to the content of traumatic events. In such instances, the client's trauma-related symptoms appear to be largely resolved. Nevertheless, it may be clear that problems persist in areas such as sexual activity, excessive expressions of or avoidance of anger, or a sense of vulnerability. When these areas of difficulty are clearly associated with what occurred during traumatic incidents, examining these occurrences is likely to yield a better understanding of what underlies the problem areas and how to address them therapeutically.

This process usually starts with identification of a problem occurring in the present that brings up associations to childhood experiences of threat. Examination of these traumatic experiences then help to clarify the origins of the problem and help to draw attention to a reasonable strategy for resolving the present-day difficulty. Often the more obvious and direct approaches are present oriented rather than center on extensive processing of traumatic events in the past.

**Challenging Unhelpful Beliefs Using Cognitive Processing Therapy**

A clearly structured approach to cognition-centered trauma processing is *cognitive processing therapy* (Resick, Monson, & Chard, 2017), a 12-session manualized treatment approach primarily aimed at targeting trauma-related cognitive distortions in a systematic fashion. Clients are taught how to identify and challenge maladaptive beliefs about the traumatic event and their reactions to it. The objective is to not only help survivors accomplish this process of identifying and challenging during treatment but to acquire a skill they can continue to apply following termination. During therapy, challenging trauma-related cognitive distortions is sequentially applied to a series of specific areas, such as trust, safety, and intimacy.

Originally, cognitive processing therapy included event-centered processing that consisted of writing out a detailed account of the targeted traumatic incident between sessions and then reading it aloud in the following session. However, more recently, this element is sometimes omitted from cognitive processing therapy so that cognition-centered processing is almost exclusively the focus of therapy.

## CUE-CENTERED TRAUMA PROCESSING

In cue-centered trauma exposure in contrast to event-centered trauma exposure, the survivor repeatedly and progressively intentionally pictures or behaviorally approaches cues of the traumatic event (i.e., desensitization to external reminders). Cues might consist of locations (e.g., for someone who was in a plane crash, being near or in an airport), activities (e.g., for someone who was in a rollover car accident, driving), people (e.g., someone who physically or behaviorally resembles an assailant), objects (e.g., for a shooting victim, a gun), or situations (e.g., for someone who has survived a hurricane, being outside away from shelter when it is cloudy).

The graded exposure cue-centered procedure is similar to classic systematic desensitization. In imaginal exposure, the client pictures each item on the hierarchy, starting with the lowest rated, and working up until that item no longer elicits distress. In in vivo exposure, the client behaviorally approaches or engages in each item until it no longer elicits distress. The major difference is that classic systematic desensitization as originally designed includes training in a distress reduction technique. After each round of imaginal exposure, the client uses a relaxation technique to reduce any distress evoked by picturing or approaching the disturbing item. Graded exposure, though, does not include use of a relaxation technique. The client simply imagines or engages in the item repeatedly until it no longer elicits distress.

Cue-centered trauma processing tends to carry much less risk of counter-therapeutic reactions than event-centered trauma exposure probably because the targets of exposure are cues associated with the trauma but not the traumatic event itself. That it carries less risk is also probably because the procedure is graded from least to most distressing. In approaches to event-centered exposure, such as prolonged exposure (PE; Foa, Hembree, & Rothbaum, 2007), the trauma narrative in its entirety is the target, which therefore has a higher likelihood of being overwhelming.

## EVENT-CENTERED TRAUMA PROCESSING

When people think of trauma processing, what they commonly have in mind and what is widely regarded as the essence of trauma treatment are interventions entailing exposure to recollections of the traumatic event. In contrast to cognition-centered processing, which focuses on arriving at a rational understanding of the traumatic event or disputing distorted beliefs that evolved from it, event-centered exposure techniques consist of overt expression about or mental concentration on the event. In some approaches, the focus of concentration is on the entire sequential narrative of the traumatic event; in others, it is on salient aspects of the traumatic experience.

The underlying principle is that the adverse psychological consequences of traumatization are perpetuated (or even intensified) when thinking about the event or when the survivor avoids encountering external reminders of the event. By systematically and repeatedly being exposed to details of the event (in the case of event-centered trauma processing) or external reminders of the event (in the case of cue-centered trauma processing), the association of the event with danger is progressively dissipated, and posttraumatic stress reactions are extinguished. In effect, what is being extinguished is the fight–flight–freeze response reaction to thoughts and reminders of the traumatic event.

### Timing: Client Readiness for Event-Centered Trauma Exposure

When, then, is it time for survivors of CTr to engage in intensive trauma work? How can we know that they are ready? What can clinicians do to augment and assess clients' preparedness to productively process traumatic material? The combination of deprivation and traumatization that characterizes CTr necessitates careful consideration of what functional capacities, especially coping abilities, need to be in place to maximize the likelihood that trauma processing is beneficial rather than detrimental. Generally speaking, bolstering resiliency is a higher priority than, and often a prerequisite for, productive trauma processing in cases of CTr.

It is not unusual for survivors of CTr to rely on one or more forms of addictive and compulsive behaviors as a means of attempting (often unsuccessfully) to manage their distress and suppress intrusive recollections of traumatic events. These behaviors could include any of the dysfunctional patterns addressed in the previous chapter. Before initiating exposure procedures, the practitioner should engage in a concerted effort to assist the client in reducing their dependence on these strategies and, at minimum, substantially diminish the frequency and intensity of these patterns. Failure to help the client moderate, if not eliminate, regular reliance on these behaviors before starting a course of trauma exposure is highly likely to trigger relapse and marked intensification of addictive and compulsive patterns without any gains in trauma resolution.

Similarly, some survivors fairly consistently present with multiple episodes of crisis when they first begin treatment. They may report spikes in suicidal ideation or attempts; bouts of nonsuicidal self-injury; eating-disordered behaviors, such as restricting or purging; or episodes of intense interpersonal conflict up to or including physical violence. As with addictive and compulsive behaviors, presentations of this type are contraindications for entry into a course of trauma-focused exposure. Initiating exposure when the client is susceptible to crises due to a relative lack of effective coping skills does not result in a reduction in the intensity and frequency of these occurrences; instead, it certainly leads to an increase in both their rate and severity, again without progress toward resolution of traumatization.

A positive sign that treatment has reached a juncture at which trauma exposure is likely to be productive is that a confluence of indicators suggest that the client has achieved stabilization. Even though trauma-related symptoms may persist, the client has consistently demonstrated the capacity to regulate affect, restrain destructive impulses, and maintain a reasonable degree of focus and awareness (i.e., disrupt, or at least modulate, dissociative reactions) under stressful conditions. In the absence of these abilities, trauma exposure is likely to exacerbate rather than lead to resolution of traumatic stress. In effect, the attainment of these proficiencies places the survivor in a position of psychological parity with clients with "simple" PTSD in that the relative absence of these abilities is a common consequence of the experiences of deficiency associated with the disturbances in self-organization (DSO) component of CTr.

Recent research on complex trauma that distinguishes deficit-related DSOs from threat-related PTSD symptoms offers a powerful rationale for the long-standing caveat by trauma specialists that to benefit from trauma processing, survivors of complex trauma must first be provided with an often extended period of treatment aimed at stabilization (Gold & Brown, 1997; Gomez-Perales, 2015; Herman, 1992b). The purpose of the stabilization phase is to appreciably reduce the severity of DSOs, which otherwise not only undermine attempts at trauma resolution via exposure but in all likelihood cause them to backfire.

The timing of trauma processing, then, is not determined by the clock, calendar, or number of sessions that have accumulated but is based on the client's level of resilience and readiness. Trauma survivors with PTSD of mild to moderate severity are more likely to have the emotional hardiness to successfully undergo exposure relatively early in treatment—in some instances, as soon as the first session. Those with CTr, in contrast, are much less likely to be equipped to do so. The DSO aspects of CTr—emotional dysregulation, negative self-image, and disturbances in relationships—appreciably heighten the probability that trauma exposure will trigger addictive and compulsive, self-destructive, dissociative, or interpersonally conflictual reactions to exposure that interfere with its effectiveness and exacerbate rather than ameliorate problems in adjustment.

### Rationale: Is Event-Centered Trauma Exposure Indicated?

As seen in the case of Jeanette (see Chapter 1), in instances in which CTr encompasses symptom patterns other than PTSD (in her case, experiences of threat were associated with depression rather than PTSD), regardless of timing, trauma exposure is not only irrelevant but may do more harm than good. Trauma exposure techniques are not necessarily indicated for all forms of reaction to experiences of threat but are indicated for specifically targeted PTSD-related symptoms. Therefore, if a survivor of CTr originally met diagnostic criteria for C-PTSD, and PTSD symptoms remain, once substantial progress has been made toward resolving DSOs, exposure techniques are likely to be indicated.

By this point in treatment, the survivor who began therapy with C-PTSD may not only have overcome DSOs to a considerable extent but also may no longer be plagued by intense avoidance or chronic arousal symptoms. However, when in the presence of cues associated with the traumatic events in their history, they still may be susceptible to intrusion symptoms, such as flashbacks, nightmares, or physiological and emotional reexperiencing. In these instances, exposure treatment is strongly recommended.

Even when PTSD symptoms are relatively mild or may seem to have ceased altogether, event-centered trauma processing may be helpful if aspects of the trauma continue to seem unresolved. One instance in which event-centered trauma processing may be indicated is when client and therapist deduce that persisting difficulties are related to the content of traumatic events. Depending on the nature of the trauma, these problems may be in areas such as sexual preoccupation or activity, excessive expressions of or avoidance of anger, or an enduring sense of vulnerability. When the difficulty is clearly associated with what occurred during traumatic incidents, examining these occurrences likely yields a better understanding of what underlies the problem areas and how to address it therapeutically. Closer cognitive exploration of the relationship between past traumatic experiences and the current difficulty helps clarify whether present-oriented intervention for the problem itself, cognition-centered processing, cue-centered process, or event-centered processing is most likely to be effective.

Once it has been established that the client is stabilized, has acquired adequate coping skills, and can benefit from event-centered trauma exposure, a procedure designed for this purpose can be safely initiated. When these three conditions have been met, the same interventions that may have led to decompensation earlier in treatment are likely to instead foster trauma resolution. Of the number of approaches to event-focused trauma exposure, four are discussed here. Given the importance of tailoring interventions to the particular needs and characteristics of the individual survivor, once therapist and survivor conclude that event-centered trauma exposure is indicated, they should jointly consider which procedure is most appropriate before proceeding.

## Prolonged Exposure

The most widely researched and generally most highly regarded event-centered exposure method is PE (Foa et al., 2007). A highly structured, manualized treatment of nine to 12 sessions, PE combines imaginal exposure to a detailed account of the traumatic event with in vivo exposure to trauma-related cues, often referred to as *triggers*. As described in the section Event-Centered Trauma Processing, the survivor repeatedly describes the original traumatic event in session while simultaneously progressively exposing themselves to cues outside of therapy.

In Session 3 of the nine- to 12-session PE treatment, after receiving an explanation of the rationale for the imaginal exposure procedure, the client begins recounting the traumatic event to the therapist in session. In addition, the session is audio recorded, and the client is instructed to listen to the recording at least once a day every day until the following session. In effect, then, the survivor is confronting the narrative of the traumatic situation on a daily basis. At the same time, they are progressively approaching external reminders of the traumatic event outside of session. This dual exposure—to the trauma narrative in session and cue-centered exposure outside of session—continues in Sessions 4 through 8. In Session 8, the client is administered the Posttraumatic Diagnostic Scale (PDS; Foa, Cashman, Jaycox, & Perry, 1997), a measure of PTSD symptom severity. If the score on the scale reflects that PTSD symptoms are below the diagnostic cutoff score, then treatment ends in Session 9. If the score is higher, then treatment continues for another three sessions, and the same interventions used in Sessions 3 through 8 are repeated.

One alternative to PE is eye-movement desensitization and reprocessing (EMDR; Shapiro, 2017). Unlike PE, EMDR does not require that the survivor review the entire traumatic event. Instead, the survivor attends to salient features of the event. Therefore, EMDR may be more appropriate for clients for whom the detailed trauma narrative in its entirety might be overwhelming.

## Eye-Movement Desensitization and Reprocessing

EMDR (Shapiro, 2017) is another widely used exposure-based approach for resolving PTSD symptoms.[1] Exposure in EMDR is not applied to the entire

---

[1] EMDR is a multiphase treatment that is much more extensive than reflected in the description here, which pertains exclusively to the trauma processing phase of this approach.

trauma narrative but, rather, to key elements of the traumatic incident. The client identifies an image, an emotion, and a sensation that was especially salient for them during the traumatic incident. For instance, someone who was sexually molested as a child might isolate the image of the assailant looming over them, the emotion of fear, and the sensation of the assailant's breath on their face. These three components of the traumatic situation are the focus of processing along with a fourth component, a negative cognition associated with the event.

EMDR (Shapiro, 2017) aims to both desensitize the survivor's distress-related reactions to the traumatic event and hasten cognitive processing of the trauma. The negative cognition provides a means of assessing progress in cognitive processing. It is elicited by asking the client, "What does the [traumatic] incident say about you as a person?" The aim is to capture the survivor's critical self-appraisal in response to the trauma. Common responses might include, "It says I can't protect myself," or "That I am weak." The client is also asked to formulate an alternate, positive cognition, that is, what they would like to believe instead. Often it is the opposite of the negative cognition, such as, "I am able to protect myself."

Before initiating the EMDR processing procedure, the practitioner asks the client to provide three ratings, usually on a scale of 1, the lowest, to 10, the highest, of their level of (a) subjective distress when thinking about the traumatic event, (b) belief in the negative cognition, and (c) belief in the positive cognition. These three indices are a means of assessing the progress of trauma processing. They enable the practitioner and client to track the degree to which trauma-related distress is diminishing, belief in the negative cognition is lowering, and belief in the positive cognition is increasing.

Processing begins by using one of a number of possible forms of stimulation while the client attends to the trauma-related image, emotion, sensation, and negative cognition. The original mode of stimulation, reflected in the name of this form of therapy, was eye movements. In this form of stimulation, the client gazes from side to side in rapid succession (guided by the therapist, who moves their finger side to side or moves a point of light back and forth horizontally) while thinking about the four elements of the trauma.

The eye movements were originally thought to hasten both desensitization to the distress associated with the traumatic event and processing of the survivor's negative self-appraisal in relation to the event. It was later proposed that any type of bilateral stimulation serves the same purpose (Shapiro, 2017). Modes of sensory stimulation other than eye movement that are now used in EMDR include alternately tapping both sides of the body (e.g., the right and left knees) or alternately presenting finger snapping or other sounds to the right and left ears (Shapiro, 2017).

Following each series of eye movements, the clinician asks, "What are you noticing now?" or some slightly alternately worded variant of that question. (The implication of this inquiry is that a progression has occurred, so the client is now experiencing something other than the original conglomeration of image, emotion, sensation, and negative cognition.) The client's response becomes the focus of the next round of stimulation. Processing is considered to be complete when the client experiences a sense of resolution, the 10-point distress level is down to a rating of 2 or below, belief in the negative cognition is no higher than 3, and belief in the positive cognition is 7 or above.

Yet another event-centered form of trauma processing is traumatic incident reduction (TIR; French & Harris, 1998). Like PE, TIR consists of a repeated review of the entire trauma narrative. Unlike PE, the process of review is much more under the control of the client, and cue-centered exposure is not part of the procedure.

**Traumatic Incident Reduction**

Traumatic incident reduction (French & Harris, 1998) is not as well-known and therefore not as widely used as PE and EMDR, but it possesses several features that make it especially compatible with a contextual treatment approach. In essence, TIR consists of having the client silently review the traumatic incident, as if they were watching a video, and then describing out loud to the therapist what they just observed. As soon as the survivor has finished describing the event to the practitioner, they repeat the sequence of mentally tracking in silence what happened during the traumatic event from start to finish; they then retell that sequence. This cycle of viewing and recounting is repeated as many times as necessary until thinking about the incident no longer elicits distress. The practitioner assesses this outcome by periodically asking the client, "How does the incident seem to you now?" and by asking them to identify their Subjective Units of Distress Scale (Wolpe, 1958; see also Chapter 8, this volume) level intermittently during the procedure.

A feature of TIR that is especially consistent with the CTT perspective is that, to a large degree, it is client directed. While the client cycles between recollection and retelling, the practitioner does not ask questions or encourage discussion. Furthermore, the practitioner does not probe for or encourage disclosure of more details than the client is spontaneously reporting. It is left to the survivor to determine how much or how little to say, and only the survivor decides the level of specificity with which they silently recall the traumatic event. A situation that was by definition outside of the client's control is processed in a manner that is very much under their control.

Something about TIR that impresses me is the remarkably consistent manner in which clients describe reaching a point of trauma resolution. It is sometimes difficult for survivors to imagine that they could possibly overcome traumatization without somehow obliterating their recollection of the trauma. If there is no way to undo what happened, they think, how could the fallout from such a powerful event be neutralized? Frequently, when TIR is completed, clients signal this completion by saying, almost word for word, that the traumatic event "seems just like any other memory." What they mean is that they can think about the trauma without it's evoking the experiences of revivification and intensely disturbing emotions that had before.

They may still have feelings about the event, just as they might about other occurrence, but they are not disruptively overwhelmed by it.

Like PE and TIR, the counting method of event-centered exposure consists of review of the entire event. As described in the next session, it differs in that the review process is structured to occur in fast-forward as a means of titrating the impact of exposure. This can make this approach a particularly suitable one for survivors of CTr.

**The Counting Method**

The counting method (Ochberg, 1996) is an approach to event-centered trauma processing that is explicitly designed to moderate the impact of exposure to make it easier for the survivor to tolerate the procedure and thereby to reduce the likelihood of adverse effects. While the client is mentally reviewing the traumatic event, the practitioner counts from 1 to 100, with an approximate 1-second interval between numbers. The client is asked to time the speed at which they mentally viewed the incident so that they reach the conclusion of the event by the time the clinician reaches the end of the count. After reaching 100, the therapist is initially silent to allow the client to express whatever occurs to them. If the client does not say anything for several minutes and does not appear to be about to speak spontaneously, the clinician then asks them to recount what they just remembered.

The technique of counting to 100 is presumed to have several salutary effects (Ochberg, 1996). While the client is reviewing the past, the counting method helps them to stay oriented to the present so they are not pulled into reexperiencing the past. And rather than picturing the event in silence, hearing the count helps the client simultaneously attend to the therapist. Reaching the end of the event by the time the practitioner hits 100 also requires the client to time the recall of the trauma memory at a prescribed pace that necessitates picturing it in sped up, fast-forward fashion. In addition, as the count gets increasingly closer to 100, the client has the reassurance that cessation of the period of exposure to mentally reviewing the traumatic event is approaching. All of these aspects of counting help to moderate the impact of focusing on the traumatic incident and thereby make it less likely that the client is overwhelmed by thinking about it.

After mentally reviewing the event, the client has the opportunity to discuss whatever occurred to them when they pictured and then described the incident. Toward the end of the session is a period of debriefing during which therapist and client consider what was accomplished during the recall, report, and discussion process. Ochberg (1996) emphasized that it is important that the client leave the session feeling positive about the session and what they achieved.

As mentioned previously in this chapter, it is crucial that therapists thoroughly familiarize themselves with these differing methods of event-centered trauma processing by following their respective procedures closely. Once the practitioner has applied the each of the models as written with several CTr survivors, however, it may be desirable to be more flexible in their application. Considerations in approaching event-centered trauma processing in this way are discussed in the following section.

**A Contextual Perspective on Event-Centered Trauma Processing**

When CTT practitioners who are working with a survivor of CTr assess that event-centered trauma processing is therapeutically indicated and that the client is ready to constructively engage in it, the question arises of how exactly to execute this phase of treatment. Although PE, EMDR, TIR, and the counting method are event-centered trauma processing procedures, their mode of implementation differ in various respects. Being conversant in all of these forms of event-centered exposure (and others; these are just the most common and widely accepted approaches) is useful. The variations among them allow the practitioner (in consultation with the client) to consider how these differing features may be particularly well matched or may be unsuitable to the individual survivor's traumatic experiences, preferences, characteristics, and needs. Can the client tolerate the fine-tuned, explicit level of detail of description of the traumatic event associated with PE? Are they likely to fare better with the level of self-direction and, therefore, control allowed for in TIR? Is the nature of the event or its effects such that they would benefit more from attending to the particular elements that are the focus of EMDR rather than attending to the entire incident? Would they benefit more from the combination of event-centered exposure and cue-centered exposure included in PE? Or from the grounding and containment emblematic of the counting method?

To knowledgeably make these determinations and effectively carry out these methods, it is necessary that the practitioner thoroughly familiarize themselves with and use the manuals associated with each method with several clients. In this way, the practitioner can acquire a sense of the characteristics inherent in each of these event-centered exposure forms and how these features may make these alternate approaches well suited or contraindicated for a particular client. Once the therapist has become thoroughly conversant with each approach by executing it several times (and only after having done so), it becomes clear that elements of the various event-centered exposure protocols can be brought together in novel combinations to optimize effectiveness for individual clients. Combining the protocols can be particularly appropriate when working with a client who has an especially prolonged and severe trauma history, and is easily triggered into decompensation in response to the more demanding variations of event-centered exposure.

However, it is possible to treat traumatic events in a fashion similar to the graded exposure of cue-centered trauma processing. The practitioner can ask the client to break down the account of the trauma into sections or "chapters" and then address these sections as if they were separate items from the rest of the trauma narrative. It is important to keep in mind that the client would need to rate each section in this modification for the degree of distress they evoke. The client would then address the sections not in chronological sequence but in the order of how distressing they find them, from least to most distressing. In addition, some clients possess sufficient skill in modulating mental imagery to picture the traumatic event as if they were viewing it from a distance, projected on a small screen, or in black and white. Proponents of event-centered exposure methods of trauma processing such as PE may view these types of modifications as modes of avoidance and therefore disapprove of them. However, adjustments in methods such as these can make event-centered trauma exposure less arduous and potentially destabilizing so that it can be more safely used with CTr survivors.

## FINAL CONSIDERATIONS ABOUT TRAUMA PROCESSING

In this chapter, I have examined three different forms of trauma processing: cognition-centered, cue-centered, and event-centered. All other things being equal, cognition-centered trauma processing strategies are likely to carry the least degree of destabilization of the three cue-centered processing has slightly more risk of eliciting treatment-disruptive reactions. Unquestionably, event-centered trauma processing approaches carry the greatest risk. I am not speaking here of the likelihood that distress will increase in response to these methods. One can expect that with any exposure technique, distress heightens when the procedure begins, and then gradually declines over time. That in itself is not disruptive.

Survivors of CTr are particularly susceptible to adverse reactions in response to event-centered exposure. Nevertheless, it is important to emphasize that this is not a reason to scrupulously avoid the use of event-centered processing in this population. CTr survivors can benefit immensely from event-centered trauma work when it is applied at the right time and in a planful manner. The practitioner must ensure, however, that the client has adequately mastered the requisite coping skills beforehand and assess whether event-centered trauma processing needs to be conducted in a titrated fashion. It is not necessary, though, to presume that event-centered processing is an essential component of treatment for every CTr survivor. In my own work with CTr survivors and in a number of cases treated at the Nova Southeastern University Trauma Resolution & Integration Program, my team and I have observed that extensive CTT-oriented Phase 1 treatment (see the discussion on phases of treatment in the section The Necessity of Therapist Self-Care in Chapter 6) can result in the elimination of PTSD symptoms and thus renders event-centered trauma processing unnecessary.

# 13

# Enhancing the Life Trajectory

*Trauma Integration and Competency Consolidation*

We now turn our attention to Phase 3 of treatment. Phase 3 consists of assisting the client to approach a quality of life they have not attained before. Contextual trauma therapy (CTT) emphasizes that what has interfered with the complex traumatization (CTr) survivor's life adjustment is not only the consequence of having endured pervasive trauma but also having been deprived of basic developmental resources. In Phase 3 of CTT, having first achieved a reasonable degree of stabilization and security, and then having resolved their traumatization to an appreciable degree, the survivor can now turn their full attention toward working to create a level of adult functioning that was previously beyond their grasp. Although it is Phase 3 of CTT that is the focus of this chapter, it is helpful to first look back on Phases 1 and 2 (see the discussion of these phases in Chapter 6) to trace the progression of treatment leading up to Phase 3.

I hesitate to refer to Phase 3 of treatment as the "final" phase. That is not entirely accurate if one thinks of phases as strictly sequential. Framing treatment as phase oriented is a helpful rubric, but in practice, the so-called phases of therapy can and often do overlap. Frequently, treatment for CTr survivors moves back and forth between the three phases, too. For instance, once a certain degree of trauma processing occurs, it may be necessary to return to Phase 1 stabilization and remediation before moving on to further trauma-focused work.

---

http://dx.doi.org/10.1037/0000176-014
*Contextual Trauma Therapy: Overcoming Traumatization and Reaching Full Potential,* by S. N. Gold
Copyright © 2020 by the American Psychological Association. All rights reserved.

## TAKING STOCK: PHASES 1 AND 2 OF TREATMENT

In Chapter 3, we encountered the case of Chet, who explained to his therapist that although his physical appearance was that of a man in his fifties, his inner experience was that of a 9-year-old boy. Due to the adverse impact on psychological development of experiences of deficit, most survivors of CTr enter therapy with limited capacities to live as fully functional adults. CTT proposes that this is a central reason why confrontation with traumatic material can be counterproductive for this cohort when initiated early in treatment. They have been deprived of the interpersonal support and guidance every child needs to master the myriad capabilities needed for effective adult functioning. Usually among those capacities is the ability to adequately cope with the extraordinary levels of stress required to confront past traumatic events and tolerate the high levels of stress aroused by them long enough to extinguish the conditioning of the fight–flight–freeze response.

When Herman (1992a, 1992b) proposed the complex posttraumatic stress disorder (C-PTSD) diagnosis, she suggested that it was the consequence of repeated or prolonged traumatic experiences. She therefore indicated that before survivors with C-PTSD address their traumatization in a second phase of treatment, they need a preliminary treatment phase to first establish a sense of safety and security. She further endorsed the provision of a third phase subsequent to trauma processing in which the now resolved traumatic event could be integrated into the survivor's larger life story and sense of self as a foundation for moving on to a live a meaningful existence.

Based on both empirical evidence and clinical observation, CTT builds on and refines Herman's (1992b) formulation of the nature of the three phases of treatment. Although CTr is related to multiple instances of trauma, it appears to be specifically associated with trauma that occurs in childhood (Hyland et al., 2017). In addition, the diagnostic criteria that distinguish CTr from posttraumatic stress disorder, the disturbances in self-organization (DSO), seem to be related to experiences of deficit in particular (McLaughlin & Sheridan, 2016; McLaughlin, Sheridan, & Lambert, 2014) rather than being the result of experiences of threat (i.e., trauma). CTT maintains, therefore, that CTr survivors suffer not just from prolonged traumatization but also from developmental deprivation.

Therefore, although CTT adheres to a three-phase model parallel to Herman's (1992b), it construes the function of Phase 1 somewhat differently. Its function is not merely stabilization but also identification and remediation of the particular gaps and warps in development, socialization, and enculturation manifested by the CTr survivor as a result of their having been reared with the deprivation that characterized their particular family of origin environment. CTT is directed throughout the course of treatment toward assisting the CTr survivor to not only resolve the symptoms of traumatization but to acquire, master, and expand the capacities required for a productive and gratifying life as a socially and pragmatically competent adult.

It is difficult to enumerate all the possible types of knowledge and abilities needed to function effectively that may be lacking in each particular CTr survivor's background. Generally speaking, the consequences of traumatization are much more easily catalogued than the myriad possible conglomerations of knowledge and skills deficits that can result from having been reared with the idiosyncrasies of a uniquely inadequate family environment. Recent research related to the adoption of the C-PTSD diagnosis in the 11th edition of the *International Classification of Diseases* (World Health Organization, 2018) specifically highlights the three areas of difficulty subsumed by the DSO designation: emotional dysregulation, negative self-concept, and disturbed interpersonal relationships. CTT, however, proposes that the range of potential difficulties associated with C-PTSD, in particular, and CTr, in general, is much broader. The distress created by difficulty managing daily living makes it nearly impossible for CTr survivors to tolerate the extraordinary distress entailed in revisiting the traumatic episodes that were beyond their coping capacities when they originally occurred.

Working to improve the survivor's quality of life in the present before intensely focusing on the most disturbing events in the survivor's past helps to ensure that when Phase 2 work is initiated, it is constructive rather than destabilizing. Attainments such as improved functioning in the areas encompassed by the DSO—emotional regulation, self-concept, and interpersonal relationships (the interpersonal relationships form a foundation for establishing a network of social support)—help prepare CTr survivors to approach trauma work productively; however, more is often needed. Acquisition of more effective coping skills than the survivor possesses on embarking on treatment and enhancement of quality of life in the present help equip the survivor to revisit historical trauma without being experientially engulfed by it. As treatment proceeds and life in the present becomes more manageable, and trauma-related sources of destabilization are resolved, more and more time and attention are freed up to address and remediate the developmental gaps that have restricted the survivor's potential to pursue a more optimal life trajectory. This objective can then become the primary focus of Phase 3 of therapy.

## ENHANCING THE LIFE TRAJECTORY: PHASE 3

Perhaps as a consequence of the controversy regarding whether CTr survivors need an initial period of stabilization before starting intensive trauma work, much more attention has been given to Phases 1 and 2 of three-phase treatment than to Phase 3 (Cloitre et al., 2011, 2012; Cloitre, Garvert, Brewin, Bryant, & Maercker, 2013; Courtois, Ford, & Cloitre, 2009; De Jongh et al., 2016; Herman, 2012). Herman (1992b) referred to this third phase as *reconnection*, a term that nicely captures the need, following trauma processing, for the survivor to turn attention to and align themselves with the elements and routines of ordinary (i.e., nontraumatic) daily living. Others have referred to this phase of trauma-related treatment as *integration and rehabilitation* (Steele, van der Hart, & Nijenhuis, 2005), *functional reintegration* (Ford, Courtois, Steele, van der Hart, & Nijenhuis, 2005), and *rehabilitation* (Gelinas, 2003).

Herman (1992a) called this phase *reconnection* because, for the survivor to attend to daily living, they need to overcome the sense of alienation from others who have not been touched by trauma and therefore cannot adequately comprehend what the survivor has been through. In addition, like the combat veteran returning home from war, reconnection requires contending with the challenge of resuming the regularity of everyday life after having lived under extraordinary conditions (Shay, 2002). And perhaps most demanding, reconnection entails finding meaning and direction in a life that was profoundly interrupted and unsettled by the impact of traumatic events. All of these transitions require a dedicated period of adjustment.

As arduous as these tasks may be, to a great degree they are in some respects more pertinent to survivors of posttraumatic stress disorder than to survivors of CTr. For CTr survivors, Phase 3 of trauma therapy is not a matter of returning to the circumstances of ordinary daily living, nor is it about reconnection, reintegration, reentry, or recovery. Survivors of CTr do not have the luxury of "re-"—of "once again" participating in life from a position of sound adjustment. They are not returning to the status quo that existed before trauma. So-called ordinary circumstances and functioning as exhibited by most people untouched by complex trauma never existed for CTr survivors. From their earliest days, most of these survivors have endured a life marred by the twin forces of abuse trauma and developmental deprivation that precluded the predictability, routine, and structure commonly associated with the term *status quo*. For survivors of CTr, instead of reconnection, Phase 3 is one of connection: Instead of reintegration, it is one of integration. And instead of recovery, this phase is one of *covery*—coverage and assimilation of the capacities needed for effective adult functioning. In Phase 3, CTr survivors are not returning to a normative, stable life structure; instead, they are creating and solidifying one for the first time.

The vast project of forming a productive and gratifying life structure does not begin subsequent to trauma processing. It starts at the beginning of CTT and continues throughout. This is why tentatively identifying the potential revised life trajectory of the CTr survivor occurs during the initial intake meeting by asking the question "If we are wildly successful, what will *your life* look like when we are done?" Beyond resolving the effects of traumatization, redirecting the existing ineffective and unrewarding life trajectory is the ultimate goal of CTT. Phase 1 concentrates on remediating developmental areas of deficit and thereby markedly improving the survivor's quality of life in the present. From the platform of greater resiliency in the present, the survivor is sufficiently equipped to tackle the formidable tasks of Phase 2. They can face past experiences of threat that have continued to haunt them and come to terms with them. Often for CTr survivors, Phase 2 consists of back-and-forth movement between resolving some titrated facet of traumatization that they have the coping skills and stamina to address, and then returning to a Phase 1 focus to further refine their developmental or adaptive capacities before further pursuing trauma processing.

By the time that all or almost all of the CTr survivor's traumatization is resolved so that they are no longer appreciably encumbered by either experiences of threat or experiences of deprivation, Phase 3 treatment can primarily be devoted to helping them approximate the life trajectory they might have taken if they had grown up in more favorable circumstances. In this phase, the focus can increasingly be on aiding the client to actualize their potential. It is difficult for CTr survivors first entering therapy to envision the direction their lives could take if they were not constrained by the limitations imposed by CTr. Many of them have not been able to imagine a life beyond struggling to get by. The expanse traversed by Lorna in the case example that follows provides an especially distinct example of a course of treatment in which acquisition of the capacities for effective adult functioning was particularly salient.

### Case Example: A Radical Shift in Life Trajectory

Lorna's initial phone contact with me is described in Chapter 5. She called me on my university office phone to ask about trauma treatment in the Nova Southeastern University Trauma Resolution & Integration Program (TRIP) that I direct and to assess whether it was likely to meet her needs. She did decide to commit to a course of therapy at TRIP, where doctoral trainees are placed in practicum, internship, or residency for 12 months. As with most clients with CTr, her course of treatment extended over several years. She therefore received CTT from a succession of therapists still in training. Taking into account that most of them were practicum trainees in their second year of supervised clinical work, Lorna's progress is even more impressive than it otherwise would have been.

At the end of her course of therapy at TRIP, Lorna agreed to participate in a videotaped exit interview with me and the clinical trainee who had worked with her during her final year of treatment. As she describes in the transcribed segment of the interview that follows, by this time, she not only was employed and free of the restrictions of agoraphobia but her dissociative difficulties had subsided appreciably. In terms of Phase 3 outcomes, she had by now attained her lifelong dream of teaching at the college level. She already had a master's degree, but at the time of this interview, was about halfway through a doctoral program. I had been told by her TRIP therapist about an excursion to England that Lorna had taken in connection with her graduate program.

**AUTHOR:** Do you want to fill us in on your recent success abroad?

**LORNA:** Oh, yeah! Yes! Damn! That was so . . . can you imagine? I went to London! It's like, "Whoa, through the looking glass!" I absolutely, you know, when I met you, I couldn't go around the block if I didn't have an escort and a good reason.

AUTHOR: Out the front door I think, right?

LORNA: Yeah. I couldn't go out the front door unless I was coming here or to work.

> **AUTHOR'S COMMENT:** When we had first "met" over the phone, Lorna had been unemployed for about 10 years. Her return to work occurred after she had completed therapy with her first TRIP clinician.

LORNA: And, um, yeah, I went to London. As it began, the study abroad offered the opportunity for my husband to go with me.

> **AUTHOR'S COMMENT:** When she started at TRIP, Lorna was not married to her partner because she was phobic about signing her name, one of many difficulties she surmounted during the course of therapy.

LORNA: And, so, we set it up that way. But then it turned out that he couldn't go, which was actually almost better. [*Laughs*] Or maybe I can just say, yes, it was better. It was unbelievable. I went to London. I was there for a little more than 2 weeks. I saw 11 colleges and schools. I traveled all over England and Ireland myself, and I got lost.

> **AUTHOR'S COMMENT:** Due to her severe dissociation when she first came to TRIP, Lorna had been terrified of going places alone, in part because she feared she would become disoriented and end up hopelessly lost. Here, she conveys how free she was by now of both a disabling degree of dissociation and her fear of getting around on her own.

LORNA: And I got found! And I was able to deal with the world around me just fine.

AUTHOR: Did you panic at all when you got lost?

LORNA: Yeah, I panicked. But not the level of panic that I have had in the past. And I had a couple of funny experiences. I was talking to myself, reading a map, and a police officer came up behind me and he said, "Do you want me to join the conversation?" And I cracked up, you know? It was okay. And he disarmed me completely by talking. If he would have touched me or something, that probably would have been bad. But, um, yeah, it was okay. And it wasn't any more than anybody else panicked—at least to my understanding.

**AUTHOR:** Sure. As far as you could see from the outside.

**LORNA:** Yeah. And I was with a group of people and I actually, I went to Oxford two ways. First time I went by bus. And so that's not the smart way to go. The smart way to go is by train, or it's cheaper, whatever, and a shorter distance. But the trip by bus was such a cool ride. . . . [*Briefly digresses to describe her travels through the English countryside*] But, anyway, the bottom line is [that it was] better than any kind of Disneyland could ever be. I "punted on the ham." I rented a little boat and rode on the river. Me! Got into a boat! In England! And, I remember all this. I chose to do these things. And I did them. And it was so wonderful. And, of course, now it has started something, and my [adult] kids are all in an uproar because I'm definitely traveling next summer. I have no idea where. And I may be going back to England because of the relationships I started. But that's only the beginning. There's Greece and Italy, and, I don't know, Tibet? [*Laughs with delight*] I have no clue.

> **AUTHOR'S COMMENT:** Not surprisingly, these Phase 3–related accomplishments had been reached not instead of but in addition to trauma resolution. The absence of paralyzing fear and disruptive dissociative experiences she refers to are in themselves evidence that Lorna's life is no longer hampered by lingering traumatization. But a little later in the interview, in relating a dream about her mother, the primary childhood abuser of both her and her siblings, Lorna spontaneously describes more directly how free she is now of the impact of trauma.

**LORNA:** This past Christmas, I had this weird dream where Evelyn [here, as she habitually did, she refers to her mother by her first name] showed up. My mother showed up in my mind in the middle of the night. Christmas Eve, actually, 25 years [to the day on the anniversary] of her death. And in this . . . this vision, I could see her face like anyone's face, but her body was like a whole series of blue tubes. And she came to me saying "Look at me. Look at me, Lorn. Look at me." And that's all that she said, and I was screaming in my mind, "Get away from me!"

But I woke up feeling like, "Aren't there doctors there?" "Are you okay?" You know, "Do you need a blanket?" Whatever. And I spoke to my sister about it, and she said, "Well, if you're forgiving her, that's it. I can't talk to you." You know? And it started a whole series of, uh, her being anxious about me. And me being anxious, too. But bottom line is, uh, not about forgiving her and not about evoking fear in my kid sister. It kind of set me free from a whole lot of chains of pain that I didn't need to hang on to. And, actually, if I did come upon her in this moment of my life, I know that I would be kind to her. And that I, that I, uh, I'm okay with that. I get that.

**AUTHOR:** What did you make of that image when she said, "Look at me"?

**LORNA:** I got that she was in pain. That she was suffering. Where her heart should have been was like a smoky hole. And I, you know, whatever your mind creates for you. . . . I got that she is mired in the . . . the result of her life.

> **AUTHOR'S COMMENT:** She goes on a bit later to talk about how much things have changed for her, because she used to be obsessed with trying to prove to other people what had happened to her at the hands of her mother and others. She recognizes how far she has come in contrast to little sister, who did not have therapy and who for much of her adulthood isolated herself from other people.

**LORNA:** But, anyway, when I told my sister about it, and actually told them all [i.e., all of her siblings] about this, I realized that for them, for my little sister, she can't let go of this. It's like that whole struggle, and as I watched the video yesterday [of a debriefing video she did after therapy with her first TRIP clinician], it was so clear to me how much of a burden proving what happened is. It's like a huge force in [her little sister's] life today. And it's so not part of my day anymore. And that's, you know, like a major quotient [of her sister's progress].

> **AUTHOR'S COMMENT:** A few minutes later, as she continues to discuss the extent that the obsession to prove what she'd been through is no longer there, she explains the following:

LORNA: Now I really don't think about proving what my childhood was. But there are times when I have to say what my childhood was.

**AUTHOR'S COMMENT:** Ironically, although she had been preoccupied with somehow proving how awful her upbringing had been, she would not discuss it with other people because she was afraid they would either not believe her or would look down on her.

LORNA: There was an incident while I was in Britain. One of the women in the graduate group just believ[ed] that since I was Jewish, I had this fabulous childhood. And, you know, 200 times she said it, and I let it go. The 201st time, I was like, "Whoa. No, stop." But whatever I said to her did not upset my evening, I didn't lose time [by slipping into a profound dissociative state, as she had in the past], I didn't, um, feel like, uh, my trip was now fragmented or anything. I just felt like somebody pissed me off, and I needed to say something. And that's all there was to that. So it wasn't this whole, "I have to prove to you that what I've just said to you is true." That's gone.

**AUTHOR'S COMMENT:** Toward the end of the interview, I ask her the following:

AUTHOR: Okay, this is a subtle thing. It's hard to put into words. And I always question myself about whether what I'm experiencing is accurate. But one of the things that I think happens as people move through this process is that the nature of their experience changes in that they're much more present, they're much more focused, they're much more in contact with their surroundings, they're much more here.

LORNA: I think that's true, absolutely.

AUTHOR: Okay, because it seems to me, as I was sitting here with you today, as wonderful and positive and exciting as our last discussion was, I got that sense that you're much more here and involved.

LORNA: . . . this is much more. . . . Today, *x* years later, realizing how my life has developed to what it is at this moment allows me to be in the moment. I don't usually reflect on that. But I am aware that if there's a group of people, you know, you walk into work in the morning, "Hey, how you doing?" "Hey, how are you?" [*Imitates somebody grumbling incoherently*] That's not me. I am in a good mood. I'm interested in what's happening today. I'm really where I want to be today, deliberately. So I think that's part of it. . . . Here I am. I have three grown children who are good human beings in the world. And I have grandchildren coming up right behind them, magnificent human beings. And I have this wonderful career and my marriage. I mean, I'm feeling all that because I have all that. And I had no clue that you really can have all that. I was actually looking for pain lowered, being able to focus enough to understand a conversation and get a job.

AUTHOR: Okay, so you didn't have a picture of all this.

LORNA: No, I didn't really. I had a dream of being an academic, but I never expected the dream to be fulfilled, you know? I really never expected the dream to be fulfilled.

> **AUTHOR'S COMMENT:** Early in therapy at TRIP. Lorna indicated that her ambition was to become a forensic anthropologist so that she could study the unimaginably extreme types of maltreatment she and her siblings had been subjected to growing up. She wanted to help people understand it. She indicates here that this career no longer interests her and is not the path she ended up taking.

LORNA: And I felt like an obligation, and I heard myself say, "Forensic anthropology." I felt that if I could be a credit to the world, it would only be in response to what happened to me as a child. That's not true. And, actually, if you look at the whole realm of academia [here, she names the field of academia she is in], it is not exactly brain surgery or molecular genetics or anything, uh, that, you know, [is so] intensely knowledge bearing that it's going to help mankind. But it is, um, a credible area. And it is enjoyable just in that abstract sense that people learning [names her field again] have no tragedy. It's . . . it's actually more interesting because of that. For me. So, it turns out that my dream is not as dreary as it was at that time. Because at that time, if my hope could be realized, then I would be spending my whole life talking about these horrible situations, and I don't want to do that. I had enough of that.

> **AUTHOR'S COMMENT:** What Lorna is emphasizing is that she is neither haunted by her traumatic childhood nor obsessed with it. It is resolved to the point that she is much more interested in engaging in life in the present and all the positive qualities it has to offer. Once freed of the burden of CTr, Phase 3 CTT work endowed her with the capacity to embark on and pursue a life trajectory that approximated the one that she might have followed if she had grown up in much more favorable circumstances and to realize a potential beyond her imagining.[1]

## HELPING SURVIVORS OF COMPLEX TRAUMATIZATION EMBARK ON A MORE FAVORABLE LIFE TRAJECTORY

From the first therapy session, CTT is oriented to envisioning what the client's life can be like one they have improved their present circumstances in Phase 1; freed themselves from the constraints of CTr in Phase 2; and set themselves on a new, more productive and gratifying life trajectory in Phase 3. Although most clients are unable to envision what that ultimate life trajectory might look like, encouraging them to do their best to progressively move toward envisioning it from the outset of treatment serves an important function. It conveys that much more is attainable. As Lorna put it, "I had no clue that you really can have all that. I was actually looking for pain lowered, being able to focus enough to understand a conversation and get a job." Even this is more than many CTr survivors can picture. But conveying from early on that a decidedly better quality of life is possible carries the implicit message that if this is so, then the goal of no longer being plagued by traumatization, which itself is often difficult to imagine, is achievable, too.

To the degree that trauma is successfully processed and resolved in Phase 2, survivor and therapist are freed up to focus more intently on the quality of life the client aspires to and the personal and external resources the client needs to marshal to attain it. The approaches outlined in Chapter 7 on collaborative conceptualization can be appropriated to help the client clarify what they want their life structure to be, whether it is realistic to construct the life to which they aspire, and some idea of how to attain it. The encouragement and validation encapsulated in the collaborative relationship are crucial resources in all phases of CTT. By Phase 3 of treatment, however, sufficient reduction in the three components of DSO will have been achieved such that the survivor will have or should be encouraged to solidify a circle of support outside of therapy to help them reach the goals that compose the life

---

[1] It is a welcome coincidence that on the same day I was completing the final edits on this volume, I received word from Lorna that she had passed her doctoral dissertation defense, her committee had signed off on her dissertation, and, after several years of teaching college, she officially became "Dr. Lorna."

structure they wish to move toward creating. In Phase 3, the practical intervention sphere is directed primarily toward helping the survivor absorb the particular capacities needed to put the various aspects of their desired life structure into place. This territory is likely to embrace a range of possible tasks, from learning to better manage finances, to investigating possible career paths and associated education and training, to improving the skills required in forming and maintaining emotionally intimate connections.

Over time, the importance of the therapy and reliance on the practitioner are likely to gradually wane as the new and gratifying life structure comes to take precedence over treatment, as it should. The intensity of the collaborative alliance still requires a period of disengagement to free the client to increasingly turn their attention to daily living. This is a process, given the strength of the collaborative relationship, that frequently requires that the therapist intentionally let go of and mourn the loss of the hard-won connection that has been formed. Doing so furthers the ultimate aim of therapy: for it to outlive its usefulness in favor of allowing the client to explore their new life trajectory with the support of the social network they have established.

To sum up, the three phases of CTT, slightly revised from those originally posed by Herman (1992b), can be described in the following terms:

- Phase 1: Stabilization Through Developmental Remediation;
- Phase 2: Titrated Trauma Processing; and
- Phase 3: Establishment of an Enhanced Life Trajectory.

# Epilogue
## Applying Contextual Trauma Therapy to Short-Term Treatment

Contextual trauma therapy (CTT) is an ambitious form of treatment. Whenever possible, it aspires for more than a reduction or elimination of the forms of impairment commonly referred to as *symptoms*. It seeks to help clients attain a level of functioning that was previously restricted by a far-reaching scarcity of knowledge and skills attributable to having grown up in an interpersonal context that inadequately prepared them to effectively manage adult living. An overarching goal of this magnitude is not realistically reached in a matter of weeks. However, there are undoubtedly instances for a number of possible reasons that the number of sessions available to a client is severely limited. When this is the case, the conceptually driven treatment approach that typifies CTT becomes especially relevant. Short-term CTT is guided by the following questions:

- Within a limited time frame, for this particular individual in these specific circumstances, what is most important to accomplish?

- What can be realistically be achieved? How might this goal most effectively be attained?

- In what ways can the relational, conceptual, and practical intervention spheres be mobilized to optimize treatment outcome under the constraints of a limited time frame?

The brief course of therapy described in the following case example demonstrates how the principles and intervention strategies of CTT can be applied

---

http://dx.doi.org/10.1037/0000176-015
*Contextual Trauma Therapy: Overcoming Traumatization and Reaching Full Potential,* by S. N. Gold
Copyright © 2020 by the American Psychological Association. All rights reserved.

to short-term treatment. A particular intervention was used; however, much more important than the specific techniques used is that a solid collaborative alliance was able to be forged despite the limited duration of treatment. That factor was decisive in determining the client's eventual responsiveness and, in turn, the ultimate outcome of therapy.

**Case Example: An Addendum to the Case of Jeanette**
In Chapter 1, we examined the case of Jeanette, and how a failure to recognize the nature of her traumatization, the prominence of depressive rather than posttraumatic symptoms in her clinical picture, and an ill-advised and immediate leap into exposure-based trauma treatment led to severe decompensation. Here, we return to a subsequent, albeit extremely brief, phase of her treatment. Her second therapist, after several rounds of attempts to conduct trauma-focused exposure therapy, grew increasingly frustrated. Approximately every 3 months, he was able to convince Jeanette to once again engage in exposure. Each time she did, she lapsed into an unresponsive dissociative stupor. Although he did not outright refuse to continue to work with her, he referred her elsewhere for treatment for a 6-week period with a practitioner whom he knew had experience working with trauma survivors. According to Jeanette, his stated rationale to Jeanette was that he needed "a break" so that he could "recover" from the stress of working with her.

Jeanette contacted the practitioner to whom her second therapist had referred her and tried to briefly explain what had transpired up to that point. Although somewhat hesitant to agree to the terms of treatment being proposed, after hearing her account, the third clinician could not in good conscience refuse to work with her knowing how distressed she was and that her current therapist was unwilling to make himself available to her for several weeks. The new therapist was conversant in CTT and able to recognize that Jeanette was a survivor of complex traumatization (CTr).

In the initial intake session, the new therapist surmised that despite Jeanette's extensive history of trauma and her impressive previous level of functioning, the death of her grandmother had activated a sense of vulnerability stemming from considerable childhood experiences of deficit. She also deduced that although Jeanette had initially presented with a predominantly depressive clinical picture when she began treatment with her first therapist, acute anxiety and severe dissociation episodes were now her central sources of impairment. The circumstances in which Jeanette lapsed into dissociative states suggested that they were triggered not only by sessions in which trauma-focused exposure was conducted but in general by anxiety-provoking circumstances. The therapist concluded, therefore, that what made the most sense with only five remaining sessions after the initial intake was to make distress reduction the focus of their time together.

In the second session, she explained the rationale for the regular practice of an anxiety reduction technique and taught Jeanette diaphragmatic breathing. This method worked well for Jeanette and resulted in session in a drop of four points on the Subjective Units of Distress Scale (Wolpe, 1958): from

# REFERENCES

Abrams, J. (Ed.). (1990). *Reclaiming the inner child*. Los Angeles, CA: Tarcher.

Ainsworth, M. D. (1985). Patterns of attachment. *Clinical Psychologist, 38*, 27–29.

Alain, M., Marcotte, J., Desrosiers, J., Turcotte, D., & Lafortune, D. (2018). The thin line between protection and conviction: Experiences with child protection services and later criminal convictions among a population of adolescents. *Journal of Adolescence, 63*, 85–95. http://dx.doi.org/10.1016/j.adolescence.2017.12.010

Alessandri, S. M., & Lewis, M. (1996). Differences in pride and shame in maltreated and nonmaltreated preschoolers. *Child Development, 67*, 1857–1869. http://dx.doi.org/10.2307/1131736

Allen, J. G., Coyne, L., & Huntoon, J. (1998). Complex posttraumatic stress disorder in women from a psychometric perspective. *Journal of Personality Assessment, 70*, 277–298. http://dx.doi.org/10.1207/s15327752jpa7002_7

American Psychiatric Association. (1980). *Diagnostic and statistical manual of mental disorders* (3rd ed.). Washington, DC: Author.

American Psychiatric Association. (2013). *Diagnostic and statistical manual of mental disorders* (5th ed.). Washington, DC: Author.

Anda, R. F., Butchart, A., Felitti, V. J., & Brown, D. W. (2010). Building a framework for global surveillance of the public health implications of adverse childhood experiences. *American Journal of Preventive Medicine, 39*, 93–98. http://dx.doi.org/10.1016/j.amepre.2010.03.015

Andresen, R., Caputi, P., & Oades, L. G. (2010). Do clinical outcome measures assess consumer-defined recovery? *Psychiatry Research, 177*, 309–317. http://dx.doi.org/10.1016/j.psychres.2010.02.013

Ardino, V. (2014). Trauma-informed care: Is cultural competence a viable solution for efficient policy strategies? *Clinical Neuropsychiatry, 11*, 45–51.

Asay, T. P., & Lambert, M. J. (1999). The empirical case for the common factors in therapy: Quantitative findings. In M. A. Hubble, B. L. Duncan, & S. D. Miller

(Eds.), *The heart and soul of change: What works in therapy* (pp. 23–55). Washington, DC: American Psychological Association. http://dx.doi.org/10.1037/11132-001

Ataria, Y. (2015). Trauma from an enactive perspective: The collapse of the knowing-how structure. *Adaptive Behavior, 23*, 143–154. http://dx.doi.org/10.1177/1059712315578542

Baldock, J., & Leichner, P. (1995). Re: Psychiatrists' attitudes to multiple personality disorder: A questionnaire study [Comment]. *Canadian Journal of Psychiatry, 40*, 495. http://dx.doi.org/10.1177/070674379504000816

Barach, P. M. (1991). Multiple personality disorder as an attachment disorder. *Dissociation: Progress in the Dissociative Disorders, 4*, 117–123.

Barch, D. M., Belden, A. C., Tillman, R., Whalen, D., & Luby, J. L. (2018). Early childhood adverse experiences, inferior frontal gyrus connectivity, and the trajectory of externalizing psychopathology. *Journal of the American Academy of Child & Adolescent Psychiatry, 57*, 183–190. http://dx.doi.org/10.1016/j.jaac.2017.12.011

Barlow, M. R., & Freyd, J. J. (2009). Adaptive dissociation: Information processing and response to betrayal. In P. F. Dell, & J. A. O'Neil (Eds.), *Dissociation and the dissociative disorders:* DSM–V *and beyond* (pp. 93–105). New York, NY: Routledge.

Barth, J., Bermetz, L., Heim, E., Trelle, S., & Tonia, T. (2013). The current prevalence of child sexual abuse worldwide: A systematic review and meta-analysis. *International Journal of Public Health, 58*, 469–483. http://dx.doi.org/10.1007/s00038-012-0426-1

Beck, A. T., Rush, A. J., Shaw, B. F., & Emery, G. (1979). *Cognitive therapy of depression.* New York, NY: Guilford Press.

Bell, V., Robinson, B., Katona, C., Fett, A.-K., & Shergill, S. (2018). When trust is lost: The impact of interpersonal trauma on social interactions. *Psychological Medicine, 49*, 1041–1046. http://dx.doi.org/10.1017/S0033291718001800

Bennett, D. S., Sullivan, M. W., & Lewis, M. (2010). Neglected children, shame-proneness, and depressive symptoms. *Child Maltreatment, 15*, 305–314. http://dx.doi.org/10.1177/1077559510379634

Benson, H., & Friedman, R. (1996). Harnessing the power of the placebo effect and renaming it "remembered wellness." *Annual Review of Medicine, 47*, 193–199. http://dx.doi.org/10.1146/annurev.med.47.1.193

Bentzen, M. (2015). Dances of connection: Neuroaffective development in clinical work with attachment. *Body, Movement and Dance in Psychotherapy, 10*, 211–226. http://dx.doi.org/10.1080/17432979.2015.1064479

Bernstein, E. M., & Putnam, F. W. (1986). Development, reliability, and validity of a dissociation scale. *Journal of Nervous and Mental Disease, 174*, 727–735. http://dx.doi.org/10.1097/00005053-198612000-00004

Bhalla, I. P., Stefanovics, E. A., & Rosenheck, R. A. (2019). Polysubstance use among veterans in intensive PTSD programs: Association with symptoms and outcomes following treatment. *Journal of Dual Diagnosis, 15*, 36–45. http://dx.doi.org/10.1080/15504263.2018.1535150

Black, M. C., Basile, K. C., Breiding, M. J., Smith, S. G., Walters, M. L., Merrick, M. T., . . . Stevens, M. R. (2011). *The National Intimate Partner and Sexual Violence Survey (NISVS): 2010 summary report.* Atlanta, GA: National Center for Injury Prevention and Control, Centers for Disease Control and Prevention.

Blackwell, D. (2005). Psychotherapy, politics and trauma: Working with survivors of torture and organized violence. *Group Analysis, 38*, 307–323. http://dx.doi.org/10.1177/0533316405052386

Bloom, B., & Lipetz, M. (1987). *Revisions on the self-report measure of family functioning* (Technical Report No. 2). Boulder: University of Colorado, Center for Family Studies.

Bowlby, J. (1977). The making and breaking of affectional bonds. I. Aetiology and psychopathology in the light of attachment theory. *British Journal of Psychiatry, 130,* 201–210. http://dx.doi.org/10.1192/bjp.130.3.201

Bowlby, J. (1980). *Attachment and loss: Vol. 3. Loss: Sadness and depression.* Middlesex, England: Penguin Books.

Bowlby, J. (1988). *A secure base: Parent–child attachment and healthy human development.* New York, NY: Basic Books.

Brady, K. T., Killeen, T. K., Brewerton, T., & Lucerini, S. (2000). Comorbidity of psychiatric disorders and posttraumatic stress disorder. *Journal of Clinical Psychiatry, 61,* 22–32.

Brand, B. L., & Frewen, P. (2017). Dissociation as a trauma-related phenomenon. In S. N. Gold (Ed.), *APA handbook of trauma psychology: Foundations in knowledge* (Vol. 1, pp. 215–241). Washington, DC: American Psychological Association. http://dx.doi.org/10.1037/0000019-013

Brand, B. L., Lanius, R., Vermetten, E., Loewenstein, R. J., & Spiegel, D. (2012). Where are we going? An update on assessment, treatment, and neurobiological research in dissociative disorders as we move toward the *DSM–5. Journal of Trauma & Dissociation, 13,* 9–31. http://dx.doi.org/10.1080/15299732.2011.620687

Brand, B. L., Loewenstein, R. J., & Spiegel, D. (2014). Dispelling myths about dissociative identity disorder treatment: An empirically based approach. *Psychiatry: Interpersonal and Biological Processes, 77,* 169–189. http://dx.doi.org/10.1521/psyc.2014.77.2.169

Brand, B. L., Myrick, A. C., Loewenstein, R. J., Classen, C. C., Lanius, R., McNary, S. W., . . . Putnam, F. W. (2012). A survey of practices and recommended treatment interventions among expert therapists treating patients with dissociative identity disorder and dissociative disorder not otherwise specified. *Psychological Trauma: Theory, Research, Practice, and Policy, 4,* 490–500. http://dx.doi.org/10.1037/a0026487

Breiding, M. J., Black, M. C., & Ryan, G. W. (2008). Prevalence and risk factors of intimate partner violence in eighteen U.S. states/territories, 2005. *American Journal of Preventive Medicine, 34,* 112–118. http://dx.doi.org/10.1016/j.amepre.2007.10.001

Bremner, J. D., Randall, P., Vermetten, E., Staib, L., Bronen, R. A., Mazure, C., . . . Charney, D. S. (1997). Magnetic resonance imaging-based measurement of hippocampal volume in posttraumatic stress disorder related to childhood physical and sexual abuse—A preliminary report. *Biological Psychiatry, 41,* 23–32. http://dx.doi.org/10.1016/S0006-3223(96)00162-X

Bremner, J. D., Steinberg, M., Southwick, S. M., Johnson, D. R., & Charney, D. S. (1993). Use of the Structured Clinical Interview for DSM–IV Dissociative Disorders for systematic assessment of dissociative symptoms in posttraumatic stress disorder. *The American Journal of Psychiatry, 150,* 1011–1014. http://dx.doi.org/10.1176/ajp.150.7.1011

Brende, J. O. (1987). Dissociative disorders in Vietnam combat veterans. *Journal of Contemporary Psychotherapy, 17,* 77–86. http://dx.doi.org/10.1007/BF00946278

Brewin, C. R., Cloitre, M., Hyland, P., Shevlin, M., Maercker, A., Bryant, R. A., . . . Reed, G. M. (2017). A review of current evidence regarding the ICD–11 proposals for diagnosing PTSD and complex PTSD. *Clinical Psychology Review, 58,* 1–15. http://dx.doi.org/10.1016/j.cpr.2017.09.001

Briere, J. (2006). Dissociative symptoms and trauma exposure: Specificity, affect dysregulation, and posttraumatic stress. *Journal of Nervous and Mental Disease, 194,* 78–82. http://dx.doi.org/10.1097/01.nmd.0000198139.47371.54

Briere, J., & Rickards, S. (2007). Self-awareness, affect regulation, and relatedness: Differential sequels of childhood versus adult victimization experiences. *Journal of Nervous and Mental Disease, 195,* 497–503. http://dx.doi.org/10.1097/NMD.0b013e31803044e2

Briere, J., & Runtz, M. (1988). Symptomatology associated with childhood sexual victimization in a nonclinical adult sample. *Child Abuse & Neglect, 12,* 51–59. http://dx.doi.org/10.1016/0145-2134(88)90007-5

Briere, J., Runtz, M., Eadie, E. M., Bigras, N., & Godbout, N. (2018). The Disorganized Response Scale: Construct validity of a potential self-report measure of disorganized attachment. *Psychological Trauma: Theory, Research, Practice, and Policy, 11,* 486–494. http://dx.doi.org/10.1037/tra0000396

Brown, D. W., Anda, R. F., Edwards, V. J., Felitti, V. J., Dube, S. R., & Giles, W. H. (2007). Adverse childhood experiences and childhood autobiographical memory disturbance. *Child Abuse & Neglect, 31,* 961–969. http://dx.doi.org/10.1016/j.chiabu.2007.02.011

Brown, D. W., Anda, R. F., Tiemeier, H., Felitti, V. J., Edwards, V. J., Croft, J. B., & Giles, W. H. (2009). Adverse childhood experiences and the risk of premature mortality. *American Journal of Preventive Medicine, 37,* 389–396. http://dx.doi.org/10.1016/j.amepre.2009.06.021

Brown, L. S. (2008). *Cultural competence in trauma therapy: Beyond the flashback.* Washington, DC: American Psychological Association. http://dx.doi.org/10.1037/11752-000

Brown, L. S. (2017). Contributions of feminist and critical psychologies to trauma psychology. In S. N. Gold (Ed.), *APA handbook of trauma psychology: Foundations in knowledge* (Vol. 1, pp. 501–526). Washington, DC: American Psychological Association. http://dx.doi.org/10.1037/0000019-025

Brown, P. J., Recupero, P. R., & Stout, R. (1995). PTSD substance abuse comorbidity and treatment utilization. *Addictive Behaviors, 20,* 251–254. http://dx.doi.org/10.1016/0306-4603(94)00060-3

Bryant, R. A. (2017). Acute stress disorder and posttraumatic stress disorder. In S. N. Gold (Ed.), *APA handbook of trauma psychology: Foundations in knowledge* (Vol. 1, pp. 161–184). Washington, DC: American Psychological Association. http://dx.doi.org/10.1037/0000019-010

Bryant, R. A., Guthrie, R. M., & Moulds, M. L. (2001). Hypnotizability in acute stress disorder. *The American Journal of Psychiatry, 158,* 600–604. http://dx.doi.org/10.1176/appi.ajp.158.4.600

Burgess, A. W., & Holmstrom, L. L. (1974). Rape trauma syndrome. *The American Journal of Psychiatry, 131,* 981–986. http://dx.doi.org/10.1176/ajp.131.9.981

Butler, L. D., Carello, J., & Maguin, E. (2017). Trauma, stress, and self-care in clinical training: Predictors of burnout, decline in health status, secondary traumatic stress symptoms, and compassion satisfaction. *Psychological Trauma: Theory, Research, Practice, and Policy, 9,* 416–424. http://dx.doi.org/10.1037/tra0000187

Carello, J., & Butler, L. D. (2014). Potentially perilous pedagogies: Teaching trauma is not the same as trauma-informed teaching. *Journal of Trauma & Dissociation, 15*, 153–168. http://dx.doi.org/10.1080/15299732.2014.867571

Caretti, V., & Craparo, G. (2009). Psychopathological issues of technological addiction: New diagnostic criteria for addiction. In B. K. Wiederhold & G. Riva (Eds.), *Annual review of cybertherapy and telemedicine 2009: Advanced technologies in the behavioral, social and neurosciences* (pp. 277–280). Washington, DC: The Interactive Media Institute and IOS Press.

Carlson, E. A., Yates, T. M., & Sroufe, L. A. (2009). Dissociation and development of the self. In P. F. Dell, & J. A. O'Neil (Eds.), *Dissociation and the dissociative disorders:* DSM–V *and beyond* (pp. 39–52). New York, NY: Routledge.

Carlson, E. B., & Putnam, F. W. (1993). An update on the Dissociative Experiences Scale. *Dissociation: Progress in the Dissociative Disorders, 6*, 16–27.

Carnes, P. J., & Delmonico, D. L. (1996). Childhood abuse and multiple addictions: Research findings in a sample of self-identified sexual addicts. *Sexual Addiction & Compulsivity, 3*, 258–268. http://dx.doi.org/10.1080/10720169608400116

Carrion, V. G., Garrett, A., Menon, V., Weems, C. F., & Reiss, A. L. (2008). Post-traumatic stress symptoms and brain function during a response-inhibition task: An fMRI study in youth. *Depression and Anxiety, 25*, 514–526. http://dx.doi.org/10.1002/da.20346

Carrion, V. G., & Wong, S. S. (2012). Can traumatic stress alter the brain? Understanding the implications of early trauma on brain development and learning. *The Journal of Adolescent Health, 51*, S23–S28. http://dx.doi.org/10.1016/j.jadohealth.2012.04.010

Chan, K. L., Brownridge, D. A., Yan, E., Fong, D. Y. T., & Tiwari, A. (2011). Child maltreatment polyvictimization: Rates and short-term effects on adjustment in a representative Hong Kong sample. *Psychology of Violence, 1*, 4–15. http://dx.doi.org/10.1037/a0020284

Chaney, M. P., & Burns-Wortham, C. (2014). The relationship between online sexual compulsivity, dissociation, and past child abuse among men who have sex with men. *Journal of LGBT Issues in Counseling, 8*, 146–163. http://dx.doi.org/10.1080/15538605.2014.895663

Chapman, D., Dube, S. R., & Anda, R. (2007). Adverse childhood events as risk factors for negative mental health outcomes. *Psychiatric Annals, 37*, 359–364.

Chu, J. A., Frey, L. M., Ganzel, B. L., & Matthews, J. A. (1999). Memories of childhood abuse: Dissociation, amnesia, and corroboration. *The American Journal of Psychiatry, 156*, 749–755.

Clark, G. I., & Egan, S. J. (2015). The Socratic method in cognitive behavioural therapy: A narrative review. *Cognitive Therapy and Research, 39*, 863–879. http://dx.doi.org/10.1007/s10608-015-9707-3

Cleveland, J. M., Korman, B. M., & Gold, S. N. (2015). Are hypnosis and dissociation related? New evidence for a connection. *International Journal of Clinical and Experimental Hypnosis, 63*, 198–214. http://dx.doi.org/10.1080/00207144.2015.1002691

Cloitre, M., Courtois, C. A., Charuvastra, A., Carapezza, R., Stolbach, B. C., & Green, B. L. (2011). Treatment of complex PTSD: Results of the ISTSS expert clinician survey on best practices. *Journal of Traumatic Stress, 24*, 615–627. http://dx.doi.org/10.1002/jts.20697

Cloitre, M., Courtois, C. A., Ford, J. D., Green, B. L., Alexander, P., Briere, J., . . . van der Hart, O. (2012). *The ISTSS expert consensus treatment guidelines for complex*

*PTSD in adults*. Retrieved from http://www.traumacenter.org/products/pdf_files/ISTSS_Complex_Trauma_Treatment_Guidelines_2012_Cloitre,Courtois,Ford,Green,Alexander,Briere,Herman,Lanius,Stolbach,Spinazzola,van%20der%20Kolk,van%20der%20Hart.pdf

Cloitre, M., Garvert, D. W., Brewin, C. R., Bryant, R. A., & Maercker, A. (2013). Evidence for proposed ICD–11 PTSD and complex PTSD: A latent profile analysis. *European Journal of Psychotraumatology, 4*, 1. http://dx.doi.org/10.3402/ejpt.v4i0.20706

Cloitre, M., Scarvalone, P., & Difede, J. A. (1997). Posttraumatic stress disorder, self- and interpersonal dysfunction among sexually retraumatized women. *Journal of Traumatic Stress, 10*, 437–452. http://dx.doi.org/10.1002/jts.2490100309

Cloitre, M., Shevlin, M., Brewin, C. R., Bisson, J. I., Roberts, N. P., Maercker, A., . . . Hyland, P. (2018). The International Trauma Questionnaire: Development of a self-report measure of ICD–11 PTSD and complex PTSD. *Acta Psychiatrica Scandinavica, 138*, 536–546. http://dx.doi.org/10.1111/acps.12956

Colton, M., Roberts, S., & Vanstone, M. (2010). Sexual abuse by men who work with children. *Journal of Child Sexual Abuse, 19*, 345–364. http://dx.doi.org/10.1080/10538711003775824

Conway, F., Oster, M., & Szymanski, K. (2011). ADHD and complex trauma: A descriptive study of hospitalized children in an urban psychiatric hospital. *Journal of Infant, Child, and Adolescent Psychotherapy, 10*, 60–72. http://dx.doi.org/10.1080/15289168.2011.575707

Cook, J. M., Schnurr, P. P., & Foa, E. B. (2004). Bridging the gap between posttraumatic stress disorder research and clinical practice: The example of exposure therapy. *Psychotherapy: Theory, Research, & Practice, 41*, 374–387. http://dx.doi.org/10.1037/0033-3204.41.4.374

Cotsell, M. (2005). *The theater of trauma: American modernist drama and the psychological struggle for the American mind, 1900–1930*. New York, NY: Lang.

Courtois, C. A., & Ford, J. D. (2013). *Treatment of complex trauma: A sequenced, relationship-based approach*. New York, NY: Guilford Press.

Courtois, C. A., Ford, J. D., & Cloitre, M. (2009). Best practices in psychotherapy for adults. In C. A. Courtois & J. D. Ford (Eds.), *Treating complex traumatic stress disorders: An evidence-based guide* (pp. 82–103). New York, NY: Guilford Press.

Courtois, C. A., & Gold, S. N. (2009). The need for inclusion of psychological trauma in the professional curriculum: A call to action. *Psychological Trauma: Theory, Research, Practice, and Policy, 1*, 3–23. http://dx.doi.org/10.1037/a0015224

Creamer, M., Burgess, P., & McFarlane, A. C. (2001). Post-traumatic stress disorder: Findings from the Australian National Survey of Mental Health and Well-Being. *Psychological Medicine, 31*, 1237–1247. http://dx.doi.org/10.1017/S0033291701004287

Dalenberg, C. J. (2000). *Countertransference and the treatment of trauma*. Washington, DC: American Psychological Association. http://dx.doi.org/10.1037/10380-000

Dalenberg, C. J., Brand, B. L., Gleaves, D. H., Dorahy, M. J., Loewenstein, R. J., Cardeña, E., . . . Spiegel, D. (2012). Evaluation of the evidence for the trauma and fantasy models of dissociation. *Psychological Bulletin, 138*, 550–588. http://dx.doi.org/10.1037/a0027447

Danieli, Y. (2005). Guide: Some principles of self care. *Journal of Aggression, Maltreatment & Trauma, 10*, 663–665. http://dx.doi.org/10.1300/J146v10n01_23

De Bellis, M. D., Keshavan, M. S., Clark, D. B., Casey, B. J., Giedd, J. N., Boring, A. M., . . . Ryan, N. D. (1999). Developmental traumatology: II. Brain development. *Biological Psychiatry, 45,* 1271–1284. http://dx.doi.org/10.1016/S0006-3223(99)00045-1

De Bellis, M. D., Keshavan, M. S., Shifflett, H., Iyengar, S., Beers, S. R., Hall, J., & Moritz, G. (2002). Brain structures in pediatric maltreatment-related posttraumatic stress disorder: A sociodemographically matched study. *Biological Psychiatry, 52,* 1066–1078. http://dx.doi.org/10.1016/S0006-3223(02)01459-2

De Jongh, A., Resick, P. A., Zoellner, L. A., van Minnen, A., Lee, C. W., Monson, C. M., . . . Bicanic, I. A. E. (2016). Critical analysis of the current treatment guidelines for complex PTSD in adults. *Depression and Anxiety, 33,* 359–369. http://dx.doi.org/10.1002/da.22469

Del Casale, F., Munilla, H. L., Rovera de Del Casale, L., & Fullone, E. (1982). Defective parenting and reparenting. *Transactional Analysis Journal, 12,* 181–184. http://dx.doi.org/10.1177/036215378201200302

Delker, B. C., & Freyd, J. J. (2014). From betrayal to the bottle: Investigating possible pathways from trauma to problematic substance use. *Journal of Traumatic Stress, 27,* 576–584. http://dx.doi.org/10.1002/jts.21959

Dell, P. F. (1988). Professional skepticism about multiple personality. *Journal of Nervous and Mental Disease, 176,* 528–531. http://dx.doi.org/10.1097/00005053-198809000-00002

Dell, P. F. (2013). Three dimensions of dissociative amnesia. *Journal of Trauma & Dissociation, 14,* 25–39. http://dx.doi.org/10.1080/15299732.2012.724762

DeRose, L. M., Shiyko, M., Levey, S., Helm, J., & Hastings, P. D. (2014). Early maternal depression and social skills in adolescence: A marginal structural modeling approach. *Social Development, 23,* 753–769. http://dx.doi.org/10.1111/sode.12073

Desmarais, S. L., Reeves, K. A., Nicholls, T. L., Telford, R. P., & Fiebert, M. S. (2012). Prevalence of physical violence in intimate relationships, Part 1: Rates of male and female victimization. *Partner Abuse, 3,* 140–169. http://dx.doi.org/10.1891/1946-6560.3.2.140

Dienes, Z., Brown, E., Hutton, S., Kirsch, I., Mazzoni, G., & Wright, D. B. (2009). Hypnotic suggestibility, cognitive inhibition, and dissociation. *Consciousness and Cognition, 18,* 837–847. http://dx.doi.org/10.1016/j.concog.2009.07.009

Di Nicola, M., Ferri, V. R., Moccia, L., Panaccione, I., Strangio, A. M., Tedeschi, D., . . . Janiri, L. (2017). Gender differences and psychopathological features associated with addictive behaviors in adolescents. *Frontiers in Psychiatry, 8,* Article 256. http://dx.doi.org/10.3389/fpsyt.2017.00256

Dong, M., Anda, R. F., Dube, S. R., Giles, W. H., & Felitti, V. J. (2003). The relationship of exposure to childhood sexual abuse to other forms of abuse, neglect, and household dysfunction during childhood. *Child Abuse & Neglect, 27,* 625–639. http://dx.doi.org/10.1016/S0145-2134(03)00105-4

Dong, M., Anda, R. F., Felitti, V. J., Dube, S. R., Williamson, D. F., Thompson, T. J., . . . Giles, W. H. (2004). The interrelatedness of multiple forms of childhood abuse, neglect, and household dysfunction. *Child Abuse & Neglect,* 771–784. http://dx.doi.org/10.1016/j.chiabu.2004.01.008

Dorahy, M. J., Corry, M., Shannon, M., Macsherry, A., Hamilton, G., McRobert, G., . . . Hanna, D. (2009). Complex PTSD, interpersonal trauma and relational consequences: Findings from a treatment-receiving Northern Irish sample. *Journal of Affective Disorders, 112,* 71–80. http://dx.doi.org/10.1016/j.jad.2008.04.003

Dorahy, M. J., Brand, B. L., Şar, V., Krüger, C., Stavropoulos, P., Martinez-Taboas, A., . . . Middleton, W. (2014). Dissociative identity disorder: An empirical overview. *Australian & New Zealand Journal of Psychiatry, 48*, 402–417. http://dx.doi.org/10.1177/0004867414527523

Dorahy, M. J., Shannon, C., Seagar, L., Corr, M., Stewart, K., Hanna, D., . . . Middleton, W. (2009). Auditory hallucinations in dissociative identity disorder and schizophrenia with and without a childhood trauma history: Similarities and differences. *Journal of Nervous and Mental Disease, 197*, 892–898. http://dx.doi.org/10.1097/NMD.0b013e3181c299ea

Draijer, N., & Langeland, W. (1999). Childhood trauma and perceived parental dysfunction in the etiology of dissociative symptoms in psychiatric patients. *The American Journal of Psychiatry, 156*, 379–385.

Driessen, M., Herrmann, J., Stahl, K., Zwaan, M., Meier, S., Hill, A., . . . Petersen, D. (2000). Magnetic resonance imaging volumes of the hippocampus and the amygdala in women with borderline personality disorder and early traumatization. *Archives of General Psychiatry, 57*, 1115–1122. http://dx.doi.org/10.1001/archpsyc.57.12.1115

Dube, S. R., Anda, R. F., Felitti, V. J., Croft, J. B., Edwards, V. J., & Giles, W. H. (2001). Growing up with parental alcohol abuse: Exposure to childhood abuse, neglect, and household dysfunction. *Child Abuse & Neglect, 25*, 1627–1640. http://dx.doi.org/10.1016/S0145-2134(01)00293-9

Dutra, L., Bureau, J. F., Holmes, B., Lyubchik, A., & Lyons-Ruth, K. (2009). Quality of early care and childhood trauma: A prospective study of developmental pathways to dissociation. *Journal of Nervous and Mental Disease, 197*, 383–390. http://dx.doi.org/10.1097/NMD.0b013e3181a653b7

Ellason, J. W., Ross, C. A., & Fuchs, D. L. (1996). Lifetime axis I and II comorbidity and childhood trauma history in dissociative identity disorder. *Psychiatry: Interpersonal and Biological Processes, 59*, 255–266. http://dx.doi.org/10.1080/00332747.1996.11024766

Enoch, M.-A. (2011). The role of early life stress as a predictor for alcohol and drug dependence. *Psychopharmacology, 214*, 17–31. http://dx.doi.org/10.1007/s00213-010-1916-6

Escalona, R., Achilles, G., Waitzkin, H., & Yager, J. (2004). PTSD and somatization in women treated at a VA primary care clinic. *Psychosomatics, 45*, 291–296. http://dx.doi.org/10.1176/appi.psy.45.4.291

Evren, C., Şar, V., & Dalbudak, E. (2008). Temperament, character, and dissociation among detoxified male inpatients with alcohol dependency. *Journal of Clinical Psychology, 64*, 717–727. http://dx.doi.org/10.1002/jclp.20485

Evren, C., Umut, G., Bozkurt, M., Evren, B., & Agachanli, R. (2016). Mediating role of childhood emotional abuse on the relationship between severity of ADHD and PTSD symptoms in a sample of male inpatients with alcohol use disorder. *Psychiatry Research, 239*, 320–324. http://dx.doi.org/10.1016/j.psychres.2016.03.049

Fassler, I. R., Amodeo, M., Griffin, M. L., Clay, C. M., & Ellis, M. A. (2005). Predicting long-term outcomes for women sexually abused in childhood: Contribution of abuse severity versus family environment. *Child Abuse & Neglect, 29*, 269–284. http://dx.doi.org/10.1016/j.chiabu.2004.12.006

Felitti, V. J. (2002). Belastungen in der Kindheit und Gesundheit im Erwachsenenalter: Die Verwandlung von Gold in Blei [The relationship of adverse childhood experiences to adult health: Turning gold into lead]. *Zeitschrift für Psychosomatische Medizin und Psychotherapie, 48*, 359–369. http://dx.doi.org/10.13109/zptm.2002.48.4.359

Felitti, V. J., Anda, R. F., Nordenberg, D., Williamson, D. F., Spitz, A. M., Edwards, V., . . . Marks, J. S. (1998). Relationship of childhood abuse and household dysfunction to many of the leading causes of death in adults. The Adverse Childhood Experiences (ACE) Study. *American Journal of Preventive Medicine, 14*, 245–258. http://dx.doi.org/10.1016/S0749-3797(98)00017-8

Ferguson, J. M., Marquis, J. N., & Taylor, C. B. (1977). A script for deep muscle relaxation. *Diseases of the Nervous System, 38*, 703–708.

Fertuck, E. A., Tsoi, F., Grinband, J., Ruglass, L., Melara, R., & Hien, D. A. (2016). Facial trustworthiness perception bias elevated in individuals with PTSD compared to trauma exposed controls. *Psychiatry Research, 237*, 43–48. http://dx.doi.org/10.1016/j.psychres.2016.01.056

Figley, C. R. (1978). *Stress disorders among Vietnam veterans: Theory, research and treatment*. New York, NY: Brunner/Mazel.

Figley, C. R. (2002). Compassion fatigue: Psychotherapists' chronic lack of self care. *Journal of Clinical Psychology, 58*, 1433–1441. http://dx.doi.org/10.1002/jclp.10090

Figley, C. R. (Ed.). (2006). *Mapping trauma and its wake: Autobiographical essays by pioneer trauma scholars*. New York, NY: Routledge.

Foa, E. B., Cashman, L., Jaycox, L., & Perry, K. (1997). The validation of a self-report measure of posttraumatic stress disorder: The Posttraumatic Diagnostic Scale. *Psychological Assessment, 9*, 445–451. http://dx.doi.org/10.1037/1040-3590.9.4.445

Foa, E. B., Hembree, E. A., & Rothbaum, B. O. (2007). *Prolonged exposure therapy for PTSD: Emotional processing of traumatic experiences—Therapist guide*. New York, NY: Oxford University Press. http://dx.doi.org/10.1093/med:psych/9780195308501.001.0001

Foa, E. B., Keane, T. M., Friedman, M. J., & Cohen, J. A. (Eds.). (2009). *Effective treatments for PTSD: Practice guidelines from the international society for traumatic stress studies* (2nd ed.). New York, NY: Guilford Press.

Foa, E. B., Zoellner, L. A., Feeny, N. C., Hembree, E. A., & Alvarez-Conrad, J. (2002). Does imaginal exposure exacerbate PTSD symptoms? *Journal of Consulting and Clinical Psychology, 70*, 1022–1028. http://dx.doi.org/10.1037/0022-006X.70.4.1022

Ford, J. D., Courtois, C. A., Steele, K., van der Hart, O., & Nijenhuis, E. R. (2005). Treatment of complex posttraumatic self-dysregulation. *Journal of Traumatic Stress, 18*, 437–447. http://dx.doi.org/10.1002/jts.20051

Ford, J. D., Pinazzola, J., van der Kolk, B., & Grasso, D. J. (2011). Toward an empirically based developmental trauma disorder diagnosis for children: Factor, structure, item, characteristics, reliability, and validity of the Developmental Trauma Disorder Semi-Structured Interview. *Journal of Clinical Psychiatry, 79*, 17m11675. http://dx.doi.org/10.4088/JCP.17m11675

Ford, J. D., Racusin, R., Ellis, C. G., Daviss, W. B., Reiser, J., Fleischer, A., & Thomas, J. (2000). Child maltreatment, other trauma exposure, and posttraumatic symptomatology among children with oppositional defiant and attention deficit hyperactivity disorders. *Child Maltreatment, 5*, 205–217. http://dx.doi.org/10.1177/1077559500005003001

Forrest-Bank, S., Jenson, J. M., & Trecartin, S. (2015). The revised 28-item racial and ethnic microaggressions scale (R28REMS): Examining the factorial structure for Black, Latino/Hispanic, and Asian young adults. *Journal of Social Service Research, 41*, 326–344. http://dx.doi.org/10.1080/01488376.2014.987944

French, G. D., & Harris, C. J. (1998). *Traumatic incident reduction*. Boca Raton, FL: CRC Press.

Freudenberger, H. J. (1977). Burn-out: Occupational hazard of the child care worker. *Child Care Quarterly, 6*, 90–99. http://dx.doi.org/10.1007/BF01554695

Freyd, J. (1994). Betrayal trauma: Traumatic amnesia as an adaptive response to childhood abuse. *Ethics & Behavior, 4*, 307–329. http://dx.doi.org/10.1207/s15327019eb0404_1

Frischholz, E. J., Lipman, L. S., Braun, B. G., & Sachs, R. G. (1992). Psychopathology, hypnotizability, and dissociation. *The American Journal of Psychiatry, 149*, 1521–1525. http://dx.doi.org/10.1176/ajp.149.11.1521

Ganzel, B. L., Kim, P., Gilmore, H., Tottenham, N., & Temple, E. (2013). Stress and the healthy adolescent brain: Evidence for the neural embedding of life events. *Development and Psychopathology, 25*, 879–889. http://dx.doi.org/10.1017/S0954579413000242

Garb, H. N., Lilienfeld, S. O., & Fowler, K. A. (2005). Psychological assessment and clinical judgment. In J. E. Maddux, & B. A. Winstead (Eds.), *Psychopathology: Foundations for a contemporary understanding* (pp. 85–108). Mahwah, NJ: Erlbaum.

Gelinas, D. J. (2003). Integrating EMDR into phase-oriented treatment for trauma. *Journal of Trauma & Dissociation, 4*, 91–135. http://dx.doi.org/10.1300/J229v04n03_06

Gilbar, O., Hyland, P., Cloitre, M., & Dekel, R. (2018). ICD–11 complex PTSD among Israeli male perpetrators of intimate partner violence: Construct validity and risk factors. *Journal of Anxiety Disorders, 54*, 49–56. http://dx.doi.org/10.1016/j.janxdis.2018.01.004

Gleaves, D. H., May, M. C., & Cardeña, E. (2001). An examination of the diagnostic validity of dissociative identity disorder. *Clinical Psychology Review, 21*, 577–608. http://dx.doi.org/10.1016/S0272-7358(99)00073-2

Gobin, R. L. (2012). Partner preferences among survivors of betrayal trauma. *Journal of Trauma & Dissociation, 13*, 152–174. http://dx.doi.org/10.1080/15299732.2012.642752

Gobin, R. L., & Freyd, J. J. (2014). The impact of betrayal trauma on the tendency to trust. *Psychological Trauma: Theory, Research, Practice, and Policy, 6*, 505–511. http://dx.doi.org/10.1037/a0032452

Goff, D. C., & Simms, C. A. (1993). Has multiple personality disorder remained consistent over time? A comparison of past and recent cases. *Journal of Nervous and Mental Disease, 181*, 595–600. http://dx.doi.org/10.1097/00005053-199310000-00003

Gold, S. N. (2000). *Not trauma alone: Therapy for child abuse survivors in family and social context*. New York, NY: Brunner-Routledge.

Gold, S. N. (2004a). Fight club: A depiction of contemporary society as dissociogenic. *Journal of Trauma & Dissociation, 5*, 13–34. http://dx.doi.org/10.1300/J229v05n02_02

Gold, S. N. (2004b). The relevance of trauma to general clinical practice. *Psychotherapy: Theory, Research, Practice, Training, 41*, 363–373. http://dx.doi.org/10.1037/0033-3204.41.4.363

Gold, S. N. (2009). Contextual therapy. In C. A. Courtois, & J. D. Ford (Eds.), *Treating complex traumatic stress disorders: An evidence-based guide* (pp. 227–242). New York, NY: Guilford Press.

Gold, S. N. (2017). Growing together: A contextual perspective on countertrauma, counterresilience, and countergrowth. In R. B. Gartner (Ed.), *Trauma and countertrauma, resilience and counterresilience: Insights from psychoanalysts and trauma experts* (pp. 112–125). New York, NY: Routledge.

Gold, S. N., & Bacigalupe, G. (1998). Interpersonal and systems theories of personality. In D. F. Barone, M. Hersen, & V. B. Van Hasselt (Eds.), *Advanced personality* (pp. 57–79). Boston, MA: Springer. http://dx.doi.org/10.1007/978-1-4419-8580-4_3

Gold, S. N., & Brown, L. S. (1997). Therapeutic responses to delayed recall: Beyond recovered memory. *Psychotherapy: Theory, Research, Practice, Training, 34*, 182–191. http://dx.doi.org/10.1037/h0087814

Gold, S. N., Dalenberg, C. J., & Cook, J. M. (2017). Future directions: Consensus and controversies. In S. N. Gold (Ed.), *APA handbook of trauma psychology: Foundations in knowledge* (Vol. 1, pp. 595–600). Washington, DC: American Psychological Association. http://dx.doi.org/10.1037/0000019-030

Gold, S. N., Elhai, J. D., Rea, B. D., Weiss, D., Masino, T., Morris, S. L., & McIninch, J. (2001). Contextual treatment of dissociative identity disorder: Three case studies. *Journal of Trauma & Dissociation, 2*, 5–36. http://dx.doi.org/10.1300/J229v02n04_02

Gold, S. N., & Ellis, A. E. (2017). Contextual treatment of complex trauma. In S. N. Gold (Ed.), *APA handbook of trauma psychology: Trauma* (Vol. 2, pp. 327–342). Washington, DC: American Psychological Association.

Gold, S. N., Hyman, S. M., & Andrés-Hyman, R. C. (2004). Family of origin environments in two clinical samples of survivors of intra-familial, extra-familial, and both types of sexual abuse. *Child Abuse & Neglect, 28*, 1199–1212. http://dx.doi.org/10.1016/j.chiabu.2004.07.001

Gold, S. N., & Seibel, S. L. (2009). Treating dissociation: A contextual approach. In P. F. Dell, & J. A. O'Neil (Eds.), *Dissociation and the dissociative disorders:* DSM–V and beyond (pp. 625–636). New York, NY: Routledge.

Gold, S. N., & Seifer, R. E. (2002). Dissociation and sexual addiction/compulsivity: A contextual approach to conceptualization and treatment. *Journal of Trauma & Dissociation, 3*, 59–82. http://dx.doi.org/10.1300/J229v03n04_04

Golier, J. A., Yehuda, R., Bierer, L. M., Mitropoulou, V., New, A. S., Schmeidler, J., . . . Siever, L. J. (2003). The relationship of borderline personality disorder to posttraumatic stress disorder and traumatic events. *The American Journal of Psychiatry, 160*, 2018–2024. http://dx.doi.org/10.1176/appi.ajp.160.11.2018

Gomez-Perales, N. (2015). *Attachment-focused trauma treatment for children and adolescents: Phase-oriented strategies for addressing complex trauma disorders*. New York, NY: Routledge.

Grabe, H. J., Rainermann, S., Spitzer, S., Gänsicke, M., & Freyberger, H. J. (2000). The relationship between dimensions of alexithymia and dissociation. *Psychotherapy and Psychosomatics, 69*, 128–131. http://dx.doi.org/10.1159/000012380

Grant, J. E., Schreiber, L. R. N., & Harvanko, A. M. (2012). Neurobiology of addiction: Support for a syndrome model of addiction. In H. J. Shaffer, D. A. LaPlante, & S. E. Nelson (Eds.), *APA addiction syndrome handbook: Vol. 1. Foundations, influences, and expressions of addiction* (pp. 121–146). Washington, DC: American Psychological Association. http://dx.doi.org/10.1037/13751-006

Griffin, M. L., & Amodeo, M. (2010). Predicting long-term outcomes for women physically abused in childhood: Contribution of abuse severity versus family environment. *Child Abuse & Neglect, 34*, 724–733. http://dx.doi.org/10.1016/j.chiabu.2010.03.005

Grubbs, J. B., Chapman, H., Milner, L., Gutierrez, I. A., & Bradley, D. F. (2018). Examining links between posttraumatic stress and gambling motives: The role of positive gambling expectancies. *Psychology of Addictive Behaviors, 32*, 821–831. http://dx.doi.org/10.1037/adb0000399

Guideline Development Panel for the Treatment of PTSD in Adults, American Psychological Association. (2019). Summary of the clinical practice guideline for the treatment of posttraumatic stress disorder (PTSD) in adults. *American Psychologist, 74*, 596–607. http://dx.doi.org/10.1037/amp0000473

Handshake. (n.d.). In *Wikipedia*. Retrieved October 8, 2018, from https://en.wikipedia.org/wiki/Handshake

Hannan, S. M., & Orcutt, H. K. (2013). Emotion dysregulation as a partial mediator between reinforcement sensitivity and posttraumatic stress symptoms. *Personality and Individual Differences, 55*, 574–578. http://dx.doi.org/10.1016/j.paid.2013.04.028

Hartman, R. (Producer). (1999). Strive: A second look [Television series episode]. *60 Minutes*. New York, NY: Columbia Broadcasting System.

Hauffa, R., Rief, W., Brähler, E., Martin, A., Mewes, R., & Glaesmer, H. (2011). Lifetime traumatic experiences and posttraumatic stress disorder in the German population: Results of a representative population survey. *Journal of Nervous and Mental Disease, 199*, 934–939. http://dx.doi.org/10.1097/NMD.0b013e3182392c0d

Hayes, S. C., Strosahl, K. D., & Wilson, K. G. (2012). *Acceptance and commitment therapy: The process and practice of mindful change* (2nd ed.). New York, NY: Guilford Press.

Herman, J. L. (1992a). Complex PTSD: A syndrome in survivors of prolonged and repeated trauma. *Journal of Traumatic Stress, 5*, 377–391. http://dx.doi.org/10.1002/jts.2490050305

Herman, J. L. (1992b). *Trauma and recovery: The aftermath of violence—From domestic abuse to political terror*. New York, NY: Basic Books.

Herman, J. (2012). CPTSD is a distinct entity: Comment on Resick et al. (2012). *Journal of Occupational and Organizational Psychology, 25*, 256–257. http://dx.doi.org/10.1002/jts.21697

Hill, E. L., Gold, S. N., & Bornstein, R. F. (2001). Interpersonal dependency among adult survivors of childhood sexual abuse in therapy. *Journal of Child Sexual Abuse, 9*, 71–86. http://dx.doi.org/10.1300/J070v09n02_05

Hooper, L. M., Stockton, P., Krupnick, J. L., & Green, B. L. (2011). Development, use, and psychometric properties of the Trauma History Questionnaire. *Journal of Loss and Trauma, 16*, 258–283. http://dx.doi.org/10.1080/15325024.2011.572035

Hsieh, Y., Shen, A. C., Wei, H., Feng, J., Huang, S. C., & Hwa, H. (2016). Associations between child maltreatment, PTSD, and Internet addiction among Taiwanese students. *Computers in Human Behavior, 56*, 209–214. http://dx.doi.org/10.1016/j.chb.2015.11.048

Hughes, C., Roman, G., Hart, M. J., & Ensor, R. (2013). Does maternal depression predict young children's executive function?—A 4-year longitudinal study. *Journal of Child Psychology and Psychiatry, 54*, 169–177. http://dx.doi.org/10.1111/jcpp.12014

Hulsey, T. L., Sexton, M. C., & Nash, M. R. (1992). Perceptions of family functioning and the occurrence of childhood sexual abuse. *Bulletin of the Menninger Clinic, 56,* 438–450.

Hyland, P., Shevlin, M., Elklit, A., Murphy, J., Vallières, F., Garvert, D. W., & Cloitre, M. (2017). An assessment of the construct validity of the ICD-11 proposal for complex posttraumatic stress disorder. *Psychological Trauma: Theory, Research, Practice, and Policy, 9,* 1–9. http://dx.doi.org/10.1037/tra0000114

Imperatori, C., Innamorati, M., Lamis, D. A., Farina, B., Pompili, M., Contardi, A., & Fabbricatore, M. (2016). Childhood trauma in obese and overweight women with food addiction and clinical-level of binge eating. *Child Abuse & Neglect, 58,* 180–190. http://dx.doi.org/10.1016/j.chiabu.2016.06.023

International Society for the Study of Trauma and Dissociation. (2011). Guidelines for treating dissociative identity disorder in adults, third revision. *Journal of Trauma & Dissociation, 12,* 115–187. http://dx.doi.org/10.1080/15299732.2011.537247

Kabat-Zinn, J. (2003). Mindfulness-based stress reduction (MBSR). *Constructivism in the Human Sciences, 8,* 73–107.

Kalmakis, K. A., & Chandler, G. E. (2014). Adverse childhood experiences: Towards a clear conceptual meaning. *Journal of Advanced Nursing, 70,* 1489–1501. http://dx.doi.org/10.1111/jan.12329

Karatzias, T., Cloitre, M., Maercker, A., Kazlauskas, E., Shevlin, M., Hyland, P., . . . Brewin, C. R. (2017). PTSD and Complex PTSD: ICD-11 updates on concept and measurement in the UK, USA, Germany and Lithuania. *European Journal of Psychotraumatology, 8,* 1418103.

Karatzias, T., Shevlin, M., Fyvie, C., Hyland, P., Efthymiadou, E., Wilson, D., . . . Cloitre, M. (2016). An initial psychometric assessment of an ICD-11 based measure of PTSD and complex PTSD (ICD-TQ): Evidence of construct validity. *Journal of Anxiety Disorders, 44,* 73–79. http://dx.doi.org/10.1016/j.janxdis.2016.10.009

Karatzias, T., Shevlin, M., Fyvie, C., Hyland, P., Efthymiadou, E., Wilson, D., . . . Cloitre, M. (2017). Evidence of distinct profiles of posttraumatic stress disorder (PTSD) and complex posttraumatic stress disorder (CPTSD) based on the new ICD-11 trauma questionnaire (ICD-TQ). *Journal of Affective Disorders, 207,* 181–187. http://dx.doi.org/10.1016/j.jad.2016.09.032

Kardefelt-Winther, D., Heeren, A., Schimmenti, A., van Rooij, A., Maurage, P., Carras, M., . . . Billieux, J. (2017). How can we conceptualize behavioural addiction without pathologizing common behaviours? *Addiction, 112,* 1709–1715. http://dx.doi.org/10.1111/add.13763

Kattari, S. K. (2019). The development and validation of the Ableist Microaggression Scale. *Journal of Social Service Research, 45,* 400–417. http://dx.doi.org/10.1080/01488376.2018.1480565

Kazlauskas, E., Gegieckaite, G., Hyland, P., Zelviene, P., & Cloitre, M. (2018). The structure of ICD-11 PTSD and complex PTSD in Lithuanian mental health services. *European Journal of Psychotraumatology, 9,* Article 1414559. http://dx.doi.org/10.1080/20008198.2017.1414559

Kealy, D., Rice, S. M., Ogrodniczuk, J. S., & Spidel, A. (2018). Childhood trauma and somatic symptoms among psychiatric outpatients: Investigating the role of shame and guilt. *Psychiatry Research, 268,* 169–174. http://dx.doi.org/10.1016/j.psychres.2018.06.072

Kessler, R. C., Sonnega, A., Bromet, E., Hughes, M., & Nelson, C. B. (1995). Posttraumatic stress disorder in the National Comorbidity Survey. *Archives of General Psychiatry, 52,* 1048–1060. http://dx.doi.org/10.1001/archpsyc.1995.03950240066012

Kilpatrick, D. G., Badour, C. L., & Resnick, H. S. (2017). Trauma and posttraumatic stress disorder prevalence and sociodemographic characteristics. In S. N. Gold (Ed.), *APA handbook of trauma psychology: Foundations in knowledge* (Vol. 1, pp. 63–85). Washington, DC: American Psychological Association. http://dx.doi.org/10.1037/0000019-004

Kilpatrick, D. G., Resnick, H. S., Milanak, M. E., Miller, M. W., Keyes, K. M., & Friedman, M. J. (2013). National estimates of exposure to traumatic events and PTSD prevalence using *DSM–IV* and *DSM–5* criteria. *Journal of Traumatic Stress, 26,* 537–547. http://dx.doi.org/10.1002/jts.21848

Kinsler, P. J. (2017). *Complex psychological trauma: The centrality of relationship.* New York, NY: Routledge. http://dx.doi.org/10.4324/9781315651910

Kluemper, N. S., & Dalenberg, C. (2014). Is the dissociative adult suggestible? A test of the trauma and fantasy models of dissociation. *Journal of Trauma & Dissociation, 15,* 457–476. http://dx.doi.org/10.1080/15299732.2014.880772

Kluft, R. P. (1987). First-rank symptoms as a diagnostic clue to multiple personality disorder. *The American Journal of Psychiatry, 144,* 293–298. http://dx.doi.org/10.1176/ajp.144.3.293

Kluft, R. P. (2005). Diagnosing dissociative identity disorder. *Psychiatric Annals, 35,* 633–643.

Kluft, R. P. (2012). The same old elephant. . . . *Journal of Trauma & Dissociation, 13,* 259–270. http://dx.doi.org/10.1080/15299732.2011.652347

Kong, S. S., Kang, D. R., Oh, M. J., & Kim, N. H. (2018). Attachment insecurity as a mediator of the relationship between childhood trauma and adult dissociation. *Journal of Trauma & Dissociation, 19,* 214–231. http://dx.doi.org/10.1080/15299732.2017.1329772

Kulka, R. A., Schlenger, W. E., Fairbank, J. A., Hough, R. L., Jordan, B. K., Marmar, C. R., & Weiss, D. S. (1990). *Trauma and the Vietnam War generation: Report of findings from the National Vietnam Veterans Readjustment Study.* Philadelphia, PA: Brunner/Mazel.

Laddis, A., Dell, P. F., & Korzekwa, M. (2017). Comparing the symptoms and mechanisms of "dissociation" in dissociative identity disorder and borderline personality disorder. *Journal of Trauma & Dissociation, 18,* 139–173. http://dx.doi.org/10.1080/15299732.2016.1194358

Laible, D. (2007). Attachment with parents and peers in late adolescence: Links with emotional competence and social behavior. *Personality and Individual Differences, 43,* 1185–1197. http://dx.doi.org/10.1016/j.paid.2007.03.010

La Mott, J., & Martin, L. A. (2019). Adverse childhood experiences, self-care, and compassion outcomes in mental health providers working with trauma. *Journal of Clinical Psychology, 75,* 1066–1083. http://dx.doi.org/10.1002/jclp.22752

Lancaster, C. L., Teeters, J. B., Gros, D. F., & Back, S. E. (2016). Posttraumatic stress disorder: Overview of evidence-based assessment and treatment. *Journal of Clinical Medicine, 5,* 105. http://dx.doi.org/10.3390/jcm5110105

Lanning, K. V. (2010). *Child molesters: A behavioral analysis for professional investigating the sexual exploitation of children* (5th ed.). Alexandria, VA: National Center for Missing and Exploited Children.

Liao, K. Y., Weng, C. Y., & West, L. M. (2016). Social connectedness and intolerance of uncertainty as moderators between racial microaggressions and anxiety among Black individuals. *Journal of Counseling Psychology, 63*, 240–246. http://dx.doi.org/10.1037/cou0000123

Linehan, M. M. (2015). *DBT skills training manual*. New York, NY: Guilford Press.

Liotti, G. (1992). Disorganized/disoriented attachment in the etiology of the dissociative disorders. *Dissociation: Progress in the Dissociative Disorders, 5*, 196–204.

Litvin, J. M., Kaminski, P. L., & Riggs, S. A. (2017). The complex trauma inventory: A self-report measure of posttraumatic stress disorder and complex posttraumatic stress disorder. *Journal of Traumatic Stress, 30*, 602–613. http://dx.doi.org/10.1002/jts.22231

London, K., Bruck, M., Ceci, S. J., & Shuman, D. W. (2007). Disclosure of child sexual abuse: A review of the contemporary empirical literature. In M. Pipe, M. E. Lamb, Y. Orbach, & A. Cederborg (Eds.), *Child sexual abuse: Disclosure, delay, and denial* (pp. 11–39). Mahwah, NJ: Erlbaum.

Ludy-Dobson, C., & Perry, B. D. (2010). The role of healthy relational interactions in buffering the impact of childhood trauma. In E. Gil (Ed.), *Working with children to heal interpersonal trauma: The power of play* (pp. 26–43). New York, NY: Guilford Press.

Luoni, C., Agosti, M., Crugnola, S., Rossi, G., & Termine, C. (2018). Psychopathology, dissociation and somatic symptoms in adolescents who were exposed to traumatic experiences. *Frontiers in Psychology, 9*, 2390. http://dx.doi.org/10.3389/fpsyg.2018.02390

Luthar, S. S., & Latendresse, S. J. (2005). Children of the affluent: Challenges to well-being. *Current Directions in Psychological Science, 14*, 49–53. http://dx.doi.org/10.1111/j.0963-7214.2005.00333.x

Luyten, P., Assche, L. V., Kadriu, F., Krans, J., Claes, L., & Fonagy, P. (2017). Other disorders often associated with psychological trauma. In S. N. Gold (Ed.), *APA handbook of trauma psychology: Foundations in knowledge* (Vol. 1, pp. 243–280). Washington, DC: American Psychological Association. http://dx.doi.org/10.1037/0000019-014

Lynn, S. J., Lilienfeld, S. O., Merckelbach, H., Giesbrecht, T., McNally, R. J., Loftus, E. F., . . . Malaktaris, A. (2014). The trauma model of dissociation: Inconvenient truths and stubborn fictions. Comment on Dalenberg et al. (2012). *Psychological Bulletin, 140*, 896–910. http://dx.doi.org/10.1037/a0035570

Ma, X., Yue, Z. Q., Gong, Z. Q., Zhang, H., Duan, N. Y., Shi, Y. T., . . . Li, Y. F. (2017). The effect of diaphragmatic breathing on attention, negative affect and stress in healthy adults. *Frontiers in Psychology, 8*, 874. http://dx.doi.org/10.3389/fpsyg.2017.00874

Maercker, A., Neimeyer, R. A., & Simiola, V. (2017). Depression and complicated grief. In S. N. Gold (Ed.), *APA handbook of trauma psychology: Foundations in knowledge* (Vol. 1, pp. 185–194). Washington, DC: American Psychological Association. http://dx.doi.org/10.1037/0000019-011

Majohr, K. L., Leenen, K., Grabe, H. J., Jenewein, J., Nuñez, D. G., & Rufer, M. (2011). Alexithymia and its relationship to dissociation in patients with panic disorder. *Journal of Nervous and Mental Disease, 199*, 773–777. http://dx.doi.org/10.1097/NMD.0b013e31822fcbfb

Mann, B. J., & Sanders, S. (1994). Child dissociation and the family context. *Journal of Abnormal Child Psychology, 22*, 373–388. http://dx.doi.org/10.1007/BF02168080

Mason, O., Tyson, M., Jones, C., & Potts, S. (2005). Alexithymia: Its prevalence and correlates in a British undergraduate sample. *Psychology and Psychotherapy: Theory, Research and Practice, 78*, 113–125. http://dx.doi.org/10.1348/147608304X21374

McKenzie-Mohr, S., Coates, J., & McLeod, H. (2012). Responding to the needs of youth who are homeless: Calling for politicized trauma-informed intervention. *Children and Youth Services Review, 34*, 136–143. http://dx.doi.org/10.1016/j.childyouth.2011.09.008

McLaughlin, K. (2017, April). *The long shadow of adverse childhood experiences: Adverse environments early in life have lasting consequences for children's health and development* [Psychological Science Agenda science brief]. Retrieved from https://www.apa.org/science/about/psa/2017/04/adverse-childhood

McLaughlin, K. A., & Sheridan, M. A. (2016). Beyond cumulative risk: A dimensional approach to childhood adversity. *Current Directions in Psychological Science, 25*, 239–245. http://dx.doi.org/10.1177/0963721416655883

McLaughlin, K. A., Sheridan, M. A., & Lambert, H. K. (2014). Childhood adversity and neural development: Deprivation and threat as distinct dimensions of early experience. *Neuroscience and Biobehavioral Reviews, 47*, 578–591. http://dx.doi.org/10.1016/j.neubiorev.2014.10.012

McLaughlin, K. A., Sheridan, M. A., & Nelson, C. A. (2017). Neglect as a violation of species-expectant experience: Neurodevelopmental consequences. *Biological Psychiatry, 82*, 462–471. http://dx.doi.org/10.1016/j.biopsych.2017.02.1096

Meins, E. (2003). Emotional development and early attachment relationships. In A. Slater & G. Bremner (Eds.), *An introduction to developmental psychology* (pp. 141–164). Malden, MA: Blackwell.

Merskey, H. (1994). The artifactual nature of multiple personality disorder: Comments on Charles Barton's "Backstage in psychiatry: The multiple personality disorder controversy." *Dissociation: Progress in the Dissociative Disorders, 7*, 173–175.

Mersky, J. P., & Reynolds, A. J. (2007). Child maltreatment and violent delinquency: Disentangling main effects and subgroup effects. *Child Maltreatment, 12*, 246–258. http://dx.doi.org/10.1177/1077559507301842

Miller, R. G. H., & Spence, J. (2013). The impact of breathing and music on stress levels of clients and visitors in a psychiatric emergency room. *Arts in Psychotherapy, 40*, 347–351. http://dx.doi.org/10.1016/j.aip.2013.06.002

Modestin, J., Lötscher, K., & Erni, T. (2002). Dissociative experiences and their correlates in young non-patients. *Psychology and Psychotherapy: Theory, Research and Practice, 75*, 53–64. http://dx.doi.org/10.1348/147608302169544

Moene, F. C., Spinhoven, P., Hoogduin, K., Sandyck, P., & Roelofs, K. (2001). Hypnotizability, dissociation and trauma in patients with a conversion disorder: An exploratory study. *Clinical Psychology & Psychotherapy, 8*, 400–410. http://dx.doi.org/10.1002/cpp.293

Mollerstrom, W. W., Patchner, M. A., & Milner, J. S. (1992). Family functioning and child abuse potential. *Journal of Clinical Psychology, 48*, 445–454. http://dx.doi.org/10.1002/1097-4679(199207)48:4<445::AID-JCLP2270480404>3.0.CO;2-2

Moormann, P. P., Bermond, B., & Albach, F. (2004). The reality escape model: The intricate relation between alexithymia, dissociation, and anesthesia in victims of child sexual abuse. In I. Nyklíček, L. Temoshok, & A. Vingerhoets (Eds.), *Emotional expression and health: Advances in theory, assessment and clinical applications* (pp. 82–98). New York, NY: Brunner-Routledge.

Moos, R. H., & Moos, B. S. (1986). *Family Environment Scale manual* (2nd ed.). Palo Alto, CA: Consulting Psychologists Press.

Morris, D. J. (2015). *The evil hours: A biography of post-traumatic stress disorder.* New York, NY: Houghton Mifflin Harcourt.

Moss, T. A. (2017, October 18). A guide to kissing etiquette around the world. *Condé Nast Traveler.* Retrieved from https://www.cntraveler.com/story/a-guide-to-kissing-etiquette-around-the-world

Najavits, L. M. (2015a). The problem of dropout from "gold standard" PTSD therapies. *F1000prime Reports, 7,* 43. http://dx.doi.org/10.12703/P7-43

Najavits, L. M. (2015b). Trauma and substance abuse: A clinician's guide to treatment. In U. Schnyder & M. Cloitre (Eds.), *Evidence based treatments for trauma-related psychological disorders: A practical guide for clinicians* (pp. 317–330). Cham, Switzerland: Springer International. http://dx.doi.org/10.1007/978-3-319-07109-1_16

Nash, M. R., Hulsey, T. L., Sexton, M. C., Harralson, T. L., & Lambert, W. (1993). Long-term sequelae of childhood sexual abuse: Perceived family environment, psychopathology, and dissociation. *Journal of Consulting and Clinical Psychology, 61,* 276–283. http://dx.doi.org/10.1037/0022-006X.61.2.276

Nijenhuis, E. R. S., Vanderlinden, J., & Spinhoven, P. (1998). Animal defensive reactions as a model for trauma-induced dissociative reactions. *Journal of Traumatic Stress, 11,* 243–260. http://dx.doi.org/10.1023/A:1024447003022

Norman, S. B., Tate, S. R., Anderson, K. G., & Brown, S. A. (2007). Do trauma history and PTSD symptoms influence addiction relapse context? *Drug and Alcohol Dependence, 90,* 89–96. http://dx.doi.org/10.1016/j.drugalcdep.2007.03.002

Ochberg, F. M. (1996). The counting method for ameliorating traumatic memories. *Journal of Traumatic Stress, 9,* 873–880. http://dx.doi.org/10.1002/jts.2490090415

Ogawa, J. R., Sroufe, L. A., Weinfield, N. S., Carlson, E. A., & Egeland, B. (1997). Development and the fragmented self: Longitudinal study of dissociative symptomatology in a nonclinical sample. *Development and Psychopathology, 9,* 855–879. http://dx.doi.org/10.1017/S0954579497001478

Olson, L. N., Daggs, J. L., Ellevold, B. L., & Rogers, T. K. K. (2007). Entrapping the innocent: Toward a theory of child sexual predators' luring communication. *Communication Theory, 17,* 231–251. http://dx.doi.org/10.1111/j.1468-2885.2007.00294.x

Ouimette, P., & Brown, P. J. (Eds.). (2003). *Trauma and substance abuse: Causes, consequences, and treatment of comorbid disorders.* Washington, DC: American Psychological Association. http://dx.doi.org/10.1037/10460-000

Ouimette, P. C., Kimerling, R., Shaw, J., & Moos, R. H. (2000). Physical and sexual abuse among women and men with substance use disorders. *Alcoholism Treatment Quarterly, 18,* 7–17. http://dx.doi.org/10.1300/J020v18n03_02

Paley, A. M. (1988). Growing up in chaos: The dissociative response. *American Journal of Psychoanalysis, 48,* 72–83. http://dx.doi.org/10.1007/BF01252923

Palic, S., Zerach, G., Shevlin, M., Zeligman, Z., Elklit, A., & Solomon, Z. (2016). Evidence of complex posttraumatic stress disorder (CPTSD) across populations with prolonged trauma of varying interpersonal intensity and ages of exposure. *Psychiatry Research, 246,* 692–699. http://dx.doi.org/10.1016/j.psychres.2016.10.062

Palmer, S. E., Brown, R. A., Rae-Grant, N. I., & Loughlin, M. J. (1999). Responding to children's disclosure of familial abuse: What survivors tell us. *Child Welfare, 78,* 259–282.

Paulson, D. S., & Krippner, S. (2007). *Haunted by combat: Understanding PTSD in war veterans including women, reservists, and those coming back from Iraq.* Westport, CT: Praeger Security International.

Pearlman, L. A., & Saakvitne, K. W. (1995). Treating therapists with vicarious traumatization and secondary traumatic stress disorders. In C. R. Figley (Ed.), *Compassion fatigue: Coping with secondary traumatic stress disorder in those who treat the traumatized* (pp. 150–177). New York, NY: Brunner/Mazel.

Penta, C. R. (2000). Dissociation among patients diagnosed with addictive disorders: A comparative and follow up study. *Dissertation Abstracts International, 60,* 9-B, 4902.

Pereda, N., Guilera, G., Forns, M., & Gómez-Benito, J. (2009). The prevalence of child sexual abuse in community and student samples: A meta-analysis. *Clinical Psychology Review, 29,* 328–338. http://dx.doi.org/10.1016/j.cpr.2009.02.007

Perry, B. D., Pollard, R. A., Blakley, T. L., Baker, W. L., & Vigilante, D. (1995). Childhood trauma, the neurobiology of adaptation, and "use-dependent" development of the brain: How "states" become "traits." *Infant Mental Health Journal, 16,* 271–291. http://dx.doi.org/10.1002/1097-0355(199524)16:4<271::AID-IMHJ2280160404>3.0.CO;2-B

Pietrzak, R. H., Goldstein, R. B., Southwick, S. M., & Grant, B. F. (2012). Psychiatric comorbidity of full and partial posttraumatic stress disorder among older adults in the United States: Results from wave 2 of the National Epidemiologic Survey on Alcohol and Related Conditions. *American Journal of Geriatric Psychiatry, 20,* 380–390. http://dx.doi.org/10.1097/JGP.0b013e31820d92e7

Pitman, R. K., Altman, B., Greenwald, E., Longpre, R. E., Macklin, M. L., Poiré, R. E., & Steketee, G. S. (1991). Psychiatric complications during flooding therapy for posttraumatic stress disorder. *Journal of Clinical Psychiatry, 52,* 17–20.

Platt, M. G., & Freyd, J. J. (2015). Betray my trust, shame on me: Shame, dissociation, fear, and betrayal trauma. *Psychological Trauma: Theory, Research, Practice, and Policy, 7,* 398–404. http://dx.doi.org/10.1037/tra0000022

Powers, A., Fani, N., Carter, S., Cross, D., Cloitre, M., & Bradley, B. (2017). Differential predictors of *DSM–5* PTSD and ICD–11 complex PTSD among African American women. *European Journal of Psychotraumatology, 8,* 1338914. http://dx.doi.org/10.1080/20008198.2017.1338914

Price, D. A. (1996). Inner child work: What is really happening? *Dissociation: Progress in the Dissociative Disorders, 9,* 68–73. Available at https://scholarsbank.uoregon.edu/xmlui/handle/1794/1772

Putnam, F. W. (1997). *Dissociation in children and adolescents: A developmental perspective.* New York, NY: Guilford Press.

Ray, K. C., Jackson, J. L., & Townsley, R. M. (1991). Family environments of victims of intrafamilial and extrafamilial child sexual abuse. *Journal of Family Violence, 6,* 365–374. http://dx.doi.org/10.1007/BF00980539

Resick, P. A., Monson, C. M., & Chard, K. M. (2017). *Cognitive processing therapy for PTSD: A comprehensive manual.* New York, NY: Guilford Press.

Resnick, H. S., Kilpatrick, D. G., Dansky, B. S., Saunders, B. E., & Best, C. L. (1993). Prevalence of civilian trauma and posttraumatic stress disorder in a representative national sample of women. *Journal of Consulting and Clinical Psychology, 61*, 984–991. http://dx.doi.org/10.1037/0022-006X.61.6.984

Rind, B., Tromovitch, P., & Bauserman, R. (1998). A meta-analytic examination of assumed properties of child sexual abuse using college samples. *Psychological Bulletin, 124*, 22–53.

Rosenkranz, S. E., Muller, R. T., & Henderson, J. L. (2014). The role of complex PTSD in mediating childhood maltreatment and substance abuse severity among youth seeking substance abuse treatment. *Psychological Trauma: Theory, Research, Practice, and Policy, 6*, 25–33. http://dx.doi.org/10.1037/a0031920

Ross, C. A. (1991). Epidemiology of multiple personality disorder and dissociation. *Psychiatric Clinics of North America, 14*, 503–517. http://dx.doi.org/10.1016/S0193-953X(18)30286-7

Ross, C. A., Joshi, S., & Currie, R. (1990). Dissociative experiences in the general population. *The American Journal of Psychiatry, 147*, 1547–1552. http://dx.doi.org/10.1176/ajp.147.11.1547

Ross, C. A., & Ness, L. (2010). Symptom patterns in dissociative identity disorder patients and the general population. *Journal of Trauma & Dissociation, 11*, 458–468. http://dx.doi.org/10.1080/15299732.2010.495939

Rossi, E. L., & Ryan, M. O. (Eds.). (1992). *Mind-body communication in hypnosis: The seminars, workshops, and lecture of Milton H. Erickson* (Vol. 111). New York, NY: Irvington.

Roth, S., Newman, E., Pelcovitz, D., van der Kolk, B., & Mandel, F. S. (1997). Complex PTSD in victims exposed to sexual and physical abuse: Results from the *DSM–IV* field trial for posttraumatic stress disorder. *Journal of Traumatic Stress, 10*, 539–555. http://dx.doi.org/10.1002/jts.2490100403

Rothbaum, B. O., Foa, E. B., Riggs, D. S., Murdock, T., & Walsh, W. (1992). A prospective examination of post-traumatic stress disorder in rape victims. *Journal of Traumatic Stress, 5*, 455–475. http://dx.doi.org/10.1002/jts.2490050309

Sakagami, H., & Suganuma, M. (2001). Attachment and emotion regulation: Attachment and conscious attitudes toward four discrete emotions. *Japanese Journal of Educational Psychology, 49*, 156–166. http://dx.doi.org/10.5926/jjep1953.49.2_156

Şar, V., Alioglu, F., Akyuz, G., & Karabulut, S. (2014). Dissociative amnesia in dissociative disorders and borderline personality disorder: Self-rating assessment in a college population. *Journal of Trauma & Dissociation, 15*, 477–493. http://dx.doi.org/10.1080/15299732.2014.902415

Şar, V., Alioglu, F., Akyuz, G., Tayakisi, E., Öğülmüş, E. F., & Sönmez, D. (2017). Awareness of identity alteration and diagnostic preference between borderline personality disorder and dissociative disorders. *Journal of Trauma & Dissociation, 18*, 693–709. http://dx.doi.org/10.1080/15299732.2016.1267684

Şar, V., Yargiç, L. I., & Tutkun, H. (1996). Structured interview data on 35 cases of dissociative identity disorder in Turkey. *The American Journal of Psychiatry, 153*, 1329–1333. http://dx.doi.org/10.1176/ajp.153.10.1329

Schaffer, J., & Rodolfa, E. (2016). *A student's guide to assessment and diagnosis using the ICD-10-CM: Psychological and behavioral conditions.* Washington, DC: American Psychological Association. http://dx.doi.org/10.1037/14778-000

Schilpzand, E. J., Sciberras, E., Alisic, E., Efron, D., Hazell, P., Jongeling, B., . . . Nicholson, J. M. (2017). Trauma exposure in children with and without ADHD:

Prevalence and functional impairment in a community-based study of 6–8-year-old Australian children. *European Child & Adolescent Psychiatry, 27*, 811–819. http://dx.doi.org/10.1007/s00787-017-1067-y

Schmidt, N. B., Richey, J. A., Zvolensky, M. J., & Maner, J. K. (2008). Exploring human freeze responses to a threat stressor. *Journal of Behavior Therapy and Experimental Psychiatry, 39*, 292–304. http://dx.doi.org/10.1016/j.jbtep.2007.08.002

Schottenbauer, M. A., Glass, C. R., Arnkoff, D. B., Tendick, V., & Gray, S. H. (2008). Nonresponse and dropout rates in outcome studies on PTSD: Review and methodological considerations. *Psychiatry: Interpersonal and Biological Processes, 71*, 134–168. http://dx.doi.org/10.1521/psyc.2008.71.2.134

Seedat, S., Stein, M. B., Oosthuizen, P. P., Emsley, R. A., & Stein, D. J. (2003). Linking posttraumatic stress disorder and psychosis: A look at epidemiology, phenomenology, and treatment. *Journal of Nervous and Mental Disease, 191*, 675–681. http://dx.doi.org/10.1097/01.nmd.0000092177.97317.26

Segal, Z. V., Williams, J. M., & Teasdale, J. D. (2002). *Mindfulness-based cognitive therapy for depression: A new approach to preventing relapse.* New York, NY: Guilford Press.

Segal, Z. V., Williams, J. M., & Teasdale, J. D. (2013). *Mindfulness-based cognitive therapy for depression* (2nd ed.). New York, NY: Guilford Press.

Semiz, Ü. B., Öner, Ö., Cengiz, F. F., & Bilici, M. (2017). Childhood abuse and neglect in adult attention-deficit/hyperactivity disorder. *Psychiatry and Clinical Psychopharmacology, 27*, 344–348. http://dx.doi.org/10.1080/24750573.2017.1367551

Serrano-Sevillano, Á., González-Ordi, H., Corbí-Gran, B., & Vallejo-Pareja, M. (2017). Psychological characteristics of dissociation in general population. *Clínica y Salud, 28*, 101–106. http://dx.doi.org/10.1016/j.clysa.2017.09.003

Shapiro, F. (2017). *Eye movement desensitization and reprocessing (EMDR) therapy: Basic principles, protocols, and procedures* (3rd ed.). New York, NY: Guilford Press. http://dx.doi.org/10.1007/978-3-319-46138-0_13

Sharkansky, E. J., Brief, D. J., Peirce, J. M., Meehan, J. C., & Mannix, L. M. (1999). Substance abuse patients with posttraumatic stress disorder (PTSD): Identifying specific triggers of substance use and their associations with PTSD symptoms. *Psychology of Addictive Behaviors, 13*, 89–97. http://dx.doi.org/10.1037/0893-164X.13.2.89

Shay, J. (2002). *Odysseus in America: Combat trauma and the trials of homecoming.* New York, NY: Scribner.

Sheridan, M. A., & McLaughlin, K. A. (2014). Dimensions of early experience and neural development: Deprivation and threat. *Trends in Cognitive Sciences, 18*, 580–585. http://dx.doi.org/10.1016/j.tics.2014.09.001

Shirar, L. (1996). *Dissociative children: Bridging the inner and outer worlds.* New York, NY: Norton.

Siegel, D. J. (2012). *The developing mind: How relationships and the brain interact to shape who we are* (2nd ed.). New York, NY: Guilford Press.

Simeon, D. (2014). Depersonalization/derealization disorder. In G. O. Gabbard (Ed.), *Gabbard's treatments of psychiatric disorders:* DSM–5 edition (5th ed., pp. 459–470). Arlington, VA: American Psychiatric Publishing. http://dx.doi.org/10.1176/appi.books.9781585625048.gg25

Simeon, D., & Abugel, J. (2006). *Feeling unreal: Depersonalization disorder and the loss of the self.* New York, NY: Oxford University Press.

Simeon, D., Kozin, D. S., Segal, K., & Lerch, B. (2009). Is depersonalization disorder initiated by illicit drug use any different? A survey of 394 adults. *Journal of Clinical Psychiatry*, *70*, 1358–1364. http://dx.doi.org/10.4088/JCP.08m04370

Smith, P. H., Potenza, M. N., Mazure, C. M., McKee, S. A., Park, C. L., & Hoff, R. A. (2014). Compulsive sexual behavior among male military veterans: Prevalence and associated clinical factors. *Journal of Behavioral Addictions, 3*, 214–222. http://dx.doi.org/10.1556/JBA.3.2014.4.2

Somer, E. (2003). Prediction of abstinence from heroin addiction by childhood trauma, dissociation, and extent of psychosocial treatment. *Addiction Research & Theory, 11*, 339–348. http://dx.doi.org/10.1080/1606635031000141102

Spiegel, D., Hunt, T., & Dondershine, H. E. (1988). Dissociation and hypnotizability in posttraumatic stress disorder. *The American Journal of Psychiatry, 145*, 301–305. http://dx.doi.org/10.1176/ajp.145.3.301

Spores, J. M. (2013). *Clinician's guide to psychological assessment and testing: With forms and templates for effective practice*. New York, NY: Springer.

Sprang, G., Ford, J., Kerig, P., & Bride, B. (2019). Defining secondary traumatic stress and developing targeted assessments and interventions: Lessons learned from research and leading experts. *Traumatology, 25*, 72–81. http://dx.doi.org/10.1037/trm0000180

Stanton, H. E. (1984). A comparison of the effects of a hypnotic procedure and music on anxiety level. *Australian Journal of Clinical & Experimental Hypnosis, 12*, 127–132.

Steele, K., van der Hart, O., & Nijenhuis, E. R. S. (2005). Phase-oriented treatment of structural dissociation in complex traumatization: Overcoming trauma-related phobias. *Journal of Trauma & Dissociation, 6*, 11–53. http://dx.doi.org/10.1300/J229v06n03_02

Steenkamp, M. M., Litz, B. T., Hoge, C. W., & Marmar, C. R. (2015). Psychotherapy for military-related PTSD: A review of randomized clinical trials. *JAMA, 314*, 489–500. http://dx.doi.org/10.1001/jama.2015.8370

Stein, D. J., Koenen, K. C., Friedman, M. J., Hill, E., McLaughlin, K. A. Petukhova, M., . . . Kessler, R. C. (2013). Dissociation in posttraumatic stress disorder: Evidence from the World Mental Health Surveys. *Biological Psychiatry, 73*, 302–312. http://dx.doi.org/10.1016/j.biopsych.2012.08.022

Stein, M. B., Koverola, C., Hanna, C., Torchia, M. G., & McClarty, B. (1997). Hippocampal volume in women victimized by childhood sexual abuse. *Psychological Medicine, 27*, 951–959. http://dx.doi.org/10.1017/S0033291797005242

Stein, P. T., & Kendall, J. C. (2004). *Psychological trauma and the developing brain: Neurologically based interventions for troubled children*. New York, NY: Haworth Press.

Steinberg, M. (1995). *Handbook for the assessment of dissociation: A clinical guide*. Washington, DC: American Psychiatric Press.

Steinberg, M., & Schnall, M. (2000). *The stranger in the mirror: Dissociation—The hidden epidemic*. New York, NY: HarperCollins.

Stevens, J. E. (2012, October 3). The Adverse Childhood Experiences Study—the largest, most important public health study you never heard of—began in an obesity clinic. *ACES Too High News*. Retrieved from https://acestoohigh.com/2012/10/03/the-adverse-childhood-experiences-study-the-largest-most-important-public-health-study-you-never-heard-of-began-in-an-obesity-clinic/

Stoltenborgh, M., van IJzendoorn, M. H., Euser, E. M., & Bakermans-Kranenburg, M. J. (2011). A global perspective on child sexual abuse: Meta-analysis of prevalence around the world. *Child Maltreatment, 16*, 79–101. http://dx.doi.org/10.1177/1077559511403920

Sue, D. W. (Ed.). (2010). *Microaggressions and marginality: Manifestation, dynamics, and impact.* New York, NY: Wiley.

Sue, D. W., Capodilupo, C. M., Torino, G. C., Bucceri, J. M., Holder, A. M. B., Nadal, K. L., & Esquilin, M. (2007). Racial microaggressions in everyday life: Implications for clinical practice. *American Psychologist, 62*, 271–286. http://dx.doi.org/10.1037/0003-066X.62.4.271

Sullivan, H. S. (1953). *The interpersonal theory of psychiatry.* New York, NY: Norton.

Sullivan, J., & Beech, A. (2004). A comparative study of demographic data relating to intra- and extra-familial child sexual abusers and professional perpetrators. *Journal of Sexual Aggression, 10*, 39–50. http://dx.doi.org/10.1080/13552600410001667788

Swann, G., Minshew, R., Newcomb, M. E., & Mustanski, B. (2016). Validation of the sexual orientation microaggression inventory in two diverse samples of LGBTQ youth. *Archives of Sexual Behavior, 45*, 1289–1298. http://dx.doi.org/10.1007/s10508-016-0718-2

Swingle, J. M., Tursich, M., Cleveland, J. M., Gold, S. N., Tolliver, S. F., Michaels, L., . . . Sciarrino, N. A. (2016). Childhood disclosure of sexual abuse: Necessary but not necessarily sufficient. *Child Abuse & Neglect, 62*, 10–18. http://dx.doi.org/10.1016/j.chiabu.2016.10.009

Szymanski, K., Sapanski, L., & Conway, F. (2011). Trauma and ADHD—Association or diagnostic confusion? A clinical perspective. *Journal of Infant, Child, & Adolescent Psychotherapy, 10*, 51–59. http://dx.doi.org/10.1080/15289168.2011.575704

Tanaka, S. (2018). What is it like to be disconnected from the body? A phenomenological account of disembodiment in depersonalization/derealization disorder. *Journal of Consciousness Studies, 25*, 239–262.

Teicher, M. H., Dumont, N. L., Ito, Y., Vaituzis, C., Giedd, J. N., & Andersen, S. L. (2004). Childhood neglect is associated with reduced corpus callosum area. *Biological Psychiatry, 56*, 80–85. http://dx.doi.org/10.1016/j.biopsych.2004.03.016

Terhune, D. B., & Cardeña, E. (2015). Dissociative subtypes in posttraumatic stress disorders and hypnosis: Neurocognitive parallels and clinical implications. *Current Directions in Psychological Science, 24*, 452–457. http://dx.doi.org/10.1177/0963721415604611

Terr, L. C. (1979). Children of Chowchilla: A study of psychic trauma. *Psychoanalytic Study of the Child, 34*, 547–623. http://dx.doi.org/10.1080/00797308.1979.11823018

Thanos, K., Cloitre, N., Maercker, A., Kazlauskas, E., Shevlin, M., Hyland, P., . . . Brewin, C. R. (2017). PTSD and complex PTSD: ICD-11 updates on concept and measurement in the UK, USA, Germany and Lithuania. *European Journal of Psychotraumatology, 8*, Article 1418103. http://dx.doi.org/10.1080/20008198.2017.1418103

Thomas, J. L., Wilk, J. E., Riviere, L. A., McGurk, D., Castro, C. A., & Hoge, C. W. (2010). Prevalence of mental health problems and functional impairment among active component and National Guard soldiers 3 and 12 months following combat in Iraq. *Archives of General Psychiatry, 67*, 614–623. http://dx.doi.org/10.1001/archgenpsychiatry.2010.54

Thompson, K. L., Hannan, S. M., & Miron, L. R. (2014). Fight, flight, and freeze: Threat sensitivity and emotion dysregulation in survivors of chronic childhood maltreatment. *Personality and Individual Differences, 69*, 28–32. http://dx.doi.org/10.1016/j.paid.2014.05.005

Thomson, P., & Jaque, S. V. (2018). Depersonalization, adversity, emotionality, and coping with stressful situations. *Journal of Trauma & Dissociation, 19*, 143–161. http://dx.doi.org/10.1080/15299732.2017.1329770

van der Hart, O., Nijenhuis, E. R. S., & Steele, K. (2005). Dissociation: An insufficiently recognized major feature of complex posttraumatic stress disorder. *Journal of Traumatic Stress, 18*, 413–423. http://dx.doi.org/10.1002/jts.20049

van der Kolk, B. A. (2005). Developmental trauma disorder: Toward a rational diagnosis for children with complex trauma histories. *Psychiatric Annals, 35*, 401–408. http://dx.doi.org/10.3928/00485713-20050501-06

van der Kolk, B. A. (2014). *The body keeps the score: Brain, mind, and body in the healing of trauma*. New York, NY: Viking.

van der Kolk, B. A., Roth, S., Pelcovitz, D., Sunday, S., & Spinazzola, J. (2005). Disorders of extreme stress: The empirical foundation of a complex adaptation to trauma. *Journal of Traumatic Stress, 18*, 389–399. http://dx.doi.org/10.1002/jts.20047

van Dijke, A., Ford, J. D., Frank, L. E., & van der Hart, O. (2015). Association of childhood complex trauma and dissociation with complex posttraumatic stress disorder symptoms in adulthood. *Journal of Trauma & Dissociation, 16*, 428–441. http://dx.doi.org/10.1080/15299732.2015.1016253

van Harmelen, A. L., van Tol, M. J., van der Wee, N. J., Veltman, D. J., Aleman, A., Spinhoven, P., . . . Elzinga, B. M. (2010). Reduced medial prefrontal cortex volume in adults reporting childhood emotional maltreatment. *Biological Psychiatry, 68*, 832–838. http://dx.doi.org/10.1016/j.biopsych.2010.06.011

Vio, C. G., Vivanco, A. F., & Morales, C. H. (2009). Efectos de una intervención cognitivo-conductual en el aumento de conductas de autocuidado y disminución del estrés traumático secundario en psicólogos clínicos [Effects of a cognitive-behavioral treatment on the increase of self-care behaviors and decrease of secondary traumatic stress on clinical psychologists]. *Terapia Psicológica, 27*, 73–81. Retrieved from http://search.proquest.com.ezproxylocal.library.nova.edu/docview/852908396?accountid=6579

Vrana, S., & Lauterbach, D. (1994). Prevalence of traumatic events and post-traumatic psychological symptoms in a nonclinical sample of college students. *Journal of Traumatic Stress, 7*, 289–302. http://dx.doi.org/10.1002/jts.2490070209

Walker, L. E. (1979). *The battered woman*. New York, NY: Harper & Row.

Walling, D. P., & Baker, J. M. (1996). Hypnosis training in psychology intern programs. *The American Journal of Clinical Hypnosis, 38*, 219–223. http://dx.doi.org/10.1080/00029157.1996.10403341

Wamser-Nanney, R., & Vandenberg, B. R. (2013). Empirical support for the definition of a complex trauma event in children and adolescents. *Journal of Traumatic Stress, 26*, 671–678. http://dx.doi.org/10.1002/jts.21857

Wechsler-Zimring, A., & Kearney, C. A. (2011). Posttraumatic stress and related symptoms among neglected and physically and sexually maltreated adolescents. *Journal of Traumatic Stress, 24*, 601–604. http://dx.doi.org/10.1002/jts.20683

Whittle, S., Dennison, M., Vijayakumar, N., Simmons, J. G., Yücel, M., Lubman, D. I., . . . Allen, N. B. (2013). Childhood maltreatment and psychopathology affect brain development during adolescence. *Journal of the American Academy of Child & Adolescent Psychiatry, 52,* 940–952.e1. http://dx.doi.org/10.1016/j.jaac.2013.06.007

Widom, C. S. (1999). Posttraumatic stress disorder in abused and neglected children grown up. *The American Journal of Psychiatry, 156,* 1223–1229.

Winnicott, D. W. (1971). *Playing and reality.* New York, NY: Routledge.

Wolpe, J. (1958). *Psychotherapy by reciprocal inhibition.* Stanford, CA: Stanford University Press.

World Health Organization. (2018). *International classification of diseases* (11th ed.). Retrieved from https://icd.who.int/browse11/l-m/en

Yama, M. F., Tovey, S. L., & Fogas, B. S. (1993). Childhood family environment and sexual abuse as predictors of anxiety and depression in adult women. *American Journal of Orthopsychiatry, 63,* 136–141. http://dx.doi.org/10.1037/h0079399

Yama, M. F., Tovey, S. L., Fogas, B. S., & Teegarden, L. A. (1992). Joint consequences of parental alcoholism and childhood sexual abuse, and their partial mediation by family environment. *Violence and Victims, 7,* 313–325. http://dx.doi.org/10.1891/0886-6708.7.4.313

Yan, N., Zhou, N., & Ansari, A. (2016). Maternal depression and children's cognitive and socio-emotional development at first grade: The moderating role of classroom emotional climate. *Journal of Child and Family Studies, 25,* 1247–1256. http://dx.doi.org/10.1007/s10826-015-0301-9

Yehuda, R., & Hoge, C. W. (2016). The meaning of evidence-based treatments for veterans with posttraumatic stress disorder. *JAMA Psychiatry, 73,* 433–434. http://dx.doi.org/10.1001/jamapsychiatry.2015.2878

Zayfert, C., & Black, C. (2000). Implementation of empirically supported treatment for PTSD: Obstacles and innovations. *Behavior Therapist, 23,* 161–168.

Zettle, R. D. (2007). *ACT for depression: A clinician's guide to using acceptance and commitment therapy in treating depression.* Oakland, CA: New Harbinger.

Zlotnick, C., Zakriski, A. L., Shea, M. T., Costello, E., Begin, A., Pearlstein, T., & Simpson, E. (1996). The long-term sequelae of sexual abuse: Support for a complex posttraumatic stress disorder. *Journal of Traumatic Stress, 9,* 195–205. http://dx.doi.org/10.1002/jts.2490090204

Zucker, M., Spinazzola, J., Blaustein, M., & van der Kolk, B. A. (2006). Dissociative symptomatology in posttraumatic stress disorder and disorders of extreme stress. *Journal of Trauma & Dissociation, 7,* 19–31. http://dx.doi.org/10.1300/J229v07n01_03

# INDEX

## A

Abstinence, 42, 235, 236
Acceptance and commitment therapy (ACT), 190
ACEs. *See* Adverse childhood experiences
ADD (attention-deficit disorder), 64
Addictive and compulsive behaviors (ACBs), 233–244. *See also specific headings*
  contextual understanding of, 233–235
  and event-centered trauma processing, 259–260
  interventions for, 110
  SCAN-R procedure for treatment of, 235–244
  and structure in childhood, 58
Adverse childhood experiences (ACEs)
  and brain development, 64
  and causation of complex PTSD, 83
  and conceptualization of psychological difficulties, 80
  and dissociation, 184
  overview, 53–57
  providers with, 144
  subcategories of, 67
Adverse Childhood Experiences Questionnaire, 101
Adverse Childhood Experiences Study, 54, 67, 83, 101
Affective blunting, 30
Aggression, 59
Alcohol use. *See* Substance use
Alexithymia, 128, 189, 197, 213
Alienation, 41, 109, 272

Amnesia
  in complex dissociation case example, 206
  and continuum of dissociation, 187
  as form of dissociation, 184
  and functional impairment, 78
  processing of, 201
  and SCAN-R procedure, 243
  theoretical conceptualizations of, 188
Amodeo, M., 71
Anderson, K. G., 42
Andresen, R., 5
Anesthesia (dissociative phenomenon), 189
Anger
  and developmental deprivation, 59
  as form of client distress, 167, 169, 170, 177–178
  and trauma processing, 257
Anxiety, 169, 170, 197, 200
Arnkoff, D. B., 17
Arousal symptoms
  and client distress, 168
  effects of chronic, 78–79
  and event-centered trauma processing, 261
Assessment and case formulation, 89–112
  collaboration with client in, 159–161
  and complex dissociation case example, 203–231. *See also* Dissociation
  developmental context in, 99–102
  inclusion of client strengths in, 102–105
  and initiating conceptually guided treatment, 89–98

orientation toward success in, 98–99
steps for, 105–107
three spheres for, 107–112, 147
Attachment
and attention, 63
and dissociation, 189
and relational sphere of treatment, 114–116, 128–129
Attentional abilities, 63–64
and client distress reduction, 179
and dissociation, 191
disturbances in, 78
Attention-deficit disorder (ADD), 64, 69
Authoritarian control, 72
Automatic thoughts, 192
Avoidance behaviors, 15, 40, 69, 261

**B**

Barach, P. M., 128, 186, 187
Bedtime rituals, 57–58
Behavioral activation, 110
Behavioral patterns, 58–59
Being mode, 190
Betrayal, 117, 118
Between-session contact, 126–127
Bilateral stimulation, 263
Binge-eating behaviors, 234
Black, C., 17
Bodily experiences
and effects of trauma, 28, 30–31. *See also* Fight–flight–freeze response
and modulation of dissociation, 195–196
Body language, 193
Body ownership, 64
Body scan exercises, 196
Borderline personality disorder, 37, 40, 84, 185
Bowlby, J., 128, 186, 189
Brain development, 64–65, 151
Breathing techniques, 172–173
Brewin, C. R., 69
Brief, D. J., 42, 233
Brown, L. S., 14, 127, 145
Brown, S. A., 42
Bullying, 207, 209–210
Bureau, J. F., 187
Burnout, 144
Butler, L. D., 144

**C**

Caputi, P., 5
Carello, J., 144
Carlson, E. A., 187–188
Case formulation. *See* Assessment and case formulation
Centers for Disease Control and Prevention, 55

Chandler, G. E., 56–57
Childhood physical abuse (CPA)
and dissociative identity disorder, 189
and families of abused children, 70, 71
and vulnerability to revictimization, 73
Childhood sexual abuse (CSA)
and adverse childhood experiences, 54
and dissociation, 186
and dissociative identity disorder, 189
and families of abused children, 70–71
prevalence of, 32
and vulnerability to revictimization, 73
Choice, 192
Clark, G. I., 152
Clay, C. M., 71
Coercive control, 41, 72
Cognition-centered trauma processing, 247–258
Cognitive behavior therapy, 152
Cognitive distortions, 252–254, 258
Cognitive functioning, 61, 114, 150–151
Cognitive processing therapy (CPT)
challenging unhelpful beliefs with, 258
function of, 13
training in, 17
Collaborative conceptualization, 149. *See also* Conceptual sphere of treatment
Collaborative therapeutic relationship, 99, 114, 116. *See also* Relational sphere of treatment
Combat trauma, 32, 39, 101
Compassion fatigue, 143
Complex dissociation. *See* Dissociation
Complex posttraumatic stress disorder (C-PTSD). *See also specific headings*
conceptualization of causation with, 84
differentiation of PTSD vs., 24, 40–47, 67–70
lack of clinician familiarity with, 37–38
original conceptualization of, 3, 15, 49
Complex traumatization (CTr), 11–26. *See also specific headings*
differential treatment for, 15–18
early identification and conceptualization of, 4
experiential and existential nature of, 12–14
limitations of intervention-focused therapy for, 23–26
prevalence of, 12
and respecting survivors' experience, 18–23
Compulsions. *See* Addictive and compulsive behaviors
Concentration difficulties, 168
Conceptually guided treatment, 89–98
Conceptual sphere of treatment, 149–165
applications of collaboration in, 159–162
domains of understanding in, 162–164

"following the thread" in, 155, 157–159
and integration with other spheres, 111–112, 147, 164–165
overview, 107–110
principles of, 151–157
and reasoning abilities, 150–151, 165
Conflict management, 59
Consciousness, 41, 68
Consultation, 144
Context, 26
Contextual trauma therapy (CTT). *See also specific headings*
core proposition of, 11–12, 49–50
differentiating impact of abuse trauma and neglect in, 65–67
guiding principles of, 4–6
overview, 3
short-term, 281–284
and two-pronged causation model, 19
Cook, J. M., 17
Coping skills
and developmental deprivation, 74
and event-centered trauma processing, 260
and readiness for event-centered trauma processing, 260–261
and session frequency, 126
and stabilization, 16
Corpus callosum (brain area), 151
Corry, M., 68
Count method (trauma processing), 265–266
CPA. *See* Childhood physical abuse
CPT. *See* Cognitive processing therapy
C-PTSD. *See* Complex posttraumatic stress disorder
Criminal assaults, 101
CSA. *See* Childhood sexual abuse
CTr. *See* Complex traumatization
CTT. *See* Contextual trauma therapy
Cue-centered trauma processing, 247, 248, 258–259

**D**

Danieli, Y., 144
DBT (dialectical behavior therapy), 190
Death, 12
Decision-making abilities, 7, 61, 65, 151
Deduction, 162–164
Deep muscle relaxation (DMR), 173
Delker, B. C., 234
Dell, P. F., 184–185
Denmark, 69
Dependency, 123–127
Depersonalization
in complex dissociation case example, 208
on continuum of dissociation, 187
dissociative dial intervention for management of, 197
overview, 185
theoretical conceptualizations of, 188
Depression
and causation of PTSD, 84
and childhood sexual abuse, 70
and conceptual sphere of treatment, 161
as co-occurring with PTSD, 41
and dissociative dial intervention, 197
maternal, 64
strategies for overcoming of, 179–182
trauma-related, 15
Deprivation. *See* Developmental deprivation
Derealization
on continuum of dissociation, 187
overview, 185
theoretical conceptualizations of, 188
Desensitization, 258
Detachment (dissociative experience), 186–187
Developmental deprivation, 49–75
and adverse childhood experiences, 53–57
characteristics of, 70–75
and complex PTSD as discrete diagnosis, 67–70
as component of complex traumatization, 27
and conceptual sphere of treatment, 154
differentiating impact of trauma vs., 65–67
and dissociation, 187–188. *See also* Dissociation
features and consequences of, 57–65
and reasoning abilities, 150–151
and relational sphere of treatment, 114, 116
role of, 50–53
and trauma processing, 246
*Diagnostic and Statistical Manual of Mental Disorders (DSM–5)*
addictive and compulsive behaviors in, 234
and complex PTSD as separate entity, 41
and conceptualizations of therapeutic treatment, 25
and previous categorization of PTSD, 167
PTSD classification in, 32, 38–40, 65
*Diagnostic and Statistical Manual of Mental Disorders (DSM–III)*, 31, 39, 49, 80, 184
Dialectical behavior therapy (DBT), 190
Diaphragmatic breathing, 173, 283
DID (dissociative identity disorder), 184, 186, 189
Disability, 140–141
Disbelief, 132–135
Disembodiment, 185
Disenfranchisement, 143
Disorganized attachment, 63

Dissociation, 183–201
  and attentional abilities, 64
  case example, 203–231
  and causation of PTSD, 84
  contextual conceptualization of, 187–191
  defined, 186
  and diagnosis of complex PTSD, 37, 40
  as experiential distance and disconnection, 186–187
  as form of client distress, 167, 170
  and history of trauma, 15
  and phases of treatment, 16
  and relational sphere of treatment, 127–132
  and SCAN-R procedure, 237
  and sexual compulsivity, 235
  strategies for modulation and extinguishment of, 191–201
  triggers of, 182
  varieties of, 184–186
*Dissociative Children: Bridging the Inner and Outer Worlds* (Shirar), 207
Dissociative dial intervention, 192, 197–199
Dissociative disorders, 37, 42
Dissociative Experiences Scale, 228
Dissociative identity disorder (DID), 184, 186, 189
Distorted beliefs, 161–162
Distress, client, 167–182
  depression as, 179–182
  reduction of baseline, 169–179
  relief for immediate spikes in, 178–179
Distrust. *See* Trust
Disturbances in self-organization (DSO)
  causes of, 18
  and conceptual sphere of treatment, 150
  and developmental deprivation, 69
  and diagnosis of complex PTSD, 15, 41
  and event-centered trauma processing, 260, 261
  and life trajectory of clients, 270, 271
  and relational sphere of treatment, 114, 132
Diversity, 139–143
Divorce, 184
DMR (deep muscle relaxation), 173
Doing mode, 190
Domestic violence. *See* Intimate partner violence
Dorahy, M. J., 68
DSM. *See Diagnostic and Statistical Manual of Mental Disorders* headings
DSO. *See* Disturbances in self-organization
Dual impact model of complex trauma, 77–88
  bidirectional and circular causation in, 80–88
  case formulation based on, 90
  components of. *See* Developmental deprivation; Traumatic events
  overview, 18, 19, 50, 77–80
Dutra, L., 187, 188
Dysphoria, 168–169, 243

**E**

Eating disorders, 234, 260
Economic status, 140–141
Educational history, 101
Egan, S. J., 152
Egeland, B., 187
Ellis, M. A., 71
EMDR. *See* Eye-movement desensitization and reprocessing therapy
Emergency contact information, 126–127
Emotional arousal
  and bodily experiences, 30
  and PTSD diagnostic criteria, 40
Emotional awareness, 195
Emotional control, 15
Emotional equilibrium, 5
Emotional expressiveness, 70, 72
Emotional object constancy, 109, 131
Emotional regulation
  and brain development, 65
  and conceptual sphere of treatment, 151
  and definitions of complex PTSD, 68
  and developmental deprivation, 61–63, 69
  and life trajectory of clients, 271
  and substance use, 233
Emotional responsiveness, 114
Employment history, 101
Enculturation
  and developmental deprivation, 50
  and effects of trauma, 78, 79, 81–82
  in life trajectory of clients, 270
Entitlement, 136
Erickson, Milton, 110
Erikson, M., 197
Erni, T., 188
Ethnicity, 140–141
Event-centered trauma processing, 247, 248, 254, 259–267
*The Evil Hours* (Morris), 17
Existential, 12–14
Experiential nature of trauma, 12–14
Exposure therapy. *See also* Cue-centered trauma processing; Prolonged exposure
  as central strategy for PTSD, 15–16
  and developmental deprivation, 68
  possible negative consequences of, 17
  and practical intervention sphere, 110
  successful applications of, 246
Eye contact, 193

Eye-movement desensitization and
    reprocessing (EMDR) therapy, 262–264
    and developmental deprivation, 65
    function of, 13
    training in, 17
    for treatment of client distress, 173

**F**

Family cohesiveness, 70–72
Family Environment Scale, 71
Family Functioning Scale, 71
Family history, 101
Family upbringing. *See* Developmental
    deprivation
Fassler, I. R., 71
Felitti, V., 54–56, 83
Fight–flight–freeze response
    and client distress, 167, 169–170
    components of, 28–30
    and conceptual sphere of treatment,
        151
    deconditioning of, 133–134
    and dissociation, 188, 190
    overview, 15–16
Figley, C. R., 143
Financial difficulties, 79
Flashbacks
    and client distress, 168
    and event-centered trauma processing,
        261
    and fight–flight–freeze response, 188
    functional impairment from, 78
    and phases of treatment, 16
Foa, E. B., 17
Focus, 63–64
Fogas, B. S., 70
"Following the thread" (conceptual sphere
    of treatment), 155, 157–159
Freyd, J. J., 234
Functional behavior analysis, 110
Functional impairment, 78, 80–88
Functional reintegration, 272. *See also*
    Life trajectory of clients

**G**

Gambling, 101, 234
Gender, 140–141
Glass, C. R., 17
Graded exposure cue-centered processing,
    258
Grant, J. E., 234
Greetings, 163–164
Griffin, M. L., 71
Grounding techniques
    modulating dissociation with, 191
    overview, 191–197
Guilt, 167, 169, 253

**H**

Handshakes, 163–164
Harvanko, A. M., 234
Health-risk behaviors, 55
Heart rate, 29
Herman, J.
    and complex PTSD diagnosis, 37–41, 49,
        69, 145
    and difficulties with complex PTSD, 68
    and dissociative identity disorder, 186
    and life trajectory of clients, 270–272
    and phases of treatment for trauma, 280
    pioneering ideas of, 3, 15
    and safety, 18
    and treatment of complex PTSD, 16
Hippocampus, 65
Holmes, B., 187
Household dysfunction, 55–56. *See also*
    Developmental deprivation
Hulsey, T. L., 71
Hygiene, 58
Hypervigilance
    and client distress, 168
    in clinical settings, 91–92
    effects of, 78–79
Hypnosis, 173–174, 197

**I**

ICD. *See International Classification of Diseases*
Identity. *See* Self-perception and self-image
Identity alteration
    in complex dissociation case example,
        208–209, 228
    on continuum of dissociation, 187
    overview, 186
    theoretical conceptualizations of, 188
Identity confusion
    in complex dissociation case example,
        206, 211, 227–228
    on continuum of dissociation, 187
    overview, 185
    theoretical conceptualizations of, 188
Imaginal approaches to stress reduction, 173
Imaginal exposure, 252, 258, 262
Impulse control. *See also* Addictive and
    compulsive behaviors
    assessment of, 101
    and conceptual sphere of treatment, 151
    and developmental deprivation, 61–63
    and differentiation of complex PTSD, 15
Indecision, 219
Inferior frontal gyrus (brain region), 64
Inner-child work, 114
Insomnia, 78, 168
Integration and rehabilitation phase, 272.
    *See also* Life trajectory of clients
    (phase 3 of treatment)

Internal working model, 114
*International Classification of Diseases* (ICD)
  assessment of PTSD categories in, 69
  and causation of complex PTSD, 83
  complex PTSD in, 4, 38, 41, 271
International Society for the Study of Trauma and Dissociation, 186
International Trauma Questionnaire (ITQ), 69
Internet addiction, 234, 238–240
Internet resources, 163
Interpersonal conflict, 70, 79, 233, 260
Interpersonal connectedness
  assessment of, 101
  deficits in, 5, 59–61, 69. *See also* Developmental deprivation
  and diagnosis of complex PTSD, 41, 68
  and differentiation of complex PTSD, 15
  and dissociation, 128–129
  and families of abused children, 72
  and life trajectory of clients, 271
  and relational sphere of treatment, 114
  with therapist, 100
Interpersonal psychiatry, 146
Interpersonal violence traumas, 123
Intervention-focused therapy
  and developmental deprivation, 65
  limitations of, 23–26
Intimate partner violence
  assessment of, 101
  and criteria for PTSD, 39
  prevalence of, 32
  and revictimization, 73
Intrusive thoughts
  and event-centered trauma processing, 261
  and PTSD diagnostic criteria, 40
In vivo exposure, 252, 262
Irritability, 78–79
Isolation, 109
Israel, 69
ITQ (International Trauma Questionnaire), 69

## J

Janet, Pierre, 3, 189
Judgment competencies, 61

## K

Kaiser Permanente, 54, 55
Kalmakis, K. A., 56–57
Karatzias, T., 69
Kidnapping, 39

## L

Laddis, A., 186
Learning deficits
  and developmental deprivation, 50
  and effects of trauma, 78, 79, 81–82
  interventions for, 162–163

Legal history, 101
Life expectancy, 55–56
Life trajectory of clients (phase 3 of treatment), 269–280
  case example, 273–279
  and earlier phases of treatment, 270–271
  overview, 271–273
  steps for helping with, 279–280
Liotti, G., 187
Lithuania, 69
Lötscher, K., 188
Lyons-Ruth, K., 187
Lyubchik, A., 187

## M

Ma, X., 173
Maguin, E., 144
Maltreatment. *See* Developmental deprivation
Mann, B. J., 188
Mannix, L. M., 42, 233
Marginalization, 143
Mason, O., 189
Maternal depression, 64
Maternal unresponsiveness, 187
McLaughlin, K., 66–68, 150
Meaning in life, 41
Medial prefrontal cortex (brain region), 65
Medical difficulties, 55
Medication, 97
Meditation, 179
Meehan, J. C., 42, 233
Memory lapses, 184–185
Mental illness, parental, 184
Microaggressions, 142–143
Mindfulness
  and being mode, 190
  and bodily awareness, 196
  defined, 179
  and dissociation, 188
Mindfulness-based stress reduction, 190
Modestin, J., 188
Morales, C. H., 144
Morris, David, 17
Music, 174

## N

Najavits, L. M., 17
Narcissistic personality disorder, 136
Nash, M. R., 71
Natural disasters, 101
Negative thoughts
  and conceptualization of complex PTSD, 15

functional impairment from, 78
and PTSD diagnostic criteria, 40
Neglect and negligence, 27, 65–66.
  *See also* Developmental deprivation
Nelson, C. A., 150
Nightmares
  and client distress, 168
  and conceptualization of complex PTSD, 15
  and event-centered trauma processing, 261
  functional impairment from, 78
Nonsuicidal self-injury, 37, 101, 234
Norman, S. B., 42
*Not Trauma Alone: Therapy for Child Abuse Survivors in Family and Social Context* (Gold), 3–4
Nova Southeastern University Trauma Resolution & Integration Program, 15, 92, 234, 267, 273

## O

Oades, L. G., 5
Ochberg, F. M., 265
Ogawa, J. R., 187, 188

## P

Palic, S., 69
Parenting difficulties, 79
PDS (Posttraumatic Diagnostic Scale), 262
PE. *See* Prolonged exposure
Peirce, J. M., 42, 233
Penta, C. R., 235
Perceptual blunting, 30
Perceptual changes, 41
Peritraumatic dissociation, 185
Personality disorders, 84. *See also specific headings*
Phone calls, 92–93
Physical pain and discomfort, 197, 233
Political torture, 69
Posttraumatic Diagnostic Scale (PDS), 262
Posttraumatic stress disorder (PTSD)
  assessment of, 90. *See also* Assessment and case formulation
  central strategies for treatment of, 15–16
  complex. *See* Complex posttraumatic stress disorder
  conceptualization of causation with, 84
  development of terminology for, 31
  differentiation of complex PTSD vs, 24, 40–47, 67–69
  fight–flight–freeze response with, 30
  and secondary traumatic stress symptoms, 144
  and trauma processing, 246

Practical intervention sphere of treatment.
  *See also specific interventions*
  and integration with other spheres, 111–112, 147
  overview, 107–111
Prefrontal cortex, 151
Pretreatment assessment. *See* Assessment and case formulation
Prolonged exposure (PE)
  and developmental deprivation, 65
  function of, 13
  overview, 262
  risks with, 258
  training in, 17
PTSD. *See* Posttraumatic stress disorder

## Q

Quality of life, 5–6. *See also* Life trajectory of clients

## R

Race, 142
Rage reactions, 37
Rape trauma
  assessment of, 101
  and criteria for PTSD, 39
  prevalence of PTSD with, 33
  and revictimization, 73
Reactivity
  and characteristics of trauma, 28
  and conceptualization of complex PTSD, 15
  as protective response, 29
Reasoning abilities, 61, 150–151, 165, 180
Reconnection phase, 271. *See also* Life trajectory of clients
Reexperiencing symptoms
  and conceptualization of complex PTSD, 15
  and developmental deprivation, 69
  and event-centered trauma processing, 261
Reflexive responsivity, 29
Rehabilitation, 272. *See also* Life trajectory of clients (phase 3 of treatment)
Relational sphere of treatment, 113–147
  centrality of, 145–147
  and challenges to therapeutic alliance, 117–143
  and integration with other spheres, 111–112, 147
  overview, 107–109
  philosophy for navigating gaps and warps in, 114–117
  and therapist self-care, 143–145
Relaxation techniques, 110, 179, 258.
  *See also specific headings*

Reparenting, 114
Resilience, 74
Revictimization, 73
Risk assessment, 234

**S**

Safe place imagery, 173
Safety
  and client distress, 168
  and dissociation, 194
  and diversity, 140
  and life trajectory of clients, 270
  and phases of treatment, 18
  and therapeutic relationship, 24, 100
  and trauma-informed staff, 91
Sanders, S., 188
Şar, V., 186
SCAN-R (select, cue, analyze, note, and revise) procedure, 235–244
  analysis of episodes in, 240–241
  effects of, 243–244
  getting started with, 236–237
  identification of cues in, 237–238
  inconsistencies in, 241–243
  and introducing technique to client, 235–236
  overview, 110
  sampling multiple instances in, 238–240
Schemas, 161–162
Schizophrenia, 186
Schneiderian symptoms, 186
Schnurr, P. P., 17
Schottenbauer, M. A., 17
Schreiber, L. R. N., 234
Scotland, 69
Secondary traumatic stress symptoms (STSS), 143–144
Secure attachment, 115–116, 129
Security
  and life trajectory of clients, 270
  and therapeutic relationship, 100
  and trauma-informed staff, 91
Segal, Z. V., 190
Select, cue, analyze, note, and revise procedure. *See* SCAN-R procedure
Self-blame, 252–254
Self-care, therapist, 143–145
Self-destructiveness, 234
Self-esteem, 72, 115, 136, 140
Self-help groups, 127
Self-monitoring, 229
Self-perception and self-image
  and conceptual sphere of treatment, 150
  and definitions of complex PTSD, 68
  and developmental deprivation, 69
  and differentiation of complex PTSD, 15
  and dissociation, 64
  effects of trauma on, 5
  and life trajectory of clients, 271
  and trauma processing, 253
Self-sabotage, 136, 216–217
Sensory analgesia, 197
Sensory experiences, 194, 195
Sensory shutdown, 128
Sequestration, 142–143
Session frequency, 126
Sexton, M. C., 71
Sexual adjustment, 79
Sexual behavior
  compulsive, 101, 234–235, 237–238, 240–243
  and trauma processing, 257, 261
Sexual orientation, 140–141
Shame, 167, 169, 252–253
Sharkansky, E. J., 42, 233
Sheridan, M. A., 150
Shevlin, M., 69
Short-term contextual trauma therapy, 281–284
Siegel, D. J., 189
Single parents, 66
*60 Minutes* (TV show), 141, 164
Sleep disturbances, 78
Social conventions, 163–164
Socialization
  and developmental deprivation, 50
  and effects of trauma, 78, 79, 81–82
  in life trajectory of clients, 270
Social learning, 78
Socratic interviewing method, 152, 162
Somatization disorders, 42
Somatoform disorders, 37, 40
Sroufe, L. A., 187
Stabilization phase of treatment
  and event-centered trauma processing, 260
  function of, 16
  and life trajectory of clients, 270
Startle response, 168
Stein, D. J., 183, 184
Strengths, client, 102–105, 114
Stress reduction techniques, 144, 172–175
Strive (employment program), 141, 142, 164
Structure (developmental deprivation), 57–58
STSS (secondary traumatic stress symptoms), 143–144
Subjective Units of Distress Scale (SUDS), 170–172, 175–176, 264, 282–283
Substance use. *See also* Addictive and compulsive behaviors
  assessment of, 101
  and conceptual sphere of treatment, 161
  as co-occurring with PTSD, 42
  and developmental deprivation, 62
  and dissociation, 184, 185

and history of trauma, 15, 233–234
and maladaptive habits, 58
Success orientation, 98–99
SUDS. *See* Subjective Units of Distress Scale
Sue, D. W., 142
Suggestibility, 222
Suicidal ideation, 260
Sullivan, Harry Stack, 146
Support circles, 127

## T

Tate, S. R., 42
Teasdale, J. D., 190
Technology, 174, 175
Teicher, M. H., 151
Therapeutic alliance
  challenges to, 117–143
  collaborative, 99, 114, 116–143
  importance of, 25
  and practical intervention sphere of treatment, 111
  and relational sphere of treatment, 108–109. *See also* Relational sphere of treatment
  and safety, 24
Threat, sense of, 69, 167
TIR (traumatic incident reduction), 264–265
Totalitarian control, 41
Tovey, S. L., 70
Trauma, 27–47. *See also specific headings*
  defined, 34
  obstacles to accessing treatment for, 34–38
  paradoxical nature of, 28–31
  surge in clinical recognition of, 31–34
Trauma History Questionnaire, 101
Trauma processing, 245–267
  cognition-centered, 247–258
  cue-centered, 247, 248, 258–259
  difficulties with benefiting from, 74
  event-centered, 247, 248, 254, 259–267
  overview, 245–247
  and practical intervention sphere, 110
  and relational sphere of treatment, 115
Trauma-related disorders, 84
Trauma Resolution & Integration Program, 3, 16, 99
Traumatic events, 38–47
Traumatic Events Questionnaire, 101
Traumatic incident reduction (TIR), 264–265

Traumatization
  complex. *See* Complex traumatization
  and conceptual sphere of treatment, 154
  defined, 34
  vicarious, 144–145
Treatment nonresponsiveness, 17
Trust
  client discernment of, 109
  and dissociation, 194
  as potential barrier to collaborative therapeutic alliance, 117–122
  and therapeutic relationship, 24, 100
  and trauma-informed staff, 91
Two-pronged model of complex trauma. *See* Dual impact model of complex trauma

## U

Unresponsiveness, 28

## V

VA (Veterans Administration), 17
Validation, 114
Veterans Administration (VA), 17
Vicarious traumatization, 144–145
Vigilance, 201
Vio, C. G., 144
Violence, 123, 184, 260. *See also* Intimate partner violence
Vivanco, A. F., 144
Vulnerability, 257

## W

Weinfield, N. S., 187
Whittle, S., 65
WHO (World Health Organization), 38
Widom, C. S., 68
Williams, J. M., 190
Winnicott, D. W., 154
Work status, 140–141
World Health Organization (WHO), 38

## Y

Yama, M. F., 70

## Z

Zayfert, C., 17

# ABOUT THE AUTHOR

**Steven N. Gold, PhD,** is a professor in the College of Psychology at Nova Southeastern University and director of the Trauma Resolution & Integration Program, which he established in 1990. He was a founding coeditor of the *Journal of Trauma Practice*, inaugural editor of the American Psychological Association journal *Psychological Trauma*, editor-in-chief of the two-volume *APA Handbook of Trauma Psychology*, and author of the book *Not Trauma Alone: Therapy for Child Abuse Survivors in Family and Social Context*. He served as president of the American Psychological Association Division 56 (Trauma Psychology) in 2009, has held other professional leadership roles, and has lectured throughout the United States and internationally. A certified traumatologist and consultant in clinical hypnosis, Dr. Gold maintains an independent psychology practice in Plantation, Florida, and has regularly been retained as an expert witness in legal cases.